KIERKEGAARD'S
RELATION TO HEGEL

Kierkegaard's Relation to Hegel

NIELS THULSTRUP

TRANSLATED BY
GEORGE L. STENGREN

PRINCETON UNIVERSITY PRESS
PRINCETON, NEW JERSEY

CONTENTS

Contents

THE SECONDARY LITERATURE on Kierkegaard in English generally recognizes some relationship between Kierkegaard and Hegel, and Kierkegaard's vehement rejection of Hegelian thought is familiar to all his readers. But there has been no comprehensive treatment of this complex issue in any language prior to Professor Thulstrup's book. There has, indeed, been much written on this topic, as Professor Thulstrup has shown with his customary thoroughness in another work: *Kierkegaards Verhältnis zu Hegel: Forschungsgeschichte* (Stuttgart: Verlag W. Kohlhammer, 1970).

In translating this book, I have tried to render the thought content of the original accurately. I have not felt called upon to rewrite or radically alter the style of the original except where Danish syntax simply would not do in English. In many instances where a Danish word or phrase might be translated in various ways I have enclosed the original in square brackets. Square brackets have also been used around my additions and explanations. I have also translated (except where the meaning is obvious) all quotations, terms, and book titles directly from the original Danish, German, Latin, Swedish, etc. Books that have been translated into English are identified by the English title alone. For others, the original title is given, followed by my English translation of that title in square brackets. Particularly in the case of works by Kierkegaard and Hegel, I have translated quotations directly from the Danish of the *Samlede Værker* and from the German of the Glockner *Jubiläumsausgabe*. I have, of course, consulted available English translations of these works, but mainly so as to give page references to these translations. Unfortunately it has not been possible to give page references to two new English translations of Hegel's *Aesthetics* and the *Phenomenology of the Spirit*, inasmuch as they were published after the present translation was completed.

The numbered footnotes to the text are Professor Thulstrup's. Translator's footnotes are indicated by letters.

Translators, like authors, owe many debts of gratitude to various individuals. First and foremost, I should like to express my profound indebtedness to Professor Thulstrup and to Ms. Carol Orr of the Princeton University Press for their confidence in me, their encouragement, and their incredible patience during the unexpectedly lengthy period during which this translation was done. Professor Thulstrup has not only responded promptly and cordially to my many questions but has also been most kind and generous in a variety of ways. Various colleagues, particularly Professor Charlotte Evans, Chairman of the Department of Foreign Languages at Central Michigan University, have helped me with some of the more difficult passages in German. Mrs. Marjorie Farmer has patiently typed and retyped the bulk of this manuscript. Professor Howard V. Hong generously provided an advance copy of his "Collation of Entries" for his magnificent edition and translation of the *Journals and Papers* so that I was able to include references to the volumes of his translations which were not yet published while the present translation was in progress.

Professor Hong has also read the first chapter critically and made a number of valuable suggestions. Mr. Robert Widenman has carefully scrutinized the entire text and has suggested a great many corrections and changes. No doubt this translation has been vastly improved through the efforts of these two gentlemen, and I am most grateful to them both. However, since I have not followed all of their suggestions, the responsibility for any defects that remain is, of course, mine.

My wife and children have cheerfully endured many inconveniences while I was working on this translation and I wish to take this opportunity to express my appreciation to them.

THIS BOOK is properly the middle volume in a trilogy, but it can be read separately.

In the first part of the book, which was published in German under the title *Kierkegaards Verhältnis zu Hegel. Forschungsgeschichte* (Stuttgart: Verlag W. Kolhammer, 1970; 2nd ed., 1972, 204 pp.), I have critically examined the extensive prior research into the complex of issues in the relation of Kierkegaard and Hegel.

Dissatisfied with the results of the investigations by my numerous predecessors, finding them neither historical nor fundamentally systematic, I began my own investigation, basing it upon the primary sources: Hegel's treatises, works, and posthumously published lectures, as well as the many publications of the Hegelians (for the sake of accuracy, I have used the same editions Kierkegaard himself owned and read) and Kierkegaard's *Samlede Værker*, *Papirer*, and *Breve og Aktstykker* (the latter two in my own Danish editions).

That Kierkegaard was a severe critic of Hegel and "the System" —or "speculation," as he most frequently called philosophic, speculative idealism—has been recognized from Kierkegaard's own day. Yet no Kierkegaard scholar appears to have posed with sufficient care and to have answered the simple questions: How did Kierkegaard get to know about "speculation"? What did he read of Hegel's own works? How did he understand them in their details and as a whole? How did he respond, critically and constructively, to that with which he became acquainted?

My answer to these and related questions is in this book, which thus constitutes the central, historical portion of my work. This part was published in Danish under the title *Kierkegaards Forhold til Hegel og til den spekulative Idealisme indtil 1846* (Copenhagen: Gyldendal, 1967, 354 pp.). It was published in German under the title *Kierkegaards Verhältnis zu Hegel und zum spekulativen Idealismus 1835-46* (Stuttgart: Verlag W. Kolhammer, 1972, 320 pp.).

In my opinion, it is impossible to determine precisely the relation between these two giants in the world of thought unless the person undertaking the investigation has a specific, albeit unstated, basis—namely, a well-founded integral conception of Kierkegaard and Hegel, each on his own terms. Without this basis, one will get lost in details and mere words, as do so many scholars. On the other hand, a close reading of the texts is stringently required unless one is satisfied with generalities, as so many others are who have written about this complex of issues.

My integral conception of Hegel has been elaborated, documented, and, after continual discussion with earlier Hegel scholars, set forth in an unpublished prize treatise (University of Copenhagen, 1947). This has been published in abridged form in my little book *Hegel* (Copenhagen: G.E.C. Gads Forlag, 1967, 83 pp.) trans. into English in *Bibliotheca Kierkegaardiana*, vol. 4 (Copenhagen: C. A. Reitzels Boghandel, 1979). My integral conception of Kierkegaard is fundamental to my introductory and annotated editions of his works, especially of *Philosophical Fragments* (Copenhagen: Munksgaards Forlag, 1955; 2nd rev. ed., C. A. Reitzels Forlag, 1977; English translation by Howard V. Hong, Princeton University Press, 1962) and of *Concluding Unscientific Postscript* (I-II, Copenhagen: Gyldendal, 1962), and it is directly expressed several places therein, as in this book. It is my aim to present this integral conception in detail in part three of the trilogy, the systematic-critical portion.

In the present volume, little reference is made to the many books and treatises on both Hegel and Kierkegaard that have appeared in many languages during the last ten years. The explanation is simple—none of these many books with which I have become acquainted (some of which I have reviewed in *Kierkegaardiana*) has given me reason to alter my interpretation. In the last volume of the trilogy, however, there will be occasion for discussion with Hegel scholars, such as Findlay and Taylor, and with Kierkegaard scholars, such as Malantschuk, Crites, Mark Taylor, Hügli, and others, who in the last years have published scholarly and insightful books.

For their contributions to the preparation of this English edition, I warmly thank George L. Stengren, who has graciously assumed the huge task of clothing it in the English language; Robert Widenmann, who has kindly scanned the translation in order to harmonize the terminology with that of the forthcoming edition of *Kierkegaard's Writings*; and last but not least Princeton University Press, which has accommodatingly undertaken the publication.

Niels Thulstrup
2900 Hellerup, Denmark
February 1978

SV: *Søren Kierkegaards Samlede Værker*. References to the second Danish edition, 15 vols. (1920-1936) given as, for example: SV IX, 22. Volume is in Roman numerals, page in Arabic numerals.

References to the third Danish edition, 20 vols. (1962-1964) given as, for example: SV 5, 22. Volume number first, followed by a comma, then page number, both in Arabic.

SW: Georg Wilhelm Friedrich Hegel, *Sämtliche Werke* (Jubiläumsausgabe), herausgegeben von Hermann Glockner, 20 vols. (1958) given as, for example: SW VIII, 222. Volume is in Roman numerals, page in Arabic.

Ktl: *Katalog over Søren Kierkegaards Bibliotek* (1957). See also: H. P. Rohde, *Auktionsprotokol* . . . and Niels Thulstrup, *S.K.s Bibliotek* (listed in the bibliography).

DBL: *Dansk Biografisk Leksikon*

DTT: *Dansk teologisk Tidsskrift*

KIERKEGAARD'S
RELATION TO HEGEL

1. One of Kierkegaard's well-known Diapsalmata points out: "What the Philosophers say about reality is often as disappointing as a sign you see in a shop window that reads: Pressing Done Here. If you brought your clothes to be pressed, you would be fooled; for the sign is only for sale" (*Either/Or*, I, 31).

It can also turn out to be, if not disappointing, then surely a bit confusing to see a whole group of books that have similar titles, but that only partly deal with the same thing and not in the same way at all.

If we consider a number of books on the philosophy of religion published during the last ten years or so—as for example, those of Henry Duméry, Johannes Hessen, Emmanuel Hirsch, Søren Holm, Ulrich Mann, N. H. Søe, and Willem F. Zuurdeeg—we will soon discover that apart from the title *Philosophy of Religion* they have almost nothing in common. Points of departure, topics chosen, methods, evaluations, and conclusions are different from one another, in some cases so different that they are incompatible.

It is not strange that this is so. It corresponds to the situation we encounter if we are tempted to presume that perhaps there lived not just a single retiring thinker by the name of Søren Kierkegaard, but a whole great crowd with the same name, when we become acquainted with a few of the many books whose titles seem to indicate that they deal with a thinker by the name of Søren Kierkegaard. Works such as G. G. Graus's *Die Selbstauflösung des christlichen Glaubens, eine religions-philosophische Studie über Kierkegaard* (1963) and E. Tielsch's *Kierkegaards Glaube* (1964)[1] would surely confirm such an impression.

It is not surprising that this is the case with the philosophy of religion when this discipline contains so much diversity. We may see this diversity if we examine a long series of actual problems and groups of problems, which seen from one angle do not essentially belong to the other traditional disciplines of either philosophy or theology, but which, seen from another perspective, often arise and

[1] Cf. Lars Bejerholm's review of the first in *Kierkegaardiana*, 1964, 8ff., and Klaus Schäfer's review of the latter in *Kierkegaardiana* (1966), 152ff.

must be discussed, perhaps be solved, perhaps be put aside as insoluble or at any rate unsolved, perhaps be dissolved as pseudo-problems.

Johannes Sløk has held that the philosophy of religion does not have the same function now as earlier. In the ancient and medieval world "the topic of the philosophy of religion [was] ... man's epistemological and ethical relation to God apart from and independent of revelation, and the method which came to be used in treating this area was pure speculation." From the Renaissance on, it became "the task of the philosophy of religion to reestablish the whole religious life" so that both reality and validity could be attributed to it, and the method in this—frequently apologetical—philosophy of religion consisted in trying to demonstrate "how religiosity emanates from basic actions in humanity itself and in virtue of that is indispensable and valid."[2] This point of view got its best expression in Kant's thought, which, considered on the whole, has dominated thinking in the philosophy of religion up to the present.[3] Two factors particularly in the contemporary scene have meant a decisive change in the understanding of the problems of the philosophy of religion and the procedures for solving those problems. Sløk gives as the first factor the comparative history of religion and ethnography, and as the second factor the theological development in the time after the First World War. Both of these factors have meant that the philosophy of religion is no longer understood as speculative, or normative, or only apologetical, but as "a place for revision and confrontation; in the philosophy of religion among other things, analysis and criticism of the received cultural consciousness and interpretation of life has been expressed" (Sløk, p. 208). It should be stressed, as indeed Sløk explicitly does, that the philosophy of religion is understood as a discipline within theology, and this is in fact the way it is arranged and functions in Danish universities. Thus it has turned out, Sløk continues, "that now the philosophy of religion is not so much one discipline which deals with a single, firmly defined theme but a collective term for a group of topics that have in common that they are all located in the area between Christianity and the non-Christian aspects of life, but that moreover can even be quite different from one another . . . the unity of the subject may be relinquished because of the actual

[2] In an article, "Religionsfilosofi," *Teologien og dens fag* (1960), 201ff.
[3] Cf. e.g. Søren Holm's *Religionsfilosofi* (1955), 11ff.

nature of its themes." He then identifies some of the groups of areas with which the philosophy of religion deals nowadays, such as the relation between Christianity and other religions, between Christianity and scientific-philosophical concepts, between Christianity and philosophical notions of life.

Regardless of whether one, as theologian, deplores, approves, or is indifferent to this situation, it is a fact that, from the first days of the Church to the present, philosophic thought has played a very significant role in theological thought. Included in this is the philosophy of religion, in its first, second, and latest development—as Sløk, for instance, has sketched it. Platonism, Aristotelianism, Stoicism, and neo-Platonism in ancient times, Cartesianism, Wolffianism, Kantianism, and Hegelianism in the modern period, Phenomenology, Existentialism, and—so far to a less prominent degree —Empiricism and Linguistic Philosophy in the contemporary period, are philosophical schools, movements, or veritable systems that for good or ill have unquestionably been not only influential but often dominant in the work of systematic theology, especially with respect to the philosophy of religion (viewed as coming within the scope of theology). Christianity and philosophy, or, as we frequently put it, faith and knowledge [*Viden*], are an old combination, and their reciprocal relation has certainly become most diverse. They are seen as harmonious, as complementary, as identical, as disharmonious, as completely irrelevant to one another; and these different determinations of their mutual relations have thus naturally occurred from the changing conceptions of their distinct content. The classic figures in the history of theology, from Paul to Augustine and Thomas to Luther, from Pascal and Hamann to Kierkegaard have been just as much in disagreement in the evaluation of philosophical schools (and their representatives) insofar as they knew about them, as are contemporary theologians, e.g., Tillich, Bultmann, and Barth.

2. If we now—with some hesitation, for the difficulties can be formidable—approach such sets of problems anew, for example, the problems of the relation between a notion of existence determined by Christianity and a philosophic view of the world, we can proceed in several ways.

We can take up the problem in a purely systematic way. Then, we must try to clarify what a notion of existence proceeding from Christianity in general contains and implies, and what is a philosophic attitude toward the world as a matter of pure principle. Having done this, we might try to determine their reciprocal relation and whether they can be harmonized, whether they must be incompatible, or whether they are, so to speak, irrelevant phenomena for each other.

If we approach the problem in this way, then obviously on the way to the solution we are seeking, we shall use both the history of theology and the history of philosophy as data which, among other things, can furnish examples of mistakes to avoid as well as examples of fruitful approaches, and we can put ourselves in the best position to arrive at a resolution of the problem that will be free of contradiction.

This is not a particularly unusual procedure. It is frequently used in different elaborations in systematic expositions of the philosophy of religion. In using it, however, we can very quickly encounter significant difficulties, for even if we are so optimistic as to suppose that we can say clearly, unequivocally, and undeniably what true Christianity is (without taking a position on the question of the truth of Christianity), and which notion of human existence is harmonious with true Christianity, we can hardly provide in a corresponding way any main definition of what a philosophical worldview is when only a number of specific elaborations of philosophical world-views actually exist. Moreover, the latter situation corresponds to the claim of some that the chief reason it is impossible to answer the question of what true Christianity is, is that there exist a host of different interpretations of Christianity from the primitive Church to our own time, so that we are forced to pick and choose among them, certainly not arbitrarily and haphazardly but by means of a criterion.[4]

We can also tackle the problem by means of a purely historical approach.

If we choose this procedure, then we can, for example, adopt a particular body of writings in which this problem is treated with one or another resolution as the outcome, and we can analyze this body of writings in detail and as a whole, explore its presuppositions, perhaps also give an account of its influence, evaluate its resolution of the problem, and stop there.

---

[4] Just as Kierkegaard did not seek examples in distant times and countries but used those closest to hand, so we can refer here simply to Søren Holm's *Religionsfilosofi* (1955), 99-120, and his *Dogmatik* (1962), 29ff.

This is not a particularly unusual procedure either. But if we approach the works of a particular author in a purely historical fashion, we easily slide into a situation in which the treatment of the problem becomes unimportant in the notion that, seen from a purely historical perspective, every treatment is equally valid simply by its presence alone, similar to the way certain forms of modern psychology and sociology will speak only of various behavior patterns in individual men and groups, but not of any qualitative distinction among them.

As a third possibility we can investigate the problem by using both the historical and the systematic approach and with constant, albeit not always explicit, reference to their limitations.

If we choose this method, then we can, moreover, clothe the chief problem in historical garb, as it is described in the *Concluding Unscientific Postscript*, so that we constantly strive to keep the chief problem in view.

3. If then, one has chosen to dress the problem in historical garb, as is done here, the next question becomes, which approach shall we choose? Once the choice has been made, it is, of course, an expression of an evaluation, and it will point toward the chief problem.

There are many possible choices. We could, for example, investigate the problem in a theologian such as Thomas, or Schleiermacher, or Bultmann, who each, although in the most disparate ways, assumes a harmonious relation between what is in a purely provisional way called here "a notion of existence determined by Christianity and a philosophic view of the world." Perhaps these theologians do not assume beforehand that this harmonious relation exists; but according to their respective interpretations, by the paths they take themselves and advise others to follow, it can be established.[a] Or we could study the question in a theologian such as Luther or Barth, who at a certain stage made it a point of their theological honor, so to speak, to reject all philosophy without ex-

[a] Thomas Aquinas is quite explicit in expressing his conviction of the essential harmony and reciprocal autonomy of Christian faith and philosophic endeavor throughout his writings. See e.g., *Summa Theologiae*, Ia, q.1, art. 5; *Summa Contra Gentiles*, Bk. II, ch. 2-4; and *Expositio super librum Boethii De Trinitate*, II, 3. Among twentieth-century adherents of Aquinas, Etienne Gilson has stressed this point most vigorously. See Gilson's *The Christian Philosophy of St. Thomas Aquinas* (New York: Random House, 1956).

amining it,[5] and thus it happened that their "notion of existence determined by Christianity" simply excludes validity and legitimacy from any philosophic view of the world, whether any such philosophic view would include or exclude Christianity. Or we could take up the question in a philosopher such as Karl Jaspers, who both in his earlier writings and in his mature work *Der philosophische Glaube angesichts der Offenbarung* (1962) has made a significant contribution to the contemporary debate.

The possibility also exists of dressing the problem in historical garb by choosing as the object of the investigation a thinker who cannot correctly be described as a theologian in either the traditional or the modern sense nor a technical philosopher in either sense; but one who argued as an existing thinker and who was a psychologist and poet as well,[b] a thinker, namely, Kierkegaard, who formulated his thoughts out of a pronounced, theologically based anthropology in unceasing confrontation with the dominant thought of his time, which was intended to be a Christian speculative idealism, especially as formulated by Hegel and the right-wing Hegelians.

If this possibility is chosen, the problem does not exactly become easier to deal with than if we had chosen a consistent, straightforward [*monologisk*] thinker as a point of departure; but it can become more interesting than if we had chosen one of the other available possibilities, since in this instance we can not only arrive at a finished result in Kierkegaard, but we can also follow both how the problem came to be worked out and how it came to be solved in an original way. This was through a direct and indirect reckoning with a brilliant representative of both the older and the more recent tradition in the philosophy of religion described above, a reckoning accomplished by an entirely different type of genius, who by his status as a philosopher of religion anticipated one position concerning the philosophy of religion which has adherents today. This is not to say that originality and contemporaneity (or lack thereof) in itself tells us anything at all about the thinker's validity, invalidity—or irrelevance.

[5] On Luther, references can be made to, for example, W. Link's *Das Ringen Luthers um die Freiheit der Theologie von der Philosophie* (2nd ed., 1955) and to P. Althaus's *Die Theologie Martin Luthers* (1962); on Barth, to B. E. Benktson's *Den naturliga teologiens problem hos Karl Barth* (1948), as well as to N. H. Søe's *Religionsfilosofi* (2nd ed., 1963, *passim*), among others.

[b] Cf. Louis Mackey, *Kierkegaard: A Kind of Poet* (Philadelphia: University of Pennsylvania Press, 1971).

Kierkegaard's conflict with speculative idealism, especially in Hegel's version, his clash with its comprehensive view of existence from the standpoint of a fixed concept of Christianity and concept of man, his sharp distinction between Christian faith and speculative, philosophical knowledge [*Viden*], are interesting, although complex, objects for investigation in themselves. They can also furnish points of departure for research into new considerations particularly in the philosophy of religion.

Certainly it can be claimed that Kierkegaard's clash [*Opgør*] with Hegel, for example, has, if not exclusively, then surely mainly historical interest today, when scarcely anyone accepts Hegel's method and system as valid in its entirety, and when, for some contemporary thinkers, elements of Kierkegaard's thought play a positive role as a source of inspiration or simply as an arsenal, but as a whole it is just as passé and lacking current interest as Hegel's. Quite apart from the hazard of letting the history of the world be the judge of the world in this case, by doing what in every age the prevalent group or at least the trendiest opinions among professional philosophers and theologians do, viz., sit as a Supreme Court to judge what is significant or insignificant to concern oneself about, we cannot entirely a priori foreclose the possibility that the point of departure chosen here can open certain perspectives, and that Kierkegaard's answers to certain questions can, perhaps, shed a unique light on some contemporary endeavors.

It can also be maintained that Kierkegaard's reckoning [*Opgør*] with Hegel has already been analyzed and interpreted exhaustively and satisfactorily in the quite significant research done in the last couple of generations, so that a new investigation of this topic can only be a repetition of the familiar.

To this objection, the results of this investigation must speak for themselves; everyone is free to undertake a comparison between this study and the earlier ones.[6]

[6] I have worked up a critical history of the research on this topic up to 1959. [Niels Thulstrup, *Kierkegaards Verhältnis zu Hegel: Forschungsgeschichte* (Stuttgart: Verlag W. Kolhammer, 1969).] In the present investigation there is a brief evaluation in passing of earlier investigators' viewpoints and results, but only in instances where it seems worthwhile, partly because the research on Kierkegaard in these areas probably can be presumed to be known in its broad outlines, partly because I have gradually become convinced that a position can certainly be presented with complete clarity without being put into relation on every point with other views more or less akin to it, when the decisive point in any case is that an investigation of this

4. It is obvious to every informed reader of Kierkegaard's Authorship, especially the pseudonymous works up to and including *Concluding Unscientific Postscript*, that his language, his philosophical
vocabulary, is redolent of Hegel and his contemporaries. Although
some (especially Bohlin among the earlier scholars, and Anz among
the more recent) have maintained that Kierkegaard's position and
main problematic are largely determined by the system of thought
he so critically turned against, nevertheless there is a simple question about what detailed knowledge and what general understanding Kierkegaard had of his adversary, hitherto not exhaustively
answered, although his attitude toward Hegel may be presumed to
be determined both by his own positive viewpoint and by his actual
knowledge of Hegel and of the whole speculative system of
thought. There is also a question of whether Kierkegaard's understanding of Hegel's own system was decisively influenced by direct
contact or by the interpretations and applications of it that he encountered quite early in his student years.

These questions ought to be answered, and the answer can be
discovered only by an inquiry into his notes, both published and
unpublished,[7] and into his works.[8]

The arrangement and the approach used in this study is the
simplest possible, namely, chronological and analytical. The point
of departure for this investigation is always the Kierkegaardian
texts, and the first chapter, which is mostly devoted to a rather complete treatment of Hegelianism in Denmark up to 1835, provides
background for what follows.[9]

---

type must be based on what the sources say, what can be derived from them
through a historical perspective, and what are the chief conclusions we can
draw from them.

[7] Simultaneously with the development of the present investigation I have
been engaged in editing the hitherto unpublished *Papirer*. The manuscript
for this edition is ready for the printer, but since publication will be delayed
somewhat, in what follows I have quoted and given an account of the manuscripts rather completely, instead of just referring to them. [These texts have
now been published as Volumes XII and XIII (Supplementbind 1 & 2) of
the latest edition of the *Papirer* (Copenhagen: Gyldendal, 1970).]

[8] Those works of Kierkegaard for which I have written introductions and
furnished historical information, notably for his *Philosophical Fragments*
(Princeton University Press, 2nd edition, 1962) and for his *Afsluttende
uvidenskabelig Efterskrift* [Concluding Unscientific Postscript] (1962), I
have—referring to my editions—treated more briefly in what follows than
other texts.

[9] In particular instances, naturally, it has had to be a matter of judgment

This study is confined to the period of about ten years, from the summer of 1835 when the young student Kierkegaard took stock of himself intellectually and spiritually and set a particular goal for himself that he pursued on a long and roundabout way until the winter of 1846, when he published *Concluding Unscientific Post-script*, a parting shot at the whole speculative, idealistic philosophy and theology, which had promised so much and delivered so little —of what Kierkegaard once had expected of it.

The topical scope of this study is not narrowly taken, since it has been difficult, in some cases impracticable, to sort out areas (e.g., according to today's theological or philosophical classifications and delimitations of topics) which naturally belong together for both Hegel and Kierkegaard (and their contemporaries).[10] Some questions, such as those which belong exclusively to theoretical aesthetics, for example, are either passed over or treated very briefly.

A close examination of the texts reveals that the most difficult thing to get clear concerning Kierkegaard's relation to Hegel, and to the thinkers influenced by Hegel, is not with respect to the Authorship itself, but rather in regard to the preceding time, especially in connection with his first large book, *On the Concept of Irony*. A further consideration is that it was during his student years that Kierkegaard's existential problematic sprang forth and began to be formulated, and it is important to follow this process step by step, point for point. If we then proceed to the sources from the time following his dissertation up to the beginning of the pseudonymous Authorship, the problematic, and with it our investigation, will be constantly simplified.

We have no intention of giving a complete exposition of Hegel's

whether to employ quotations, paraphrases, and summaries, or only references to the sources and to the literature. The norm for this judgment has been that where it is a matter of easily accessible and presumably relatively familiar printed sources, references and brief summaries have usually been considered sufficient. Where there is a question of texts that must be studied in a special way, quotations and paraphrases have been used to the extent required. The same principle is followed when the issue concerns unpublished sources or books and treatises from Kierkegaard's time that are probably unfamiliar. Since this whole investigation was originally written with a view to publication in a common language [*Hovedsprog*], Danish sources in particular are quoted and paraphrased comparatively more extensively than German sources, for example, for a purely practical reason.

[10] Cf. The preliminary remarks to my introduction to the *Efterskrift* [Postscript], II, 1962, 1-3.

philosophical system nor of Kierkegaard's world of thought in this study, but only to give an account in sufficient detail of the parts of each that have something to do with each other, so that these accounts will explicitly and implicitly be compatible with a complete understanding of Hegel's and Kierkegaard's thoughts, which may be considered to be consistent with their own intention and achievement. With this it naturally follows that along the way there will be occasions to take a position on the question of how Kierkegaard's understanding of Hegel can be characterized.

In this study, only in a very limited way is a direct position taken concerning the very rich body of research on Hegel as well as of that on Kierkegaard. But specialists will immediately recognize that the present investigation would have turned out differently, probably essentially poorer than it is, if I had not incurred a very significant indebtedness to many of those who through the years have been concerned with Hegel, Kierkegaard, and with the chief topic of this study.

5. There is an extraordinary relation between quotations, allusions, and references to Hegel in the entire first period of Kierkegaard's Authorship up to and including the *Postscript*, on the one hand, where they seem to occur rather sporadically and by chance, and on the other hand in the whole of this Authorship, which can very well be read as a great counterpart to Hegel. A clarification of this must be sought.

Hegel, especially in *Phenomenology of Spirit, Science of Logic*, and *Encyclopedia of the Philosophical Sciences*, presents the stages from immediacy to absolute knowledge as a development that proceeds with absolute necessity and in such a way that the singular human individual threatens to vanish completely in the world-historical development.

Kierkegaard presents the stages from immediacy to faith as a development that must take place in a leap, in freedom and in such a way that the individual, the singular existing human, is all-important. The world-historical process, on the contrary, has no special significance.

Thus seen, Hegel and Kierkegaard have in the main nothing in common as thinkers, neither as regards object, purpose, or method, nor as regards what each considered to be indisputable principles.

This can be designated this investigation's chief and major thesis.

Historically seen, the knowledge of this fundamental incompatibility was, for Kierkegaard, the result of a process of clarification, both with respect to his own problematic and the whole realm of thought and with respect to its relation to Hegel and to the school of speculative idealism. This process of clarification was essentially completed around the time of the publication of *Either/Or*.

This can be called the second thesis of this investigation.

The Authorship in its first period (up to and including the *Postscript*) may be understood, consonant with the above, as Kierkegaard's radical cure for a contemporary age suffering from an attack of "speculation."

This can be called the third thesis of this study.

Kierkegaard's knowledge of Hegel and of his disciples' thought was complete and accurate on the points he was interested in attacking; but beyond that, it can scarcely be correctly described as particularly extensive or exhaustive. His understanding of Hegel continued to bear the mark of the interpretations of right-wing Hegelians, as he had learned to know them in his final years as a student. His estimate of Hegel became unsympathetic, first in individual respects, and—gradually, as his own theology and anthropology were clarified and got a firm formulation—then in every respect. Although he retained respect for Hegel, his disdain for Hegel's adherents increased from year to year.[11]

This can be called the fourth thesis of this investigation.

[11] Figuratively speaking, it can be said that Kierkegaard considered Hegel to be a wolf in sheep's clothing, while he regarded the Hegelians as a flock of sheep pure and simple.

CHAPTER I

Hegelianism in Denmark until the Summer of 1835 and Kierkegaard's Relation Thereto

1. POINT OF DEPARTURE

IN A DRAFT of a letter sent to his distant relative P. W. Lund, dated June 1, 1835,[1] and in an entry in the *Papirer* (I A 75)[a] of August 1 the same year, we find Kierkegaard's first detailed reckoning of intellectual and spiritual accounts.

It is natural, then, to let these documents serve as a focal point for an interpretation of Kierkegaard's perspective, interests, and problems as a young theological student. Obviously in this investigation such an interpretation must concentrate especially on Kierkegaard's possible knowledge of Hegelianism such as he could have encountered it in the intellectual environment of Copenhagen. But before interpreting Kierkegaard's notes it is necessary to discuss the background so as to exhibit the main lines of the history of Hegelianism in Denmark up to the summer of 1835.

2. HEIBERG'S HEGELIANISM

In his *Autobiografiske Fragmenter*, written in November-December 1839, J. L. Heiberg recounted his philosophical conversion to Hegel's system.[2] Previously he knew about Hegel partly by having heard about him at the University of Kiel and partly by having read one of the Master's chief works, and finally he had become personally acquainted with Hegel and his leading disciple in Berlin. As Heiberg tells it:

[1] *Papirer,* I A 72; *Breve og Aktstykker vedrørende Søren Kierkegaard,* No. 3 with commentary.

[a] An English translation of much of this important "Gilleleie entry" will be found in Alexander Dru's selections from *The Journals of Kierkegaard* (New York: Harper Torchbooks, 1959).

[2] Johan Ludvig Heiberg, *Prosaiske Skrifter,* XI (1862), 498ff. Kierkegaard had read these "prose writings" when they were first published: see the *Postscript,* pp. 163-164. [SK's unmerciful and hilarious satire of Heiberg's account of his conversion to Hegelianism will be found on these pages.]

I heard Hegel mentioned by the teachers at the University of Kiel, but in a way which would discourage me from getting acquainted with his writings. Only Etatsraad Berger, the Professor of Philosophy, mentioned him as an extraordinary man, who had brought philosophy to a higher plateau, but whose writings required a great effort and a very serious resolve to understand. He enjoined me especially (in a letter, which I still have),[3] on this point when he, at my request, loaned me Hegel's *Encyclopedia*. When I began to read the book I had to affirm his remark, and I would likely have given up the endeavor, had I not believed that in some spots I glimpsed a guiding star, so as to suspect a connection between the thoughts which struck a responsive chord with my own views, and led me to give them a more conscious expression than I had previously formed. At the same time (the summer of 1824) I had to travel to Berlin on private business; and since together with other introductions I had obtained, I also had got from Berger an oral greeting to Hegel, and since I should soon meet him face to face, it was doubly urgent for me to make myself somewhat familiar with his system. Before my departure I had to return the book Berger loaned me; but as soon as I arrived in Hamburg, I bought a copy, which I took with me in the stage-coach, where I, sitting next to the driver, alternately chatted with him and studied the *Encyclopedia*, which I just finished reading the moment we rolled within the gates of Berlin. During the two months I stayed in the city I became ever more and more engrossed in the new system, not only through cursory reading of many [*endeel*] of Hegel's writings, but also and chiefly through conversations with the most distinguished local Hegelians, especially Gans, and not least with Hegel himself, who answered my immature observations with the greatest good nature, and in whose home I also enjoyed many pleasant hours. Yet on my departure from Berlin I was still somewhat confused about the new material I had acquired: I could not find the right pivotal point from which the whole manifested itself in its inner structure. When now on the journey home I stopped off to rest in Hamburg, where I stayed for six weeks before returning to Kiel, during this time I constantly brooded over

[3] *Breve og Aktstykker vedrørende Johan Ludvig Heiberg*, ed. Morten Borup, I (1946), No. 115, with commentary in Vol. V, 1950. On this whole matter, see Borup's biography of Heiberg, especially I (1947), 137ff.

what was still obscure to me, it happened that one day while I was sitting in my room in the "König von England," with Hegel on my table and Hegel in my thoughts, and at the same time listening to some beautiful hymns which almost constantly sounded from the choir of St. Peter's Church, suddenly, in a way which I have never before or since experienced, I was gripped by a moment of inner vision, like a flash of lightning, which suddenly illuminated the whole region for me and awakened in me the previously concealed central thought. From that moment on, the system in its large outlines was clear to me, and I was completely convinced that I had grasped it in its innermost nucleus, however much more there could be in the details, which I still had not grasped, and would perhaps never acquire. I can truly say that this wonderful moment was the most important event in my life, for it gave me a peace, a security, which I had never before known. Immediately upon my arrival in Kiel, when I became aware of the deterministic controversies taking place in Copenhagen at the time, and realized that the point of contention would appear in an absolutely new light if considered from a Hegelian perspective, I wrote my treatise on human freedom, the first Danish work which gave a glimpse of the Hegelian philosophy. When one considers that this work came out in December 1824, and that in the month of May in the same year I scarcely knew that there was a philosopher named Hegel, then the fact that in such a short time I could achieve so much as that otherwise imperfect work contains, can best show with what voraciousness I had devoured the new wisdom, and from this again one could imagine the desire I must have felt for it before I knew it, and—when indeed on such an important point I could not be entirely different from my contemporaries—how much the world was filled with the same desire. It is certain that the new light which arose for me, has had a decided influence on all my subsequent undertakings, even those in which one would not suspect a connection. Thus, for example, I would never have come to write my comedies, and would never have become a writer for the theater at all if I had not through Hegelian philosophy learned to perceive the relation between the finite and the infinite, and thereby acquired a respect for finite things which I did not previously have, but which the dramatist cannot possibly do without, and if, again, I had not learned to understand the meaning of limitation through the same philosophy, for without that I would neither have limited myself nor chosen small and limited things, having previously disdained limits to my expression.

There can hardly be any doubt that Heiberg has sketched here his philosophical conversion and its psychological significance for his attitude toward life and activity in the main credibly. With the help of Hegel's philosophy he got a grip on himself. That this is the case can be gathered from his writings and correspondence from subsequent years and requires—in this connection—no further substantiation. Unfortunately we must point out an important omission—or mistake perhaps—in Heiberg's otherwise so valuable, learned, faithful, and loyal biographer and editor, Morten Borup. In his great work, which is certainly detailed and careful but does not display enough psychological and philosophical understanding, Borup describes both Heiberg's encounter with Hegel's philosophy and Heiberg's understanding, interpretation, and use of it; at the same time he frequently allows himself to express regret precisely over Hegel's influence and meaning for Heiberg.[4]

If it is correct that Hegel's importance for Heiberg may be described as chiefly positive in the sense that, with the help of Hegel, Heiberg found enlightenment and security, then it is still appropriate to correct along with Borup a demonstrable mistake in Heiberg's *Autobiografiske Fragmenter*, which has been accepted uncritically in many places, and thereby pose the question of how Heiberg interpreted Hegel in 1824.

Heiberg says that he borrowed Hegel's *Encyclopedia of the Philosophical Sciences* from Johann Erick von Berger, who in his later years had turned away from Schelling's and Steffens's thought to Hegel's system.[5]

It was, as it appears from the cited[b] letter from Berger—printed in Borup—not Hegel's *Encyclopedia*, but his *Science of Logic* that Heiberg borrowed from him and read first. That makes a difference; but how great the significance of this difference is for understanding Heiberg's first Hegelian treatise can be established only

[4] Morten Borup, *Johan Ludvig Heiberg*, e.g., I (1947), 152-53.

[5] S. V. Rasmussen in *Dansk Biografisk Leksikon*, II, 455-56, cf. e.g., J. E. Erdmann, *Grundriss der Geschichte der Philosophie*, II, 3rd ed. (1878), 532, and Ueberweg, IV, 13th ed. (1951), 101.

[b] See note 3 *supra*.

approximately, when there is no reason to doubt the correctness of
Heiberg's assertions that before, during, and after his sojourn in
Berlin he had perused other works of Hegel.

In the summer of 1824 the following major philosophical works
of Hegel were available—the treatises published by Hegel himself
prior to *Phenomenology of the Spirit* are not particularly important
in this context—*Phenomenology of the Spirit, Science of Logic,
Encyclopedia of the Philosophical Sciences,* and *Elements [Grund-
linien] of the Philosophy of Right.* Rubow correctly asserts that this
last work especially made a profound impression on Heiberg.[6]

It is not necessary to go into the Howitz controversy itself here.[7]
Only Heiberg's position in its relation to Hegel must be clarified.

Only twice in the treatise on free will does Heiberg refer explicitly to Hegel, *viz.* on page 7, where he recommends that Howitz
read Hegel's account of the concept of the will in *Philosophy of
Right,* and on page 22, where he quotes in translation the famous
passage from *Phenomenology of the Spirit* (SW II, 12)[8c] about the
blossom that yields to the bud, which in turn yields to the fruit,
illustrating the unfolding of a concept both in the microcosm and
in the macrocosm.[9]

Both references are full of significance. The theme of the treatise

[6] *Dansk litterær Kritik i det nittende Aarhundrede,* 1921, 96.

[7] This dispute concerning the freedom of the will has been treated in various places, among others, by Harald Høffding in *Danske Filosofer* (1909),
81-88, and by Oluf Thomsen, *F. G. Howitz og hans Strid om "Villiens
Frihed"* (1924); see also e.g., Jens Himmelstrup, *Sibbern* (1934), 175.

[8] Herman Glockner's *Jubiläumsausgabe,* I-XX, of the works of Hegel is
used here, which gives the text Heiberg and Kierkegaard knew. Lasson's and
Hoffmeister's editions are much to be preferred from a philological viewpoint; but Kierkegaard and his contemporaries could have known only part
of the text as contained there. In the summary account of the philosophy of
freedom in Hegel's philosophy of right no consideration is given to the additions taken from students' notebooks in the edition of Hegel's complete
works. Heiberg could not have known about them when he wrote his treatise on Freedom.

[c] In the revised second edition of J. B. Baillie's translation of this work
(the title is rendered as *The Phenomenology of Mind,* although I think that
"Spirit" would be a better choice for Hegel's use of *"Geist"*) into English
(London: George Allen & Unwin, 1949), this passage appears on p. 68. In
what follows, I shall give page references to this edition of the English translation of *Phänomenologie des Geistes* although I may alter some of the translations from German into English.

[9] The page references are to the printed version of *Om den menneskelige
Frihed* in Heiberg's *Prosaiske Skrifter,* I (1861).

is precisely the problem of human freedom, the freedom of the will, and Heiberg wishes to show there that the positions of Howitz and his opponents are stages—with a relative legitimacy—on the way of dialectical unfolding toward the summit of speculation, represented by Hegel and presented by Heiberg, who closes his treatise with the claim (page 70) that all speculation consists of a leap out of time into the world of ideas. With this assertion Heiberg ignores, in the first place, that there can be no talk about a leap in Hegelian philosophy and, in the second place, that the world of ideas, identical with the Hegelian philosophy of spirit, the third and highest part of the system, consisting of art, religion, and philosophy, is precisely declared to be in and not above time, namely within the fixed limits of the objective spirit.

In the detailed footnotes of the treatise, Heiberg refers to Hegel more frequently. Also from the Preface of *Phenomenology of the Spirit* is the remark about the absolute (of Schelling) understood as the night where all cats are gray (SW II, 22)[d], and in one place in the treatise (page 26) where Heiberg tries to explain that there is a gradual transition in Nature from the lowest matter to the highest rational being, the human, he refers—in connection with his claim that "even the animal behaves as a subject, as it consumes the plants, which it sets as its object"—to Hegel's statement in the section "Sensory Certainty" (SW II, 90-91) [Eng. pp. 158-159] with its curious juxtaposition of the Eleusinian mysteries and the behavior of animals. Heiberg could be right in calling that passage in Hegel remarkable. Further on Heiberg suggests that mental illness [*Sindssygdomme*] really ought to be called dislocation [*Forrykthed*] (p. 84), "because all mental illness consists in this, that the objective ego becomes dislocated or torn away from its normal position in relation to the subjective," and in this connection he refers to Hegel's *Encyclopedia of the Philosophical Sciences* §321 (2nd ed., §408);[10] but there is no need to delve further into this point here. Heiberg also gives a significant reference to *Philosophy of*

---

[d] This is certainly a minor point, but Glockner's *Jubiläumsausgabe* gives this as: ". . . die Nacht . . . , worin, wie man zu sagen pflegt, alle Kühe schwarz sind. . ." English translation, p. 279.

[10] Cf. on this Søren Holm in *Religionsfilosofiske Essays* (1943), 98, where it is reported that Heiberg's copy of the third edition of the *Encyclopedia* "does not bear the mark of having been thoroughly studied." [Hegel's *Philosophy of Mind* (Part III of the *Encyclopedia*) trans. William Wallace (Oxford: Clarendon Press, 1894), pp. 36-39. Page references to the English translation of the Third Part of the *Encyclopedia* will be according to this edition.]

Right (§99-103) where Hegel discusses the concept of punishment and holds that Hegel's theory is "the only reasonable [one]."[11]

These are the explicit quotations and references to Hegel's three chief works, or, more correctly, three of his chief works. *Science of Logic* is not expressly named.

If we proceed from these secure points of contact between Heiberg and Hegel to the total philosophical view that Heiberg presents, then we can derive some observations that will not be without meaning for the broader investigation not only of Heiberg's Hegelianism but of the chief theme, namely Kierkegaard's relation to Hegel.

Thus we can take Heiberg's definition of man as a point of departure:

> Man is a substance, or that which has an existence in itself, not in something external and alien. Or, with respect to the external, man is essentially subject, just as the external is essentially object. Man's striving for detachment from restraint is therefore—when the restraint is the external—the subject's striving for detachment from the object . . . man is the subjective, restraint is the objective; this I, that not I; this intelligence, that nature; this spirit, that matter (pp. 19-20).

The spirit strives with an eternal urgency to obtain what it already possesses, and it must do that because it is immersed in the stream of time. "The eternal idea must, in this changeable realm, go out of itself, squander its indivisible power in discrete successions, and be pleased that in the extended it can disclose something of its intensity" (p. 21). As essentially spirit, man is free, although under the apparent restraint of space, he must constantly strive to become so in time (p. 22). A little further on it is said that man is the good, and therefore he cannot will what is opposed to himself. Insofar as man wills something, he must will the good (p. 24). Evil, considered in its innermost nature, is "pure matter, stripped of all intelligence . . . that which man cannot imagine, and which therefore cannot be for man either" (p. 25). In spite of such a statement, Heiberg identifies several types of manifestations of evil.

---

[11] Heiberg, p. 67. There is no reason to go into Hegel's discussion of Beccaria and the elder Feuerbach on the theory of penal law here. [Cf. Hegel's *Philosophy of Right*, trans. T. M. Knox (Oxford: The Clarendon Press, 1952), pp. 69-73. See also pp. 246-247.]

In the material world, evil expresses itself as sickness, in which the inferior, organic matter battles against the superior, the more intelligent. In the moral world, evil shows itself in the life of the individual as vice, in civil society as injustice. The basis for both is egoism, and it expresses itself in the first instance as rebellion against the law which governs all things, in the second case as despotism. In art evil manifests itself as the ugly, in science [*Videnskaben*] as the false or error in opposition to the truth; but all error contains a portion of truth, without which it would never find room in our consciousness, and if it cannot do that, then it recedes back to nothing (pp. 37-41).

Man wills the good and, as essentially spirit, possesses freedom for that; but freedom—which must not be understood as a single individual's *libertas indifferentiae*[e]—is at one and the same time positive and negative (p. 44); positive in its reality as Idea, negative in man's effort to actualize the Idea as Ideal, in time.

> Man *is* free (in the Idea), but he must necessarily work for his liberation (in time). Or, in other words: man is free in the Idea, but on the other hand, in time he is subjected to necessity, but this necessity itself impels him toward freedom, which is the principle of both necessity and liberty. Only the principle remains on this highest standpoint; its disclosure in time, under the forms of necessity and liberty, disappears, and, so too, with them evil. Here man is *absolutely free* (p. 44).

Absolute freedom is identical with the good. Man's striving for freedom is virtue, in which he is at once free and constrained, for in part duty implies freedom to be able both to fulfill and to infringe, partly the word itself suggests something that may, ought, and should be, i.e., a necessity (p. 47). But sin consists in simultaneously relinquishing freedom and eluding necessity. Freedom and necessity condition each other reciprocally as the principle and

[e] "Liberty of indifference." This refers to the theory of free will that holds that the human will is free with respect to particular goods, to which there can always be alternatives. Since I am neither more nor less strongly inclined to one rather than the other, I am, as it were, "indifferent" to each, and so my choice of one is free inasmuch as I determine the choice. St. Augustine regarded this as the lowest degree of freedom. Cf. St. Thomas Aquinas, *Summa Theologiae*, Ia, q. 82 art. 2, *corpus articuli*; Francis Suarez, *Disputationes Metaphysicae*, disp. XIX; and Descartes, *Meditations*, IV, for various points of view concerning "liberty of indifference."

its consequences, so that we can say both that necessity is free and freedom is necessary. Life is the contradiction between the Idea and the phenomenon, and to cancel this contradiction requires something more than the absolute, which is nothing other than its empty abstraction. It can be canceled only by annihilating the world of phenomena (p. 55), and the will's empirical freedom rests on the difference between the world of Ideas and the incorrectly so-called reality. The will balances on this line of demarcation (p. 57).

In a letter to H. C. Ørsted on March 25, 1825,[12] Heiberg tries on the one hand to point out his independence in relation to Hegel; on the other hand, he does not conceal his admiration and his actual approval of Hegel's philosophy. The independence in the treatise on human freedom should in any case manifest itself in the method. It is quite evident that, to as great a degree as was possible for him, he wished to adopt not only the content of Hegelian philosophy but also in some way its form. The works of Hegel that he explicitly cited and quoted were his chief sources and guides. Not the least of them was *Philosophy of Right*, which played a decisive role for Heiberg, as Rubow correctly asserts.

If the facts are as stated here, then there is good reason to point out something about the special character of Heiberg's Hegelianism, as it was expressed in the treatise on human freedom.

At the beginning of this treatise Heiberg raises the objection that Howitz had not understood Schelling's treatise on human freedom "for everything that Schelling intended in an ideal sense Howitz took in an empirical meaning" (p. 7).[f]

Now we cannot correctly make the same sort of objection against Heiberg in connection with Hegel that Heiberg makes against Howitz concerning Schelling. For there can be little doubt about Heiberg's intention, nor about his ability by and large to reproduce Hegel's view in a formally correct way and to apply it validly in a particular instance, viz., the philosophical debate about Howitz. But we can maintain that Heiberg's Hegelianism, as expressed in *this* treatise, does not—despite all his honest efforts—give evidence of a complete understanding of the unique character of Hegelian

[12] Number 126 in Borup's edition [see note 3 *supra*].

[f] This is not surprising, since unlike his opponents (Heiberg, Sibbern, et al.) who took a generally German, and particularly Kantian, philosophical viewpoint, Howitz was oriented toward Hume in general and was to some extent influenced by the deterministic view of Spinoza.

philosophy. When Hegel uses concepts such as spirit [*Aand*], freedom, necessity, compulsion, etc., in his systematic writings, these
concepts are primarily qualified by the fact that they are speculative
determinations, i.e., links, elements of what he intended to be an
exhaustive description of the Absolute, i.e., God. So also with the
concept of man in Hegel. It is not a general concept for a group of
living substances, but a portion of the speculative essential determination of God, about which the whole philosophy of Hegel
wishes to treat. Hegel's anthropology is a part of his theology.

This does not seem to have occurred to Heiberg when he wrote
his treatise on freedom. Heiberg sees Hegel as "one of the greatest
geniuses, with whom philosophy has reached such a development
that I cannot envision what new direction it should take henceforth to develop further . . . for everything is found in his system,
without the least lack."[13] At this stage Heiberg has not seen that
Hegel, even when he seems just to be speaking of concrete
phenomena, nevertheless constantly speaks abstractly and speculatively. This is the case in Hegel's systematic works, not in the
political and aesthetical-historical periodical articles during his last
years. One instance of this is Hegel's doctrine of the objective spirit,
concerning which *Philosophy of Right* forms one major part, while
Philosophy of History is the other. This may be found also in
Hegel's teaching on the subjective spirit as well as in his doctrine of
the absolute spirit, where he constantly speaks in an abstract-
speculative way, although empirical-concrete material can be
pointed out. Thus the state, which he exhibits in *Philosophy of
Right*, is not basically identical with Prussia at the time of the
Restoration. Although for Hegel Prussia could be the earthly city
—not the devil's city!—his speculative state was the city of God.
Civil society, which Heiberg places highest in his treatise, is [for
Heiberg] only a transitional point, a stage in the Absolute Spirit's
effort toward complete unfolding of itself within the given con-
straints of matter, space, and time.

In *Groundwork of the Metaphysic of Morals*,[g] Kant had held that
there are three conditions for the possibility of ethics:

---

[13] Letter to Ørsted. See note 12 *supra*.

[g] This work has been translated into English under a number of titles. In
addition to the one above other versions of the title are: *The Moral Law;
Foundations of the Metaphysics of Morals*; and *Fundamental Principles of
the Metaphysics of Morals*.

1) there must be found one common moral law for all rational beings,

2) respect for the moral law, and

3) the postulate of man's freedom to follow the moral law.

As part of the phenomenal world, man is causally determined; as a part of the noumenal world, man, as an intelligent being, has freedom and therefore duty and responsibility. From this Kant's thought goes on to the doctrine of the categorical imperative.

As is well known, Kierkegaard complained that the Hegelian system had one decisive omission, namely, an ethics. But the problem of freedom, even as a major issue in ethics, is treated by Hegel especially in the work that played such an important role for Heiberg, namely *Philosophy of Right*.[14]

We said above that *Philosophy of Right* is one part of the doctrine of the objective Spirit. The work elaborates a philosophy of freedom. It was written and published after *Encyclopedia of the Philosophical Sciences*, and can be regarded as a further development of one of the main sections of the *Encyclopedia*, namely the second section of the third part (in the third edition, §§483-552), and indicates the negation in the triad: subjective spirit, objective spirit, Absolute Spirit. Within the confines of this negation (narrow limits insofar as Hegel's ideal state is not a universal state, but a national state bounded by others), the Absolute Spirit must unfold itself in art, religion, and philosophy.

In *Philosophy of Right* §1, it is said that "The philosophical science of right is concerned with the idea of right, the concept of right and its actualization." Right, which according to Hegel may take the form of a positive right, has a certain Idea, namely freedom. Its basis is the mental, and its place and point of departure is the will, which is free (§4), understood in such a way that freedom constitutes the substance and goal of right, and "the system of right is the realm of actualized freedom."[h] What is meant by this, Hegel has put in the most concise possible form in the *Encyclopedia* (2nd and 3rd editions) §487, where he says that "The free will is:

"A. First itself immediate, and hence as a single individual,—

[14] A monograph on Hegel's ethics has been done by H. A. Reyburn, *The Ethical Theory of Hegel* (Oxford, 1921).

[h] A convenient English translation is Knox's translation: Hegel's *Philosophy of Right*, although my translation of the passages quoted from Hegel's German differs slightly from that of Knox.

the person; the presence [*Daseyn*] which the individual gives to its freedom is property. The right as such is formal, abstract right." This is treated in detail in *Philosophy of Right*, First Part: "Abstract Right" (Property, Contract, Wrong).

"B. Reflected in itself, so as to be present within itself, and in this way at the same time is defined as a particular,—the right of subjective will, morality." This is dealt with in *Philosophy of Right*, Second Part: "Morality" (Purpose and Responsibility, Intention and Welfare, Good and Conscience, with the significant concluding section on the moral structure of evil).

"C. The substantial will as reality according to its concept in the subject and as a totality of necessity, morality, the family, civil society, and the State."[i] This is handled in *Philosophy of Right*, Third Part, the three sections of which deal with the family, civil society, and the state.

The philosophy of freedom that, according to the above, Hegel develops in his *Philosophy of Right* thus also contains a section on the individual human's will; but—quite characteristically—this problem is dealt with in the dialectical development of the concept under negation, that is the negation of abstract right. Only because the development must proceed with necessity through negation does the individual human will have its philosophical place and, with that, legitimacy. Moreover, since it is Hegel's notion that this dialectical development proceeds with an immanent necessity, then, whatever else he says about the individual human's will, it is totally indifferent whether it is described as bound or free, since each individual human as a totality with necessity participates in this inexorable development. The freedom that in this respect can be spoken of as individual is illusory, when every individual with necessity must as a matter of principle, theoretically and in the practical order accept the development, of which he himself as an individual plays a negligible role.

The difference from Kant is so immediately obvious that it is hardly necessary to emphasize it here. But Kierkegaard's complaint

[i] I must admit that I despair of rendering Hegel's German in "C" into intelligible and accurate English. The Wallace translation, Hegel's *Philosophy of Mind*, gives it thus: "When the free will is the substantial will, made actual in the subject and conformable to its concept and rendered a totality of necessity—it is the ethics of actual life in family, civil society and State." Granted that this is smooth and clear, I don't see how it is justified on the basis of the original.

that the Hegelian system lacks an ethics is—seen from the Hegelian perspective—not warranted. The system contains a descriptive ethics, which also can be called normative, insofar as we inconsistently (from the Hegelian point of view) wish to describe the Idea as ideal.

If we now compare individual points in Heiberg with individual points in Hegel, indeed, even his whole doctrine of freedom with that of Hegel, then we will see that Heiberg wanted to be a faithful disciple of Hegel and that he wanted to say the same thing as his master. If we then ask whether Heiberg, when he wrote his treatise on freedom, understood Hegelian philosophy in its proper totality, as it is sketched here, then the answer must be that Heiberg's treatise does not bear witness to any exhaustive understanding. This observation is significant for the larger investigation, since there is a question, which has not been raised and answered satisfactorily in previous research, of what role Heiberg's and other Hegelians' understanding of Hegel played for Kierkegaard. It is a possibility that has not been thoroughly analyzed that the Hegelians', particularly the Danish Hegelians', understanding of Hegel radically influenced Kierkegaard's understanding or, more correctly, gave him a prejudiced view which he retained when he began to read Hegel's own works.

It is, moreover, characteristic of Heiberg—cf. the letter to Ørsted —that he understood Hegel's thought as the crown on the development of philosophy despite the fundamental break with modern philosophy—that which begins with Descartes—that Hegel represents by leaving aside the problem of the theory of knowledge for the sake of the ontological problem. *Phenomenology of the Spirit* marks the break.

This should not in and of itself place the blame on Heiberg, since the understanding of Hegel he presents was and is a common one, one praised by Hegel himself (*Lectures on the History of Philosophy*, III, 545ff.). It cannot be called absolutely incorrect, but we can correctly speak of it as a variation on the norm even if we— in line with the usual presentations of the history of modern philosophy, in which Kant is described as a critical idealist, Fichte as a subjective idealist, Schelling as an objective idealist, and Hegel as an absolute idealist—can mention many grounds that can testify to the advantage of an interpretation such as the one Heiberg has undertaken. It can also turn out that Kierkegaard's understanding of Hegel's situation in the historical development of philosophy is an assessment like Heiberg's. Moreover, without anticipating the outcome of this investigation, it can already be said, that when Kierkegaard so frequently in the first period of the Authorship mocks Martensen's (among others') attempt to "go beyond" Hegel, this is an important indication of the way Kierkegaard understood Hegel, both as regards his place in history and his systematic rank.

Heiberg's treatise on the problem of freedom was written for a particular occasion. His *Ledetraad ved Forelæsningerne over Philosophiens Philosophie eller den speculative Logik*,[j] which was printed for private circulation in 1831-1832, has the character of a textbook, while the prospectus *Om Philosophiens Betydning for den nuværende Tid*[k] was a manifesto intended not only for specialists but also for the general, cultivated reader. This appeared in 1833 as a prospectus for a series of philosophical lectures that was canceled for lack of audience.[15]

Heiberg's position is that one finds himself in a crisis situation, and that there is only one salvation in this unstable situation, namely, speculative, Hegelian philosophy.

At this point, in order to clarify for his readers what he means by saying that speculative philosophy is the salvation of the age, Heiberg first develops what, according to his understanding, philosophy is. "Philosophy is nothing other than the knowledge of the eternal or the speculative Idea, the Reason, the Truth; these different expressions all signify the same Substance. Philosophy exhibits the Idea as the only Cause, and consequently can find no other than it in all finite effects" (pp. 385-386). The various philosophical systems—given that they are permeated with the speculative Idea—all contain the same philosophy, only seen from diverse stages of civilization in the development of mankind "just as the different religions all contain the same God, regarded from diverse perspectives in the religious Idea" (386). Every age that is not in a critical transition, but that finds itself in an orderly and peaceful condition, has its philosophy, which is the outcome of all previous experience and of the knowledge that fund of experience had produced. The raw material of philosophy is the past as something finished, something at hand, which philosophy by its treatment

[j] [Guide to the Lectures on the Philosophy of Philosophy or Speculative Logic.] As far as I know, this has not been translated.

[k] [On the Significance of Philosophy for the Present Age.]

[15] J. L. Heiberg's *Prosaiske Skrifter*, I (1861), 381ff. References in the sequel are to this edition.

turns into something present. We cannot say that philosophy is the work of the philosophers, because it is not individual philosophers who have created ideas, truth, and reason; but they have discovered them and expressed them in the changing forms of changing eras. This corresponds, according to Heiberg, to the fact that teachers of religion did not themselves produce the religion they teach (p. 388),

> indeed, not anyone will even dare to claim this about the founders of religions, when thereby one must also maintain that truth was lacking in some of the religions. Least of all can we as Christians accept the notion that the founder of our religion was its producer, when he has himself explicitly proclaimed himself to be the Son who was sent forth by the Father. But the Father did not send the Son before the fullness of time had come, i.e., when the present was ended and completed, and thus belonged to the past, to the dead, then there was also a raw material, a formless substance, which in the acquisition of a new form could find a revival of the dead (388-389).

The influence of Hegel's *Philosophy of History* on Heiberg is obvious here and in what follows. The divine must turn back to mankind,

> and thus the finite is reconciled with the Infinite; it was necessary that the divine as human should take up His abode among mankind. Therefore we can correctly say that the Christian religion was a work, not of Christ, but of humanity; this is just why the Son was sent, not by Himself, but by the Father, for whatever is a work of mankind is thereby also a work of God (390).

The same may be said about art and poetry. Neither art, poetry, religion, nor philosophy gives people anything really new, but opens their eyes to what they already have. The individuals in whom human consciousness is awakened to a higher clarity are the artists, poets, teachers of religion, and philosophers, who all "hold up the mirror in which mankind sees itself and becomes conscious of itself as its own object" (391).

If, as has been said earlier, it is true that philosophy cannot arise before it has a content available, then it is clear, Heiberg maintains, in the first place that the present age cannot yet have its own philosophy, when the age itself is in a state of crisis, in a transition, in which the content is still present and not incorporated into the realm of the dead; in the second place, this is a lack that the various efforts of the period strive to overcome.

The question thus becomes, what is the past and what is the present? Whether something is classified present or past varies with the context and with the point of view of the person classifying. If we look at the present age, we find that something considered present or contemporary by the uneducated is considered past by the educated. As an example of this Heiberg adduces (p. 395) the theological controversies of the time which are, no doubt, carried on by the educated but which are of present concern for the un-educated. Heiberg does not hold that the theologians are un-educated, but he maintains that "the educated, who have gone beyond this standpoint, are almost unaffected by it, but find their heaven and their hell in political agitation" (395). "There is no use in our wanting to conceal or gloss over the truth: we must admit to ourselves that in our time religion is for the most part a concern only of the uneducated, while for the cultured world it belongs to the past, to the rejected" (396). Now it is politics that occupies the educated class, a situation Heiberg deplores on the basis of principle: "for after having abandoned religion and the recogni-tion of the Infinite, they [i.e., contemporary political characters] have only finite categories left, and with these they nevertheless wish to construct an eternal state and an eternal constitution" (397). To return to religion in its earlier form is no answer, no refuge in the situation of crisis, and art and poetry fare no better; but "Philos-ophy . . . shall put an end to the confusion" (402), and it can do that because truth is both its content and its structure, indeed, its only content and its only structure. We can neither doubt nor deny the truth, everyone must yield to it; and since the truth is adequate-ly expressed in philosophy, then obviously philosophy must become the supreme judge and rescue. Surely art, poetry, and religion con-tain the same truth as philosophy, but not according to the proper structure of truth: "That is, in [art, poetry, and religion] truth is substantially present, and has there various accidental forms; but in [philosophy] truth is present as concept, and the concept has only one form, just as matter does" (404).

In addition to politics Heiberg also identifies natural science as an interest of the age. Like politics, it [natural science] is an activity in the finite world, whereas art, poetry, and religion are realizations of the infinite in the finite, and also represent a reconciliation, although only in accidental ways. Only philosophy is in a position both to provide recognition for art, poetry, and religion, not to mention natural science and politics, but also to confirm their legitimacy. Philosophy is the integrating factor both for the infinite endeavors, art, poetry, religion, and for the finite ones, of which politics is the dominant one.

All three—art, poetry, and religion—contain the truth, and philosophy is thereby their integrating factor, which must now develop itself into the concept (410). As far as religion is concerned, to a certain extent it coincides with philosophy, as religion itself contains philosophy, i.e., the truth; but it differs from philosophy with respect to form. Philosophy exhibits the same content as religion, but in a form that is not distinct from its content, unlike religion. It is the nature of religion to be a particular religion, while it is the case that for philosophy in each of its systems to be a particular philosophy is something accidental to the nature of philosophy. The distinction between the systems is dissolved by philosophy itself, properly so-called (p. 412), while the same may not be said for religion, which exhibits the infinite from the standpoint of the finite. The relations art and poetry have to philosophy are different. In them the accidental form is unimportant: "One type of literature does not stand as an enemy against another; all are equally good, for they all have substantially the same nature" (413), by which they are distinct from religion and in harmony with philosophy.

"Philosophy is thus the foundation in which our finite as well as our infinite goals find their truth and thereby their justification and claim to validity" (414). The sickness of the age, which is identical with a crisis, cannot be cured except by philosophy (415).

Heiberg will then maintain that Goethe and Hegel are the two greatest minds produced in the modern period. Having described Goethe's superiority over other poets, Heiberg asserts (430) that Hegel's system is the same as Goethe's. Just as the poetry of Goethe does, it reconciles the ideal with the real, which is precisely the task of philosophy at the present moment. With that Heiberg has shown why he wishes to deliver the planned series of lectures, and he even says directly that he will adhere to the Hegelian system (431), "but in such a way that he will be sure to distinguish between that which can only be thought to be peculiar to Hegel and that which he has expressed in the name of humanity; for only the latter, not the former, is our common property, our true philosophy" (432). This philosophy must not be described as something new nor as something individual. It is the point of departure and measure of all intellectual endeavors, and philosophy is nothing but the recognition of the truth already arrived at by these endeavors. Hegel's system has the merit that it is the most comprehensive thus far. That it has not gained its merited dissemination and recognition is in this connection insignificant.

It is clear that by comparison with his essay on freedom there is in Heiberg's prospectus described above evidence of progress made toward an assimilation of Hegel's philosophy. But here, too, we find a treatment of Hegel that basically is extremely simple, in fact even trite. The famous statement in the preface of *Philosophy of Right* that "What is rational is actual and what is actual is rational"[16] could well be placed as a motto over Heiberg's prospectus with the understanding that actuality is identified with concrete empirical actuality, which is not the case for Hegel himself.[17] As in

[16] SW VII, 33 (Eng. trans. p 10).

[17] On this point *cf.* for example, Karl Rosenkranz, *Hegel's Leben*, 1844, 335: "He [Hegel] was later in the second edition of his *Encyclopedia* required to give the clarification that by actuality [*Wirklichkeit*] he understood not only the empirical, with the contingent, but also mixed with the inferior and non-necessary existence [*Dasein*], but on the contrary the concept of reason identical with existence. Then if the actual is taken according to his view, the common appearance and immediate reality are subsumed under it, so that there is no question but that these cannot be irrational either." [T. M. Knox, trans., *Philosophy of Right*, has added an explanatory footnote to this statement of Hegel, and it is well worth adding here: "This statement is further explained and defended in Enc., §6. Note that Hegel is not saying that what exists or is 'real' is rational. By 'actuality' (see Translator's Foreword, §3) he means the synthesis of essence and existence. If we say of a statesman who accomplishes nothing that he is not a 'real' statesman, then we mean by 'real' what Hegel calls 'actual.' The statesman exists as a man in office, but he lacks the essence constitutive of what statesmanship ought to be, say effectiveness. Conversely, and in Hegel's view no less important, if effectiveness were never the quality of an existing statesman, then it would not be the rational essence of statesmanship, but a mere ideal or dream. Hegel's philosophy as a whole might be regarded as an attempt to justify his identification of rationality with actuality and vice versa, but his doctrine depends ultimately on his faith in God's Providence, his conviction that history is the working out of His rational purpose. That purpose, as the purpose of the Almighty, is not so impotent as to remain a mere ideal or aspiration, and conversely, what is genuinely actual or effective in the world is simply the working of that purpose. It follows that Hegel's identifica-

Heiberg's treatise on freedom we cannot deny that he wanted to reproduce Hegel and that he obviously had no greater desire than to follow his philosophical teacher faithfully. And there is no denying that Hegel's "practical" philosophy in particular permits a reading and use as an interpretation and philosophical justification of contemporary phenomena, and thus, e.g., as a defense of political conservatism. Nor can we deny Heiberg's right to consider all earlier philosophy, and (especially as concerns his own age) Hegel's philosophy, as an exponent of the culture of the time, to put it in modern terms. However, what we can reproach Heiberg for in his interpretation and development of Hegel's philosophy is that he so obviously thinks that Hegel's speculative deity has been able to control concrete empirical reality, and that this should be evident to all cultivated people. Insofar as he thought that, his Hegelianism became a cultural optimism, in which everything at bottom is exceedingly good. This understanding of Hegel can be defended. It is not difficult to find expressions in the Master's own writings that—if read in isolation, in their narrower context—would seem to furnish a basis for such an understanding. The notable statement just quoted from *Philosophy of Right* invites just such an interpretation—and the invitation has frequently been accepted.[18] Nevertheless, if it is the case that Hegel's speculative deity has not vanquished the concrete, material, empirical world, then a cultural optimist interpretation and use of his philosophy becomes a dubious affair. Since it is unquestionably Hegel's notion that his philosophy is the crowning achievement of the whole development of the history of philosophy, then it follows that he cannot consider any further development to be possible, that the perspective of a future is excluded. Nor is it possible either, if the general understanding of Hegel's philosophy sketched here is correct, to allow cultural optimism to be a hope for a future Utopia.

Heiberg's Hegelianism, as expressed in his prospectus, may be described as a certainly close, yet ultimately inadequate understanding and development of Hegel's philosophy. Hence there is no particular value in describing in detail the points on which he is in harmony with Hegel. His view of religion in general and of

tion of the actual and the rational is not a plea for conservatism in politics. The actualization of God's purpose is not yet complete. See the addition to paragraph 270 and the closing pages of the *Philosophy of History*."]

[18] See, for example, Søren Holm: *Søren Kierkegaards Historiefilosofi* (1952), 16ff.

Christianity in particular correspond by and large to Hegel's. Just like the Master, he wishes to consider the course of historical events as governed by metaphysical necessity, and just like the Master he holds that there is a harmony between the content of religion and philosophy, while philosophy also contains and expresses the truth in its adequate form.

3. SIBBERN'S AND POUL MØLLER'S RELATION TO HEGEL

While Heiberg described himself as a Hegelian and was understood as such, the same cannot be said of other Danish thinkers during this period, i.e., until the summer of 1835, which is the terminal date for the present chapter. Actually, there are only two other Danish thinkers who can be mentioned in this context: Frederick Christian Sibbern (1785-1872) and Poul Martin Møller (1794-1838). Sibbern's historian, Jens Himmelstrup, maintains (without discussing it further) that in Sibbern's involvement in the Howitz controversy there is "no trace of a Hegelian mode of thinking. And in the course of the twenties and thirties Sibbern's attitude toward Hegel's philosophy became more and more severe."[19] Sibbern's extensive, thorough critique of Hegel dating from 1838 will be spoken of later.

According to the extant attendance records, which Ammundsen has examined (*SK's Ungdom*, 1912, 78ff.), in the winter semester, 1830-1831, Kierkegaard attended Sibbern's lectures on basic psychology, and in the summer semester, 1831, his survey of logic and psychology (SK attended both courses as preparation for the philological-philosophical examination, the so-called "second examination"). Neither as logician nor as psychologist was Sibbern a Hegelian. This is manifested both by his textbooks in the subjects and, particularly as regards logic, by his major critique of Hegel in 1838.

During the winter semester of 1833-1834, Kierkegaard attended Sibbern's lectures on "The Philosophy of Christianity."[20] These lectures were never printed, but attempts have been made to get a summary sketch of them.[21] According to these reconstructions,

[19] Jens Himmelstrup, *Sibbern* (1934), 83. This monograph is referred to in general in what follows.

[20] *Papirer*, I xxvi.

[21] Skat Arildsen, *H. L. Martensen* (1932), 42-45; cf. Himmelstrup, *Sibbern*, pp. 227ff. It is scarcely possible to reconstruct a coherent presentation of

Sibbern's philosophy of Christianity takes its point of departure in the Faith as the central, all-determining principle of the spiritual life; subsidiary to that is thought. Philosophy analyzes the historically given fact of revelation and interprets its content. Christianity and philosophy can and should be combined. When Christ is taken as the universal principle for both life and philosophy, then philosophy itself may become Christian. The difference from Hegel is evident. Hegel recognizes the fact of the revelation of Christ, takes it as a metaphysically necessary fact; but, in his view, thought should not take its point of departure in faith in that revelation and its content, nor does he hold revelation and the Faith as his norm. According to Hegel, speculative philosophy leads to the pure way of thought, with no need for any historical datum. It leads to the absolute truth, which is certainly also expressed in the absolute religion, as Hegel calls Christianity. While, for Sibbern, the philosophy of Christianity has its source and norm outside of itself, as something given and beyond dispute, Hegel's philosophy, subsuming under it his philosophy of religion, has its source and norm in itself; and while for Sibbern the revelation of Christ is supreme in his thought (during this period), for Hegel it is taken as a moment within the system.

That Sibbern's view of the method and purpose of philosophy was, on the whole, divergent from that of Hegel needs no further proof in this context. Jens Himmelstrup has said all that is required.

Then there is Poul Møller. During his sojourn as professor of philosophy at Oslo from 1826 until 1831 he also became acquainted with Hegel's philosophy, and traces of this familiarity can be found in the works he wrote toward the end of his life. Most of these works were not printed until after his death.

The sources for our knowledge of Poul Møller's philosophical position during the years from 1831 until 1835 can be found in his *Efterladte Skrifter* [Posthumous Works].[22] Here we can only speak of studies, treatises, and reviews, which Møller himself allowed to be printed during this period, and which Kierkegaard also had the opportunity to know. There is not much to take into consideration. *Forelæsnings-Paragrapher over Moralphilosophien* [Paragraphs

---

Sibbern's "philosophy of Christianity" from his extant manuscripts and notes alone (which are preserved in the manuscript collection of the Royal Library in Copenhagen).

[22] The third edition, 1856, to which references will be made in the sequel, is employed here.

from Lectures on Moral Philosophy] was printed on the basis of notebooks dating from 1837 correlated with the author's manuscript, and can therefore be used only with caution. The review of Sibbern's *Logik som Tænkelære* [Logic as Doctrine of Thinking] (2nd ed., 1827) was first printed in 1842; and the noteworthy treatise *Om Muligheden af Beviser for Menneskets Udødelighed* [On the Possibility of Proofs of Human Immortality] belongs to a later period. Thus there remain only the reviews of F.L.B. Zeuthen's *Noget om Philosophien og dens Dyrkelse, tildeels med Hensyn paa Danmark* [Something about Philosophy and its Cultivation, with Particular Reference to Denmark], which came out in 1831 (Poul Møller's review appeared in the *Maanedsskrift for Litteratur* [Literary Monthly] in the same year), Peter Christian Kierkegaard's[1] *De Notione atque Turpitudine Mendacii Commentatio* [Dissertation on the Meaning and Baseness of Lying], published in 1829 (Møller's review of this appeared in the same periodical in 1832) and of Sibbern's *Om Poesie og Konst* [On Poetry and Art], I, 1834 (Møller's review appeared in *Dansk Litteraturtidende* [Danish Literary Times] in 1835). Random thoughts from various periods cannot be taken into consideration here, nor can the various sketches that were published under the title *Brudstykker* [Fragments] in the *Efterladte Skrifter* [Posthumous Writings] (III). Poul Møller's extensive draft of *Forelæsninger over den ældre Philosophies Historie* [Lectures on the History of Ancient Philosophy] Kierkegaard had known later—when it was published.[23]

The relevant sources in this context do not contain much material for determining Poul Møller's own philosophical position and its relation to that of Hegel. One clear statement—in the review of Zeuthen's little work—says:

> the various systems that have been able to gain acceptance in the history of philosophy have never been completely wrong, but each has interpreted the Idea from the perspective of a single facet; they obviously neither should nor could exclude one another, but they may be described as diverse stages in the development of mankind which should not be rejected but

[1] This was, of course, SK's older brother, later Bishop of Aalborg in Jutland. P. C. Kierkegaard received the doctorate in theology at the University of Göttingen in Germany with this dissertation.

[23] See *Papirer*, IV B 13:7 and 13:22, and my Commentary on *Philosophical Fragments* (Princeton: Princeton University Press, 1962), p. 166.

recognized as subordinate movements in a multifaceted system.[24]

Such a view of the history of philosophy is genuinely Hegelian.
In the otherwise very appreciative review of P. C. Kierkegaard's
dissertation, only at the end does Poul Møller offer some considerations on the relation of isolated conceptual analysis to (speculative)
moral philosophy; but the few indications given do not permit any
sure conclusions concerning the relation to Hegel. In the detailed
discussion of the first volume of Sibbern's work on aesthetics,
Om Poesie og Konst, published in 1834, Hegel is named (p. 204)
with significant respect. Møller speaks there of "the frank, sarcastic
Preface, which is found before Hegel's *Phenomenology of the
Spirit*" which "has gone a long way toward making the present
age aware of his extraordinary power of mind," and a little further
on Hegel is spoken of as "the strongest logician who has ever
lived," but who has nevertheless allowed himself to stray from "the
proper methodical development of the concept" (p. 205). The criticism is soon expressed more clearly (pp. 212f.):

> Hegel held that the continued reference to the real sciences and
> the common experiences of life that enliven the philosophical
> presentations of the ancients, now must be seen as superfluous,
> when skill in abstraction has become so great, and the exem-
> plification of this is surely evident. But many facts show that he
> was mistaken in this respect, for having judged his contem-
> poraries by himself. Thus it must be striking to any diligent
> reader of the important philosophical literature what a signifi-
> cant role the few examples and comparisons which are found
> here and there in the writings published by Hegel himself have
> played for most of the authors who have adhered to his system.

Then follows a remark that is vintage Poul Møller:

> If anyone shall say here that genuine knowledge or the pure
> concept in its immanent dynamism has nothing to do with the
> sphere of experience, then we without picking any quarrel
> about the meaning of these words, will take the position that
> pure knowledge according to their usage, is a one-sided cogni-
> tion, that it can become true cognition only when a living ex-
> perience penetrates it; and in this respect, naturally, we think

[24] *Efterladte Skrifter*, V, 179. The two following reviews will be found in
the same volume.

not only of the interpretation of the phenomena of Nature outside of us, but much more of the moral, poetical, and religious
experiences of the interior life (213).

The last part of the review is concerned with praising Sibbern's
vitality as a philosopher and is an appreciation of his style of presentation.

Had the task here been to give a fundamental exposition of Poul
Møller's philosophical position during these years, then we naturally
would have had to introduce the sources printed later, such as
Vilhelm Andersen has done in his classical biography.[25] In Møller's
reviews, he accepts Hegel on individual issues, such as the notion of
the historical development of philosophy; but critical comments
predominate.

During the summer term of 1831 Kierkegaard participated in a
course on moral philosophy conducted by Poul Møller, in preparation for the second part of the Second Examination. As has already
been pointed out, in Poul Møller's *Efterladte Skrifter* (V, 141-162)
we find *Forelæsnings-Paragrapher over Moralphilosophien*, given
according to notebooks dating from 1827 collated with the author's
manuscript. It has not been determined whether the printed text
corresponds to what Poul Møller had conveyed in the summer of
1831; therefore, only with reservations is it possible to characterize
his interpretation of moral philosophy as it was presented to Kierkegaard. In any case, if we venture to assume agreement on basic
principles, then it is clear that even if traces of Hegel's influence on
Poul Møller can be found, even on a central issue, still it would
not be legitimate to describe his moral philosophy as Hegelian in its
entirety. Having defined moral philosophy, and discussed the problem of freedom, Poul Møller divides his treatment into the topics
of responsibility, happiness, and, finally, of true good, and the conclusion (in §47) is that

> The good should not be known through subjective thought
> alone, but should be found in its actuality and development in
> the state, and the individual fulfills his purpose only by func-
> tioning as a link in such a rationally organized society. Indi-
> vidual freedom is not thereby abolished or restricted; for the
> individual must be able to discover the same Reason as it de-

[25] *Poul Møller, Hans Liv og Skrifter*, 3rd ed. (1944). Reference is made
particularly to pp. 302ff.

velops itself in itself, in the laws, ordinances, and arrangements of the state. There is found therein only a boundary for his capriciousness, because the primary forms of rational freedom, which the true conscience cannot command mankind to transgress, have therein their objective presence. In the life of the state the natural satisfaction of activities obtains its ethical significance, because activities become means for the life and progress of the state, and the most free development of individual action advances the perfection and happiness of society.[26]

This conclusion seems to be typically Hegelian; but there is an omission in it which prevents us from correctly characterizing Poul Møller's moral philosophy as wholly Hegelian. Møller speaks of the notion that the good should be found in its actuality in the state; but he does not say in which state, i.e. in what type of state. Since what has already been considered in the foregoing discussion of Heiberg's Hegelianism is not in harmony with Hegel's intention to identify his ideal state with some actual state, then it is a dubious enterprise, even after such a clear expression as Poul Møller's, to describe him as a Hegelian on the basis of the conclusion of his moral philosophy. Moreover, its development and the definitions of concepts we find there are thoroughly out of conformity with the corresponding ones in Hegel, just as the moral philosophy of Poul Møller, in spite of the discussion of the state, is not incorporated—and thereby given justification and validity—into a total system as is the case in Hegel.

4. The Attitude of the Theologians toward Hegel

If we now turn from the philosophers to the theologians, we must, of course, consider not only the Faculty of Theology at the University of Copenhagen but also, for example, Mynster and Grundtvig and their followers and disciples. In this connection it may be asked whether any of them can be spoken of as being disciples of Hegel during the period under discussion. This question would have to be answered in the negative. The basis for this answer is not difficult to give, and it can be treated quite briefly here.

In his book on Kierkegaard's youth (pp. 79ff.) Valdemar Ammundsen has sketched the positions of Mynster, Grundtvig and of the Faculty of Theology during these years. We must pass over

[26] *Efterladte Skrifter*, V, 162.

Ammundsen's sketch here and consider only the question of whether research into the history of the church and the history of theology since 1912, when Ammundsen's book appeared, correctly contends, in opposition to Ammundsen, that during this period, *viz.* until the summer of 1835, we should speak of Hegel's philosophy as having in one way or another any significance for the Danish theologians.

We can follow the same sequence we find in Ammundsen. Thus Mynster comes first. No special study of Mynster as philosopher has appeared since O. Waage's book, published in 1867 and still worth reading: *J. P. Mynster og de philosophiske Bevægelser paa hans Tid* [J. P. Mynster and the Philosophical Movements of his Time]. In addition, Bjørn Kornerup, Henry Ussing, N. M. Plum, and Hal Koch have investigated and described Mynster's place in the history of the Danish church, his preaching, and his development as Christian and theologian.[27] Like Sibbern—and Kierkegaard—Mynster was an outspoken opponent of Hegelian logic and a decided adherent of classical logic. He was in general especially well oriented in the theological and philosophical thought of the age; but still in the time around 1830, when he had just completed his treatise on dogmatics (*Grundrids af den christelige Dogmatik*)[28] he seems to have had in the main only a second-hand knowledge of Hegel. Thus he writes in a letter (22 October 1830) to the learned pastor in Lyderslev, his friend W. F. Engelbreth, that

> I know only a little about Hegel's system; however, if it is based on that of Schelling, its tendency can hardly be pantheistic; on the other hand, it could well be that "the Hegelian Philosopher" is an altogether incorrect use of words, so as to draw all from all, to affirm and deny, as the circumstances require. Hardly any philosopher has developed a worse school than Hegel.[29]

[27] *Vor Frue Kirkes og Menigheds Historie* [History of Our Lady Church and Parish] ed. by Bjørn Kornerup (1930), 334-341. 369-387 (Ussing on Mynster's preaching), N. M. Plum, *Schleiermacher i Danmark* (1934), esp. pp. 72ff.; *J. P. Mynsters Visitatsdagbøger 1835-53* [J. P. Mynster's Journals of Pastoral Visitations], ed. Bjørn Kornerup, esp. Introduction to Vol. I (1937); N. M. Plum, *Jakob Peter Mynster som Kristen og Teolog* (1938); Bjørn Kornerup's article on Mynster in DBL, XVI, 322-333; Hal Koch: *Den danske Kirkes Historie VI: Tiden 1800-1848*, 1954, esp. pp. 141-155 and 285-315. Børge Ørsted's *J. P. Mynster og Henrich Steffens*, I-II, only goes up to 1807.
[28] Printed in *Blandede Skrivter* [Miscellaneous Writings] (1857), 1-400.
[29] *Kirkehistoriske Samlinger*, IV Rk., vol. IV (1895-1897), 713.

The statement does not indicate first-hand knowledge. Not until the conflict on the principles of logic did Mynster take an explicit position on the thought of Hegel and the Hegelians; on the whole, there is no reason to suppose that during this period Kierkegaard received any impression of Hegelianism through Mynster, at least not a positive one. There is no further reason to delve into Mynster's views during these years.

In the case of Grundtvig and his followers and disciples, among whom P. C. Kierkegaard was surely predominant, there is on the face of it no great likelihood either that Kierkegaard could have been brought into any contact with Hegelianism. In this area one might say the same about Ammundsen's sketch of Grundtvig as about the sketch of Mynster, that on every point it can be made more thorough and complete; but with respect to the question of Hegel, nothing of any new significance has appeared.[30]

Høirup is undoubtedly correct in considering Grundtvig's conflict with the romantic philosophy of identity represented by Schelling as an antecedent and parallel of Kierkegaard's much later clash with Hegel and Hegelianism. But there is no evidence that Kierkegaard had any particular knowledge of Grundtvig's philosophical controversy almost a generation previously. Nor is it likely that we can assume that Grundtvig himself nor his disciples at the beginning of the 1830s, when the conflict with H. N. Clausen still filled their thoughts and writings, had given Hegel and Hegelianism any attention. The break with idealistic philosophy had occurred much earlier as far as they were concerned. On his great journey abroad, P. C. Kierkegaard had also been in Berlin and became acquainted with some of the prominent men at the university there;[31] but

---

[30] C. I. Scharling, *Grundtvig og Romantiken* (1947), illuminates Grundtvig's relation to Schelling, while H. Høirup, *Grundtvigs Syn paa Tro og Erkendelse* [Grundtvig's View of Faith and Knowledge] (1949), expressly (esp. pp. 85-89) emphasizes Grundtvig's conflict with Schelling's philosophy of identity as a precursor in intellectual history of Kierkegaard's conflict with Hegelianism. Neither W. Michelsen (in *Tilblivelsen of Grundtvigs Historiesyn* [The Genesis of Grundtvig's View of History], 1954) nor K. E. Bugge (in *Skolen for Livet* [The School for Life], 1965) names Hegel in connection with Grundtvig, while K. Thaning (in *Menneske først* [Humanity First], 1963) furnished individual quotes and speaks of Hegel in passing, most often in the familiar triad Fichte-Schelling-Hegel, as representatives of the intellectual position Grundtvig rejected.

[31] In his article on P. C. Kierkegaard in DBL, XII, 416, Carl Weltzer identifies Hengstenberg, Schleiermacher, Neander, and Herder. The last-named should certainly be the faithful Hegelian Karl Werder.

nothing has appeared that would prove or even suggest that Kierkegaard had got any orientation on Hegel through his older brother Peter.[32]

5. THE FACULTY OF THEOLOGY AND PARTICULARLY H. N. CLAUSEN

The leading figure in the Faculty of Theology during these years was H. N. Clausen. He was not a Hegelian, and he was not likely to become one at all, and certainly not in the early 1830s.[33]

Kierkegaard attended Clausen's lectures on dogmatic theology during the winter 1833-1834 and summer 1834 terms (Ammundsen, p. 82 and 90f.), and he also went to Clausen's lectures and discussions of New Testament exegesis and the disciplines ancillary to the study of the New Testament.

It would be natural to imagine that in his lectures on dogmatic theology Clausen would present a confrontation between his own points of view and, if not those of the Hegelian left, then certainly those of the right-wing Hegelian dogmatic theologians Daub and Marheineke. Nor would it have been without good reason if Clausen in his teaching on the New Testament had, in any case, taken a position with regard to F. C. Baur's publications, which had just developed at the beginning of the 1830s.[34] In Kierkegaard's sum-

[32] On this point cf. Carl Weltzer, *Grundtvig og Søren Kierkegaard*, 1953. As far as Grundtvig himself is concerned, we must yield to the specialized research into the earliest history of Grundtvigianism to clarify the possible Hegel-problem in this connection. Judging by the available conclusions of such research, it appears that neither Mynster nor Grundtvig nor their respective disciples and adherents in the early 1830s had paid any attention to Hegelian philosophy. It has not, of course, been the function of this section to give a general description of Mynster's and Grundtvig's philosophical and theological views during these years.

[33] On this point, cf. the literature subsequent to Ammundsen's book: M. Neiiendam's article in DBL, V, 288-293; N. M. Plum's book on *Schleiermacher i Danmark* (*supra cit.*); J. Larsen, *H. N. Clausen*, I (1945); L. Bergmann's critique of this monograph in *Kirkehistoriske Samlinger* (1946); Søren Holm's critique in DTT (1945); Hal Koch in *Den danske Kirkes Historie, VI: Tiden 1800-1848*, 1945, especially pp. 197ff.

[34] It may also be noted that in his *Det nye Testaments Hermeneutik*, 1840 (Ktl. 468), Clausen very clearly dissociated himself from "speculation," cf. p. iv: "If theology should derive the right benefit from the link which binds it more intimately than ever before with philosophy, then it will not dare to allow itself to be overwhelmed by a speculation which means that the dialectical fountain of life—which often is as rich in sand as it is in

mary of the lectures on dogmatic theology (*Papirer* I C 19)[m] Marheineke is named only twice (p. 61 and p. 77), Daub not at all, and nowhere in this text is there any discussion of them. In a marginal note (p. 74) the contributions of Richter, Weisse, I. H. Fichte, and Göschel to the controversy over human immortality are mentioned; but Clausen did not enter into any discussion of this precise point either. It is not our task here to describe Clausen's dogmatic position in relation to the "speculative" approach at the time of the lectures.[35] It can be observed only that a comparison of these lectures and those of Martensen a few years later, which Kierkegaard likewise summarized in large measure, not only as regards individual points of doctrine but as a totality, clarifies fundamental disagreements. The young Kierkegaard's actual profit from Clausen's lectures on dogmatics (apart from his simultaneous and later disagreement with Clausen) was that he got a rather thorough, but not particularly original orientation in and knowledge of the areas of biblical theology, history of dogma, and systematic theology, which he would later make free use of.[36]

There is no need in the present context to further discuss the other members of the Faculty of Theology—Jens Møller, M. H. Hohlenberg, N. Fogtmann, C. T. Engelstoft, and C. E. Scharling— who in 1836 began a critical reckoning with F. C. Baur. From what is known of them it cannot be assumed that Kierkegaard got any urge to concern himself with Hegel's thought from them, and, from the available evidence, it must be taken as doubtful that Kierkegaard got any overall impression of Hegelian thought from them, or any impression of attempts to employ Hegelian thought outside of philosophy alone.

water—makes everything superfluous . . . ," and especially in a section beginning on p. 370 about the Hegelian school and scriptural interpretation, where, among other things, Clausen expresses the fear that the Hegelian school will give reinterpretations instead of clarifications of the Biblical texts, a point he amplifies in a criticism of Strauss and Weisse.

[m] This will be found in the latest edition of the *Papirer*; *Søren Kierkegaards Papirer*, anden forøgede Udgave ved Niels Thulstrup, XII (Supplementbind I) (Copenhagen: Gyldendal, 1969), 52-125.

[35] See the introductory remarks to my edition of these lectures in *Kierkegaards Papirer*, Supplementbind I, 49-51.

[36] See esp. Arild Christensen's article in DTT (1953), 216ff., on *Kierkegaards Individuationsprincip*. It can be noted in passing that August Hahn's *Lehrbuch des christlichen Glaubens*, published in 1828, has obviously played a more prominent role, particularly as a compendium of the history of dogma, both for Clausen and for Kierkegaard, than has been hitherto recognized.

6. MARTENSEN

During the period under consideration Martensen had not yet become a member of the Faculty of Theology. Was he influenced by Hegel during this period, and did he thus influence Kierkegaard? Indeed, they had a connection with one another. Since the appearance of Ammundsen's book on Kierkegaard's youth, which, naturally, is not mentioned here as outstanding in regard to research on Martensen, Skat Arildsen's monograph has appeared, as well as Oskar Andersen's presentation of Martensen's youth, which is frequently critical of Arildsen.[37]

Arildsen, who thinks that, on the whole, Martensen at an extraordinarily early point in time sought an exhaustive world- and life-view, maintains that an important influence on the quite young Martensen came from Lindberg and Steffens, and indeed also from Rudelbach. According to Arildsen, Sibbern had the greatest philosophical influence on Martensen. Martensen's concern with Schleiermacher is spoken of, after which Arildsen asserts (*Martensen*, p. 54) that

> what Martensen failed to find in Schleiermacher, he thought he could more likely find in Hegel, where he obviously became impressed by [Hegel's] recognition of thought as the objective, the divine, as the basic moving force of existence, and hence also of religion. He was also clearly captivated by Hegel's insistence on an objective world view, in which all the orthodox dogmas, reproduced in "a new and fresh form" achieved new honor and worth, recognized in their objective validity. During his studies of Hegel Martensen thus got an "inkling" of a "view which against the background of the Trinity understands Christ as the midpoint in creation, understands the universe as a system of concentric circles which all point to the innermost circle, where Christ is, and only in Him do they find their transfiguration and comprehension."

Arildsen bases this on Martensen's own remarks in *Af mit Levnet*, I [From My Life], and in this way places Martensen's encounter with Hegel's writings—which ones Arildsen does not mention —at the time prior to Martensen's final university examination. In

---

[37] Respectively, *Biskop Hans Lassen Martensen, hans Liv, Udvikling og Arbejde*, I, 1932, and "Biskop H. L. Martensens Ungdom" in *Kirkehistoriske Samlinger*, 6 ser., I (1933), 130-237.

the passage in his autobiography referred to here, Martensen names only Hegel's *Logic*.

In his discussion and summary of Martensen's entry (December 1833) for the Faculty of Theology's prize essay on the topic "Quodnam est fundamentum theologiae naturalis, quis ambitus & quaenam relatio ejus ad theologiam positivam" [What is the foundation and scope of natural theology, and what is its relation to positive theology], Arildsen says quite explicitly (p. 69) that Martensen

> has allied himself with Hegel and with speculative theology. He has to a certain degree adopted Hegel's speculative-dialectical method, of which he has made abundant use in his resolution of the problem [posed by the Faculty of Theology], as well as in his view on the relation between faith and knowledge —the idea of God can be elevated from the form of faith to the form of knowledge, and human knowledge is not only subjective, but objective idealism—and [in his view] on history, the development of which is understood logically.

Even if this is the case, Arildsen nevertheless thinks that Martensen's independence prevented him from embracing Hegel completely. This is the case with regard to Martensen's view of knowledge, "according to which comprehensive knowledge consists of concept + attitude [*Anskuelse*]," and his view of the philosophical concept of God as not completely satisfactory. Moreover, Arildsen thinks that

> there is still a point where it was possible that Martensen would part company with Hegel. That is with reference to the objectivity given in the whole of creation as in sacred history, he wanted the given to be respected in every case, and therefore employed every sense which he thought necessary for complete knowledge.

Arildsen thinks that this attitude

> consequently consistently sees beyond Hegel's treatment of scriptural and ecclesiastical studies and can be clearly considered an anticipation of Martensen's future defense as a University teacher of historical Christianty against, among others, D. F. Strauss's mythologizing consideration of Christianity. (*Martensen*, p. 70)

Martensen's first publication (March 1834) was a review of

E. V. Kolthoff's dissertation (for the Licentiate) on the author of the Apocalypse. According to Arildsen's description of it, the review is permeated with speculative thought.

In opposition to Arildsen, Oskar Andersen's article brings out that both Steffens and Grundtvig may have influenced the young Martensen against speculative thought (p. 153), and that Martensen cannot correctly be called a Hegelian at any time during the period 1827-1834 (p. 157). Andersen emphasizes Rudelbach's importance for Martensen more strongly than did Arildsen (p. 163), and holds that Hegel entered the picture at a much later time, after Martensen had read Heiberg's prospectus issued in 1833 (p. 182). Oskar Andersen, who throughout his account places far greater reliance on Fr. Hammerich's recollections than on Martensen's own, holds that as late as the fall of 1832, when he took his final University examinations, Martensen still belonged to the narrow Grundtvigian circle.

As might be expected, Oskar Andersen does not discuss Martensen's relation to Hegel at any length, and that is, of course, what is relevant in the present context. Unfortunately, Arildsen is vague about Martensen's encounter with Hegel, but in his discussion of Martensen's prize essay he is somewhat more precise. If we take it that this is the only point of agreement manifested by these two Martensen scholars, then in this case Arildsen is correct to a higher degree than Oskar Andersen. In any case it is true that the views Martensen (according to Arildsen's summary) put forward in his prize essay, only with great difficulty can be interpreted as having been essentially derived from a reading of Heiberg's prospectus. In all likelihood Martensen must have read Hegel himself at the time he was writing his response for the theological prize competition, and possibly before. Thus Martensen's remarks, regrettably few as they are on this point in his autobiography, must be taken as gilding the historical fact.

Kierkegaard's relationship with Martensen during these years was, as is well known, that he took Martensen as tutor in the early summer of 1834. With Martensen, he went through—or got a survey—of the main points in Schleiermacher's *Der Christliche Glaube*. At this time there was no discussion of Hegel.

7. MOLBECH AND MONRAD

There remain only two men who could conceivably have been intermediaries between Hegel and Kierkegaard, namely Molbech and

Monrad.[38] Kierkegaard knew both of them, but naturally each in his own way. Kierkegaard knew and referred to Molbech's *Forelæsninger over den nyere danske Poesie* [Lectures on Recent Danish Poetry], but not until 1836 (*Papirer* I A 129,[n] cf. I C 88 and 90). Furthermore, the work of Molbech that, according to Borup, was most influenced by Hegel, namely his *Historiens Philosophie* [Philosophy of History] I-II, did not appear until 1840-1841 (cf. Borup's biography, pp. 351ff.). With regard to Monrad, the relationship between Kierkegaard and the two-year-older Monrad in the years prior to summer 1835 seems to have been no more than a general student's acquaintance. Monrad's activities during these years did not go in the direction of Hegel.

8. Kierkegaard's Knowledge of Hegel and Hegelianism at this point

With this background, we will attempt to answer the question of what during this period Kierkegaard knew of Hegel and Hegelianism, or, more precisely, of Danish Hegelianism, which he had the best opportunity to encounter. To do this, we must go the primary sources, viz., Kierkegaard's own comments in his *Papirer* and *Letters* during this time.

First, the letters. They say very little that is relevant to the topic under discussion. The two earliest letters from Kierkegaard (Numbers 1 and 2)[39] to his older brother Peter, both dated March, 1829, are lengthy and rather charming schoolboy letters with reports about the teachers at the Borgerdydskole, Peter's former colleagues. In this context they are important only as testimony of Kierkegaard's then naturally very narrow horizon, which did not stretch beyond the city walls, and within that limited area did not even

---

[38] Cf. Morten Borup, *Christian Molbech* (1954), and for Monrad, Povl Bagge, *D. G. Monrads Statstanker* (1936); Sv. Hauge, *Studier over D. G. Monrad som religiøs Personlighed* (1944); and A. Nyholm: *Religion og Politik, en Monrad Studie* (1947). On the two latter books see especially L. Bergmann's critical reviews in *Kirkehistoriske Samlinger* (1945), 27-130, and *ibid*. (1949), 312-349.

[n] *Søren Kierkegaard's Journals and Papers*, edited and translated by Howard V. Hong and Edna H. Hong, 7 vols., (Bloomington: Indiana University Press, 1967-1978) I, 123 (hereinafter cited as "Hong").

[39] In *Breve og Aktstykker vedrørende Søren Kierkegaard*, I-II (1953-1954). [The text of the letters will be found in vol. I, pp. 29-32; commentary and notes on them will be found in vol. II, pp. 21-24.]

extend as far as *Frue Plads*.° The official documents concerning Kierkegaard from this period contain no indication of any exposure to or knowledge of Hegel and Hegelianism, and thus need not be discussed here. The only conclusion that can be drawn from them is that, prior to his entry into the University, it appears unlikely that Kierkegaard had become aware of speculative idealism. There is nothing remarkable about this, however.

Next, the *Papirer*. Oskar Andersen, in his article on Martensen noted the plan for theological studies that the faculty of the University of Copenhagen issued in November 1831.[40] This official plan of studies seems hitherto unknown in Kierkegaard research. It appeared just after Kierkegaard had completed the second part of the Second Examination, which took place on October 27, 1831.

According to this plan of studies a student should follow lectures and exercises four hours daily for a period of six semesters, after which he could take the final examinations. As an introduction to the course of studies, the theological compendium should be gone through every other winter semester, while Old Testament exegesis in the areas necessary for the examination were allotted four semesters. Exegesis of the New Testament should continue through all six semesters, and together with this main topic, isagogics and the other ancillary exegetical disciplines belong, just as for the Old Testament. Surveys of dogmatics and ethics would alternate every other year, each survey continuing for two semesters. In addition, every other year there should be a survey of natural theology and of apologetics, each being of one semester's duration. The survey of church history should be of three semesters' length and should begin in a winter semester. Thereafter a single semester of the history of dogma should follow. In addition, there would also be a one-semester treatment of the Creed [*Symbolikken*]. Every semester, written or oral exercises should be held, these to be either as practices in disputation or as exercises in interpretation.

For the first year, the students were advised to occupy themselves with Old and New Testament exegesis and to begin on church history, regardless of the period being treated at the time. If natural theology and the theological compendium were being presented in

° At the time, Copenhagen was still a walled city. Frue Plads is the square on which the cathedral, Vor Frue Kirke, and the University are situated.

[40] *Kirkehistoriske Samlinger* (1933), 158 and 184ff. The plan was originally printed in *Tidsskrift for Kirke og Theologie*, I (1832), 305ff., and was designed for a normal three-year course in theology.

that year, then the student ought to follow these lectures also. In the second year, the student would perhaps do the two last named areas, would continue with exegesis and the historical field, and would possibly study ethics or dogmatics, if these two areas were being given. In the third year the student should continue New Testament exegesis, but in addition, study especially ethics, dogmatics and the Creed, and take part in exercises.

Oskar Andersen emphasizes that

> the prescribed three-year curriculum would be possible for instructors as well as for students only if the scope of the disciplines were confined to a quite modest level, but even presupposing that, it must be said that the determination of both [instructors and students] to work was important (p. 186).

He cites the statement in the plan of studies that private tutoring normally should be quite superfluous.

Valdemar Ammundsen was the first to investigate Kierkegaard's relation to the theological instruction at the University during his first year as a student. In the light of the above course of studies and guidance, the conclusion is that Kierkegaard, as a very talented moderately diligent student who did not need to support himself by giving lessons, should have been in a position to take the final examination in 1835. So far as is known, he did not participate in the exercises prescribed by the faculty for the final year of theological studies but, instead, in the spring of 1834 engaged Martensen as tutor. Apparently at Martensen's suggestion, they went through the chief points in Schleiermacher's *The Christian Faith*.[41]

If, armed with this knowledge, we proceed to the reading of Kierkegaard's entries in the *Papirer* from the period under investigation here, then we should not be surprised to find these entries influenced by the conditions discussed above.

The notes dealing with exegetical matters and church history can in this context be left out of consideration.[42] Only notes on sys-

[41] The topic was timely and obvious. In the first place, H. N. Clausen (who was expected to be Kierkegaard's examiner) was, before anyone else, influenced by Schleiermacher. In the second place, Schleiermacher's chief dogmatic work [Schleiermacher, *The Christian Faith* (New York: Harper Torchbooks, 1963)] had a short time previously appeared in a new edition (the renowned second edition). Finally, the Master himself had just recently visited Copenhagen—an event that naturally had evoked interest among the theology students; cf. N. M. Plum's book on Schleiermacher and Denmark.

[42] Generally speaking it is true that Kierkegaard, both among his theology

tematic theology, philosophy, and esthetics can be discussed here.

First, then, *Papirer*, I C 1-45 (Theologica).

In the group C entries there are only isolated numbers which can be brought into a relationship with Hegelianism and possibly with Hegel himself. In H. N. Clausen's lectures on dogmatic theology (*Papirer*, I C 19)[p] there is, as remarked previously, no reason to assume that Kierkegaard got any impulse in the direction of Hegel. Nor could the study of Schleiermacher lead in that direction. At some point, Kierkegaard had occupied himself somewhat with Marheineke's *Grundlehren der christlichen Dogmatik als Wissenschaft*, in the second edition published in 1827 (*Papirer*, I C 25,[q] cf. I A 273),[43] but most likely this was not until 1836.

This presentation of dogmatic theology by Marheineke is known as a classical writing of right-wing Hegelianism, and it was Marheineke who undertook the editorial work for Hegel's *Vorlesungen über die Philosophie der Religion*.[44] If, prior to the summer of 1835, Kierkegaard had already read Marheineke's *Dogmatik* at least in part, then it is obvious that in that way he would have got a purer presentation of Hegelian thought than he would have been able to get from the native Danish side. Both the Trinitarian construction of the *Dogmatik* in Marheineke and his efforts to pass from the immediate data [*Forestillinger*] to speculative concepts, as well as his attempt to transcend the traditional opposition between rationalism and supernaturalism are in their development decisively

---

teachers in these areas and in the commentaries and other aids he employed, on the whole became acquainted with a mild conservatism.

[p] It should be pointed out again that the complete text of this entry will be found in vol. XII (Supplementbind I) of the new edition of the *Papirer*.

[q] The text of I C 25 will also be found in vol. XII (Supplementbind I) of the new edition of the *Papirer*.

[43] Ktl. 644, acquired by Kierkegaard December 14, 1836. If the editors' dating of the excerpts is correct, Kierkegaard must have worked with a borrowed copy in 1834-1835. *Papirer*, I A 273, indicates November 1836, which is reasonably explained by the fact that Marheineke took part in the observance of the Jubilee of the Reformation at the University of Copenhagen that year. This was probably when Kierkegaard first became aware of him.

[44] On Marheineke in general, the reader is referred to the more recent presentations in the history of theology, e.g., Horst Stephan, *Geschichte der evangelischen Theologie seit dem Deutschen Idealismus* (1938), 74ff. (in the second, "neubearbeitete Auflage" by Martin Schmidt [1960], 81f.); Karl Barth, *Die protestantische Theologie im 19. Jahrhundert* (1947), 442-450; Em. Hirsch, *Geschichte der neuern evangelischen Theologie*, V, 154, esp. pp. 366-372.

marked with Hegel's thought, both by the method and by the system. The likelihood is that Kierkegaard did not begin to study Marheineke's *Dogmatik* until the fall of 1836. Judging by the extant excerpts from Marheineke and notes in the *Papirer* he had read only the first few pages of that work. Nor through Clausen and Hohlenberg's *Tidsskrift for udenlandsk theologisk Litteratur* [Journal of Foreign Theological Literature] (1833 ff.), to which Kierkegaard had a subscription, could he have been exposed to Hegelian thought during this period.

Do these group C entries in the *Papirer* give evidence of other possibilities for contacts with Hegelianism or perhaps even with Hegel himself?

Kierkegaard had written out excerpts from Baader's *Vorlesungen über speculative Dogmatik* (cf. *Papirer*, I C 27-33);[r] but then these excerpts probably belong to a later period, very likely the summer of 1836 (cf. *Papirer*, I A 174), and Baader was not an entirely uncritical admirer of Hegel.

The question must be answered in the negative: none of the extant entries in the category of systematic theology in group C shows that Kierkegaard had any contact with Hegelianism or with Hegel through any of the professors of theology, from books or elsewhere during this period.

Curiously enough, the first work from which Kierkegaard wrote down excerpts as a student was Marheineke's history of the Reformation (*Papirer*, I C 1);[s] but neither in this nor in those which follow (*Papirer*, I C 2, 3, 7, 8, 11-12, 13, 16, 18, 20-24, 24)[t] is there anything of direct relevance to our study. On the other hand, these entries have considerable significance for a richer, more precise understanding of the whole development of Kierkegaard's youth, which we shall not attempt to sketch in this context. In them, his intellectual horizon can be seen clearly and quite accurately delineated. We can see there that the theological school learning, especially in the exegetical and historical fields (but to a far lesser degree in the area of systematic theology) very soon lost interest for him, but their actual meaning, positive as well as negative, for him and for his later authorship must not for that reason be ignored or even underestimated.[45]

---

[r] Anden forøgede Udgave, XII (1. Supplementbind).

[s] *Ibid.*

[t] *Ibid.*

[45] Valdemar Ammundsen, in *Søren Kierkegaards Ungdom* (1912), under-

We now proceed to group A in the same volume of the *Papirer*, i.e., I A 1-71, and examine these entries in the same way. They fill a time frame between April 15, 1834, and the beginning of August 1835, so that the important draft of a letter to Peter Wilhelm Lund dated June 1, 1835, does not fall within the otherwise often uncertain chronology of many entries, and considering that in some instances Kierkegaard later turned back and made additions to earlier entries.

Just as our examination of the group C entries revealed, so also, as might be expected, the group A entries from this period show Kierkegaard's intellectual horizon as quite limited. Schleiermacher is the only foreign thinker to whom he devoted attention over an extended period, and it was the doctrine of predestination and Judaism as a problem in its relation to Christianity that particularly concerned him. It is quite probable, indeed the only likely possibility, that if at this time Kierkegaard had acquired even a cursory knowledge of Hegel's philosophy, then in his reflections on these problems he would have mentioned and taken a position on this philosophy, which furnishes a parallel to the strict doctrine of predestination and in whose philosophy of history and philosophy of religion Judaism is considered in relation to Christianity.

The other notes of a theological character from the period (e.g., I A 27, 33, 45, 46, 49) are understandably in connection with Clau-

---

took a fundamental account of Kierkegaard's studies up to the end of the summer of 1838. Ammundsen can be supplemented here and there, as is done in the present and the following chapter (without giving an explicit indication of this each time), but to correct Ammundsen is not germane to the area dealt with here. The situation is somewhat different with respect to Em. Hirsch, who in his *Kierkegaard-Studien*, esp. in vol. II (1933), 451-477, has treated of the same period. In note 1, on page 459, Hirsch emphasizes that unlike Ammundsen, who on many points limited his efforts to presenting the material, he will provide a penetrating dialectical interpretation. Hirsch himself observes, in this note and elsewhere, that he was not able to do complete justice to Kierkegaard's particularly Danish assumptions and milieu because of a lack of knowledge of the sources. But unfortunately, often in the course of his intended penetrating dialectical interpretation, the reader of his learned and incisive work, a classic in Kierkegaard research, is given a not entirely correct impression of the thinkers and trends which in one respect or another influenced Kierkegaard. In the section *"Der werdende Denker"* (II, 451-602), Hirsch gives considerable importance to Schleiermacher, J. G. Fichte and I. H. Fichte, Erdmann, Daub, and other German-speaking thinkers, while, for example, Clausen, Martensen, Poul Møller, Sibbern and others with whom in one way or another Kierkegaard had come into closer living contact, are not handled nearly so satisfactorily.

sen's lectures on dogmatics, and have no relation to Hegel or Hegelianism. The same holds true of his noted critique of Grundtvig's
theory of the Church (I A 60)[u] which was written on May 28, 1835.

As was said at the beginning of this chapter, the draft of a letter
to P. W. Lund, dated June 1, 1835 (I A 72)[v] is a focal point in this
investigation.

In this draft, we find a clear account by Kierkegaard of his intellectual situation if we pay close attention not only to what he
says but also to what he does not say.

Kierkegaard is in a situation of doubt and seeks a way out of the
doubt. As other entries show, he had recently begun a study of the
Faust character (cf. I C 46ff.),[w] and here he interprets Faust as
"doubt personified." Even if he does not identify himself with this
character, it is quite clear that he is immersed in a fundamental
doubt. In this situation, when he seeks to choose the right way out
of doubt, two possibilities occur to him, natural science and theology. Philosophy is not even suggested as a possibility.

Of course, he is not speaking of natural science in an empirical
sense. By the term "natural science" Kierkegaard means romantic
philosophy of nature. Just as in *Concluding Unscientific Postscript*
(p. 27 and p. 549) he expresses his respect for classical philology, so
also here he recognizes those who "have made a name for themselves in the literature by means of a tremendous collecting activity"
(I A 72). He does not plan to follow in their footsteps, although
he would like to use their conclusions, which he wishes to stand off
and observe from an Archimedian point from which the whole can
be contemplated and the part seen in the correct light. But Kierkegaard does not say that he has chosen or will choose the philosophy
of nature—only that it is one option for him, and he has described
and set forth his notion of the philosophy of nature.

Theology is the other possibility Kierkegaard raises, and here—
characteristically—he does not speak of exegetical, historical, or
practical theology, but only of systematic theology or, more accurately, of two comprehensive theological positions—orthodoxy and
rationalism, as they are rather vaguely called. He does not identify
Grundtvig, Schleiermacher, and other independent theologians
whose views had come within his field of vision, and he is on the
whole critical of both orthodoxy and rationalism, such as he understood them. For Kierkegaard, theology seems as unlikely to become

[u] Hong, V, #5089.   [v] Hong, V, #5092.   [w] Hong, V, #5077.

a way out of doubt as are the natural sciences. He points out that he was raised in orthodoxy, and there is no denying the generally orthodox character both of his father's understanding of Christianity and of the instruction he received in school.[46]

We are not concerned with how Kierkegaard understood natural science, orthodoxy, and rationalism, nor even with how he actually rejected them as possible avenues out of the situation of doubt. Of interest in this context is that he did not raise philosophy as a possibility at all. It is indeed noteworthy that he does mention Hegel (I A 72, p. 46; Breve og Aktstykker, p. 33). But there is no discussion of Hegelianism in this entire entry. This is completely in harmony with the earlier letters and entries, and from this we can derive the present conclusion, that at this time this philosophy had not come within his horizon at all.

Kierkegaard does, however, mention Hegel in this entry. He observes first (ibid.) that there are people who unwaveringly work toward a previously foreseen way without falling into doubt as to whether this is the right way for them. On the other hand, there are people who allow themselves to be governed and guided completely by their environment. To use a cliché from Kant it may be said that "just as the former class had its interior categorical imperative, so the latter recognizes an external categorical imperative" (ibid.). There are not many in the first group, Kierkegaard says, and he has no desire to belong to the second. Then he says: "greater is their number who get to try in life what this Hegelian dialectic really means."

Does this expression mean that, after all, Kierkegaard at this time had begun to acquire some familiarity with Hegelian philosophy either by reading Hegel's published works or through the orientation that the more or less genuine Hegelians could have given him through their publications or orally?

The only one who has commented on this passage up to now is Hirsch, who writes: "What is meant is the dialectic of the development from dreaming youths to their determination as rational persons."[47] This interpretation is understandable in the light of what precedes the reference to Hegelian dialectic in Kierkegaard's letter.

[46] Cf. esp. Ammundsen's book (supra cit.) pp. 21-77; Sejer Kühle, S.K. Barndom og ungdom (1950), 9-77; and Breve og Aktstykker vedrørende S.K. nos. V and VI with commentaries thereon.

[47] In his translation of a selection (taken from Breve og Aktstykker vedrørende S.K.) of Kierkegaard's Briefe, 1955, 7 note 2.

For Kierkegaard says there, using some of the same words as Hirsch, that

> Our early youth stands like a flower at dawn with a lovely drop of dew on its petals,[x] in which all the surroundings are reflected in a harmonic-melancholic way. But soon the sun comes over the horizon, and the dew drop evaporates; with it disappear life's dreams, and now it is good if the man is ready for it, again to take an example from the flowers, to develop—by one's own strength like an oleander—a drop which can stand as the fruit of his life. For this it is necessary first and foremost, that one come to stand on solid earth, where one really belongs; but this is not always so easy to find.

Thus Hirsch's interpretation coincides somewhat with this passage, just where there is a discussion of finding a possibility that will serve for an individual man and his development. In what immediately follows, quoted in part above, the train of thought is continued, as Kierkegaard discusses the various sorts of difficulties that occur for different kinds of people. The typology in the little section where Hegel turns up is static; that is, there is no discussion of whether the individual human automatically passes through the possibilities mentioned. He does say there that there are two positions, namely, being determined by an "external categorical imperative" or by an "internal categorical imperative," and then he speaks of there being in life a whole segment of mankind that gets to test "what this Hegelian dialectic really means."

Now, does this expression involve in the first place that Kierkegaard thinks that the individual human, or indeed a whole segment of mankind, is without further qualification subject to a Hegelian dialectic in life? that thus Kierkegaard partially, at least, adheres to Hegel's view of man? and in the second place that he had such a knowledge of Hegel's philosophy that an essential agreement must be presupposed?

Kierkegaard says "this" Hegelian dialectic. By that he obviously cannot have meant anything other than the classification of mankind that he has just given, according to which some are led by an interior, others by an exterior categorical imperative, while still

---

[x] The word SK uses, *Bæger*, should, of course, be translated as "calyx," which is appropriate considering that he was writing to a naturalist, but I have taken the liberty of sacrificing linguistic and botanical accuracy for the sake of enhancing the beauty of the metaphor.

others first have to get clear about to which of the two groups they belong. This classification is Hegelian. It is a little more difficult to get a clear picture of how Kierkegaard actually understood the word "dialectic" at this point. The fundamental meaning in Hegel's definitive system, such as it is set forth in the writings beginning with *Phenomenology of the Spirit*, is partly the scientific use of the regularity inherent in the nature of thinking, partly this regularity itself. Thought and being are—speculatively considered—governed by the same dialectic. This is evident in the movement of the concepts—which are understood as both the implements and the objects of thought—which, in virtue of the negative element contained in every concept, unfold themselves according to the famous schema, thesis, antithesis, synthesis. Thus all oppositions are mediated according to Hegel.

In Kierkegaard, there is no discussion at this point of any mediation in the dialectic of the concrete human being. The closest Kierkegaard comes to explaining his understanding of the word "dialectic" in this passage comes subsequently: the practical problematic, i.e., the people who have a clear recognition of whether they are led by an internal or an external categorical imperative have no problem; but the group who at a given moment in their development do not have such clarity must discover through experience ("who get to test in life") where they belong. There is no statement that the inner and outer imperative are identified or mediated to a higher unity, which must be the consequence if we are to be correct in speaking of a Hegelian dialectic. The question of what understanding Kierkegaard has here of "Hegelian dialectic" can be answered by saying that he has used the label without being clear about its meaning.

It is futile to search for a parallel or anything at all in Hegel's philosophical system that could have given Kierkegaard a reason to set forth the classification and the practical problematic cited. The main text where Hegel speaks of man is the third part of *Encyclopedia of the Philosophical Sciences, Philosophy of the Spirit*, first section: "Subjective Spirit" (§387-482, *SW*, X, 9-379);[y] but Kierkegaard could not have found a basis for his designation in this text, which is divided into "Anthropology," "Phenomenology of the Spirit," and "Psychology." The most natural interpretation, both on the basis of the precise context in which the text analyzed is situated and on the basis of the connection with the earlier entries, is that

[y] Hegel's *Philosophy of Mind*, trans. William Wallace, pp. 10-102.

Kierkegaard had not yet read Hegel. Had he done so, he could hardly have written what he did here. As a matter of fact he did not subscribe to Hegel's anthropology (here taken to mean the whole section on the subjective spirit), which is one part of Hegel's speculative conceptual world, for in this anthropology, in the first place, there is no discussion of the different types of people such as Kierkegaard gives, and, in the second place, there is no claim that the individual man at one point in his development must get clear about where he belongs. Such problems are not found in Hegel at all.

If this is correct, it is still possible that through secondary sources Kierkegaard had obtained a kind of understanding of Hegel, a bit of knowledge, according to which he had thought it proper to speak of the Hegelian dialectic in this context.

In this chapter we have surveyed the chief points in the history of Hegelianism in Denmark until the summer of 1835, and thus the closest opportunities for Kierkegaard to learn to know it. In general, we would have to say that none of the sources investigated gives evidence that during this period Kierkegaard received any knowledge of Hegelianism at all.

We have also described Heiberg's Hegelianism, and the other Danish philosophers and theologians and their relation to Hegel have been explained in a similar way. The conclusion of the investigation was that only in the case of Heiberg can we speak of a conscious and rather dominant relationship as a disciple of Hegel, combined with the fact that his Hegelianism does not witness to an adequate understanding of what is genuinely characteristic of Hegel. Among the other thinkers there are individual points of contact or similarity with Hegel, while the differences—whether they are brought out by these thinkers themselves or not—are predominant. If Kierkegaard had read Heiberg's 1883 prospectus, and if it had made even a somewhat deep impression on him, then it is likely that in his letter to P. W. Lund he also would have listed philosophy—not necessarily, but very probably Hegelian philosophy—as one option that might be a possible way out of doubt. Indeed, Heiberg saw Hegelian philosophy as the only salvation of the age. To judge from all the available evidence, however, Kierkegaard did not see it. At precisely the point where there would have been the best occasion to take it into consideration, it did not happen.

If we now reconsider the text analyzed, with its statement about Hegelian dialectic, then there is one thing which is characteristic of Kierkegaard, and that is that obviously he, on the basis of a quite casual second-hand acquaintance with Hegel's philosophy, did not hesitate to identify a certain state of affairs as being an expression of a Hegelian dialectic. Even the fact that Kierkegaard introduces Hegel into his comments at all indicates that he imagined that this philosophy dealt with the same problems that had arisen for Kierkegaard himself.

We have been considering, of course, only Hegelianism in Denmark and the Danish philosophers' and theologians' relation to Hegel as the most proximate opportunity for Kierkegaard to come into contact with Hegel's philosophy. He evidently had just as little knowledge during this period of Hegelianism in Germany. Kierkegaard's purely historical knowledge of Hegel's writings as well as those of the Hegelians by the summer of 1835, when he sought to achieve clarity about himself and his future, must be described as minimal. How it occurred to him to speak of the Hegelian dialectic just then is a question that can be answered by saying that in one way or another (whether through reading or orally it is impossible to determine), he got a very superficial, cursory, and misleading notion of Hegel, and that was enough for him to produce a comment such as the one given.

On the whole the entries from this period do not show that Kierkegaard had very much knowledge of philosophy in general, and his theological perspective was not wide either.

It is not the task of this portion of our investigation to give an account of the chief points of contact between Kierkegaard's and Hegel's thought as the two complicated totalities they are, but only the actual, historical points of contact. Until the summer of 1835 Kierkegaard had some opportunities to learn to know Hegel's philosophy; but an examination of the sources has shown that these opportunities did not come to fruition. It has become equally clear that the majority of the philosophers and theologians with whom he came into contact in one way or another did not have Hegelian views. Criticism of Hegel and Hegelianism in Denmark was just beginning in earnest during this period; but both Sibbern and Poul Møller as philosophers, Mynster and H. N. Clausen as theologians—to mention only the most important—held views that either only on individual issues or else in no respect agreed with Hegel's philosophy.

Finally there is the question of whether during this period a decisive intellectual influence on Kierkegaard from some other side can be discovered, but this question falls outside the scope of this study.

It has been pointed out that, of the non-Danish thinkers, he had acquired some familiarity with Schleiermacher. There can also be good reason, with Hirsch, to bring out the meaning which the reading of the elder Fichte's *Die Bestimmung des Menschen* very likely had for him in the summer of 1835.[48]

Neither historically nor in principle during this period, then, can there be any claim of a contact of any importance with Hegel by Kierkegaard. The historical question has been answered, but the fundamental question has only been hinted at here.

[48] Hirsch, II, 471ff., Hirsch essentially bases his interpretation on *Papirer*, I C 50 together with I A 68 and 75. SK may have borrowed the book from the library of the Student's Association or from the University Library. His own book collection included an edition from 1838 (Ktl. 500) in addition to the complete edition of Fichte's *Works*, 1834-46 (Ktl. 489-499), in which the work will be found in vol. II, which appeared in 1845.

CHAPTER II

Kierkegaard's Possible Contact with Hegel and Hegelianism from the Summer of 1835 to November 1837

1. SCOPE AND PROCEDURE

IN THE PREVIOUS CHAPTER, our investigation took as its point of departure the Danish thinkers who have had a more or less close contact with Hegel. After an account of this, we went on to an analysis of the texts of Kierkegaard with reference to his possible contact with these thinkers and with Hegel himself, and we arrived at certain conclusions. Now that the general outlines of this background have been sketched, another procedure will be employed in what follows. We shall now begin with the relevant texts of Kierkegaard and seek points of contact with the Hegelians and with Hegel.

Wherever there is an actual contact, an account will be given of the views that Kierkegaard has noted and taken a position on. The depth and elaboration of each purely historical account will vary in individual cases depending on how much seems necessary to understand Kierkegaard's relation to that point of contact.

Two questions immediately arise—the first concerning the chronological boundaries, the second, the delimitation of the topical area.

If we attempt to elucidate Kierkegaard's whole development as a youth, there can hardly be much doubt that the summer of 1838, and speaking more precisely, May 19 of that year, furnishes a natural pivotal point. But this does not mean that that date is decisive in connection with Kierkegaard's relation to Hegel. Even though Kierkegaard experienced a religious breakthrough then, this need not indicate any change in his relation to the Hegelians and to Hegel. In our investigation of this specific relationship, a more accurate limit would be Martensen's first lectures at the University of Copenhagen in which both his own and others' conception of speculative thought, strongly redolent of Hegel, were first presented to an audience. Kierkegaard followed these lectures during the winter semester 1837-1838, which means that in this chapter our investigation can terminate at November 1837.

It is not so easy to delimit the topical area. Beginning in the fall of 1835 Kierkegaard engaged in an impressive expansion of his intellectual horizon at the same time he began to work intensively on the problems that arose for him after the confrontation with theology in the summer of 1835, and he involved himself with definite sets of problems that demanded resolution. The reader may be familiar with Kierkegaard's interest in politics, his literary and esthetic studies, his work with "the three great ideas," with the concepts of irony, humor, the romantic, etc. His grappling with the problem of the relation between Christianity and philosophy is also well known.

If the goal of this investigation were to give a complete presentation of Kierkegaard's development as a thinker, then these and various other themes would have to be given a penetrating and thorough treatment; but here they can be taken into consideration only insofar as they have an evident relation to Hegel and the Hegelians. In what follows, only individual points in the texts of Kierkegaard will be taken up for a historical analysis with a view to the elucidation of the relation between Kierkegaard and Hegel.

2. *Papirer*, I A 75 Compared with Hegel

As was said earlier, in *Papirer*, I A 72 Kierkegaard did not at all suggest philosophy as a possible way out of the situation he found himself in. But that possibility did occur to him not long after in the lengthy entry—a kind of continuation of the June 1 entry— which he wrote at Gilleleie[a] on August 1, 1835 (*Papirer*, I A 75).

Here philosophy appears as a possibility for him, but as a possibility that at least in a certain mode of development, is adduced only to be rejected.

> . . . the thing is to find a truth which is true *for me, to find the idea for which I will live and die.* And of what use would it be to me if I discovered a so-called objective truth; if I worked my way through the systems of the philosophers, and if I could

---

[a] Gilleleie is on the extreme northernmost coast of Sjælland, about forty miles north of Copenhagen. Many of the sights and scenes in this beautiful area turn up in some of Kierkegaard's subsequent writings, e.g., *Either/Or, Stages on Life's Way.*

hold a review of them on demand, and demonstrate the inconsistencies within each system;—of what use would it be to
me if I could develop a theory of the state, and from the diverse
details synthesize a totality, and thereby construct a world in
which I did not live, but which I would only hold up to the
view of others; . . .[b]

This statement does not put Kierkegaard into relation with
Hegelianism or with Hegel himself. If we consider how generally
the chief points of the statement are stated, there is no need to assume any historical allusion. The only thing worth noting is what
type of philosophy Kierkegaard rejects as valueless to him in the
present situation. That is the objective, systematic philosophy. He
does not say whether he is thinking of any definite type or particular representative of this kind of philosophy. Hegel would have
been an appropriate example, but he is not named here. This can
be taken as a fresh indication that Hegel could hardly have been a
known quantity for Kierkegaard at this time, and in any case he
was not a crucial problem to be reckoned with. Kierkegaard's
knowledge of the history of philosophy at this time is still quite
narrowly circumscribed, and we cannot discover with certainty
which particular systematic philosophers he had in mind. Surely he
thinks—as the statement shows—that he has enough knowledge to
decide that in his situation it cannot help him if he were to tackle
objective, systematic philosophy, a type in the history of philosophical thought that includes many other systems in addition to
that of Hegel.

Kierkegaard looks for a truth that can become a personal truth
for him. The thing is to find a truth—an idea, as he puts it—for
which he will live and die. There is no discussion here of the
familiar distinction in the *Philosophical Fragments* between the
Socratic (the idealistic) and the Christian, in which, according to
the first position, the truth is immanent in man and, according to
the second position, the truth must be brought to man from God,
which, moreover, must put man in the condition of being able to
receive the truth. Kierkegaard does not say at this point whether he
expects to be able to find the truth he seeks within or outside of

[b] Emphasis in the original. A convenient English translation of most of
this important Gilleleie entry will be found in Alexander Dru, *The Journals
of Kierkegaard* (New York: Harper Torchbooks, 1959), pp. 44-48. My translation of the above excerpt differs slightly from that of Dru.

himself; but actually he seeks it outside, and thus, like a Faust, so to speak, he wanders through all the faculties—and thinks that what he seeks is nowhere to be found.

In the June entry Kierkegaard takes issue with theology (rationalism and orthodoxy, but not with Grundtvig, Schleiermacher, or the speculative theology). In August it is the turn for Christianity. It is not doubtful to him as a fact; but as a fact alone it is useless to him in his situation:

> what good would it do me to be able to unfold the meaning of Christianity, to be able to elucidate many individual phenomena, when it does not have any deeper meaning for me and for my life?... [and] what would it profit me if truth stood before me cold and naked, indifferent whether I recognize it or not, producing an anxious shudder rather than a trusting submission?

The problem for Kierkegaard is not whether objective truths, possibly one highest objective truth, exist, but the subjective problem of how he can find a truth that can become truth for him, become decisive for his life.

There is no conflict between this and what Kierkegaard says a little further on in the same entry when he insists that self-knowledge is the first task. This task is a continuation of the reflections begun in June, but something new has been added, namely, discussion of the irony of life and the distinction between morality [*Sædelighed*] and virtue [*Dyd*] (I A 75, pp. 56-67).

This distinction is worth noting. Kierkegaard says:

> Not until a man has understood himself and now sees the path he must follow, does his life acquire peace and meaning, not until then does he become free of that troublesome, sinister traveling companion, that irony of life, which manifests itself in the sphere of knowledge, and bids true knowledge to begin with ignorance (Socrates), just as God created the world from nothing. But they are especially adrift on the open sea of morality who have not entered into the guiding breezes of virtue.

Is Kierkegaard thinking of Hegel here? The two most important passages in Hegel that can be discussed in the present instance are sections of *Phenomenology of the Spirit* and *Philosophy of Right*.

First *Phenomenology of the Spirit*. There Hegel speaks—as does Kierkegaard in his journal entry—of virtue [*Tugend*] and ethics

[*Sittlichkeit*] (and highest, morality [*Moralität*]), but in the reverse order and rank. Virtue is a moment in the microcosmic and macrocosmic Spirit's dialectical process of development, which shows itself under "Reason" [*Vernunft*] while "the true Spirit, Ethics" is a higher form of manifestation. In *Philosophy of Right*, Hegel speaks of the abstract Right, Morality, and Ethics.

What does Hegel understand by virtue in *Phenomenology of the Spirit*? The determination of the concept proceeds from the place of the concept in the dialectical development within the section on Reason. The position [thesis] is A: Reason observing [pp. 281-283ff.]; negation [antithesis] is B: the actualization [*Verwirklichung*] of rational self-consciousness through itself [pp. 373-412]; and the higher unity [synthesis] is C: individuality, which in and for itself is real [pp. 413-453].[1] Within this triad, a less comprehensive triad is present in the moment of negation, namely, "Pleasure and Necessity," "The Law of the Heart and the Madness of Self-Conceit," and "Virtue and the Course of the World" [pp. 373-412]. Thus in the lesser triad, virtue becomes the higher unity [synthesis] according to Hegel's usual pattern of thought, and as such must be described as positive, while in the greater triad it must be called negative, and in the quite narrow context the concept also contains both a positive and a negative element, with the latter predominant.

To clarify this dialectical concept, virtue—that is, only as regards *Phenomenology of the Spirit*—we need only clarify here the development of the negation in the major triad, that is, point B.

In point A, the dialectic had led to the stage that the observing Reason must shift from a passive to an active position. Active Reason is exhibited in B, where the rational self-consciousness will actualize itself. Active Reason is first only conscious of itself as individual and as such must demand and produce its actuality in something else, i.e., in something outside of itself. Then, since its consciousness ascends from the individual to the universal, it becomes universal Reason, and the goal that is reached through this development becomes "the domain of ethics," which is defined thus (pp. 375-376):

> this is nothing other than the absolute spiritual unity of individuals in the independent reality of their essences; it is an inherently universal self-consciousness, which is so real in another

[1] Hegel, *The Phenomenology of Mind*, trans. J. B. Baillie, pp. 271-453.

consciousness, that the latter has complete independence, or is a thing for it, and that precisely therein is conscious of its unity with it, and in this unity with this objective essence first begins to be self-consciousness. This ethical substance in its abstract universality is only the law as conceived; but it is nevertheless quite immediately self-consciousness of the real or it is morals. The individual consciousness is, on the other hand, only this existing unit, in that it is aware of the universal consciousness in its unity as its being, while its action and existence is the universal morals.

The goal here, then, as usual in Hegel, is to achieve identity between the individual and the universal or—to put it better—to point out that this identity is present in his speculative, dialectical ontology. On this level of morality this means that, for a free society, reason is actualized in its law, which expresses the determination of the individual, of its common nature, with which it can, shall, and ought to live in harmony (cf. pp. 377-378). The concept of virtue, *Tugend*, arises here.

The active Reason will unfold itself in its individuality and conquer the world. This first appears as desire, and, as Hegel puts it (p. 384):

> It repudiates sense and science
> The highest gifts possessed by men—
> It has gone over to the devil,
> And must be o'erthrown.[c]

Kuno Fischer has called this stage the "Faustian," thinking of Goethe's fragment dating from 1790.[2] The active Reason first takes shape as desire and craving and achieves the enjoyment of pleasure; but—to put it briefly—this apparent unhindered self-expansion reveals that it contains a constraint, an immanent necessity, and the consciousness becomes an enigma to itself, it becomes alien to itself. The self-consciousness has thus "in itself" survived the process, for this necessity is its proper nature; but in order for the self-consciousness to obtain clarification of this, it becomes aware that this necessity is a new form of that, namely "The Law of the Heart and the Madness of Self-Conceit" (pp. 390-400). Here, unlike in the

---

[c] The translator of Hegel's *Phenomenology of Mind* (whose version has been followed here) identifies this as an adaptation from *Faust*.

[2] *Geschichte der neuern Philosophie*, VIII, 1, 2nd ed. (1911), 357.

previous stage, the self-consciousness will not allow itself to be governed by the desire that results in being subject to the enjoyment that also appears as an unavoidable necessity imposed by fate. It will now be lord and master itself, and improve the world. The law decreed by the self-consciousness is the individual goal that should be actualized. This law can thus be called the law of the heart. Opposed to this is the reality it aims to bring into harmony with the established law, and

> here there is thus no longer the levity of the previous stage [*Gestalt*], which only wanted its own pleasure, on the contrary, it is the seriousness of a noble goal, which seeks its pleasure in the manifestation of its own excellent nature and in bringing about the welfare of mankind (p. 392).

If it succeeds now in putting into effect this law of the heart, then that happens through that which is purely interior becoming purely exterior, i.e., it stops being the law of the heart and becomes something that is alien to everyone other than the individual, the self-appointed reformer, who has brought it about in the social order. The result is that

> the palpitation of the heart for the welfare of mankind changes . . . into the rage of insane self-conceit, into the frenzy of consciousness, to preserve itself from its destruction, and to do this through casting out what is the absurdity which it is itself, and to exert itself to consider and express [that absurdity] as an other. Hence it speaks of the universal ordinance as a complete perversion of the law of its heart and happiness, invented by fanatical priests, by licentious despots and their underlings, who seek to indemnify themselves for their own degradation by degrading and oppressing in their turn—a distortion practiced to the nameless misery of deluded mankind (p. 397).

This again leads to group rising up against group, each appealing to its own law of the heart, thereby bringing about the rule of lawlessness. But this is an untenable situation, which is thus only a transition, after which follows the stage of virtue, which on an introductory level may be described as follows:

> This type of consciousness, which becomes aware of itself in the law; which finds itself in what is inherently true and good not as mere individual, but only as essentially real; and which

knows individuality to be what is perverted and perverting, and hence feels bound to surrender and sacrifice individualism of consciousness—this type of consciousness is *Virtue* (p. 400).

Active Reason in its first form (Reason is always taken as self-consciousness here) had the character of pure individuality, and opposite pure individuality it found "vacuous universality." In its second form both factors, law and individuality, were found in it. The heart was the immediate unity of the factors; but a clash of interests, resulting in actual lawlessness, was the result of this stage. Here on the stage of virtue, where we speak of the relation of virtue to the course of the world, we find both aspects, the juxtaposition of individuality and law, but in opposition to one another. For the consciousness of virtue, law is the essential thing and individuality is what must be relinquished. This applies both in the proper awareness of virtue and in the course of the world (pp. 402-403), which was "perverted" in the previous stage. It must now be turned back again (p. 404) to what virtue sees as its duty: the world as that which must be fought. Virtue lives under the conviction that the authentic good is not actualized in the world, but is found only in its own consciousness, and therefore it turns against the world. The good, such as it emerges in this context, consists in talents, skills, powers; but virtue comes into conflict with the actualized goods in the course of the world:

> Where . . . virtue takes on the course of the world, it always discovers spots where the good itself exists, which in all manifestations of the course of the world, as the inherent nature [*das Ansich*] of the course of the world, is inseparably enmeshed, and has its own existence in reality itself [the course of the world]; it is thus invulnerable to [virtue] (p. 407).

Thus it turns out that virtue not only resembles the knight who strives only to keep his sword gleaming in battle, but it must also be careful not to injure the victory of the enemy—and the course of world history triumphs over the abstraction and empty declamations of virtue (pp. 407-409). The struggle of individuality against the universal is always doomed to fail. In this instance virtue is a kind of manifestation of individuality.

In this context nothing more is required for an understanding of Hegel's discussion of virtue in *Phenomenology of the Spirit*. In the lesser triad the stage of virtue represents the higher unity of the desire and law of the heart, and is to that extent something positive; but as belonging to the manifestations of individuality opposed to the universal, negative elements predominate in their concepts and lead to their abrogation [*Ophævelse*]. This becomes even clearer when virtue is seen in its place within the greater triad, where it belongs in the negation [antithesis].

Before continuing with the account of the developments of Hegel's concept, a provisional answer can be given to the question of whether the statements of Kierkegaard quoted can be regarded as having some historical, possibly even direct contact with the ideas of Hegel set forth above.

Morality designates a lower stage than virtue for Kierkegaard. For Hegel, on the other hand, it is just the reverse—virtue is a lower stage than morality. But the important issue here, obviously, turns not only on clarification of the difference of terminology, but on the definition of concepts. Thus the question is, first, whether Kierkegaard's "morality" corresponds to Hegel's "virtue"—and whether Kierkegaard's "virtue" corresponds to Hegel's "morality"; but the latter half of the question cannot be answered without first clarifying Hegel's development of "morality."

It is a commonplace that *Phenomenlogy of the Spirit* can be read both as a philosophy of history—as a description of the Absolute Spirit's gradual penetration of the course of the macrocosm with the negative as the principle of movement—and as a description of the Absolute Spirit's penetration to complete clarity in the microcosm, the human individual. If we interpret it in the latter way—in harmony with the dominant tradition in modern philosophy from Descartes up to existential philosophy in the version of Heidegger—we can describe it as Hegel's theory of knowledge. After this comes, chronologically and topically, the whole system, with *Science of Logic* as the first work. Thus it is possible to read Hegel's *Phenomenology of the Spirit* as a theory of knowledge, an account of the way by which the Absolute (universal) Spirit and the individual spirit necessarily move toward the absolute, speculative knowledge, which is the Spirit's knowledge of itself. It is possible to interpret this work of Hegel in this way, and the conviction that this way of understanding is in harmony with Hegel's intention is fortified at the outset by the fact that the preface deals precisely with "scientific knowledge." Naturally, in this context, "scientific" means "speculative." Unlike for Kant in *Critique of Pure Reason*, the fundamental question for Hegel is not how is scientific knowledge pos-

sible? but the ontological question: what is being [*det værende*]?
The answer briefly, is that Absolute Spirit is being; it is being-in-and-
for itself. Absolute Spirit is identical with Absolute Thought, and
thus thought and being are identical. The dialectical movement of
thought and being is directed toward a synthesis, in which the stages
traversed are abrogated and transcended [*ophæves og hæves op*].
The way passes from "sense-certainty" beyond "perception," "force
and understanding," "the truth of certainty itself," "truth and certainty of reason," "Spirit," "religion," up to "absolute knowledge."

It is within the context of this work in its totality that we must
understand both the greater and the lesser triad, the content of which
has been given schematically above, and within which Hegel
situates "virtue." If we set what has been developed here alongside
Kierkegaard's discussion of morality in the entry cited (I A 75),
we see that through a consideration of the problematic of the whole
entry and from the precise context, that its orientation is completely
different from that of Hegel in *Phenomenology of the Spirit*. In the
realm of self-knowledge at a definite stage, which Kierkegaard
calls that of morality, there can emerge

> that troublesome, sinister traveling companion—that irony of
> life, which manifests itself in the sphere of knowledge, and bids
> true knowledge to begin with ignorance (Socrates), just as God
> created the world from nothing.

Already in 1835 Kierkegaard had stages, just as Hegel had stages,
but Kierkegaard's stages are not Hegel's. For him, the irony of life
emerges in the sphere of knowledge, more precisely, in the sphere
of self-knowledge, "on the open sea of morality," where it "tosses
man around this most vile environment." For Hegel, the concept
"virtue" contains, as do all of Hegel's concepts, positive and negative elements; but the negative ingredient is positive in the sense
that with necessity (metaphysical necessity) it leads to the progress
of thought. The genuinely negative, the negative constant in the
concept of Hegel, if we may be allowed to use this expression in
connection with Hegel, must be found therein inasmuch as it
belongs to the way and not to the goal of the way in absolute knowledge. For Kierkegaard, the concept "morality" designates something lower than "the breeze of virtue," and the only similarity with
Hegel in this respect is that he offers a rank order. This is not what
is of interest in the present case, but rather that in Kierkegaard there

is no metaphysically necessary stride toward the higher stage such as we find in Hegel. Even if we assume—a difficult thing to do in the case of both Hegel and Kierkegaard—that each in his own way is speaking of the development of an individual man or, better, of the development of every single man, that they are thus speaking fundamentally, then a constant difference remains, namely, in anthropology. According to the present text of Kierkegaard, there is a possibility that man *can* pass from the stage in question to another and higher one, from morality with its place for the irony of life in self-knowledge. For Hegel there is a necessity that man *must* progress along the dialectical way of development. Another difference between the two thinkers is that Kierkegaard's problem is not the same as that of Hegel. Hegel poses an ontological question: what is being? Kierkegaard, however, raises an existential issue, a question of finding "the idea, for which I will live and die," as he puts it. The fundamental intention, problematic, and the definitions of concepts are so different in the two thinkers, that in the present instance there is no basis for assuming any more than peripheral connection between them.

From the standpoint of rank order, the concept "virtue" in Kierkegaard corresponds to the concept "morality" in Hegel's *Phenomenology of Spirit*, which was one of the two works where there could have been some possible contact on the part of Kierkegaard. It turns out that this is not very likely.

The other place where one might find some possible contact with Hegel is, as has been said, in Hegel's *Philosophy of Right*.[3]

The philosophy of right is a part of the teaching on the Objective Spirit, which also includes the philosophy of history, and only in this larger context do the individual definitions and elaborations of concepts get their meaning. Because they exemplify the structure of Hegel's thought, we will sketch here the essential themes and basic format of the work. Hegel's language and disposition coincide quite closely.

The teaching on the objective spirit is the teaching on the objectifications of the free will. The product of free will as objective reality is right, which Hegel understands not as a restriction, but as an

---

[3] SW (*Jubiläumsausgabe*), VII, to which references are made in what follows. [A convenient English translation is T. M. Knox, Hegel's *Philosophy of Right*. Prof. Thulstrup's page references to the Glockner edition will be converted to the pagination of the Knox translation here.]

actualization of freedom, an actualization that rises up against capriciousness. As such, the right is formal and abstract right, in which free will is immediately present.

The next stage is that of morality [*Moralitet*], i.e., the will in its self-determination as conscience, and ethics [*Sædelighed*] is found to be the third and highest stage, in which the subject knows itself to be united with the ethical substance, which consists of three parts: the family, the civil society, and the state. The state is the idea of the ethical reality, ethical substance conscious of itself, the ethical spirit, which unfolds itself toward an organic actuality in the empirical world. According to Hegel this means that the divine will is present and unfolds itself not only in the world but toward a world, an ordered whole, a cosmos in the form of a constitutional monarchy.

That, briefly, is the theme and structure of Hegel's *Philosophy of Right*.

On this basis, it is already evident that, unlike Kant, for example, Hegel did not distinguish sharply between ethics and right, but integrated both under the theory of the state.

Now the question arises of a more precise understanding of morality [*Moralität*] and ethics [*Sittlichkeit*] and their mutual relation according to Hegel, and, next, what this understanding can contribute to the resolution of the question of Kierkegaard's relation to these theories.

The stage of morality is the free will in its self-determination as conscience. Another way of putting this would be to say that we go beyond the abstract, formal right to the concrete, individual, and individualistic ethics, where the free will not only "is infinite in itself, but for itself" (§105, p. 75). Here it is the subjectivity that determines the content of the concept and exhibits the real aspect of the concept of freedom. The moral standpoint is the subjective will's right, and the manifestation of this right is the action that proceeds not according to a rule of right but from the subjective conviction of the duty to follow it (§113, p. 78). This action contains three further determinations, namely, that it is conscious as the action of the individual subjectivity, that it is traced back to duty, and, finally, that it externalizes itself and intends to become the will of another (*ibid.*).

The right of the moral will is then subdivided into three parts, viz., "Purpose and Responsibility" (§§115-118, pp. 79-81), "Intention and Welfare" (§§119-128, pp. 81-86), and "The Good and Conscience" (§§129-140, pp. 86-103).

The subjective conviction of the duty to carry out an action is the intention of the will, which is the formal right of the action; the special thing about the action is its content, which constitutes its value, which again is the goal of subjectivity. To this is added its proper content, which is to actualize "the welfare," which regarded more closely means the good, to which, in the sphere of reflection, is added evil and conscience.

The intention of the will—the motive of action as it could be called in other words—consists, finally, in the understanding that as a condition of its action the subjective will has a presupposition, an external object bound up with manifold adjacent circumstances. The action causes a change in the object, and thereby the will has [non-moral] responsibility [*Skyld*], namely, for the change. The subjective, moral will is [morally] responsible [*ansvarlig*]; but responsibility can be imputed only insofar as a given change can be traced back to a particular intention, a definite motive for acting in the person who acts. Responsibility [*Skyld*] does not automatically entail imputability [*Ansvar*], for which a definite intention is required. Therefore, we cannot without further ado charge a person with every action of which he is the cause [*Skyld*]. Furthermore, the subjective will certainly has a notion of the circumstances that are bound up with the intention of carrying out a particular action with regard to a particular object; but because of its finitude the will cannot recognize all circumstances, and thus it is its right in its action to take into account, and thereby have responsibility for, what comes within its limited purview. Correspondingly, a distinction must be made between the incidental and the necessary consequences of an action. With this, the development of the concept moves on to the next step in this triad, "Intention and Welfare."

The intention is only the intention of a single action; but the purpose of an action is not confined to the accomplishment of this individual action. The intention aims at the universal, which in this stage is determined as the satisfaction of the needs, inclinations, passions, attitudes, etc., of the individual subjective will, with the help of particular actions, and the fulfillment of this general need for the individual is thus "welfare or happiness" (§123, p. 83). To obtain these satisfactions the individual can undertake lawful actions; but it is possible also that one may trespass beyond his limits to attempt unlawful actions, e.g. theft out of need. To judge in such instances we must thus take into account the intention as well as the unlawful action.

However a collision (between the individual and the universal) intrudes not only in emergencies but in each of the actions of the individual, which indicates that subjectivity has overstepped the confines in which its legitimacy is situated and has made itself infinite in conscience, which is given an illegitimate role as supreme judge.

Hegel deals with these matters in the third and final section of "morality" under the title "Good and Conscience."

The good is the idea as the unity of the will (i.e., the universal will) and the concept of the individual will. The individual will makes itself independent and posits itself as the absolute purpose of the world (§129, p. 86). Here the will not only seeks to realize or obtain one or another good but aims at the good in itself as the moral goal toward which the conscience unconditionally commits itself (§133, p. 89). This goal is not sought just for its own sake. It now becomes important to consider not only how this good is defined, but what the determining factors are. Discussion of the absolute good and the absolute duty to make this good real can remain on the first stage, the abstract stage. According to the interpretation given by Hegel (who at the same time indicates his evaluation by the place he gives it in his own system), that is the case with Kant's ethics, which results in formalism, indeed, in empty chatter. "From this standpoint, no immanent doctrine of duties is possible" (§135, p. 90). It can also take on an entirely different form, such that an individual subjective will, sovereign in conscience, will define the good. In its self-assertion is contained the germ of its destruction; but the process of resolution has several phases.

Along the way, the good lapses into its opposite, the evil. At first this self-assertion can take on the rather innocent form of acting with a bad conscience, i.e., the good is still recognized. In the next phase, that of hypocrisy, one gives only the pretense of recognition, while Probabilism makes one at ease, when one has simply discovered one or another casually recognized norm that can be used as a good reason and defense of a particular type of action. Probabilism leads on to the phase in which one asserts that he wills the good, but at any price, so that the end justifies the means. The defining factor here is the subjective will alone, the conscience of the individual. The last phase is called irony. Here Hegel is not thinking of Socratic, but rather of romantic irony, especially as represented by Friedrich Schlegel. Kuno Fischer aptly describes this phase as follows:

> Fichte had made the absolute ego the principle of philosophy, Schlegel put the particular ego in this position, *his* particular ego and gave it the plenitude of the power of the absolute. The ego, this particular ego, knows itself as decisive above truth, right and duty, it knows itself as that which so wills and determines, even though it can also will and decide on some other good; it is not things which are important, but only this ego, which plays with things, enjoys them.[4]

It appears—as Kuno Fischer's conclusion shows—that if the good remains at the abstract stage, it becomes only a formal, empty standard, and if the will, the conscience, remains supreme in its subjective character, the process ends in total capriciousness. With that, the dialectical development has arrived at the point where the two criteria, the good and conscience, are reconciled, mediated, into a concrete identity, and we find ourselves on the threshold between morality and ethics.

On the whole it is extremely difficult and sometimes entirely impossible to declare with certainty what a particular person has *not* read. We cannot absolutely exclude the possibility that Kierkegaard had Hegel in mind here, despite the absence of compelling proof. In any case, at first glance there is a certain similarity between Hegel's and Kierkegaard's stages here.

Kierkegaard says that self-knowledge and virtue belong together as excluding the irony of life, which is found on the lower stage of ethics. The question now is whether the sphere of morality in Hegel (it will be recalled that this is the negation in the triad: abstract right, morality, ethics) has points of contact with Kierkegaard's "ethics" and "life-irony." Points of similarity are that both thinkers work with a qualitative distinction here, and thus a rank order, and that both take the lower stage as negative and temporary in character, even though Hegel's "morality"—as indeed all his concepts—contains positive elements. In spite of this, we must not ignore the difference, which clearly emerges from the question about the translation from the lower to the higher stage. At issue is whether this transition takes place freely or with necessity. There

---

[4] *Geschichte d. neuern Philosophie* [History of Modern Philosophy], VIII, 2 (2nd ed., 1911) p. 710.

can be no doubt that for Hegel it happens with necessity; but Kierkegaard, on the whole, says nothing here about the transition. So much for the points of similarity and the difference between the two thinkers. The relevant question in this part of our inquiry is whether we can or may assume that Kierkegaard formulated his statement in direct relation with Hegel or with Hegel's thought process (in *Philosophy of Right*) in mind.

On a closer view, neither seems to be the case.

In this entry (I A 75) Kierkegaard speaks of the irony of life, which in the realm of knowledge "bids true knowledge to begin with an ignorance." In a marginal note to this entry, he adds that this life-irony has an enduring significance, yet is not greater than what man can bear. He says further of life-irony that it can manifest itself in the fact that "when one most of all believes that he has understood himself, yet one actually has only memorized the life of another." Here he speaks of the effect of life-irony in knowledge, more precisely marked in the individual's struggle toward self-knowledge, and maintains that it essentially belongs to a particular stage, and, moreover, it can be found, without such profoundly negative effects, on a higher stage. A later entry (I A 125; February 1836) places life-irony in the period of childhood (that of fantasy, of the medieval, of the romantic school) while adulthood does not have so much of it. The placement of life-irony corresponds to that of the earlier entry. In a couple of still later entries (II A 38 and 112), Kierkegaard no longer speaks of life-irony, but of world-irony, an irony that has the same effect on the individual as life-irony, i.e., it mocks his efforts. What is relevant there is that it is clearly understood in the first place as a power coming from without, and in the second place as distinct from both Socratic and romantic irony—athough these two types are still not entirely clarified for Kierkegaard.[5]

Kierkegaard's concept of life-irony does not correspond to Hegel's discussion of romantic irony within the sphere of morality, nor is ethics in Kierkegaard identical with morality in Hegel. Kierkegaard's treatment of knowledge and self-knowledge does not have

[5] On this point see esp. P. A. Heiberg, *Et Segment af SK's religiøse Udvikling* [A Segment of SK's Religious Development] (1918), 30ff., 192ff., and J. Himmelstrup's *SK's Opfattelse af Sokrates* [SK's Interpretation of Socrates] (1924), 34ff., and Himmelstrup's *Terminologisk Register* (*T. Ordbog*) [Terminological Register (Dictionary)] (1936; 2nd ed. 1964), the articles "Irony" and "World-Irony."

any parallel in Hegel's philosophy of right either. For Hegel, "morality" is understood as the negative stage in the dialectical unfolding of the objective spirit, a stage represented by individuality, in which irony emerges from within necessarily while life-irony (world-irony) comes from without ("a little external circumstance" I A 75). When that is the situation, it is most unlikely that Kierkegaard formulated his thoughts with knowledge of Hegel's *Philosophy of Right*, particularly the section on morality. For Hegel, irony is a negative, and precisely for that reason, a propelling moment; while for Kierkegaard it is also negative, without anything being said about whether it should facilitate any dialectical development. Furthermore, for Hegel irony is a condition of individuality, in Kierkegaard it is taken as a condition of the world.

The next stage in Kierkegaard, virtue, is spoken of with such great brevity in I A 75 that its exact content must be inferred mainly from its positive character in relation to the foregoing. Even if we could in this way penetrate to Kierkegaard's understanding, at least approximately, that would be an inadequate foundation for a discussion of the possible historical relation to Hegel's understanding of ethics and virtue. On the basis of the present text no conclusion can be derived with certainty. But it can be said that as little likely as it is that there should be any historical link with what has already been said about Hegel's philosophy of right, it is just as little likely that there will be any indication that Kierkegaard had knowledge of what follows in *Philosophy of Right*. Kierkegaard's distinction between ethics and virtue, his description of these stages and of life-irony as belonging naturally to the first stage, seem to have developed independently of Hegel.

3. The Incompatibility of Christianity and Philosophy, and Hegel's View of Their Relationship

Based upon what has just been said, the lengthy Gilleleie entry (August 1, 1835), a continuation and expansion of I A 72 (June 1, 1835), provides no basis for any supposition that it was written in historical relation to Hegel.

The next relevant entry is I A 94 (October 17, 1835).

In that entry, the thesis is formulated thus: "*Philosophy and Christianity are always incompatible.*" The argument that follows brings out how Kierkegaard understands philosophy and Christianity and why they are incompatible.

Kierkegaard's understanding and evaluation of philosophy in this entry is not essentially different from that expressed in I A 75: philosophy "just seeks to give an account of the relation between God and the world *qua* human," and in this effort it must, as is said in a notable addition to this entry, "either assume optimism—or—despair." This pregnant description is quite interesting and concerns Hegel's philosophy to an eminent degree, since Hegel's philosophy is undeniably optimistic. But the scope of this statement is much wider, and relates to the work of many philosophers, not just Hegel. The statement describes philosophy in general and not Hegel's in particular. Yet there are a couple of words in the statement, viz., "*qua* human" and the reflections that follow, which are most noteworthy.

The philosopher can derive a conclusion only within the limits set by the fact that he is a human. The philosopher can arrive at "a conception of the sin of mankind, but it does not follow from this, that he knows that mankind needs redemption." The philosopher knows that mankind strives for redemption, but only inasmuch as this redemption is not understood as a work of God, but as man's self-redemption—a relative redemption, as Kierkegaard puts it. That means that philosophy's optimism is preserved or, better, that it must be preserved if there is to be consideration of philosophy at all.

Precisely this optimism, this confidence in man's fundamental possibility of obtaining his superior goals, is not only made dubious by Christianity but is made impossible by the assertion of "the universal sinfulness of creation." Sin makes philosophical optimism impossible and necessitates not human self-redemption, but redemption as a work of God. Kierkegaard does not elaborate an explicit theory of redemption here. As far as knowledge and thus the efforts of philosophy are concerned, the Christian dogma on sin means that knowledge is "full of gaps," a claim that philosophy cannot acknowledge in its radicality, since that would mean the capitulation of philosophy.

If redemption is maintained as occurring essentially within Christianity, and sin is maintained as corrupting not only man's "normal capacities" but also, what is relevant in this context, knowledge, then Christianity becomes incompatible with (any) philosophy whose efforts are as described and whose point of departure must be a basic optimism in its view of man and the possibility of human knowledge.

Even if Kierkegaard is working with a more comprehensive concept of philosophy here than the Hegelian version in particular, then it is not impossible at the outset that he could have consciously included the Hegelian approach in his indictment. Nor can we eliminate the possibility that, in his sharply formulated thesis, he wished precisely to express his opposition to Hegel, who is known to have wished just that—to align his philosophy with Christianity, even to identify them as regards content.

Hegel's special speculative concept of philosophy is narrower than the one Kierkegaard employs here, and certainly he could also have said that the philosopher philosophizes *qua* human. But Hegel would not be able to imagine any inherent limitation on the possibilities of knowledge because of sin, at least not in the same sense as Kierkegaard's concept of sin. This can be shown, quite briefly, from pivotal passages in Hegel's works.

In two places Hegel deals at length with the relation between philosophy and religion (which, for him, in its highest form is identical with Christianity), and in both places concludes that there is a connection between his own speculative idealistic philosophy and his intended orthodox Lutheran understanding of Christianity. One place is in the introduction to *Lectures on the Philosophy of Religion*,[6] the second is in the introduction to *Lectures on the History of Philosophy*.[7] The fundamental point of view is the same throughout, just as in *Encyclopedia of the Philosophical Sciences*, especially §573.[d] In various places in these texts Hegel indulges in polemics, as, for example, on the concept of pantheism in the *Encyclopedia*, but we can ignore that here.

"The concern of religion as of philosophy is eternal truth in its objectivity itself, God and nothing other than God and the explication of God" (*Phil. Relig.*, I, 19). Philosophy is knowledge of the

[6] Hegel, *Lectures on the Philosophy of Religion*, trans. E. B. Speirs and J. Burdon Sanderson (New York: The Humanities Press, 1962) I, 18-35. (SW, XV, 36-52).

[7] Hegel, *Lectures on the History of Philosophy*, trans. E. S. Haldane (London: Routledge and Kegan Paul, New York: The Humanities Press, 1963) I, 61-92. (SW XVII, 92-125.) Neither here nor elsewhere in the present study is account taken of Lasson and Hoffmeister's philologically superior editions of Hegel's lectures, since the point here is to give an account of Hegel's thoughts in the form in which Kierkegaard might have had the opportunity to know them, not to present the "genuine" Hegel.

[d] Cf. Hegel's *Philosophy of Mind*, (Part III of the *Encyclopedia*), trans. William Wallace (Oxford: Clarendon Press, 1894) §573, pp. 181-196.

eternal, of God and of what proceeds from the nature of God, which reveals and unfolds itself. The object of philosophy is the same as that of religion; indeed Hegel says plainly that philosophy considered from the standpoint of its function is "liturgy, religion." Philosophy and religion are identical so far as content and function are concerned; the difference between them consists solely in their method and form of expression.

Naturally Hegel understands philosophy here as his own speculative philosophy, which he explains as "the consciousness of the Idea, so that everything is apprehended as Idea; but the Idea is the True in thought, not in the mere perception or representation" (*Phil. Relig.*, I, 21). With that, the difference between religion and philosophy with respect to the form of expression is given. The form of philosophy is inseparable from its method,[8] the dialectical, which Hegel concisely sketches as follows: the true in thought is that it is concrete—i.e. speculative-concrete (Hegel uses the word "concrete" in its etymological sense: coalesced)—that it divides in two (posit-negate) and thus, that the two aspects are reciprocally opposed (as contraries not contradictories) conditions of thought, as the unity (mediation) whose Idea must be grasped in understanding. Hegel himself expresses it this way:

> To think speculatively means to resolve a reality into its parts and to oppose these to each other in such a way that the distinctions are placed in opposition according to the conditions of thought and the object is apprehended as the unity of both (*Phil. Relig.*, I, 21).

The simple view has the totality of the object (the immediate concrete) before it. The philosophy of reflection (the only rationalistic philosophy that Hegel had turned against in criticism even before the elaboration of his definitive system at the beginning of the century) can divide this totality but cannot retain its unity. At one point it forgets the totality, at another the parts, and makes it into something different. Speculative thought pioneered in conquering the immediate view (positing) and the reflexive reason (negation) in the speculative conception, which grasps the unity in

---

[8] This is decisive for Hegel, and for a correct understanding of his philosophy. Some have sought to interpret Hegel by ignoring the indissoluble connection between system and method, whereby that which is decisive and characteristic in Hegel's philosophy vanishes. An important work on this is B. Heimann, *System und Methode in Hegels Philosophie* (1927).

the contraries and expresses, formulates, this unity in the concrete concept that is both means and end in Hegel's philosophy.

The highest unity is the Absolute Idea, as it is called in philosophical terminology, and is the same as God in religious language. There is also something given there, and this given appears to consist of contraries that are reconciled (Hegel himself most frequently employs this word rather than "mediated") in harmony.

For Hegel, the absolute religion is Christianity, the absolute philosophy, his own. The content is the same, the forms differ. Philosophy and Christianity are united in Hegel. Sin and reconciliation do not, according to Hegel, hinder this union, as they do for Kierkegaard in the entry cited (I A 94). What does Hegel understand by sin and redemption (or reconciliation)? His answer emerges from his account of the Fall and Redemption in the philosophy of religion (*Phil. Relig.*, I, 276ff.).

> We find a noted representation in the Bible, in abstract fashion called the Fall—a representation that profoundly sees not merely a random history, but rather the eternal, necessary history of mankind is outwardly expressed in mythological fashion.

The account of the Fall in the third chapter of *Genesis* is interpreted by Hegel thus:

Man's immediate, primordial condition includes consciousness of the absolute, divine nature, and if man lives in harmony with that he is in the state of Paradise. Hegel asserts that man has never been a purely natural being (like plants and animals), but is essentially an intellectual being [*Aandsvæsen*] and that as such knows that God is rational, the Absolute Reason. By virtue of this constitution man is inherently the true, but this constitutive principle is still not manifested in (external) existence. The concept must make itself real, must, in accord with necessity, abandon the condition of immediacy. After immediacy comes reflection, and only after that reconciliation. In religious terminology, the first, immediate condition is called the state of innocence; but Hegel does not find this term appropriate, since the human condition there is in a state where there is responsibility. Thus the state of innocence is a condition in which there is neither good nor evil. It is also actually an animal condition, and so it is the case that:

> in truth that first natural unity as existence is not a state of inno-

cence, but one really of crudeness, greed, barbarity. The animal is not good and not evil: but man in an animal condition is wild, is evil, is what he ought not be, but what he is, he ought to be through Spirit, through knowing and willing what is right. This notion that if man exists only according to nature he is not what he ought to be, has been expressed by saying that man is evil by nature (*Phil. Relig.*, I, 276).[9]

According to the account of the Fall, man knew about God and the good, had that as an object of his consciousness, which also means that a "bifurcation" intruded between the consciousness and its object. The stage of reflection is entered necessarily as a pre-requisite of reconciliation, and this stage must be transcended. Even if evil intrudes herewith (in reflection) it is a source of cure for that evil. Hegel finds this expressed in the words (Genesis 3:22) "Man has become like one of us by knowing good and evil," by which it is said that the serpent speaks the truth. Thus the evil contains the good within itself; they are not absolute opposites. The fact that man arrives at awareness of good and evil, and also passes from immediacy to reflection, is for Hegel just as necessary as that reflection in turn must be abandoned as the intermediate link it is. It must be stressed that for Hegel it is the Fall which makes possible the knowledge that is precisely the condition for man's achieving his full development as the speculative conception of the Absolute Idea, God.[10]

What, then does reconciliation mean for Hegel? The concept of redemption does not seem to appear in his writings. Discussion of reconciliation occurs in various contexts. Here we shall speak only of his understanding of reconciliation in Christianity.[11]

[9] "Man exists essentially as Spirit; but Spirit does not exist in an immediate way, rather it is essentially that which exists for itself [not just in itself], to be free, which places the natural opposite itself, which extricates itself from its immersion in nature, to separate itself from nature and only through and from this separation does it reconcile itself with it, and not only with nature, but also with its own essence, with its truth" (*Phil. Relig.*, I, 275).

[10] In the course of his survey of the Jewish religion (the Religion of Sublimity) Hegel again deals with the account of the Fall (*Phil. Relig.*, II, 197-204). It is worth noting (cf. Kierkegaard's *The Concept of Dread*) the sentence: "It is Adam, or man in general, who appears in this story" (*Phil. Relig.*, II, 201), and also the emphasis on the fact that it was precisely from the tree of knowledge that Adam should not have eaten.

[11] The most important places where Hegel presents his teaching on recon-ciliation, are the *Lectures on the Philosophy of Religion* [see index at the end

Hegel understands the redemptive act of Christ as, above all, an illustration that the Spirit of God and man's spirit are fundamentally one. The Crucifixion is only a transitional point in the self-unfolding of the Divine Nature, a transitional point in which the human and the divine, death and life (Resurrection) are reconciled. Death is the culmination of finiteness, but here it is also its abrogation, its defeat. In an absolute sense, God cannot die, and when the God-Man Jesus Christ—Hegel is quite concerned to adhere to orthodox Christology—dies, that means (*Phil. Relig.*, III, 96, 99) that God reconciles Himself to Himself, returns to Himself and thereby abrogates finitude. The death of Christ on the cross thus becomes the pivotal point in God's self-unfolding: from his being in Himself before the creation of the world (in Hegel's logic), through His being in the world (nature and history) God returns to Himself (the world of the Spirit). The created world, to which man belongs, cannot reconcile God. God must reconcile Himself, and this reconciliation entails something that, although Hegel does not say so explicitly, is an inherent consequence of his train of thought. That is that, through God's self-reconciliation to Himself, creation is liberated from its misery, and that this illustrates how the summit of creation, man, is essentially constituted as spirit, and is fundamentally one with God. Furthermore, the pivotal point must occur with absolute necessity, since the process of God's self-unfolding requires the intermediate link of negation, and its character of "uniqueness" (*Einmaligkeit*) is, according to Hegel's theory, surely not to be denied but to be declared inessential for an understanding of its content and significance. Speculatively considered, reconciliation is an eternal phenomenon in the self-unfolding of God.

Hegel unquestionably wishes to speak of reconciliation as God's action. Although he does not put it in quite these terms, it follows that the accompanying release comes to be understood as the self-redemption of man. If we then place the development of his concepts within the larger context not only of aesthetics and the philosophy of religion but of the whole system in its definitive form in the *Encyclopedia of the Philosophical Sciences*, it becomes clear

---

of volume III of the English translation] and *Vorlesungen über die Aesthetik* (SW, XIII, 142-149). [A new English translation of Hegel's *Lectures on Aesthetics* by T. M. Knox has been published by Oxford University Press.] Of the most recent literature, we can refer here especially to Erik Schmidt, *Hegels Lehre von Gott* (1952), 201ff. and 236ff.

that reconciliation (and redemption) is really understood as man's own work. In fact, this involves saying that in Hegel's interpretation the redemptive act of Christ is an illustration of the identity of the spirit of God and the spirit of man. The three divisions of the philosophy of spirit in Hegel—aesthetics, religion, and philosophy—ultimately have the same content, and in philosophy man's thought and God's thought are one. Reconciliation occurs and is grasped by man without hindrance or restraint because of sin or imperfection. Philosophy and Christianity not only allow themselves to be united, but according to Hegel's view they have been united by the incorporation of the Christian doctrine on sin and reconciliation.

If we now return to Kierkegaard's Journal entry, it could certainly appear that he wrote it with Hegel in mind and in protest against Hegel's view. There is an absolute opposition between the viewpoints of Hegel and Kierkegaard on the relation between philosophy and Christianity. Kierkegaard's concept of philosophy is not identical with Hegel's; but insofar as the present context is concerned, the optimism of philosophy is precisely characteristic of Hegel's understanding. Hegel's optimism is undisturbed by an interpretation of Christianity in which the radicality of sin is rendered harmless by being conceived speculatively, and in which reconciliation as an action of God in reality is toned down to mean an illustration of the factual harmony between God and man, a harmony which in the Absolute philosophy itself is conceived of as an identity. Hegel wants to show that the combination, indeed, the identity of Philosophy and Christianity, and reconciliation (redemption) becomes for him not an obstacle to this union of philosophy and Christianity but precisely the relevant criterion of identity. Thus it is not so much Kierkegaard's notion of what philosophy is as his concept of Christianity, and together with that his view of man, which leads him to present the thesis of the incompatibility of the two standards. Neither in the previous entries nor in the one under scrutiny here are there passages that decisively indicate knowledge of Hegel. At this point Kierkegaard's concept of philosophy was not firmly established, but in any case it was not particularly Hegelian, nor was his understanding of Christianity. His theory was thus in all likelihood developed, and may be understood, without special reference to Hegel. This is not without significance for an understanding of the correct perspective on his subsequent development as a thinker, as Hirsch correctly observes.[12]

[12] Cf. Chap. 1 *supra*, note 45.

4. KIERKEGAARD'S CONTINUED REFLECTIONS ON THE SAME TOPIC

The theme in the entry just analyzed is taken up again in the one immediately following. Here Kierkegaard tried to consider the relation from the outside, objectively, as an observer. Several times he speaks of "the Christians" for whom reason is encountered as a spiritual trial, which "asserts its claims once more before it finally subsides" (I A 95).[e] Reason is a temptation or spiritual trial when it tries to assert its claims subsequent to the truth of Christianity's having become a man's firm conviction, while the same condition at an earlier stage, prior to faith, is called doubt. The attempt to understand in the entry just cited and the two following ones merges into a modified estimate of Christianity, while in I A 98 and 99,[f] probably also dating from October 1835, the theme is taken up again. Nearly a year later, on September 10, 1836, and again in January 14, 1837, Kierkegaard returned to these reflections and made notes on them.

On the basis of I A 98 it is clear that in October 1835 Kierkegaard was not thinking of Hegel or speculative idealism at all. He says there plainly that "the consequences of such a union [of Christianity and philosophy] can be seen in rationalism," thus the same standard which in I A 72 he declared to be such an inadequate one. It is, of course, evident that Kierkegaard was thinking of rationalism here in the context of church history and not in the sense in which it is used in the history of philosophy.

Papirer, I A 99 is a counterpart to 95 and 96. There Kierkegaard tried to see the Christian life from the standpoint of reason, from which vantage point it cuts a sorry figure. Here he wishes "to sketch how man as man apart from Christianity must appear to the Christian." The result is a confirmation of the thesis of the incompatibility of philosophy and Christianity presented in I A 94. Here for the first time we meet the category of "the leap," which later became so significant in the thought of Kierkegaard. In this respect he is also implicitly in opposition to Hegel's view, but, as far as we can see, without having a clear understanding of it himself.

---

[e] This whole entry will be found as #416 in volume I of Howard and Edna Hong's new edition and translation of selections from *Søren Kierkegaard's Journals and Papers* (Bloomington, Indiana: Indiana University Press, 1967).

[f] Hong, III, #3246, 3247.

After these entries it is interesting to read I A 108 (November 3, 1835).[g] The first half, which takes up a theme from I A 50 (February 5, 1835), is marked with an optimism about development (an opinion Kierkegaard later rejected for the sake of the contrary opinion) in the concept of Christianity which after "the course of 1800 years has permeated all life." The latter half of this entry is best understood in relation to Grundtvig.

Not until the autumn of the following year, August 1836, do we find entries that clearly stand in relation to Hegel. The problem, then, is to determine the nature and scope of that relation.

The editors of the *Papirer* concisely described Kierkegaard's "project" at this point as follows: "to collect ingredients for a characterization of the spirit of the medieval period through a general historical study of the three distinctive phenomena in all areas of the intellectual life, in literature, art, religion, science [*Videnskab*], and social relations, concentrating on a more penetrating study of the reflection of the mind of the medieval people in poetry, myths, folklore, and stories, especially of the representative ideas arising out of the world of consciousness of medieval popular life: Don Juan—Faust—the eternal Jew, and all this in the light of a concurrent, more abstract Hegelian philosophical interest, through the determination of concepts such as the ancient, the romantic ('dialectical'), the modern,—the comic, the tragic, irony, humor, resignation, etc., to fix the stages of the development of the spirit taken as a whole, within 'world-history' as well as within the single individual's 'microcosm.' "[13]

In this connection the question arises of what relation to Hegel we can speak of regarding the entries I A 170[h] and I A 211[i] and the ones immediately following each of these. It is not so easy to answer this question, partly because the several entries are rather abbreviated and only provisionally worked out, hastily jotted down, and partly because the allusions in them are frequently kept general. The sources do not always speak as clearly and unambiguously as we might wish, and sometimes several interpretations are possible, so that we cannot say with assurance that any one of them is exhaustive.

[g] Hong, I, #581.
[13] *Papirer*, I, Fortale [Preface] xv-xvi.
[h] Hong, II, #1563.
[i] Hong, II, #1564.

On June 12, Kierkegaard notes that to the same degree that necessity is advanced the romantic recedes, and thus Christianity does not remain romantic at all. With this it is said that antiquity enters into time, i.e., the contemporary, and finally he asks how this antiquity resembles the genuine, i.e., the historical antiquity (I A 170). Necessity is associated with Hegel, whose name Kierkegaard gives in parentheses. This probably means that Hegel's philosophy was progressing in the present age, it represents necessity, or more correctly: necessity dominates in his philosophy, and—without expressing any evaluation or criticism of Hegel—where the perspective of necessity prevails, the romantic cannot survive. Christianity does not recede or disappear together with the romantic, but its concept becomes decisively altered, although Kierkegaard does not say precisely how.

Here we find the beginnings of the reflections on the philosophy of history that are taken up in the period immediately following. Already on July 2 (I A 200) Kierkegaard notes that he now understands what he had often wondered about, "that Thorwaldsen[j] has arisen just in our age; he is really purely contemporaneous with Hegel. The romantic has disappeared and the present tense of necessity (the classical) has supervened . . . and thus we have resurrected a new ancient stage. The romantic is reconciled with the world." Hegel is seen as a neo-classicist. This development is then paralleled with monasticism according to the Hegelian schema, Thesis-Antithesis-Synthesis, thus: first the monks lived apart from the world (T), then in conflict with the world (A), and finally reconciled with the world like the Jesuits (S).

We can scarcely find a single place in Hegel with which this passage can be connected. On the contrary, we can assume a second-hand knowledge of Hegelian philosophy of history and aesthetics. It is most likely that Heiberg was the intermediary.[14] What is chiefly relevant in this entry is whether Kierkegaard thought that this dialectical development took place necessarily or freely. This

[j] Bertel Thorvaldsen (1768-1844), eminent Danish neo-classical sculptor, went to Rome to study in 1797. His first return to Copenhagen in 1819, via Vienna, Warsaw, and Berlin was like the return of a hero. In 1838 he again visited his native city and decided to remain. In 1839 a museum to house his work was started adjacent to Christiansborg Palace in Copenhagen. He was buried in the courtyard of the museum. I A 200 will be found in Hong, III, #3805.

[14] Cf. *supra*, Chapter I, section 2.

problem, which is presented and resolved in the "Interlude" of the *Philosophical Fragments*,[k] appears at this earlier point, but without being formulated or answered clearly at this time.

While reading Friedrich Schlegel's *Geschichte der alten und neuen Literatur* Kierkegaard comments (I A 211)[1] that the Indian teaching that God is the source of both good and evil, whereby the devil is included in the Trinity, seems to him to be Hegelianism. He does not express himself with certainty on the question. The theory belongs chiefly to another schema within speculative philosophy, identified with names such as Böhme, Baader, Schelling, and Martensen. In his *Lectures on the History of Philosophy* (Eng. trans., III, 194) Hegel sums up his attempt to describe Böhme's "raw and barbaric" thought as follows: "thus he has striven to grasp, to comprehend, the negative, evil, the devil in God." Hegel himself must consequently derive the evil from the idea of God—cf. the treatment of his teaching on sin, *supra*—but no clear statement on this point seems to have emerged, neither where we should expect it, that is, in his philosophy of religion, nor elsewhere in his writings.

In the same month, August 1836, Kierkegaard made various entries concerning Hegel and the Hegelians. This is in the series numbered I A 215-230,[m] where various problems and themes are considered.

During this period Kierkegaard thought it important to develop a definite concept of the romantic in itself and in relation to other phenomena, including Christianity. Entry I A 215 is characteristic:

> To the extent that Christianity adheres to the doctrine of the God-Man θεάνθρωπος, it is to that degree not romantic; Hegel has especially emphasized this aspect.[n]

The statement is undeniably correct. In Hegel's *Lectures on the Philosophy of History*[o] and especially in his *Lectures on the Philosophy of Religion* Christology occupies a central position, and this

---

[k] English translation, 2nd ed. (Princeton: Princeton University Press, 1962), pp. 89-110.

[1] Hong, II, #1564.

[m] Most of these will be found in vols. I and II of the Hong translation.

[n] A slightly different translation of this will be found in Hong, I, #421.

[o] Hegel, *The Philosophy of History*, trans. J. Sibree (New York: Dover Publications, 1956). A newer English translation is *Lectures on the Philosophy of World History* (Cambridge: Cambridge University Press, 1975), ed. D. Forbes and H. B. Nisbet.

doctrine of Christ as true God and true man is developed with great care. This has already been emphasized in the presentation of Hegel's teaching on redemption *supra* (pp. 80-82).[15] The question here is only this—where did Kierkegaard get his knowledge of Hegel's Christology? The importance of this point cannot be over-emphasized.

Marheineke's edition of Hegel's *Lectures on the Philosophy of Religion* first appeared in 1832, so it is possible that Kierkegaard could have read it. But this is unlikely, since Kierkegaard owned this work in the second edition, published in 1840 (Ktl., 564-565), and it is most reasonable to assume that at the time he wrote this entry Kierkegaard knew this work only from secondary sources. Whichever it may have been is of no particular interest, although it would be had the entry evidenced some special interpretation of Hegel's Christology. On this point, however, nothing can be inferred from the entry itself. Despite the brevity of the note, we can infer something about the character of its source, *viz.*, that it must have been Right Hegelian, since, for example, it does not say that Hegel's intention was to incorporate and speculatively interpret the orthodox doctrine of the twofold nature, but only that Hegel had emphasized it.

Entry I A 217[p] speaks of miracles. Miracles are found within "the romantic," but they are inconceivable within "the ancient." As a sort of conclusion to this, the Hegelians and Schleiermacher are named in parentheses. With respect to Schleiermacher, there are no problems. Kierkegaard had, in fact, gone through his *The Christian Faith*[q] with Martensen, and there is no mistaking the statement in §47 of this work:

> It can never be necessary in the interest of religion so to interpret a fact that its dependence on God absolutely excludes its being conditioned by a system of Nature.

Nor is there any difficulty regarding Hegel's own attitude: on the lower level of religion there is often talk about miracles, but on the plane of Christianity (and of speculative reason), certainly so-called

---

[15] Cf. Erik Schmidt, *Hegels Lehre von Gott*, p. 226f.

[p] This short entry (Hong, III, #3809) is: "The romantic has miracles, which the ancient cannot have (the Hegelians—Schleirmacher)."

[q] Friedrich Schleiermacher, *The Christian Faith*, ed. H. R. Mackintosh and J. S. Stewart (Edinburgh: T. & A. Clark, 1928), p. 178. This has also been published in a two-volume paperback edition by Harper Torchbooks (New York, 1963). The above quote will be found in vol. I of this edition, p. 178.

miracles are known, but they are without significance: "The main standpoint of reason in regard to miracles is that the spiritual cannot be verified externally; for the spiritual is higher than the external, it can be verified only through itself and in itself."[r] In the same passage Hegel asserts that Christ Himself had rejected the miracle as a valid criterion of truth. Since, for Hegel—in a kind of parallel with Spinoza—God is identified with His dialectical, necessary unfolding in the domains of logic, nature, and spirit, miracles are superfluous. On this point Kierkegaard was sufficiently well informed; but, again, it cannot be said with certainty whether his knowledge derived from a direct reading of Hegel's own philosophy of religion. Here he writes "the Hegelians," just as in I A 211 he wrote "Hegelianism," and here again it is most reasonable to assume a particular source. Perhaps we may suggest it as a possibility, just as in the case of I A 170, that in the course of going through Schleiermacher's dogmatics with Martensen, Hegel's views could have been brought into the discussion.

The entry I A 220 is important for the understanding of a longer draft (II B 1-21),[s] toward the interpretation of which Frithiof Brandt, Emanuel Hirsch, and later Carl Roos have made especially valuable contributions. Entry I A 221[t] again takes up an analysis of the concepts "antiquity" and "the romantic."

In this entry Kierkegaard considered it important to establish that the romantic is characterized by its infinite efforts, its efforts above and beyond what one is tempted to call the philistine reality, toward an ideal. But in antiquity, whose modern representative is Hegel (and Goethe could be put into the same tradition), just as in Heiberg's 1833 prospectus,[u] there is no striving above and beyond the given earthly actuality, in which the Idea, according to the Hegelian approach in connection with the philosophy of history, has found its highest possible and most adequate expression.

[r] Hegel, *Lectures on the Philosophy of Religion*, II, 338.

[s] II B 1-21 is a draft of Kierkegaard's play, "The Battle between the Old and the New Soap-Cellar" (1838), which will be discussed in Chapter IV. The earlier entry I A 220 (August 10, 1836), Hong, V, #5156, compares the conflict between orthodox Christianity and the rationalists with the battle between the old and the new soap-cellar. See Hong, *ibid.*, note 202 for an explanation of this curious title.

[t] A translation of I A 221 will be found in Hong, I, #852.

[u] [On the Significance of Philosophy for the Present Age.] This was discussed in Chapter I *supra* p. 27ff.

Kierkegaard juxtaposes the romantics and "the orthodox" here in opposition to the Hegelians (and the rationalists). With this there is provided a relation of opposition, which is new in comparison with the Gilleleie entries; but there is no indication of whether Kierkegaard has taken sides. Perhaps we can see here an anticipation of the method he will employ in the pseudonymous authorship, of letting various attitudes toward life, stages, emerge without the author's attitude being expressed.

The entry I A 225^v (August 19, 1836) is quite striking. In surprise, Kierkegaard writes about his new observation that the concept of the romantic, which he had worked with so long, corresponds to what he calls the dialectical in Hegel. That is the second standpoint, i.e., the sphere of reflection, which is thought about, and Heiberg has transferred Hegelianism into the domain of esthetics. Kierkegaard agrees with Heiberg ("he was right"); "but this can be accomplished on a far greater scale—ancient—romantic —absolute beauty."

Papirer I A 229^w is only a disrespectful discussion of Hegel's dialectical method ("cud-chewing process"). The following entry, from the same day (August 25, 1836), raises the question of why the present age had not followed Goethe and Hegel through the romantic to "the classical," and answers that the political development must also "live through its romantic unfolding."

This reflection on the philosophy of history, with its accent on the necessity of process, sounds like the other August entries on knowledge and [seems to show] a certain influence of the perspectives of Hegel. Yet, it is not necessary to assume that Kierkegaard had tackled Hegel's own works or his minor treatises. There are no quotations or allusions to particular passages in Hegel, and the entries are understandable entirely on the basis of the obvious assumption that Kierkegaard's knowledge of Hegel was second hand and not especially detailed or profound.

Shortly later, in September 1836, another influence from an entirely different side becomes noticeable, namely from Hamann.^{x} Kierkegaard returns to his entries of October 1835 (I A 94ff) on the

---

^{v} Hong, II, #1565.

^{w} Hong, II, #1566.

^{x} Johann Georg Hamann (1730-1788), friend of Kant, also a native of Königsberg and an adherent of Pietistic Lutheranism. His friendship with Kant caused him to mute his strong disagreement with the critical philosophy.

incompatibility between philosophy and Christianity, and makes an addition from his later reading.[16]

An entry from September 25, 1836 (I A 248)[y] shows clearly that at this time at least Kierkegaard had not read *Phenomenology of the Spirit* with understanding and acceptance. If he had, the question he raises, namely, in what relation does the development of the individual stand to the development of the world, would have been answered in that work to the effect that the development in both instances proceeds with parallel necessity toward Hegel's system.

Not until the end of the year is there another entry that we must consider here, namely, the (undated) I A 273,[z] where he declares what, according to his understanding, Schleiermacher means by "religion" and the Hegelian dogmaticians mean by "faith."

Surely the editors of the *Papirer* are correct when, in connection with the latter point, they refer to Marheineke's Dogmatics,[aa] in the renowned second edition that was influenced by Hegel. Kierkegaard had acquired this work on December 14, 1836 (I C 25, *cf.* I C 26),[bb] and I A 273 must, then, either be dated later than the middle of November, where it now stands, or it must have been inserted there.

Kierkegaard asserts that, by faith, "the Hegelian dogmaticians" do not mean anything other than "the first immediacy, the condition for everything—the vital fluid—the atmosphere that in an intellectual sense we breathe."

---

[16] To pursue Kierkegaard's relation to Hamann and the significant influence Hamann had on him, falls outside the limits of this study. In the article "Incontro di Kierkegaard e Hamann" [The Meeting of Kierkegaard and Hamann] in *Studi Kierkegaardiana*, ed. by Cornelio Fabro (Brescia, 1957), pp. 325-357, I have set forth the initial chapters of such a study, and the reader is referred to this. Earlier research is critically surveyed in its main lines. Certainly P. A. Heiberg's *Et Segment af S.K.'s religiøse Udvikling*, 1918 [A Segment of Kierkegaard's Religious Development] should be taken into account.

[y] Hong, II, #1966.

[z] Hong, II, #1096.

[aa] Philip Marheineke, *Die Grundlehren der christlichen Dogmatik als Wissenschaft* [Fundamental Doctrine of Christian Dogmatics as Science], 2nd ed. (Berlin, 1827), Ktl. #644.

[bb] Omitted from vol. I of the *Papirer*, the full text of I C 25, excerpts in Danish (presumably SK's translation) from Marheineke, will be found in vol. XII. These will also be found in Hong, V, #5065, 5066. But Hong gives only the identification of the entry from vol. I of the *Papirer*, not the complete text.

What, then, does Marheineke say about faith?

In the introduction to his *Dogmatics*[17] Marheineke defines theology as a system of knowledges that grow out of religion. Religion is related to theology as life to its concept (§6). The essence of religion consists not only in faith and knowledge but also in life and action (§8). Faith is the basis of theology, which gives knowledge, and theology is necessary for the justification of faith, so that its content may be separated from superstition and disbelief (§11). Marheineke has essentially nothing more to say about faith, and Kierkegaard's characterization may be called accurate.

On January 5, 1837, Kierkegaard returns to Hegel's logical triad, as at the end of the previous August. There is now a different tone: even if one can ridicule this triad, it retains its own truth. A couple of weeks later, on January 22, there is an entry that sounds quite Hegelian (I A 324):[cc] "The fact that Christianity has not overcome the principle of contradiction shows precisely its romantic character." Kierkegaard also thinks that Goethe wanted to illustrate this theory.

The words have a rather Hegelian sound, but the interpretation of Christianity is, nevertheless, not Hegelian. On the contrary, Hegel would have held—if we recall the survey of his teaching on redemption *supra*—that Christianity (which, as regards content, he considers to be identical with his own system) has indeed overcome the principle of contradiction, whereas Kierkegaard quite distinctly maintains that it has not. From the entry itself nothing further emerges concerning Kierkegaard's understanding of Christianity at this point, and here it is also important to point out only that Kierkegaard's understanding of Christianity did not coincide with that of Hegel.

5. MARTENSEN'S REVIEW OF HEIBERG'S
Introductory Lecture

It is important to note that Hegel actually did come within Kierkegaard's purview at this time, and that Hegelians were no longer unknown to him. Martensen, who indeed would not have described himself as a pure Hegelian, but as one who wished "to go beyond" Hegel, now enters the picture.

[17] *Supra cit.* References here are to the paragraphs (§) of this work.
[cc] Hong, I, #699.

The occasion was Heiberg's renowned *Indlednings-Foredrag til det i November 1834 begyndte logiske Cursus paa den kongelige militaire Høiskole* [Introductory Lecture for the Course in Logic Begun in November 1834 at the Royal Military College] which Martensen reviewed in *Maanedsskrift for Litteratur* [Literature Monthly] in the December 1836 issue (pp. 515-528). Kierkegaard had read this review and fixed his attention on several features in it. There is no clear evidence in Kierkegaard's *Papirer* entries that he had read Heiberg's publication when it appeared. Among other things he read there that the Hegelian system:

> appears with an infinite meaning for our time, since it contains the most complete and exhaustive development of rational knowledge whereby it seems that a whole era in the history of philosophy, which, independent of all tradition and given positiveness, sought to solve the riddles of existence, has come to an end. But the new era in knowledge [*Videnskaben*] cannot arrive until the old has run its course; and the Hegelian philosophy is the unavoidable point for everyone who has participated in the scholarly [*videnskabelige*] reflection of the modern period (p. 515).

Not content with suggesting this world-historical principle, Martensen tries to find the leading principle of all modern philosophy. He goes on to say that the Hegelian philosophy

> is the consequent and the result of the work of centuries, but understanding this requires that we discover the principle that lies at the base of the philosophical trend which can be called the dominant one in the whole of the modern period, in its opposition to the Christian philosophy of the middle ages. Medieval philosophy rested on faith, its principle is Anselm's famous *credam ut intelligam*[dd] . . . it does not relinquish the idea [*Forestillingen*], and cannot admit that above and beyond it there is another higher truth, of which it is only an incomplete expression . . . the opinion is . . . the highest form of truth, its absolute revelation.

Thus, according to Martensen, it happened in the modern period that philosophy broke away from theology, and now not faith but doubt becomes the point of departure for philosophy and

[dd] *Sic.* The usual form is "credo ut intelligam" (I believe in order that I may understand). Martensen gives the verb *credere* in the present subjunctive or future indicative tense.

Science [*Videnskaben*] now wishes to know the truth from within itself, and only what is present in the inner, essential necessity of thought can be shown to be incontestable truth, must for mankind be valid as such (p. 518).

Descartes' *cogito ergo sum* and his *de omnibus dubitandum est* also are the principles of this philosophy. Doubt is the beginning of wisdom. With the principle *de omnibus dubitandum* the claim of a presuppositionless beginning is expressed (p. 519). Martensen goes on to say that Hegel tries to carry out the dialectical doubt, and "the only point that survives [the doubt] . . . is the pure abstract self, the pure being-nothing . . . from which it is impossible to abstract." Philosophy enters now as "absolute rationalism, and it is the final, supreme consequent of the Cartesian principle. All reality proceeds from thought and to it returns." The result is that, in Hegel, God's consciousness of Himself is identified with man's consciousness of God (p. 523).

Despite all his understanding, recognition, and admiration of this philosophy, the culmination of which is Hegel, Martensen cannot rest content with it, he cannot remain stationary but thinks he must go further. Before he goes further, he inserts his criticism.

"In many aspects of reality . . . there appear irrational areas, which are not absorbed in the concept, a non-reason, which should not on that account be called unreasonable . . . for instance, this is the case with poetry and religion both of which bear the character of freedom more than of necessity" (p. 524). Quite concisely he says that "the shortcoming of the age . . . is the lack of a firm faith." Hegel's philosophy has the defect that it "knows only the eternal, but not the Holy" (p. 526), which, it goes without saying, is an apt comment. Martensen concludes in a way that Hegel would surely have called incorrect, by saying that, if Hegel "had instead of seeking the eternal thought, which man has not conceived for himself, sought the eternal Word which man has not uttered for himself, then he would have arrived at the Christian Logos" (p. 527).

Kierkegaard read and remembered this. A lengthy entry with additions (I A 328-330)[ee] and especially an undated Journal entry (II A 7)[ff] from the beginning of 1837 show this clearly.

First, let us take up the longer entry. Kierkegaard is being ironic

[ee] These entries (Hong, V, #5181, 5182, 5183) fill seven pages in the Danish.

[ff] Hong, V, #5200.

here, not so much about the Hegelians, who—as usual in Kierke-gaard—are spoken of in the third person, as about those, or more correctly the one, namely Martensen, who "has gone beyond" . . . whom? Kierkegaard does not specify, but leaves it to the reader. No great perspicacity is required to suggest that the name of Hegel be inserted. The entry seems like a draft for an article or letter.

Kierkegaard stands apart as a disinterested onlooker who ob-serves contemporary philosophical endeavors in Denmark and Copenhagen: most philosophical systems and views are of recent vintage—and cheap. It must, then, only be described as a genuine happenstance, that now it has got a long historical background from Descartes to Hegel. With this kind of historical survey—for which Kierkegaard never cared very much—we get nowhere. Only sin-gularly talented people can escape from this situation. For those "who must live off others" (I A 328, p. 140) it is more perilous, for they clutch at any terminology in passing and strive to make the system popular. Kierkegaard is surely thinking of both Heiberg and Martensen here. The outcome strikes him as tragicomic. It went badly for Kant, Kierkegaard continues, when people tried to popularize his philosophy, and now the same fate has befallen Hegel, whom Kierkegaard respects as "the one of all modern phi-losophers, who by his difficult style [*strænge Form*] surely most commands silence?" (I A 328, p. 140). If we turn from these well-meaning popularizers to the politicians, Kierkegaard says, we get a striking example of "how one can serve two masters, inasmuch as their revolutionary efforts become coupled with a life-view that is precisely a means for curing [those revolutionary efforts]" (p. 141). Kierkegaard was thinking of the liberal politicians, and wrote these lines from—in this connection sufficient—a knowledge of the conservative character of Hegelian philosophy in political matters. Whether he had a precise target in mind is not important here. It is not unlikely that he could have been thinking of Monrad, for example.[19]

In Kierkegaard's view, Christianity has fared no better than phi-losophy and politics:

> every Christian concept has become so diffused, so entirely dis-persed in a mass of fog, that it is impossible for anyone to know

[19] On Monrad we may refer especially to Poul Bagge, *Studier over D. G. Monrads Statstanker* (1936), and Asger Nyholm, *Religion og Politik, en Monrad Studie* (1947).

it again. The concepts Faith, Incarnation, Tradition, Inspiration, which in the Christian context belonged to [*ere henførte til*] a definite historical fact, the philosophers have deemed it good to give an entirely different general meaning, whereby Faith becomes the immediate consciousness, which at bottom is nothing but the vital fluid of the intellectual [*aandelige*] life, its atmosphere; tradition has become the epitome of a kind of worldly experience, while Inspiration has become nothing else but the result of God's breathing into man the breath of life, and Incarnation has become nothing but the presence of one or another's idea in one or several individuals.—And I still have not named the concept which has not only become, like the others, diffused, but even profaned: the concept of Redemption.

The expressions here are significant. They point back, especially to I A 94 and I A 273, to Kierkegaard's lecture in the Students' Union on November 28, 1835 (I B 2-7), and they point forward, toward the whole first great period of the Authorship, and they have their own intrinsic significance.

There are verbal and topical connections between the critical reckoning here and Kierkegaard's earlier remarks concerning Marheineke's *Dogmatics*. The question is whether he was thinking of someone, or perhaps several people, in particular. There is a clear allusion to Martensen in the beginning of the entry. We could also think of Baader's *Speculative Dogmatics*, which Kierkegaard had excerpted earlier (I C 27ff.).[gg] Or we could think of a work such as Valdemar Henrik Rothe's *Læren om Treenighed og Forsoning* [The Doctrine of the Trinity and Redemption] (Ktl. 746), which appeared on the occasion of the Reformation Jubilee in 1836, and which was severely treated by Heiberg in the famous critique in the first issue of *Perseus* in June 1837. Kierkegaard was one of the few subscribers to this short-lived periodical (Ktl. 569). Now Kierkegaard explicitly says "the philosophers," not the theologians. As has been pointed out already, there is no previous indication that Kierkegaard had read the most relevant [*nærmestliggende*] of Heiberg's works, namely *Introductory Lecture*, which Martensen reviewed. Nor could that have given him the occasion for the remarks here. There is only a single place (Heiberg's *Prose Writings*, II, 44ff.) in

[gg] The text of these excerpts (simply described in *Papirer*, I) will be found in full in vol. XII of the latest edition of the *Papirer*. Not in Hong.

the critique of Rothe's book,[20] namely in Heiberg's excursus in connection with Martensen's review, which could have given occasion for the remarks in Kierkegaard's entry. That is the definition (by Martensen) of faith as unmediated knowledge [*umiddelbare Erkendelse*].

Can we infer, then, that Kierkegaard was thinking of Hegel himself here? The five concepts that Kierkegaard reproaches the philosophers (and politicians) for having taken from Christianity and given an entirely different general meaning appear toward the end in Hegel. His teaching on Redemption was discussed earlier, and in connection with that his teaching on the Incarnation was indicated. With respect to the other concepts, the situation is as follows:

Individual passages, such as §72 of Hegel's *Philosophische Propädeutik* (SW III, 97)[hh] and in the so-called "lesser Logic" (The first part of the *Encyclopedia of the Philosophical Sciences*) §63 (Wallace trans. pp. 123-126) speak of faith as immediate knowledge [*umiddelbar Viden*]; but in the latter passage Hegel polemicizes against Jacobi and clearly distinguishes this concept of faith from Christian Faith. Tradition in the sense of "the epitome of a kind of worldly experience" (I A 328, p. 142) does not seem to appear in Hegel. Nor does inspiration in the sense of "God's breathing into man the breath of life" seem to be found in Hegel.

Thus there seems to be very little evidence that Kierkegaard had Hegel himself in mind when he wrote this entry. Its meaning is simply: the philosophers' seeming Christian linguistic usage, or more accurately their appropriation of Christian concepts, has effectuated a topical confusion and mixing together of two areas, philosophy and Christianity, that simply do not admit of amalgamation. Kierkegaard is a foe of mediation now as before and later.

The other entries within group I A contain nothing in relation to Hegel.[21]

6. Kierkegaard's First Theory of Stages

Nothing pertinent to our topic occurs in the group I B, which consists mostly of Kierkegaard's lecture on "our Journal Literature"

---

[20] *Perseus*, I (1837), 1-89; reprinted in *Prosaiske Skrifter*, II (1861), 1-113.

[hh] As far as I can discover, this has never been translated into English.

[21] I A 33f. and its connection with Martensen's work on Faust is cogently interpreted by Carl Roos in his *Kierkegaard og Goethe* (1955), 104ff.; cf. my review of this book in *Euphorion* (1957), 341-343.

on November 28, 1835, in the Students' Union. Kierkegaard's detailed knowledge of the liberal press of his time, its rise, history and style, and his own explicit political conservatism has been clearly described elsewhere.[22] However the lecture is of interest in showing how early Kierkegaard chose his political position and, in its evaluation of an actual situation, can be set as an example alongside some of the letters to Kolderup-Rosenvinge.[23]

Group C is in several respects rich in content, but not with respect to the chief question of this study.

In the theological entries and excerpts, only I C 25-26,[ii] which are connected with Marheineke's *Dogmatics* discussed above, are of interest.

Nor is there any reason to dwell on many passages in the esthetic entries. Discussion of the entries on Faust will be found in the most recent literature, especially that undertaken by Carl Roos, to which the interested reader is referred,[24] and the same may be said about Don Juan and Ahasuerus, who are frequently stressed in the research on Kierkegaard. They are of great importance both for understanding the history of Kierkegaard's private life as a youth and for their illumination of the origin of the theory of stages. There is undoubtedly a connection between doubt personified, Faust, and the theoretical reflections, which to no small degree are connected with Martensen's emphasis on Descartes' principle *de omnibus dubitandum*, which Kierkegaard took up much later in the Authorship. But at this point in the *Papirer* there is hardly any direct connection with Hegel to speak of.

On January 16, 1837, Kierkegaard reproduced Heiberg's outline

[22] Most recently by Sejer Kühle, *SK Barndom og ungdom* [Kierkegaard's Childhood and Youth] (1950), 100; cf. Hans Jensen, *De danske Stænderforsamlingers Historie* [History of the Danish Assembly of the Estates of the Realm], I (1931), 577ff.

[23] *Breve og Aktstykker vedrørende SK* [Letters and Documents Concerning Kierkegaard]. Numbers 184, 186, 188, 189. [J.L.A. Kolderup-Rosenvinge (1792-1850), Professor of Law, regularly strolled with SK on Monday afternoons. During summer vacations, when K-R went to the country and SK remained in the city, they continued their "walking tours" by mail, as the above letters indicate. Cf. *Breve og Aktstykker*, II, 78.]

[ii] I C 25, An excerpt (in Danish) from Marheineke's *Dogmatics* is in vol. XII of the *Papirer*. I C 26, an excerpt in German from the same is in vol. I, *Papirer* (Hong, V, #5065, 5066).

[24] *Kierkegaard og Goethe* (1955), 56-158

of the types of comedy (I C 124).[jj] The entry is taken from an article by Heiberg in *Kjøbenhavns flyvende Post* from 1828,[25] that is, antedating the publication (1835 et seq.) of Hegel's *Lectures on the Philosophy of Fine Art*. It is not without significance that Kierkegaard finds Heiberg's schema deficient.

Only the long entry dated January 27, 1837 (I C 126),[kk] a clue [*Holdepunkt*] to the reflections that received a compact description earlier (p. 83f.), must be analyzed a little more closely here. The entry is a draft of a survey and description of the stages of life.

There are four stages of life.

The first is the immediacy of childhood, in which self-consciousness [*Jeg-Bevidstheden*] has not awakened but is only found latently. Thus it is in the individual, while the world-historical parallel is mythology, more precisely, the oriental mythologies. On this stage the countless moments can not be synthesized into a unit; but they strive toward it just as the superior unity ("the eternal present of the ego") struggles against it, which shows itself as pressure against the dormant self-consciousness.

The second stage is in the boyhood of the individual, when self-consciousness is awakened. Here there is peace, idyllic well-being, contentment, in family and school, in church and state. This is the stage of equilibrium, to which Greek mythology corresponds. Here the divine enters the world "such as it never before or later in the development of the world has or will enter, whereas it certainly does in the development of the single individual" (I C 126, p. 309). As late as August 1840 Kierkegaard finds, quite in harmony with this description, "the best and most pregnant aphorism on Greekness" in the old Egyptian priest's exclamation "Ah, Solon, Solon, you Greeks are always children; an old Greek does not exist."[26]

The third stage involves an abrogation of the harmony of the second. When this third stage, which Kierkegaard calls the romantic, appears, there "arises a question of a satisfaction lying beyond the world." The conflict that emerges from this is not overcome, not resolved by a harmony according to the Hegelian pattern.

The fourth stage gives a resolution in the resignation, which indeed contains within itself a hope, which is Christianity's response.

[jj] Hong, V, #5192.

[25] Cf. Paul V. Rubow, *Dansk litterær Kritik* (1921), 112ff.

[kk] Hong, IV, #4398.

[26] III A 13 [Hong, I, #18]; the latter quotation (included in this entry) is from Plato's *Timaeus*, 22B.

In two supplementary comments Kierkegaard sets his theory off in relation to Hegel.

In the first place, he says, the system has only three stages, the immediate, the reflected, and the higher unity of both. Life, on the contrary, has four stages in Kierkegaard's present view. In the second place, Kierkegaard questions whether Hegel can merge his first two stages "when his first stage . . . as a pure abstraction really is a nothing," and when the harmony that Hegel reaches is not identical with the Greek harmony in Kierkegaard's second stage.

That is what the entry says about the four stages and the relation to Hegel. But there is more to be said on this topic. For a better understanding of this, it will be of interest first to see examples of how other researchers have dealt with the present text. For this purpose, we choose Hirsch, Lindström, and Malantschuk.[27]

Hirsch notes that earlier, in September 1836 (I A 239),[11] Kierkegaard has only three stages, contrasted with four now. These four are described there approximately as above, so that for the description of the romantic Hirsch has taken into account other statements of Kierkegaard. On the relation to Hegel Hirsch says that it is

> originally very simply done: he had simply employed the Hegelian triad to arrange the stages of life. In the mature configuration he places his third and fourth stages alongside Hegel's second and third, and determines that the contrast with Hegel consists in the fact that the empty abstract immediacy of Hegel, which is a nothing, has taken place through a living concretion, and even therein he finds the distinction of life expressed by the System.

And Hirsch's overall understanding is clearly expressed shortly thereafter, when he asserts that "the latter description of the stages on the way of life is shown as a unification of the Hegelian dialectic in a romantic-Christian philosophy of life" (*Kierkegaard-Studien*, pp. 496-497).

Lindström follows Hirsch to great degree and then concludes by

[27] Emanuel Hirsch, *Kierkegaard-Studien*, II (1933), 494ff., Valter Lindström, *Stadiernas teologi* [Theology of the Stages] (1943), 149ff. Gregor Malantschuk, especially in the essay "Das Verhältnis zwischen Wahrheit und Wirklichkeit in SKs existentiellem Denken" [The Relation between Truth and Reality in Kierkegaard's Existential Thought] in *Symposion Kierkegaardianum* (1955), 166ff., esp. p. 168 with note 8.

[11] Hong, II, #1676.

saying (p. 150) that such a system that parallels the development of the individual with the world-historical process, and which makes it appear as if the history of the individual necessarily repeats that of the species, must, after all, soon seem untenable.

Malantschuk takes it to be beyond doubt that, from the beginning of his philosophical work, Kierkegaard had received positive impulses from Hegelian philosophy; but he expressly notes that already here in this first draft of a theory of stages Kierkegaard sets it in opposition to the Hegelian position. Without explicitly arguing against other researchers Malantschuk asserts (p. 175, esp. note 24) that Kierkegaard had "a clear attitude on the world-historical context," a view also expressed elsewhere in his research.[28]

Neither in Hirsch, Lindström, or Malantschuk do we find any basis for the description of Hegel's teaching and Kierkegaard's relation to it. That is probably attributable to the fact that Kierkegaard's comments on this point have been taken to be sufficient.

But the problem is more complex than that.

In the first place we may ask the purely historical question of how Kierkegaard may have contacted Hegel. In the second place we may ask as a matter of principle where the distinction between their views on the stages lies. Finally, in the third place, what motivates the distinction? There is the question of the number of stages, of the characteristics of each individual stage, and of the parallelism between the individual and the world-historical development. Furthermore, there occurs the relevant question of the transition from one stage to another.

To answer these questions we need for the most part to discuss four of Hegel's works (or parts of the system) namely, *Phenomenology of the Spirit, Science of Logic, Lectures on the Philosophy of History*, and *Lectures on the Philosophy of Religion*. Of the last two, *Philosophy of History* is not listed in the *Auction Catalogue* and as has been said earlier, Kierkegaard owned *Philosophy of Religion* in the second edition, published in 1840.

If, with Lindström, one wishes to characterize Kierkegaard's four world-historical stages (or: kingdoms, a division that dates back to the book of Daniel 2:31ff.) as the Oriental, the classical, the romantic, and the Christian, then we can find a parallel in Hegel, whose philosophy of history is divided into the Oriental, the Greek,

[28] For example, in *Indførelse i SKs Forfatterskab* [Introduction to Kierkegaard's Authorship], 1953.

the Roman, and the Germanic[mm] worlds; but the parallelism, as we see, consists chiefly in the fact that the number of divisions is the same. Kierkegaard, like Hegel, begins with the Orient; but there is nothing particularly Hegelian or Kierkegaardian in that, since even in previous ages accounts of the history of the world began with the Oriental.[29] The Greek (classical) stage in Kierkegaard is, quite likely, divided into the Greek and Roman in Hegel. We could find a parallel between Kierkegaard's romantic stage and the Germanic world in Hegel only if the romantic in Kierkegaard is identified with the medieval, but then there arises the slight difficulty that Hegel speaks precisely of the Christian Germanic world (*Philosophy of History*, pp. 343ff.). If we remain constant to the total number of stages and turn from Hegel's *Philosophy of History* to his *Phenomenology*, then he has six or eight, depending upon which arrangement we consider. According to the most obvious one, there are six, namely, Consciousness, Self-Consciousness, Reason, Spirit, Religion, and Absolute Knowledge. Another account gives us eight, namely, Sense-Certainty, Perception, Force and Understanding, the Truth of Self-Certainty, the Certainty and Truth of Reason, Spirit, Religion, and Absolute Knowledge. The triad in Hegel, of which Kierkegaard speaks, is found in these works—only in the development of the concept in individual sections. Only *Phenomenology of the Spirit* asserts a harmony between the individual and the world-historical development leading to its culmination in Hegel's own time and thought, the Absolute Knowledge.

If we look at the description of the individual stages, then for example, we can take the first stage in Kierkegaard and in Hegel, that is, the Oriental and the stage of Oriental mythology. Here there is some similarity in the determination of content. In his *Philosophy of History* (p. 139) Hegel speaks of the "dreaming Spirit" as a characteristic of India. In the dream there is just no distinction between the finite and the infinite, between the inner and the outer, between mankind and its dream world. Hegel finds Indian mythology an expression of wild fantasy and a manifold without

[mm] This really refers to post-Roman Western European culture, not exclusively German. Hegel's word is *Germanisch* not *Deutsch*.

[29] On this point, reference may be made, for example to W. Michelsen's *Tilblivelsen af Grundtvigs Historiesyn* [The Genesis of Grundtvig's View of History] (1954), 33ff., where more extensive literature (especially H. Hjärne's and Paulus Svendsen's accounts) is cited.

unity (p. 156) and in his *Lectures on the Philosophy of Religion* (II, 1-47, especially p. 10f.) using almost the same phrases as in *Philosophy of History*, Hegel speaks of Indian religion under the heading "the Religion of Phantasy." Even if Kierkegaard did not own Hegel's *Philosophy of History*, when he died, and if he did not obtain *Philosophy of Religion* until after the publication of the second edition in 1840, we cannot eliminate the possibility that he may have read these works and thus known of Hegel's characterization of the Indian. However it is more reasonable to suggest, as Hirsch has, that Kierkegaard's source here is Friedrich Schlegel, to whom he refers in I A 211.[nn]

It is not likely that Kierkegaard's characterization of the second stage, that of the Greek, is original.[30] Certainly we can find a similarity between the harmony, which Kierkegaard identifies, and the esthetic individuality in Hegel's *Philosophy of History* (pp. 241-274). According to Hegel, this esthetic individuality is worked out in the subjective work of art, namely mankind itself; in the objective work of art, the Greek world of the divine; and in the political work of art, namely, in the constitution of the State and the individuals within it. This tripartite division is not found in Kierkegaard, and it is reasonable to assume that his description of this stage rests on sources other than Hegel. This assumption is supported to a significant degree by the fact that, in his comments, Kierkegaard raises the question of whether Hegel had joined his first two stages "since his first stage (the immediate) as a pure abstraction is really a nothing; and all philosophy within its retrograde systematic crawl must begin with the conflict," and thus not with the harmony that is disrupted in Kierkegaard's third stage, the romantic. If we turn to the other works of Hegel in which he discusses Greekness, that is—apart from *Philosophy of Religion* and *Phenomenology*—his *Lectures on the Philosophy of Fine Art* and his *Lectures on the History of Philosophy*, then we find the same fundamental description as set forth in *Philosophy of History*.

The examples show that neither in the definition of the number of stages nor in their characteristics does Kierkegaard seem to have had direct knowledge of Hegel's own works.

The same observation may be made with respect to the question of the parallels between the individual and the world-historical

[nn] Hong, II, #1564.

[30] Cf., for example, Vilhelm Andersen's clarification in *Goethe*, I-II (1915-1916).

development. We must particularly take Hegel's *Phenomenology of the Spirit* into account here. In this work the Spirit manifests itself through contrary oppositions, which are evidently reconciled in Absolute Knowledge, and these manifestations are throughout entirely identical in the microcosm and the macrocosm, in the individual dialectical development and the course of world-history. If, for example, we read the renowned section on "Lordship and Bondage" (pp. 228-240) we will be able, with the same justification and in perfect harmony with its intent, to read it as a speculative-philosophical interpretation of a social revolution at a given point in time in world-history and as a description of the struggle of the individual self-consciousness with itself and its escape through Stoicism and skepticism to the domain of reason.[31]

In Kierkegaard the parallels occur only in his first two stages, and he asserts that it is unattainable in the second two, where the individual's satisfaction is sought beyond the world.

The question of the transition from one stage to another now becomes germane. According to Hegel, the transition is determined and proceeds as the self-unfolding of the Idea, on which not much discussion is needed here. The question is not answered directly in Kierkegaard. Inasmuch as he speaks of four stages of life and the child's and the boy's stages, that is, of the ages of life, and inasmuch as the problem of transition has (still) not really arisen for him, it is reasonable to trace an employment of the theory of organism in him. It is well known how Kant, especially in the *Critique of Judgment* §65,[32] endeavored to attain an exhaustive definition of the concept "organism," and how thinkers such as Schelling and Steffens made extensive use of the concept in both the proper and the symbolic sense. Hegel employs it in several key passages,[33] which is legitimate, since the transitions there, just as in the natural development of most organisms, proceed continuously. Inasmuch as it seems we can trace the theory of organism in this entry of Kierkegaard and since the problem of transition has still not really arisen

[31] Cf. of the earlier interpreters especially Kuno Fischer, *Geschichte der neuern Philosophie* I, 326ff. and of the more recent Jean Hyppolite, *Genèse et structure de la Phénomenologie de l'espirit de Hegel* (1946), 151ff.

[32] Trans. J. H. Bernard (New York: Hafner Publishing Company, 1972), p. 218ff.

[33] *Philosophische Propädeutik*, I, 1, §23; *Philosophy of Right*, p. 287; *The Philosophy of Fine Art*, IV, 29-38; *Lectures on the History of Philosophy*, III. 464f., 501, 532f., and *passim*.

for him (whereas it later becomes a major question) we are here presented with a possibility of an actual contact with Hegel, or in any case at least with the use of this concept by the romantic thinkers. It does not seem possible to achieve a more precise resolution of this problem here.

The few extant letters written by Kierkegaard during this period contain nothing of significance for this investigation.

7. OTHER ENTRIES FROM THIS PERIOD

Both in September 1836 and in the middle of January 1837 Kierkegaard returned to his reflections of October 1835 on the relation between philosophy and Christianity (I A 95-99).[oo] By September 1836 (I A 100)[pp] Hamann has come within Kierkegaard's horizon;[34] but what that meant, both then and later on, will not be investigated here. Important in this context is the distinction Kierkegaard now raises in I A 101[qq] between the Augustinian and the Pelagian view of man.[rr] It is of very minor importance here to determine where Kierkegaard got his knowledge of Augustine's and Pelagius' interpretations of Christianity and how adequate that knowledge was. H. N. Clausen described them in his lectures on Dogmatics (I C 19, esp. §38ff.).[ss] He gives a sustained discussion of Augustine only, and thereby touches on what he calls the Pelagian system. The chief difference, which conditions the other disagree-

[oo] The first three of these will be found in Hong, I, #416-418. I A 98. 99 are in III, #3246, 3247.

[pp] Hong, II, #1539.

[34] Cf. my previously cited article in *Studi Kierkegaardiani*, 1957, especially 349ff.

[qq] Hong, I, #29.

[rr] St. Augustine (A.D. 354-430), one of the most important and influential thinkers in Western civilization, engaged in a lengthy controversy with the followers of Pelagius (fl. ca. A.D. 400-418), a British monk who was believed to have denied original sin and maintained an extreme view of the freedom of the human will. As Augustine saw it, the Pelagians held that man could by the unaided use of free will attain salvation, thereby denying the essential role of grace. Augustine's polemic against Pelagianism foreshadowed the controversies over grace and free will that were so common in the sixteenth and seventeenth centuries. His anti-Pelagian writings, taken in isolation from his other works, make him appear to be a theological determinist (which he was not).

[ss] Hong, V, #5057. This lengthy synopsis of Clausen's lectures is simply identified in vol. I of the *Papirer*, but will be found in full (filling some 72 pages) in vol. XII of the latest edition.

ments between them, appears in the notion of sin. Augustine "wishes to smash all so as to raise it up" and therefore with reference to Christianity derives three stages, namely, the Creation, the Fall, and the new Creation, while Pelagius "applies himself to mankind as it is" i.e., Christianity adapts itself to the world.

At this point Kierkegaard had not himself chosen between the two positions; but it is evident that the determination of the relation between philosophy and Christianity depends on the notion of Christianity, so that the relation essentially must be defined differently when it proceeds from a Pelagian standpoint than when based on the Augustinian position. This may also be seen as a reason for Kierkegaard's having made now an addition to his earlier entry—instead of developing a completely new account—concerning the relation, which nearly eighteen months later he had still not changed but only supplemented. His knowledge has increased in the interim; but it has not induced him to make any important change in his basic opinion. His own position with regard to Christianity, as he understood it, whether negative, neutral, or positive, did not play any role either.

In their preface to the second volume, (*Papirer*, II, vii), the editors state that immediately after the long entry I C 126 Kierkegaard began recording the entries from day to day under the heading "miscellaneous." The dating is often only approximately certain.

There are a few significant entries here.

Kierkegaard makes a critical remark about Martensen's review of Heiberg's *Introductory Lecture*: Martensen himself has gone beyond Hegel "out into a vague infinity," and his criticism of Hegel is superficial. It is worth noting that Kierkegaard clearly recognizes Martensen's close relation with Baader, even if on the whole he suggests more than develops his characterization and estimate (II A 7).[tt]

In a certain respect the entry II A 17[uu] is quite remarkable. Kierkegaard wrote this after reading Poul Møller's renowned article in the January 1837 issue of *Maanedsskrift for Litteratur*, titled *Tanker over Muligheden af Beviser for Manneskets Udødelighed, med Hensyn til den nyeste derhen hørende Literature* [Thoughts on the Possibility of Proofs of Human Immortality, with Reference to the Most Recent Literature Belonging Thereto].[35] In this article,

[tt] Hong, V, #5200.
[uu] Hong, V, #5201.
[35] Here and in what follows I have used the reprint in Poul Møller's *Efter-*

which marks his final break with Hegel, Poul Møller's main thesis is that a world-view can be developed in which the reality and immortality of the individual can be proven. But Kierkegaard says nothing about this. Not until *Concluding Unscientific Postscript* does he explain the importance of Poul Møller's reflections. Immediately after his initial reading of this article, the only thing that Kierkegaard remarks on is the author's literary art, namely the insertion of an episode, the scene with the bookkeeper and the Bachelor of Theology, which obviously struck him as noteworthy.

In any case, a partial explanation of why Kierkegaard did not at this point fasten on the main thought in Poul Møller's article is probably that he had previously become familiar with a work on the same topic by the younger Fichte. Kierkegaard writes (II A 31, March 19, 1837)[vv] that he had earlier read cursorily I. H. Fichte's *Die Idee der Persönlichkeit und der individuellen Fortdauer* [The Idea of Personality and individual duration] (Ktl. 505), which appeared in 1834. Poul Møller discusses this work in his article (pp. 118-127).

This long entry is interesting inasmuch as we get Kierkegaard's understanding and evaluation not only of the younger Fichte but also of Schleiermacher, Schelling, Baader, and the nowadays little-known Jesuit Anton Günther (1738-1863), who at the close of the 1820s emerged as an advocate of a strong theism. Kierkegaard owned several of his books (see Ktl.).

Kierkegaard acknowledges that in any case the younger Fichte has made an advance by which he has "gone beyond Hegel's Abstraction to an intuition [*Anskuelse*]"; but on the other hand, none of these thinkers, who all belong within the broad idealistic philosophical tradition in spite of the diversity between them and their differences from Hegel in particular, has risen above the common human, immediate consciousness, as it is expressed here. Later Kierkegaard would have said that they have continued in immanence. When that is actually the case, then it is incorrect for

ladte *Skrifter* [Posthumous Writings], 3rd ed., V (1856), 38-141. Of the literature we may refer especially to: Vilhelm Andersen, *Poul Møller*, 3rd ed. (1944), 358ff.; Harald Høffding, *Philosophien i Tydskland efter Hegel* [Philosophy in Germany after Hegel] (1872), 17ff.; Høffding's *Danske Filosofer* (1909), 120-121; J. E. Erdmann, *Grundriss der Geschichte der Philosophie*, 3rd ed., II (1878), 647ff.; and Gregor Malantschuk's article on Kierkegaard and Poul Møller in *Kierkegaardiana*, III (1959), 7-20.

[vv] Hong, II, #1190.

philosophers to employ Christian concepts such as faith and tradition. "All this talk about Tradition in the philosophical domain is
a fraud, an illegitimate child of Christianity" (II A 31). This entry
appears to shed light on the one analyzed earlier (I A 328). Again
it seems that it is not primarily Hegel that Kierkegaard is trying
to clarify his relation with, but rather idealistic thinkers who—as
was Hegel's own intention—stand in a closer or more remote relation to Christianity. His task with these thinkers is to no small
degree connected with his attempts to make precise what is proper
to Christianity.

A description of Hegel turns up in a slightly later entry (II A
48),[ww] where Kierkegaard says that "Insofar as Hegel was fructified
by Christianity he tried to eliminate the humorous element which is
in Christianity . . . and therefore entirely reconciled himself with
the world, and led to a quietism." The same is said to be the case
with Goethe in his *Faust*. The first time Kierkegaard sketched
the humorous element in Christianity was in an entry dating from
July 19, 1836 (I A 207),[xx] where he notes that Christianity's view
of the world, and especially of what it considers important in the
world, differs from, indeed is the contradiction of the world's own
view. What is great in the eyes of the world, is for Christianity
nothing. This transvaluation of all values is not found in Hegel's
philosophy. Far from considering the world humorous, Hegel sees
the world as the adequate manifestation of God. We could express
the difference between the two ways of considering the world thus:
while Christianity regards the relative as relative and ridicules it if
it makes itself absolute, then Hegel absolutizes precisely the relative
and sanctions the philosophical status quo. Kierkegaard's description of Hegel's notion of Christianity, as, for example, it was briefly
and somewhat popularly expressed in his *Philosophy of History* is
apposite; but just as in the other entries examined up to this point
there is no sure evidence for claiming that Kierkegaard had read
Hegel before he wrote these entries.

The same is true of the following entry (II A 49).[yy] It shows
in the broadest generality that Kierkegaard had a cursory knowledge of Hegel's dialectical method. He is clear on the fact that in
Hegel each succeeding step ingests the previous one so that it retains its relative legitimacy.

[ww] Hong, II, #1568.
[xx] Hong, II, #1674.
[yy] Hong, II, #1569.

At the end of May Kierkegaard immersed himself in an article by Karl Rosenkranz, "Eine Parallele zur Religionsphilosophie," which appeared in Bruno Bauer's *Zeitschrift für spekulative Theologie* (II, 1837, 1-31ff.), and he became even more preoccupied with Carl Daub's long article "Die Form der christlichen Dogmen-und-Kirchen-Historie" in the first and second volumes of the same journal. Hirsch has carefully examined Daub's article (*Kierke-gaard-Studien*, II, 539-551) and thinks that it is of considerable importance that, through reading this article, Kierkegaard became aware of the problem of the relation between faith and history before he read Hegel. It may be noted here that, in any event Daub's article is not the only basic source, and perhaps never was the most important one in this respect for Kierkegaard. Clausen and Hohlenberg's *Tidsskrift for udenlandsk theologisk Litteratur* [Journal of Foreign Theological Literature] had already in 1836 (IV, 80-221) presented a translation of a large portion of Strauss's *Leben Jesu*, and in 1837 the faculty of Theology of the University of Copenhagen set its Prize Essay competition on the following topic: "Cum recentiore tempore autoritas [*sic*] librorum N. T. saepius impugnata sit, ut periculum inde fidei et ecclesiae imminere visum sit, instituatur disquisitio philosophica, num et quatenus religio et ecclesia Christiana ab authentia vel axiopistia historica librorum sacrorum N. T. pendeant." [Since in recent times the authority of the books of the New Testament has been impugned, so that there seems to be a present threat to the Faith and the Church, a philosophical inquiry is posed, whether and to what extent the Christian religion and Church depend upon the authenticity and historical credibility of the sacred books of the New Testament.][36] Kierkegaard subscribed to this journal and as a theological student ought to have been aware of these contemporary topics and essay contests.

What Kierkegaard called the humoristic element in Christianity at this time is an anticipation of the later category: the paradoxical, encountered more frequently in the entries from June 1837 and subsequently. Especially significant is II A 78[zz] (June 3, 1837), to which both on April 17, 1838—when he had read Daub's *Vorlesung-en über die philosophische Antropologie*—and May 14, 1839—

---

[36] *Yearbook of the University of Copenhagen* for 1837, 91. Cf. my Introduction to the *Philosophical Fragments*, 2nd ed. (Princeton: Princeton University Press, 1962), pp. lvi-lviii.

[zz] Hong, II, #1682.

when he sat in his "longest parenthesis," studying for his examinations—he returned with supplementary comments of historical rather than essential character. He finds the humorous expressed in a fundamental principle, as he puts it, which says that the truth is concealed in mystery ($\dot{\epsilon}\nu$ $\mu\nu\sigma\tau\eta\rho\dot{\iota}\phi$ $\dot{\alpha}\pi\sigma\kappa\rho\dot{\nu}\phi\eta$)[37] which also appears in Christianity's speaking of self-denial as a light burden, and, finally appears in the ignorance of the Christian [which Kierkegaard identifies with Socratic ignorance]. There is no discussion here of whether Kierkegaard considers himself a Christian. The only thing that concerns him is the analysis and determination of the essence, and a few days later Kierkegaard summarized rather thoroughly (II A 92)[aaa] Karl Rosenkranz's article, after which he again got to work on Daub's abstruse speculations. Throughout the summer he was occupied with the phenomena irony and humor, and with theories of original sin (II A 117).[bbb] Hamann is constantly perceived more distinctly as the typical Christian humorist as Socrates was the typical pagan ironist. During these months virtually no trace of concern with Hegelian thought occurs in the Group A entries. Kierkegaard's interests led him elsewhere, and we can find various suggestions of themes and problems that are taken up, developed, and resolved much later.

Not until the beginning of November do we again find anything of central importance for this study namely, Kierkegaard's preoccupation with J. E. Erdmann's *Vorlesungen über Glauben und Wissen als Einleitung in die Dogmatik und Religionsphilosophie* [Lectures on Faith and Knowledge as Introduction to Dogmatics and the Philosophy of Religion] and his participation during the winter semester 1837-1838 in Martensen's *Forelæsninger over Indledning til den spekulativ Dogmatik* [Lectures on the Introduction to Speculative Dogmatics]. Hirsch has carefully examined the matter of Erdmann (*Kierkegaard-Studien*, II, 530ff.), while the importance of Martensen's *Lectures* has not been satisfactorily analyzed.

Group B contains the highly significant draft of *Striden mellem den gamle og den nye Sæbekielder* [The Battle between the Old and the New Soapcellar], while in Group C—apart from a short entry in connection with Heiberg's guide to *Forelæsningerne over Philosophiens Philosophie eller den speculative Logik ved den kongelige militaire Høiskole* [The Lectures on the Philosophy of

---

[37] I Corinthians 2, 7.
[aaa] Hong, V, #5222.
[bbb] Hong, IV, #3993.

Philosophy or Speculative Logic at the Royal Military College], which appeared in 1831-1832—we should note only excerpts from C. H. Weisse's article "Die drei Grundfragen der gegenwärtigen Philosophie" [The Three Fundamental Questions of Contemporary Philosophy] in I. H. Fichte's *Zeitschrift für Philosophie und spekulative Theologie*, to which Kierkegaard subscribed from 1837 until his death; Ktl. 877-911).

Around the middle of November 1837 speculative thought intruded more intimately into Kierkegaard's life, and thus we can place a dividing line here. Before we begin the investigation of the next period, we ought to confront briefly the conclusions and views of earlier researchers.

8. Discussion of Earlier Researchers and Conclusion

Reuter was the first to make a noteworthy attempt to analyze the entries from this period with respect to their relation to Hegel.[38]

When Reuter finds in the entries on the "master thief" anticipations of Kierkegaard's later thesis that the outer is not the inner, and in that respect a position contrary to Hegel, we can concede this to him, also because it is almost inconceivable that Hegel should have written anything of the sort. The same holds true of Reuter's next point, which offers the conclusion that Kierkegaard was already in opposition to Hegel relatively early. He presents an account that is in the main correct. But Reuter has not answered the question of whether the opposed position on Kierkegaard's part was developed and presented with conscious consideration (knowledge) of Hegel's own works. On the basis of our analyses here and in the foregoing the question must be answered in the negative. Not until quite late do the name Hegel and the label "the Hegelians" appear, and Kierkegaard certainly did not have a particularly extensive or profound knowledge of this speculative school. Insofar as it is possible to judge from the entries, Kierkegaard had not read Hegel himself but speaks from a second hand knowledge.

The period 1835-1837, which Reuter calls a transition period, when Kierkegaard had broken with the old and still had not chosen

[38] S. *Kierkegaards religionsphilosophische Gedanken im Verhältnis zu Hegels religionsphilosophischem System* (in Abhandlungen zur Philosophie und ihrer Geschichte, ed. R. Falckenberg, Heft 23), Leipzig, 1914.

a new standpoint, is difficult to get clear. When Reuter sees Kierkegaard's struggle against Hegelian philosophy throughout his critique of contemporary political phenomena, he doubtless reads
more into the texts than anyone with a realistic view can get out of
them. Kierkegaard primarily attacks the liberal Danish politicians,
and it is simply a distortion to see them as representatives of Hegelian philosophy. Nor is there any greater validity in Reuter's next
assertion, a claim that most recently Jean Wahl has attempted to
justify, that Kierkegaard's clash with the romantic view of life is
supported by Hegel's philosophy. In this period, it is more accurate
to speak of Kierkegaard's orienting himself within the romantic
literature of the time and seeking a complete understanding of the
phenomenon "the romantic," both in its historical forms and its
main content, than of a critical reckoning. Our analysis of the entries concerning the four stages of life concluded that there is only
an extremely flimsy basis for the hypothesis of an actual contact
with Hegel. With much greater justification we can speak of a
connection, in an independent way, with generally widespread
viewpoints and tendencies. When Reuter, in agreement with Høffding, speaks of a Hegelian period in Kierkegaard's youth, then the
correctness of this claim is neither proven nor even made probable
through the reconsideration that has been undertaken in this and
the previous section. Reuter's description of the year 1837 as a transitional year doubtless contains a correct element. It is correct inasmuch as during this time Kierkegaard gained an acquaintance with
the speculative idealism of Hegel and his adherents and simultaneously took a critical position with regard to it; but we can hardly
consider his actual knowledge of it to be particularly thorough.

Bohlin thinks,[39] frequently in line with Niedermeyer and Reuter,
that it could be maintained that there was a Hegelian influence in
Kierkegaard's attempt to characterize the intellectual life of the
medieval period, and like Niedermeyer, Reuter, and Wahl, he maintains that in Hegel Kierkegaard saw a defense against the romantic. Bohlin has not answered the purely historical question of Kierkegaard's actual knowledge of Hegel during the period of his

[39] Torsten Bohlin, *Sören Kierkegaards etiska åskådning* [SK's Ethical
View] (1918), esp. pp. 25-36, with reference to Niedermeyer's and Reuter's
writings, together with Bohlin's *Kierkegaards dogmatiska åskådning* [SK's
Dogmatic View], 1925.

youth discussed here, and his research essentially concentrates on later periods in Kierkegaard's thought.

Geismar[40] correctly stresses the Pelagius-Augustine alternative in the young Kierkegaard, and the conviction that philosophy—which is not immediately identified with that of Hegel—cannot contain the consciousness of sin in the Christian sense. For this reason, as a matter of pure principle an incompatibility must exist between Christianity and philosophy, and that is why as a purely historical matter Kierkegaard would have to come to a clash with Hegel and the Danish Hegelians who wanted to reconcile philosophy and Christianity. Geismar is correct when in a longer note (III, 111-112) he says that "Kierkegaard's knowledge of Hegelian philosophy was not in the first instance derived from the study of Hegel's works"; but Geismar has nothing more to say concerning the period under consideration here.

Hirsch[41] was the first to have undertaken a perspicacious and detailed analysis of this period. As Reuter, among others, had already held, Hirsch thinks that Kierkegaard actually rejected Hegel before he had read him; but in opposition to Reuter, Himmelstrup, and Geismar, among others, Hirsch will not go along with any talk of a Hegelianizing period in Kierkegaard at all. After what has been said about the period under consideration up to this point, it must be affirmed that Hirsch is correct. He is also correct when, in line with Geismar, he says that what Kierkegaard says about Hegelianism and speculation during these years comes from a second hand knowledge.

As far as details are concerned, Hirsch's analysis of, e.g. I A 72, unlike our own, is not undertaken with special reference to its possible relation to Hegel; he has emphasized the clarification of Kierkegaard's relation to other German thinkers. According to Hirsch, the problematic, as Kierkegaard entered it, was not entered upon via Hegel, and in this Hirsch is right. When Hirsch maintains that all of Kierkegaard's polemics in the *Papirer* during this time are exclusively concerned with Heiberg's esthetic articles and the review by Martensen discussed above, then the targets he identifies must be supplemented with others (among others, Marheineke's *Dogmatics*). Contrary to various other researchers, Hirsch does not

[40] Eduard Geismar, *Søren Kierkegaard, hans Livsudvikling og Forfattervirksomhed* [SK, the Development of His Life and Work as Author], I-VI, 1926-1928, esp. vol. I.

[41] *Kierkegaard-Studien*, I-II, 1930-1933, esp. II, 451ff.

think that Poul Møller had taught Kierkegaard very much during this time. But on this point Hirsch obviously missed the sources that would enable him to speak more accurately. Frithiof Brandt's —and to a lesser degree Vilhelm Andersen's—works tell another and truer story here. It may be taken as beyond any doubt that "Hegel and Hegelianism had been privately discussed between Kierkegaard and Møller," as Brandt says (*Den unge Søren Kierkegaard*, 1929, p. 353). Brandt cites the long note in *The Concluding Unscientific Postscript* (p. 34 [Eng. trans.]) as a completely adequate proof of the correctness of his claim. Hirsch's main view of Kierkegaard's relation to Hegel is otherwise the same as Brandt's and the one presented in this investigation, although the total view of each of the two worlds of thought, which stand in a definite mutual relation, is not identical with the one maintained here.[42]

It is worth noting Hirsch's assertion of the importance of the younger Fichte for Kierkegaard; but this matter belongs essentially to the following period.

There is no reason to dwell on the summary remarks that several other researchers have made on this period, just as there is little need to take an explicit position vis-à-vis every single opinion advanced. It is important only to note the conclusions of this study in relation to the earlier researchers, the quality of whose works may be described as essentially better than average, which directly deal with the same problems we consider here, and whose opinions and conclusions are worth discussing.

Thus the claim that in his early youth, when precisely those themes and the problematic that were to be developed extensively in the first period of the Authorship received their first and preliminary form, Kierkegaard did not have any specially close relation to Hegel or to the views and writings of the Hegelians, has been strongly confirmed. It cannot be asserted with certainty that during this period Kierkegaard had read Hegel's works, while with a

[42] Brandt writes (*Den Unge SK*, pp. 353-354) as follows: "Moreover it is known that Kierkegaard had never been a Hegelian, even in his youngest days. All his life he had great respect for 'Master Hegel,' and had technically learned very much from him, almost all of his philosophical terminology, but he never believed in 'the system.' Already in the youthful entries he pours irony down upon Hegel and the Hegelians and the Hegelian cud-chewing process with the three stomachs. While he had respect for the Master, he is full of contempt for the imitators, and especially for those who believed that they had 'gone beyond Hegel.'" On the whole, there is essentially nothing to be said against the correctness of this estimate.

degree of probability that borders on certainty it can be said that it is unlikely that he did. If this is correct, then it seems even more remarkable that the researchers have not, to a greater degree than has been the case, raised and answered the main question, of whether the worlds of thought of Kierkegaard and Hegel on the whole do not have something in common at bottom, when many of the important problems for Kierkegaard arose *before* his contact with Hegel and his disciples. At this stage of our investigation, the question cannot be definitively answered. But the analyses of the texts in which we might be tempted to assume a contact have just shown striking differences. That is sufficient for the moment. An exhaustive interpretation of the texts must enter into the many difficult and wide-ranging questions about all the many determining factors in the development of Kierkegaard's problems and their resolutions, questions which here are most frequently dealt with in passing, no matter how important they are otherwise.

The Period Between November 1837
and September 1838

1. SCOPE

IN THE MIDDLE OF NOVEMBER 1837 Kierkegaard began to follow
Martensen's *Forelæsninger over Indledning til den speculative Dogmatik* [Introductory Lectures on Speculative Dogmatics], and
scarcely ten months later he published his first book: *Af en endnu
Levendes Papirer* [From the Papers of One Still Living]. The title
of course alludes to Kierkegaard, not to Martensen.

During approximately the same time, Hegelian philosophy became actualized in earnest in Denmark. Obviously Martensen's lectures came to play an important part in this connection; but there
were several impulses. In June 1837, Heiberg began the publication
of *Perseus, Journal for den speculative Idee*, to which Kierkegaard
subscribed. The same year, in *Maanedsskrift for Litteratur*, Poul
Møller published his last long article, *Tanker over Muligheden af
Beviser for Menneskets Udødelighed*, in which he parted company
with Hegel. It was in the same periodical that shortly later Sibbern
—in the context of a review of *Perseus*—extensively and sharply
criticized both Heiberg's Hegelianism and Hegel's own system and
its dialectical method both *in toto* and in detail.

These are the most important, but by no means the only, literary
contributions for and against Hegel in Denmark during this time.

It is reasonable to assume that Kierkegaard followed this debate,
and took a position on it himself. This assumption is confirmed by
an examination of the sources, but in a way that perhaps might not
have been anticipated.

Kierkegaard's knowledge of Hegelianism undoubtedly preceded
his knowledge of the Master's own works; but this knowledge did
not come about only through Martensen's lectures and articles.
Indeed, Kierkegaard knew personally the adherents and opponents
of Hegel's philosophy in Copenhagen, and no doubt, he knew the
leading opponents, Poul Møller and Sibbern, best. We cannot be

certain about the details of Kierkegaard's participation in or direct knowledge of the debates about Hegel during this period. This would, of course, be an important source for an understanding of his attitude toward Hegel and Hegelianism.

To the oral and written Danish sources must be added Kierkegaard's reading of German articles and works, a reading we can follow quite accurately, and which became of great importance for his knowledge of and attitude toward several central problems, most often in the philosophy of religion.

In what follows, then, the investigation will pursue a somewhat chronological progress within the period. First we come to Kierkegaard's reading of Johan Eduard Erdmann, *Vorlesungen über Glauben und Wissen als Einleitung in die Dogmatik und Religionsphilosophie* [Lectures on Faith and Knowledge as Introduction to Dogmatics and Philosophy of Religion], which appeared in 1837 (Ktl. 479); next, his reading of the other German Hegelians and anti-Hegelians; then Martensen's lectures. After these points, an account will be given of other aspects and phases. Following a confrontation with the views found in earlier research, we can present the conclusion of this period.

2. KIERKEGAARD AND ERDMANN'S
Lectures on Faith and Knowledge

As has been said, Erdmann's *Lectures* were published in the summer of 1837. Kierkegaard acquired it and in the beginning of November started to work his way through it. He finished the task in the middle of December.[1]

Certainly Kierkegaard's excerpts, summaries, and especially his critical remarks (*Papirer* II C 38-49[a] and several entries in Group A) are quite detailed; but they can hardly be completely understood apart from the background of Erdmann's whole interpretation, which Hirsch has briefly and aptly, but not exhaustively, described.

It is very significant that from the beginning Kierkegaard's understanding of Hegel's philosophical system was strongly influenced

---

[1] Hirsch in particular (*Kierkegaard-Studien*, II, 530-539), as has been said, has concerned himself with Kierkegaard's reading of this work, which Erdmann himself later described as an immature product (*Grundriss der Geschichte der Philosophie*, II, 3 ed., 1878, 646).

[a] Only portions of these entries will be found in vol. II of the *Papirer*. The remainder are in vol. XIII. Some of these are in Hong, I, II, and V.

by the right-wing Hegelians' version of Hegel's thought. Therefore it is necessary to devote rather more than routine attention to a work such as that of Erdmann. Without anticipating the outcome of the investigation, it can be suggested that had Kierkegaard read a work such as F. C. Baur's *Die Christliche Gnosis* as thoroughly as he now read Erdmann's, then certainly both his understanding and his attitude toward Hegel would have sooner taken a somewhat different form. Kierkegaard owned this imposing work [of Baur] (Ktl. 421); but unfortunately he seems not to have given it the attention it deserved.

Nonetheless, there is no doubt that he had read Erdmann, and so first we must clarify the main lines of Erdmann's work.

In the introductory comments Erdmann stresses the importance of the topic and its treatment in the history of philosophy. From the most recent period he emphasizes Schelling's *Vorlesungen über das academische Studium*, Hegel's *Phenomenology of the Spirit*, and his *Encyclopedia*, and the preface to Hinrichs' *Religionsphilosophie*. He then goes on to the question of to which discipline faith and knowledge really belong, whether to theology or philosophy, and the answer he gives (p. 5) is that the problem is extrinsic to both of them, belonging instead to the introduction to the philosophy of religion and the introduction to dogmatic theology.

The question of how philosophy is related to religion is not itself a religious problem, but falls outside of the area of religion as a reflection on religion.

After these preliminary considerations, Erdmann goes on (p. 10ff.) to deal with the problem of the origin of philosophy. There seems to be a difficulty here, in that it must be maintained both that the beginning may be demonstrated and that no definite proposition can be the beginning. To escape from this dilemma, Erdmann says, people have attempted to find the beginning of philosophy not in a proposition but in something else, namely, in the postulate (p. 13). Fichte's merit is in having maintained this position. Thus philosophy is considered not only as constructing—as one builds a house out of prepared stones—but as producing—as independently creating. Hegel attempted to liberate philosophy from its plethora of postulates, which resulted from his desire to establish a single one at the center and make it all-pervasive. That was the postulate "Think, or remain thinking" (p. 15), and Erdmann holds that Hegel has shown that this postulate is not arbitrary, just as he has shown in *Phenomenology of the Spirit* that pure scientific thought is the definition [*Bestemmelse*] of man. Thus *Phenomenology* is regarded as a propaedeutic to philosophy.

In the first part of his work, Erdmann takes his point of departure from within the Christian Faith, and he defines Christianity as the religion of love, the essence of which is the union of God and man. This union has been brought about after a separation, and it is also the expression of a reconciliation: "The union with God is one which is brought about through removal of sin, through its being mediated" (p. 24).

Religion in the subjective sense is defined in this context as a frame of mind deriving from inner peace with God and the world, the awareness of being reconciled with God. Faith is precisely certitude (p. 30) and not just the affirmation of any content at all. It should also be noted that the Church is not understood as an aggregate of individuals, but as an organism that is greater than its parts.

In the objective sense, religion is the religious truth such as it is formulated in the doctrine of religion. This truth must be accessible to everyone, and it appears then as a fact about which we have immediate certitude. However, here a difficulty arises for the Hegelian Erdmann, for

> but now it is the essential [character] of every single fact, that it is something temporal and contingent . . . but the essential [character] of truth is that it is eternal and necessary. Therefore the form of the fact is not appropriate [to that] of the truth, and distorts the truth thereby (p. 37).

This fact must then be corrected by another fact which contradicts it! Erdmann finds this to be the case in the New Testament narratives, about whose content he writes thus: "The physically manifested identity of God and humanity is the God-Man. He *is* the reconciliation," but the death of Christ is the corrective, which is then corrected again in the Resurrection.

What is essential in immediate faith is that it is the awareness of a complete reconciliation with God. Now, however, man is not born into faith, but is reborn into it, and in the faith there is a recollection of the unreconciled state. One can in faith—here understood as a state of consciousness—fall back into his previous state, i.e., the immediate consciousness becomes reflected.

Faith is the same as reconciliation; but now faith becomes the object that stands over against the ego: "Faith by which" stands over against "faith which" [*fides qua staar overfor fides quae*], "and the naive faith has become Faith in that which is believed" (p. 46).

Since now religious consciousness reflects on itself, it finds on the one side the ego, on the other side the object. This object is the union of God and man, and in this union lies salvation and truth. Thus truth is on the side of the object, and the ego, insofar as it stands over against the object, lacks it. If the ego should now become a participant in the truth, then it must be related to it as a recipient. In precisely the same way the ego stands over against a fact, and thus we get the historical faith, which is something positive, and we arrive at the standpoint of dogmatism.

This shows that Erdmann develops the first standpoint on the way of thought and subsequently finds it in history, and in this instance he discovers the attitude of dogmatism represented in the orthodoxy of the seventeenth and eighteenth centuries. His own position and its meaning emerges clearly from this quote: "Dogma is truth, *although* it is history, is a fact, [but] to dogmatism it is truth, *because* it is a fact" (p. 57).

The position is further developed as follows: the truth has the essential character of positivity—but, since it is constantly defined as opposed to the ego, which is rational, it here acquires the conjoined definition of the irrational, and it is defined as truth only because it is irrational. Erdmann identifies this as the position of dogmatic superstition, and he finds it manifested, for example, in Tertullian's "credibile est quia ineptum, verum quia impossibile est," [it is believable because it is absurd, true because it is impossible] in extreme Pietism, as well as in the elder Schelling. As representative of the opposite position Erdmann refers to, among others, Malebranche,[b] who is said to have "spoken excellently on this point; what presumption lies therein, to project one's own weakness of reason to all mankind at once" (p. 70).

If the truth only is truth as opposed to the ego, or because it is in opposition to the ego, then that which makes the truth into truth is nothing but the ego itself, and the content of truth is nothing but what the ego gives it! Thus it turns out, Erdmann continues, in the closest possible connection with the noted passage on this point in Hegel's *Phenomenology of the Spirit*, that "out of the complete

[b] On Nicolas Malebranche (1638-1715) see Beatrice K. Rome, *The Philosophy of Malebranche* (Chicago: Henry Regnery Company, 1963), and Desmond Connell, *The Vision in God: Malebranche's Scholastic Sources* (New York: Humanities Press, 1967).

bondage of the ego follows its exact opposite, namely, that it is precisely the lordship over that which it serves" (p. 71). This is an example, Erdmann says, of how the dialectical concepts turn into their opposites.

The development has not arrived at the point where the object must legitimize itself for the subject, i.e., the situation is (adolescent) religious doubt.

Only in harmony with the ego does the truth exist in this position. Indeed, the greater the harmony with the ego, the greater the truth. Complete harmony with the ego is only the ego itself, and so it turns out that the absolute and primitive truth is the harmony of the ego with itself. Here the development arrives at religious nihilism or indifferentism, where the ego has no limits. If the ego is itself conscious of this, then we speak of religious irony, which is the opposite of dogmatism. As historical examples Erdmann mentions Solger and the two Schlegel brothers.

Even here the ego is still limited; but if it should become entirely independent, then it must polemicize against everything objective, *because* it is objective, and Erdmann calls this stage (p. 90) disbelief (*Unglaube*), the opposite of which is superstition. He finds historical exemplification of this in the French Revolution, in Voltaire and la Mettrie.

The dialectical development continues thus: if the truth is defined only as the opposite of the ego, then it is simply and totally dependent on the object, i.e., the truth inheres in the object!

Having come this far, Erdmann thinks that it has become evident that there is a necessity that the subject and object be conjoined. This unification cannot take place by making one dominate the other, since they are coequal. Nor can it happen by modifying something in them: thus they must both remain unchanged in the union; but—in the light of the previous developments—the unification must be brought about by force, and this position, "which possesses an unshakable Faith as something brought forth, [as if] perforce, I call the point of view of a mystic" (p. 103). Here the ego *and* the object constitute the truth, indeed, the mystical union is the identification of subject and object. Just as Faith is an immediate awareness of reconciliation, so the mystical consciousness is a powerfully evoked awareness of reconciliation.[c]

As examples of contemporary theologians who come within this

[c] Cf. Newman's distinction between "notional and real assent" in his *Essay in Aid of a Grammar of Assent*, 1870, Chap. IV.

definition Erdmann mentions Hengstenberg and Olshausen (p. 117).

We can also mention that in his dialectical scheme of development Erdmann finds room for mystical separatism.

After this consideration of faith, Erdmann goes on in the second part of his work to discuss knowledge. His procedure here, as in the first part, is first to describe the structure of one form of consciousness and then to give it a name.

By passing from faith to knowledge the development has passed from the individual to the general, from the particular to the common consciousness, to use Erdmann's terms. This also means that while, generally speaking, faith cannot be granted the predicate of "the objective." yet [objectivity] belongs to reason, for: "The concept of reason is . . . to be objective oneself, and therefore to find nothing essentially distinct from it in the object, but on the contrary, it finds itself [therein]" (p. 148).

The first stage is empirical knowledge.

In considering objects, reason does not show itself to be irrational, but reason "refers to the objects in such a way that it regains for them their original definition" (p. 151). Furthermore, through experience reason can distinguish between the essential and the accidental in objects that it knows empirically.

If we now consider the object of faith, it is not something alien to reason when it seeks the essential and finds it in the practical, in which case there arises "the theology of the so-called practical Christian" (p. 156), whose representatives are, for example, Francke and Spener.

Reason seeks and finds the general in the many individual cases, with which it can then be said to experiment. In the experiment reason proceeds from a hypothesis, which it attempts to verify. In theology this is the stage in which one wishes to produce proofs of the truth of Christian doctrine by proceeding from the miracles of Christ; and on this stage a distinction is made between articles of faith that are basic and those that are not.[d]

The development moves on to "knowledge through testimony or historical knowledge" (p. 173), and in the area of theology this is historical theology or the domain of tradition, i.e., the Roman Catholic and the historical-exegetical theology of the evangelical churches

[d] Cf. St. Thomas Aquinas: "The existence of God and other like truths about God, which can be known by natural reason, are not articles of faith, but are preambles to the articles." *Summa Theologiae*, Ia, q.2, art. 2, ad 1m.

(p. 177), in which one replaces theology, in the sense of dogmatics, with the history of dogma.

On the stage just named, the activity of reason was limited, conditioned by the object. Now it becomes the task of reason to prove that the object contains truth at all. This induces reason to establish rules according to which it will decide what is correct or incorrect. Reason itself must establish the criteria, that is, reason has become critical. In the area of theology this is the so-called natural theology or the stage of naturalism. Erdmann places the English Freethinkers, i.e., the Deists of the eighteenth century, in this category (p. 193).

In agreement with Hegel's distinction, but—as usual in Erdmann's work—without explicitly identifying it, Erdmann calls reason, insofar as it occupies itself with abstractions, understanding. In the area of theology this corresponds to the so-called "theology of common sense," that is, the theology of the Enlightenment (p. 200).

Transcendental criticism now investigates the nature and possibility of knowledge in this way: "When the object is compared with the law of thought, it is only compared with the intellect itself, that is, with the reason holding itself in abstraction. When the reason therefore examines the truth of the object, it compares the object with itself." Here reason has arrived at the point of reflecting on its relation to the object, thus to construct what Kant called a transcendental reflection. In the religious area this becomes a "theology of ignorance" (p. 211). Erdmann thinks, moreover, that both rationalists and supranaturalists are semi-Kantians. He characterizes supranaturalism, in which Faith is always put in opposition to knowledge, as a "Dogmatism proven from the standpoint of ignorance," while rationalism is described as "nihilism proven from the standpoint of ignorance" (pp. 216-219). On the other hand, Erdmann says, the Bible recognizes no opposition between faith and knowledge: "The Bible employed faith and knowledge without distinction and understood thereunder the intellectual [*geistige*] possession of truth" (p. 223).

However, the transcendental reflection rests on a contradiction, which must be overcome. The opposition between subject and object must be abrogated, for "the concept . . . of knowledge . . . is that the reason finds and knows itself again in the known . . ." (p. 233).

Kantian philosophy remains stuck in a contradiction; but Fichte resolves the contradiction (between the theoretical and practical reason), since he did not establish any being at all, but only a command [*en Skullen*] with the result that we should elicit our identity with God ourselves.

The process now arrives at the stage where the identity of the subjective and the objective is not only a command [*Skullen*], but a being [*Væren*], for "the truth is not a task alone, but it is perfect, complete" (p. 245). At that point, reason is no longer only producing but contemplating, and what it contemplates is the Absolute; that is, the process has arrived at Schleiermacher's "theology of the feeling of dependence on the Absolute." The position is compared with mysticism, and Erdmann stresses (p. 252) that, while Fichte can be called an atheist, Schleiermacher can be called a pantheist.

The identity between the subjective and the objective has been achieved, and with that the process comes to "speculative theology or science of religion" (p. 256).

It becomes clear here that we cannot attribute *"Daseyn"* to God, that is, we cannot understand Him as static, since God is actuality, and activity, life, belongs to actuality. This is grasped only in the concept, *Begriff*, which is divine thought in things and is the law of development. That means that to know is to conceive, and "speculative theology grasps God as process, that is, as living consciousness" (p. 263).

Finally, we may note Erdmann's speculative understanding of evil as something ephemeral, as a transitional point, and—obviously —he particularly emphasizes Schelling and Hegel as representatives of this position in the process, which (p. 270) is understood as the absolutely true position.

Undoubtedly, Erdmann's work means to be faithful to Hegel in its method and conclusion and any further proof of this may be regarded as superfluous. Formally—as Kierkegaard pointed out, and as Hirsch (*Kierkegaard-Studien* II, p. 533) reminds us—there is a difference between the Master and the disciple, in that the latter clearly distinguishes between the process of dialectical thought and its exemplification. But this is not so essential. What is relevant is that Erdmann understood himself as a right-wing Hegelian, and that he was understood as such by his reader, student Kierkegaard.

The Hegelianism that Erdmann's work represents must, moreover, be characterized not exactly as misleading, but as defective in relation to Hegel's own system and its crucial secret. We can also put it this way: the attitude toward the philosophy of religion expressed by Erdmann certainly parallels Hegel's own view; but its detailed context and concord lacks the crucial perspective, which is clear in Hegel, namely, the cosmic cycle of the divine—or at least the attempt to educe the cycle from the realm of logic, through that of nature, and back into the realm of spirit to itself.

Kierkegaard very carefully worked through Erdmann's book and took positions partly with regard to individual points in it, partly toward the work as a whole.

Typical of Kierkegaard as a reader and—especially—as a thinker are his remarks (II C 39)[e] on the relation between thought and life. Erdmann's definitions of irony and mysticism also caught his attention.

But more important are his concise critical judgments (II C 44ff.).[f]

In the first of these entries, Kierkegaard thinks that Erdmann has been guilty of a piece of disingenuousness in the transition from the first to the second part, in that he has unconditionally allowed the ego to disappear, to be replaced by an impersonal reason. But Kierkegaard's criticism is, characteristically enough, an illustration of his own stage at this time, only immanent here.

On the other hand, he goes a step further in what follows and—in this he takes Erdmann as a typical example—criticizes prevailing contemporary views in which "one ignores the historical aspect of Christianity" (II C 44, p. 352, [Hong, II, 520]). In this way the order of connections has to be changed around. In Christianity the concept of tradition was developed after the historical revelation had taken place, indeed, began immediately after it. Therefore, this should correctly have been placed first of all in the work, and not, as is the case here, in the second part.

On the whole, Kierkegaard takes a very skeptical view of Erdmann's linking together of dialectical thought process and historical exemplification: "in many places it seems to me that it is only a caricature" (p. 353 [Hong, II, 520-521]). In Kierkegaard's view, there is an abyss between the necessity of thought and historical reality. In this context, this appears in a question, which, simply from the fact that Kierkegaard raises it, shows at a glance the difference between philosophical idealism and Christianity. The ques-

[e] Hong, V, #5272.
[f] II C 44, Hong, II, #2250; II C 46, Hong, II, #2251; II C 48, Hong, II, #2252.

tion is whether in the same sense we can subject Christianity to an a priori judgment like any other fact (II C 46).

Hirsch is right (*Kierkegaard-Studien* II, p. 535) in finding the answer in Kierkegaard's understanding and attitude toward supranaturalism and rationalism diverging from that of Erdmann.

Both through Martensen's lectures and Erdmann's book Kierkegaard has now, in contrast with his earlier comments on rationalism and supranaturalism, become aware of Kant's importance. Erdmann describes Kant's position on the philosophy of religion, points out his importance for both theological rationalism and supranaturalism, and maintains that both Kant's and these views are anticipatory, that they were overcome and abrogated by the following development, marked with names such as Fichte, Schleiermacher, and finally Hegel.

Even though in Martensen's lectures there is a more complete presentation—from the standpoint of the pure history of philosophy —of Kant (II C 19-24),[g] and although on the whole the divergencies from Hegel, and thereby from Erdmann, are not unimportant, there is hardly any doubt that Martensen had also read Erdmann's work and that in what is decisive, the assertion of the connection and harmony between Faith and knowledge, there is agreement between them. Along both paths, which lead to the same goal, and which sometimes run parallel over long stretches, Kierkegaard became aware that in speculative thought both rationalism and supranaturalism were judged to be vanquished positions, vanquished together with Kant. Moreover, Martensen had already presented this view earlier in his disputation, and in 1839 a remark by the ill-starred J. A. Bornemann (in *Tidsskrift for Litteratur og Kritik*, 1839, p. 3) gave occasion for a discussion of the principles of logic, such as Kuhr has given an account of in *Modsigelsens Grundsætning* [The Principle of Contradiction] (1915).

Hirsch's interpretation of Kierkegaard's entry is that the linking of supranaturalism with Kantian unknowability [*ikke-Viden*] is mistaken, for that about which nothing can be known is in principle inaccessible to human consciousness, and so it cannot be believed either. Supranaturalism is an interpretation that is fundamentally deeper and independent of Kantian and other philosophy, and "Supranaturalism thinks that a complete change of consciousness must take place, a development must begin entirely from the

[g] Not in Hong.

beginning," (II C 48) which means, in other words, that a conversion is needed, and that the rebirth has total significance for the whole notion of life. Hirsch thinks that it may be said quite simply that

> Kierkegaard sees Faith not only as a marvelous new consciousness, but above all, as a consciousness that is intrinsically human: Faith is just as eternal in the Idea, just as freighted with knowledge as the first immediate consciousness. In the sharp assertion of this aspect he sees his difference from historical supranaturalism. With this the riddle of the a priori has solved itself for us, [the riddle] which is preserved in the growth of the personality through the break: the rebirth is at the same time a reawakening of all that is human,

and Hirsch ventures to call attention to what are undeniably far-reaching perspectives when he continues:

> this noteworthy, peculiarly Kierkegaardian thought clarifies in what way basically there is room in his thinking for a foundation of a general world view of Kierkegaard's reasoning about attitudes toward life. By and large the fundamentally ethical and religious objections against Speculation destroying Christianity, which Kierkegaard had raised later, are all set forth in his discussion of Erdmann . . . *Kierkegaard-Studien* II, p. 535-536).

If we set the two texts, Kierkegaard's and Hirsch's interpretation of it, side by side, it is obvious that Hirsch had read more into Kierkegaard's critical remarks on Erdmann than there is basis for.

It is certainly true that Kierkegaard had a different, and wider, concept of supranaturalism from Erdmann. It approaches the concept of orthodoxy (cf. I A 72); but the words "a development must begin from the beginning and [be] just as eternal in the Idea as the first" (II C 48) contain nothing about a reawakening of humanism. Kierkegaard actually says nothing further about the content of this development which he says must begin.

In any case, then, the question about the possibility of subjecting Christianity to an a priori judgment must be answered in the negative. For the reborn there is no possibility of, so to speak, doubling back on this decisive event, and the non-Christian's judgment is meaningless for the Christian. Kierkegaard expresses this here with his discussion of supranatural faith as a new consciousness.

If this interpretation is correct, then it is obvious why, as a matter of principle, Kierkegaard must declare himself to be at odds with the whole trend in Erdmann, that is, the inclination in the first place to assign faith a lower position than knowledge and in the second place for wanting to maintain a continuity of transition from faith, the lower sphere, to knowledge, the higher realm. On the basis of his understanding of supranaturalism Kierkegaard situates faith and knowledge opposite each other in their mutual relation, and instead of the Hegelian Erdmann's continuous transition Kierkegaard maintains that there is a complete change.

Thus it appears that already at the beginning of December 1837 after Kierkegaard had, with critical alertness, worked through a representative book from the Hegelian school's right wing, that there was a fundamental division on principle.

It is not surprising then, that he did not feel impelled to read Hegel directly through having studied Erdmann's work.

3. KIERKEGAARD AND I. H. FICHTE'S
Treatise on Speculation and Revelation

In this situation Kierkegaard got to work (Dec. 12, 1837) on the younger Fichte's new *Zeitschrift für Philosophie und spekulative Theologie* and read Fichte's monograph *Spekulation und Offenbarung* [Speculation and Revelation] (I, 1837, 1-31), which, incidentally, was immediately translated into Danish and appeared in Clausen and Hohlenberg's *Tidsskrift for udenlandsk theologisk Litteratur* (1837, 747-777).

In this article Fichte characterizes Hegel's philosophy as a modern variant of rationalism, a variant which has not desired to abandon revelation, but which, on the contrary, has wished to clarify it, conceive it, give it a speculative foundation. By pushing these efforts to their ultimate consequences, philosophy has come to a crisis. We have received rationalism's first and last comprehensive system (p. 3). The situation seems to be that reality cannot be confined within the speculative concept, and thus the basis is established for a new development in which the individual and the positive can receive their due. In this new philosophy, the post-Hegelian, the concept of a proper personal revelation finds a natural place. The question is then, how does this revelation take place. The answer is: in Nature and in history. That does not mean that God is identical with the world in which this revelation takes place.

Fichte finds these views not only in Christianity and in the Old Testament belief but also in the whole of antiquity and in all folk religions. He rejects the Hegelian position that this Faith should be only an immediate representation by which humanity objectivizes its own unity with the divine Spirit outside of itself, so that that which places it outside of the personal hypostasis is precisely that which it is in itself according to its spiritual substance. Fichte thinks that Hegel has not escaped the risk of pantheism; but perhaps, he continues, it is not only Hegel who has fallen into this ditch.

Before he examines this idea, Fichte divides the prevailing views on the philosophy of religion into two main groups, called the psychological-human and the objective-divine. As representatives of the first group Schleiermacher and Jacobi immediately come to mind, and as typical of the second group, Hegel and his disciples.

These two schools of thought mutually exclude each other, but— and here we note the Hegelian, speculative tendency toward mediation in Fichte—there is, he says, a need to find a uniting point. Concerning Schleiermacher, he says that:

> He who is being accused of having gotten bogged down in subjectivism, it was he who in that memorable work drove the subjective enmeshment of pious emotion so far beyond itself, that it had to turn to a reception of the positive with a new element and a most devoutly sincere susceptibility (p. 8).

Certainly in the beginning it was seen as a weakness that the person of Christ occupied such a large place in his thought; but this was precisely Schleiermacher's merit and not a weakness:

> Such a fully penetrating and self-evaluating pious feeling is unquestionably driven, as certainly as faith encompasses confidence and trust in that which is believed, to seek something divine beyond itself, something divine in concrete form, because only in such a way can that pious emotion originate and only in this [search for the divine] can that pious feeling find satisfaction (p. 9).

However valuable Schleiermacher's contribution is in relation to rationalism on this crucial point, Fichte still has serious doubts about it. He finds that Schleiermacher always can only give a presentation of the phenomena of religious consciousness, a knowledge of the essence of the soul, as it is highlighted in self-consciousness, not a presentation of the divine essence in its positive nature and revelation. Fichte finds that Schleiermacher constantly applies only a purely anthropological criterion.

The basic reason that man can know the eternal outside of himself, Fichte continues, is that he has something eternal, something divine within him. If there were nothing eternal in our spirit, if our consciousness were entirely of finite nature, then a knowledge of the divine would be totally impossible.

Fichte holds that there are different perspectives on this topic beginning with Schelling and ending with Hegel.

Schelling demonstrated the eternal and absolute element in human consciousness from the intellectual perspective, Hegel did the same from the standpoint of speculative thought, which has as its content the world of the categories, and which will burst through and abrogate all subjectivity.

Thus one account maintains that God is in principle unknowable, the other, on the contrary, that God can be known completely, but as impersonal. In all of Hegel's works, Fichte says, he allows religion to be absorbed by philosophy, just as is also the case with the church and the state, i.e., religion must first obtain the valid expression of its truth through speculative knowledge.

In this way, religion and revelation are deprived of a special ingredient with the result that human philosophical self-knowledge is identified with knowledge of God, which Fichte must consider the fundamental error of the system, and, as he puts it:

> not enough, that the specific content of religion must be completely absorbed into philosophy,—a position on which the Hegelian teaching is quite at one with the whole rationalistic-philosophical way of thinking of the time, having only established bolder expressions and proven it more consistently;—but, what hitherto appeared less evident to consciousness, its whole position on knowledge remains thoroughly inadequate for grasping the characteristic of that fact in its proper depth and for providing exhaustive recognition: it is not expressly rejected in that concept nor is its opposite asserted, but it appears dull and reduced from its original meaning to an abstract speculative theory (p. 15).

Fichte also sees a decisive error in Hegelian philosophy inasmuch as redemption [*Forsoningen*] is reduced to a pure and simple logical process, which is a consequence of the concept that wounds and distorts this holy relationship.

Hegelian philosophy is not indifferent to the historical given in Christianity; but it thinks that it has anticipated it. The historical given is interpreted speculatively in such a way that what is said to have happened with Christ is conceived as God Himself as part of the necessary world-process. Christ is the suffering, dying, death-conquering and resurrected God. This important and correct observation of Fichte is followed by the next, that Hegel sees this whole process as proceeding necessarily by itself, whereas the historical in Christianity is seen as God's free decision. This false basic interpretation of a great and decisive truth permeates the whole Hegelian system. A little further on, Fichte gives another essentially correct description of Hegel's philosophy when he calls it mysticism; but he uses this label in a broad, general sense of the nebulous, floating, ambiguous, deep, inscrutable.

Just as Fichte found Schleiermacher's philosophy of religion unsatisfactory, he also has crucial objections to Hegel's. Thus he finds it necessary to produce a third philosophy of religion that will do justice to both the divine and the human.

A definite and explicit distinction must be made between the divine content and the human appropriation of it. The divine element does not consist in arousing the subjective disposition or feeling and then a presentiment of the nearness of God at all. In this way man would not be able to go any further than only an abstract awareness of God as something unknown. Nor is the doctrine of a universal revelation, a primordial revelation, adequate. Not until the coming of Christ was a key given to this universal revelation, so that it becomes possible to distinguish between the divine in it and the human embellishments added in the course of time. Fichte holds that no new religion after Christianity can be historically demonstrated, and, for him, it is not conceivable either.

In the revelation of Christ is the real source and final moment of the truth, and only on that basis can the world be known in its essence and context. Man can become one with God, but not by his own, but only by God's action. Likewise, knowledge is perfected not by human artifice, but by God. Philosophy must subject itself to revelation as the objectively given and must recognize its duty to understand revelation in its purity.

There may seem to be a risk of falling back on a simple faith in authority, but Fichte rejects this danger as illusory. When the divine understanding reveals itself on the highest point, in the most concrete and genuine way, this can be accessible only to the highest exertions of the reason, with the most complete independence from the subjectivity that gradually becomes troublesome.

Fichte has great hopes for the new, third position in the philosophy of religion. Only the greatest generalities of the old positions will remain standing in his opinion; so, too, in empirical respects, the views he has presented will take on profound significance in giving a sound account of reality. For example, Fichte says

> the real paradoxes in our religious doctrine, which our fathers adhered to through rational instinct and the strength of their faith against the destructive claims of the so-called rationalization of Faith,—these paradoxes [will] be held, in our time of aggressive speculative research, precisely as the true, more deeply satisfying to reason, thus approved by the devout [*Gottgemässere*].

Reading this monograph had an effect on Kierkegaard somewhat similar to the impact of Martensen's Faust article.[2] His thoughts and plans were—particularly in connection with Erdmann—going in the same direction, toward the same sort of criticism of Hegel that he was reading about in Fichte. He found in Fichte a strengthening of his own, still only incompletely developed views. Thus on December 12, 1827 (*Papirer*, II A 204),[h] Kierkegaard writes that he had become

> quite dismayed by reading this article with which Fichte begins his periodical, when one sees a man with his mental ability preparing to fight with such earnestness . . . what, then shall the rest of us say. I believe that I will give up studying, and now I know what I will be, I shall see about being a witness for a notary public.

Kierkegaard speaks of Fichte with the greatest respect, and that was not an entirely new recognition either, although we do not know of any greater study on the part of Kierkegaard.

It appears from some entries from the end of March 1837, that Kierkegaard had read, but only "hastily," as he says himself, *Die*

[2] Cf. Hirsch, II, 524f., and *Papirer* II A 50 [Hong, II, #1183] and II A 597 [Hong, V, #5225], and especially Carl Roos, *SK og Goethe* (1955), 111ff.

[h] Hong, V, #5282.

Idee der Persönlichkeit und der individuellen Fortdauer [The Idea of Personality and of Individual Duration] (II A 31),[i] and it pleases him to see essential agreement between his views here and what he encountered in his later reading of this thinker.

We do not find Fichte mentioned in these March entries—which are a transcript or fair copy of earlier notes—and the statement of December 1837 quoted above. Then there is again a leap forward to August 2, 1838, when Kierkegaard, after having written down his famous motto on the relation between Christianity and philosophy on the previous day,[j] identifies the younger Fichte as a modern representative of Chiliasm (II A 240).[k] Nearly a year passes before Kierkegaard, on July 28, 1839, again speaks of Fichte (II A 517-519)[l] and now—in connection with the long article *Aphorismen über die Zukunft der Theologie, in ihrem Verhältnisse zu Spekulation und Mythologie* [Aphorisms on the Future of Theology, in Its Relations to Speculation and Mythology] in his periodical (Bd. 3, 1839, 199-286)—with a clearly independent, critical attitude. A note in connection with Kierkegaard's reading of Fichte's chief work, *Ueber Gegensatz, Wendepunkt und Ziel heutiger Philosophie* [On the Antithesis, Crisis, and Goal of Contemporary Philosophy] (II A 592)[m] cannot be dated with certainty, and it concerns only the philosophical classification of Jacobi, Fries, and Eschenmayer.

As critical of Fichte as Kierkegaard later became, he was just as respectful of Fichte at this early point in the middle of December 1837. In the earlier period there was a fundamental disharmony between Kierkegaard and the leading right-wing Hegelians such as Erdmann. Reading Erdmann's work did not impel Kierkegaard to a study of Hegel himself and the disharmony was further strengthened by Fichte's article, which at that particular moment seemed to discourage him. Both Kierkegaard's critical confrontation with Erdmann's work and his reading of I. H. Fichte must be later taken into account in any attempt to clarify Kierkegaard's attitude toward Martensen at this time. In any case Kierkegaard did not come into direct contact with Hegel through Fichte either. On the other hand, it is significant that in this way he did become more firmly set in a critical predisposition.

[i] Hong, II, #1190.
[j] II A 239, Hong, III, #3259.
[k] Hong, V, #5332.
[l] Hong, III, #3276-3278.
[m] Hong, II, #1191.

4. MARTENSEN'S LECTURES AND SURVEY OF HEGEL

Kierkegaard attended and summarized only the first ten of Martensen's lectures, dealing with the introduction and the history of philosophy up to and including Kant. It is not necessary in this context to go through this synopsis (*Papirer* II C 12-24).[n] However, it was chiefly through Martensen's lectures on the history of philosophy that Kierkegaard got a first impression, a summary, of the main classifications in the history of thought in the area of the philosophy of religion from Descartes to Hegel. It is also true that these lectures, both the ones he summarized himself and the ones he had only secondhand knowledge of, for that fact alone had decisive meaning for him. Kierkegaard's independent study of the major presentations of the history of philosophy (especially Tennemann's, which he bought on May 15, 1841; Hegel's posthumously published lectures, which he used for the first time while writing *On the Concept of Irony*; Michelet's; Chalybäus's; and others), and of the thinkers who caught his interest, got started in earnest only later. The last entry concerning these lectures is dated December 23, 1837. After this he borrowed a notebook from another (unknown) student, and was satisfied with that.[3]

Kierkegaard stopped attending Martensen's lectures just as Martensen was about to begin his abbreviated and somewhat critical survey of the most recent thought, with Hegel as the last and greatest name. This is relevant and calls for an explanation, which has already been implied.

The notebook mentioned above (II C 25)[o] contains in its 124 small pages a generally complete summary of Martensen's lectures on the history of philosophy from Kant to Hegel, which Martensen delivered again in the winter semester 1838-1839. We get the impression from this summary that the student who wrote it did not entirely grasp the finer nuances and that he occasionally missed the context. However, what is important in this connection is that this summary is a main source for Kierkegaard's first orientation and survey of Hegel's system as a whole, whereas his other reading in

[n] Hong, V, #5277.

[3] This notebook is in the Kierkegaard Archives at the Royal Library in Copenhagen, Gruppe C, Pakke 3, Læg 3. Martensen's own drafts of the lectures (according to Skat Arildsen, *H. L. Martensen*, I (1932), 158, note 2) are in the family archives; but they are not generally available.

[o] This item, only identified in vol. II of the *Papirer*, will be found in full in vol. XII (1st Supplementbind), Hong, V, #5353.

all essentials only gave him a glimpse of Hegelian viewpoints in limited areas or on individual problems. Since these sources have not been published before, they will be given here, although with certain individual omissions.

According to the synopsis (II C 25), the sources employed by Martensen himself for the study of the history of modern philosophy were, first and foremost, Hegel's *Lectures on the History of Philosophy*, vol. III, and then Michelet's and I. H. Fichte's two main historical works.[4]

As a general description of Martensen's lectures[5] it can be said that they give a clear, faithful, but not particularly profound or independent presentation, in which the main emphasis, reasonably enough for Martensen, is placed on Descartes, Kant, Fichte, Jacobi, Fries, de Wette, Schleiermacher, Schelling (whose positive philosophy Martensen had heard presented in Munich), and Hegel.

More specifically, Martensen emphasizes modern philosophy, beginning with Descartes, as the most important for theologians, both because, according to his interpretation, this was the most profound era for philosophy, and because it was a period in which the need to reconcile theology with philosophy had manifested itself most— an opinion that shall not be criticized here, but only noted. We can also call attention to the fact that in Martensen a thinker such as Spinoza is not treated in any distinct section, and he gives very short treatment to Leibniz, Wolff, Baumgarten, and Mendelssohn (to give them in the order Martensen lists them on the same halfpage). Only when Martensen comes to Kant does the presentation become more ample. Now in several instances it is accompanied by critical remarks deriving from a speculative position. Contra Kant, he asserts that there are not just four, but infinitely many antinomies, and a little later on he says that "Kant . . . tried . . . to meet the criticism that he reached for the objective but could not obtain it. Also he wishes to imagine conscience to be the voice of

[4] Information on these will be found in my notes on Kierkegaard's *Papirer* [vol. XII], Supplementbind I. [K. L. Michelet, *Geschichte der letzten Systeme der Philosophie in Deutschland von Kant bis Hegel*, I-II (Berlin 1833-1836) (Ktl. 678-679). I. H. Fichte, *Beiträge zur Charakteristik der neueren Philosophie*, 1828 (Kierkegaard owned the second edition, "much improved and expanded," published in 1841 (Ktl. 508); I. H. Fichte, *Ueber Gegensatz, Wendepunkt und Ziel heutiger Philosophie*, I-III (1832-1836). Michelet was also editor of Hegel's *Vorlesungen über die Geschichte die Philosophie*, I-III, Berlin, 1833-1836 (Ktl. 557-559).]

[5] Skat Arildsen's discussion, *Martensen*, p. 158, unfortunately, is very brief.

God, but he feels only himself." Martensen comes to the conclusion, at the end of the section on Kant, that we cannot stop with Kant's system, since it places a dichotomy—untenable in Martensen's opinion—between thought and being. In this way, Kant has violated the principle of Protestantism, as Martensen calls the Cartesian "cogito ergo sum." (Neither Luther nor other Reformers or theologians are named by Martensen in his specification of the principle of Protestantism.) J. G. Fichte's thought is only sketched, without criticism, while Jacobi is presented with considerable sympathy. Fries and de Wette are sketched rather thoroughly but quite naturally he devotes considerably more attention to Schleiermacher, who is described, and thereby implicitly criticized, as a one-sided transitional figure, who held to an anthropocentric, subjective position redolent of Spinoza. In Martensen's critical remarks he says, among other things, that the feeling of absolute contingency asserted by Schleiermacher presents God as the absolute Substance, not as the absolute Person, "who gives me freedom and love just as well as dependence." Martensen obviously is not interested in Schelling, like Fichte and others, and he gives a rather schematic presentation, including Schelling's later philosophy, against which he offers strongly critical comments.

After the presentation of Hegel, which comes next, Martensen recapitulates and finally, quite briefly, gives his general interpretation of the relation of philosophy to theology.[6]

In his "Recapitulation" he says that the principle of knowledge in modern philosophy has been developed in part subjectively (especially in Kant and Fichte) so that by this means one cannot get to "the thing itself," i.e., knowledge of God and with that, absolute knowledge of the truth, and in part objectively (especially in Schelling and Hegel), so that (with the help of the Intellectual Intuition of Schelling and the dialectical method of Hegel) the possibility of absolute knowledge of truth is opened up. Correspondingly, Martensen finds that there are chiefly two methods, the first, the critical (Kant's) and the second, the speculative (Schelling's and especially Hegel's). His own choice is Hegel's method and philosophy, which is, "even if not the last word, still infinitely perfectible."

Concerning the content of philosophical knowledge, Martensen again presents two main types, with Spinoza as the representative of the one for which the objective is everything, and Fichte repre-

---

[6] Martensen's *De autonomia*, etc., should be compared with this.

senting the second, for which the ego is everything. Martensen finds, furthermore, that Schelling and especially Hegel endeavored to reconcile these two extreme positions by positing a unity between the individual ego and the universal ego, which he further defines as the Absolute, which again is defined as Spirit. And—Martensen continues—"The question now becomes, whether Hegel has taken Spirit deeply enough, whether he has attributed *Personality* to it," but the question is not answered directly here.

On the relation of philosophy to theology, Martensen holds that it depends on whether the principle of knowledge is subjective or objective. Kant's position was a necessary transitional stage, he says in good speculative fashion, as was Schleiermacher's, while both the rationalists and the supranaturalists have remained fixed on these positions which have been overcome by speculation. This is an interpretation that Mynster, among others, soon turned against. Martensen lauds Schelling and Hegel for having broken down the wall of separation between the subjective and the objective and in that way having prepared the way for a speculative dogmatics in harmony with philosophy on the present stage. Finally, no doubt influenced by I. H. Fichte, Martensen holds that there are three indications that show whether one is in on the right path: first, knowledge of the personal God (the Trinity); second, knowledge of the personal Christ (God-Man); third and last, knowledge of personal immortality (in the kingdom of God).

On Hegel Martensen says that:

His philosophy is the present, because the whole philosophical attitude is permeated with this philosophy, so that nothing can be written without being traceable to it, so that it is not just the conclusions of this philosophy that are often contradicted, but its whole approach, which is used even by [his] opponents. Therefore Hegel is still not finished and we will therefore not consider the later philosophers, who wish to go out beyond Hegel; he is the last from the standpoint of universal history. Schelling, with his outstanding genius, halted his productivity toward the end of his life, but Hegel, on the other hand, slowly sought to appropriate to himself philosophical formation and yet he was a great genius.

First he lived as Schelling's roommate in Tübingen; both were from Würtemberg; at this time he resembled and imitated Schelling. Then he became Rector at Nürnberg, where in 1808 he wrote *Phenomenology of the Spirit* and his *Logic*, in which he expresses his whole system's fundamental view; but at the time he was hardly noticed; Daub and Frantz Baader were the first to notice him; as Professor at Heidelberg he published his *Encyclopedia*, and from there he went to Berlin, where he began to shine.

PROLEGOMENA.

The *method* of this philosophy tends to let the thing itself speak, while the previous ones, Kant and Fichte, talked themselves. Schelling excluded the non-genius; Hegel, on the other hand, said: philosophy must be able to be learned by every scientist; and that, because he believed in beginning at the beginning and gradually making progress.—

Its relation to other systems. It recognizes them as moments in the one philosophy, so that it is itself only appropriating its heritage to itself and carrying it further if it is true. The others rejected previous systems; Schelling's was nearest to him in this, but unlike Hegel he does not go into every position; such as Hegel in his *History of Philosophy.* If he, or rather his disciples have been [a word is missing here], then this is not the fault of philosophy.

Its relation to other sciences. People raise the objection against philosophy that there is no positive material there that can be put to use in the empirical world. But Hegel's philos[ophy] has just penetrated all other sciences; there is no ph[ilosopher] who has shown such expert knowledge. Thus he has gone through all the pre-Christian positions; he has written a "history of right," a "philosophy of history," and "esthetics," so that there is hardly any man who has been so comprehensively cultured as he.—

THE SYSTEM.

It is most difficult to present the system of Hegel, because unlike the previous ones he is not one-sided. —If we look back to Schelling, we see how Hegel's system necessarily had to develop therefrom. Sch[elling] had taught that there was an identity, only the forms were different, and that only quantitatively, not qualitatively; he never defined fixed thoughts, but frequently defined one by contrast with another (e.g., architecture is frozen music, i.e., music is architecture and vice-versa, and water [is] a wet flame). In the interchange of the ideal and real (change) in Schelling, Hegel found that he resembled a painter who painted with only two colors, black and white. (But Hegel wished to come to a concrete knowledge). The lacuna in Schelling was this, that he saw the Absolute only in nature and history, Hegel wished to show and see the Absolute, this Reason, Idea, in-and-for-itself, just as it is before it ever gives itself form in nature and history. Schelling says that all opposites are in the Abs[olute]; but Hegel says that philosophy must, then, unfold these just as they are before they emerge in nature and history. —And this thought, etc., I think, Hegel says, I must think universally, or else it becomes only individual opinion, and thus I must present the absolute Universal, the logical Idea, universally. This logical Idea is the pure Thought itself, not the idea of something, nor is it a thought or an idea but the Thought [κατ’ ἐξοχην], the absolute Thought, the naked truth is the logical Idea; the logical Thought = the concrete unity of all determinations of thought. It is not thinking as immediate, for the immediate is not the true, but it is the absolute process in which the immediate is constantly abrogated and it is itself its own content, it is that which reveals itself in everything which exists. (But if there are these categories, then|: Universality, Accident, etc.:| are they not empty as in Kant? No! The real cannot consist in anything other than in the process itself in its pure universality). If one were to ask him how the log[ical] thought can be a process, he would answer: the activity of form is what matters, it is that which is genuinely Real; in nature it appears as life, in history as the great spiritual process.—

His second large section constitutes the philosophy of nature. That is, the Idea passes over into external real existence which is nature. Nature is the Idea parcelled out; but this sharing out is abrogated again in the Spirit and that is thus the third phase in Hegel. This is developed now in art, etc., but the perfectly absolute Spirit emerges only in religion and philosophy.—

THE METHOD,

by which the process comes about is the negative. Every thought contains its own negation, its own opposite, difference. But this negation must be overcome and harmony be procured. This is Hegel's main thought, thus, 1) the immediate, 2) the distinct (reflex), 3) the particular (the standpoint of the Idea). At every standpoint so gained there is developed again an opposition, straight to the Absolute Idea, where the opposition is entirely overcome. [*Comment.* Every human can discover this in himself: as a child he dwelt happy, contented in everything; now we feel unanswered questions (: in the theory of Hegel:| and unsatisfied needs|: in the practical order, according to Hegel:|). The third standpoint is now the one in which man again regains satisfaction after having gone through all doubt. Thus also in philosophy, where Kant, Fichte, Jacobi remained on the level of reflection, where a barrier|: *Das Ding an sich*:| existed for their science; on the other hand Plato and Hegel stood on the level of the Idea. Reflection: Schiller, who constantly feels needs; of the Idea: Goethe:] Objections: this schema one has without further ado imposed on everything existing, and it has thus become an object of derision, but that does not at all belong to this system. For Hegel's philosophy demands more than any other philosophy that one should develop every kind of subject from its activity; although he places logic over all, still he thinks that concrete knowledge is necessary in positive matters. Therefore one must consider both the purely logical and the real. —Finally, some have objected to Hegel's terminology; but the precision of a terminology depends upon the abstractness of the philosophy, where one must, then, choose new words, since there are no appropriate ones in ordinary usage, and the Latin and Greek languages are not to be rejected for this purpose either, since they are derived from dead languages, by which we are forced to withdraw from the immediate activities of life, so as to descend again later.|: Thus negation cannot be translated either by opposite, contradiction, difference, something other, boundary, barrier, finitude; they are all contained in negation, the negative, and this is not exhausted by any of them:|. One can just as little translate philosophy as poetry in the form of prose. Nor is it the popular philosophers| Cicero, Moses Mendelssohn|, but just such as Plato, Kant, Hegel who have carried thinking forward.—

If I begin to present theology or the doctrine of God, I cannot begin with the concrete concept of the Triune God, but must begin with the most abstract concept of God, and proceed from there to the concrete. Philosophy must thus begin with the abstract in and for itself, and that is the logical Idea. Logic (recognition of the logical Idea) must begin with the categories, which are by far the most abstract, the most empty of content, and keep going until it attains the logical Idea.

Three main divisions of philosophy 1) the doctrine of being (the universal), 2) of essence (reflection), 3) concepts (Idea). Pure being is this most abstract, most devoid of content thought, and Hegel begins with it.

The pure being is the first immediate, every other concept|: like Fichte's ego:| has presuppositions. But here we must not think of any definite being, but of that which is abstracted from all particular beings.—

If we now ask what God is, then we must say, it is the Pure Being, the predicateless, and that is = the Pure Nothing, for there is no limit, no content, no determination. I cannot make them distinct by any criterion, for there is no criterion. But yet there is a distinction, for the transition from Nothing to Being, and from Being to Nothing is the Pure Becoming. Thus in "the beginning" and "the end" Nothing passes over into Being and Being into Nothing. This unrest and transition ceases in the existing thing, which is becoming retained in the moment of being.

> (It must be remarked that this thought is
> thinking in-and-for-itself, not as it is
> found in the subject).

—The whole task of philosophy is to resolve the differences, the contradictions in the existing thing; the fundamental contradiction consists in the finitude of the existent. In general, speculative philosophy has resolved this in such a way that one has said: God must contain His negation, the finite in itself, so that that is part of His essence. Now Hegel will incorporate this radically in this [notion] of being, the first abstract expression of the Abstract; Nothing is the abstract expression of the negative; from the Abstract Nothing the determined nothing emerges, which ultimately appears as evil in opposition to God. —This concept of negation is Hegel's immortal service; J. Böhme had done it in the form of fantasy. "From nothing nothing comes," ex nihilo nihil fit, is thus contradicted here, because "nothing" is taken differently here.—

Here we will provide only an outline.
The logical Idea has these three parts:
The doctrine of being, essence, the concept—

The first book of the Logic contains the categories of
   immediacy:
Something—Other—One—Plural.
Immediate quality passes over into the concept of quantity.
Quantity—How Much—Number—Degree—Measure.

What is characteristic is that negation is placed as something
indifferent, non-independent, e.g., the difference between nothing and being. Thus, in quantity all the qualitative determinations are indifferent. In the crystal there is only being, in the
living, becoming. Quantity belongs to time and space, but the
pure points of time and space are indifferent. Now, all the empirical sciences use only the categories of quantity. But in philosophy this must not happen: God must not be described as
the absolute dimension, His omniscience [should] not [be de-
scribed] as a counting of the hairs and the sparrows, but as
something qualitative. Nor can we use the determinations of
quantity in esthetics and morals either, but the higher determinations of quality. In poetry and religion the determinations of
quantity are used as symbols. (.......)

That was the first book.

In the second book of the Logic: the determinations of reflection, the doctrine of essence. Here negation comes forth with
a real power. It is easily comprehended that the immediate
quantity and quality by being absorbed in thought pass over
from the immediacy. Thus quantity merges into quality, just
as (in the first book) quality passes over into quantity. —In the
sphere of reflection negation emerges as such; here the opposites are maintained against each other. The Essence-phenome-
non (ground and consequence), the whole-the parts—the inner
and the outer, etc., are categories of this sphere. Here we will
only consider essence and phenomenon.

Essence is that in which the abrogated immediacy has its
truth, for the truth does not inhere in the immediacy, so that
the immediacy remains as an appearance, a phenomenon, the
non-true. Only the essence is what is the truth of the phenomenon, and the phenomenon is only that in which the essence is
Essence. The essence constantly dissolves itself in the phenomenon and vice-versa. —Thus essence and phenomenon are in a
way the same. —Kant said that we do not know *Das Ding an
sich*, but only the phenomenon. But the phenomenon is nothing
without the essence, for the essence cannot appear except as

phenomenon. Many theologians say: I can know God only in His revelation, but not in His essence; but if I have God's revelation, then I have Him; if I were to conceive Him apart from His revelation, then it would not be His authentic essence I would know. —Many theologians say that they accept the essential but reject much of the concrete, but that is absurd, for the essence is nothing without its revelation. —It is also said: empiricism sticks to facts, speculation to the Idea; but the Idea is based precisely on the facts, and the facts on the Idea. Some also say: one knows only the external in nature, but there the internal and the external are the same. —Also in poetry and in philosophy both form and truth are indistinguishable. —Thus identity and difference: identity occurs only where a difference has appeared, and vice-versa. Thus we cannot separate the attributes of God, but must find that grace is justice, love is sanctity. —

All these opposites appear in a dialectically mediated unity, which is the reality. Thus we can understand Hegel's statement that "reality is the rational," so that it is not the immediacy itself in-and-for-itself which is the rational, nor is it everything which happens, for not everything which happens has the essence in itself. The reality is only the marriage of the interior with the exterior. Thus the reality is the substantial, the substance, it is the negation of the negation, it is the necessity in which all the determinations of finitude are contained. —

But the concept of reality is still interpreted unilaterally here, since the substance has still not been distinguished from its phenomena. "God the basis—the world the outcome" are the categories here, and that is pantheism. But there is a higher standpoint where they are distinguished, and that is the standpoint of the concept (of the subject), of freedom, just as the previous one was that of substance, of necessity. Thus we come to the sphere of the concept, or of freedom, or of the subject (but still we must not imagine any personality here). Concept does not mean here: a concept I have, but it has the whole reality in itself. Its moments are: the universal, the particular, and the singular. The universal is that which has the whole content in itself but it first emerges in the particular (as before it showed itself as the negative, accidents), but it is in every respect transilluminated by the universal, and there, where the universal withdraws itself from the particular, the singular arises. The universal is that which has the whole abundance of all concrete determinations in itself, from which all these could be developed. The particular is the manifold situated with the condition of being derived from the universal (hence in religion, only the religions which seem necessarily to have been derived from the universal). Thus the singular is that which is simultaneously one form and yet contains all the universal and the particular. Only then can there be talk of the concept. —These moments are in each other but they have a relative independence apart from each other. —Thus the true individual human is that which both has the universal, the particular (lives among a definite people, etc.) and yet is a definite individual, i.e., Christ. —

The concept contains its moments as ideal moments in itself. But the concept must gain objectivity, and we could therefore distinguish between the subjective and the objective concept The immediate concept must itself mediate itself to the Idea. For example, life is the concrete existence of the Idea. That is, in the living there is both the interior living, which itself produces its objectivity through the abrogation of an immediate objectivity (which is the inorganic world). Freedom made real (is the Idea), that is just the soul which produces its body, in which every part or member has its relative freedom (the particular), but the soul pulsates in the whole and takes the whole back.—Every moral man, every genuine poetic work of art in the state is an idea; for in all of these one goes over from the universal to the particular and from there to the singular, in which the spirit has obtained concrete reality, known itself.—

It has been said that the Idea is the manifestation of the infinite and eternal, but it is the infinite and eternal itself. —

This is not pantheism, for pantheism has only a duality, where God is absorbed into the world, but here God is distinguished from His world as the infinite freedom.

The logical Idea is the concrete picture of all before the world began to be, it is concerned only with the element of pure thought. —In nature the first negation of the Idea emerged, although it is also the Idea. In nature the moments of the Idea emerged separately, so that it is the fragmented Idea.

Schelling's philosophy of nature identified nature and spirit, here there is a qualitative difference, there it was only a quantitative one. Hegel says that even a criminal thought is better than all the stars in all their regularity; he also places human works above all the products of nature. He finds coincidence in nature, where others find richness and diversity; he says that it is beneath the rational and therefore it cannot be comprehended. Hegel also shows the transition of reality to the Idea. The spirit is the negation of the negation. Its essence is freedom. The ways through which the spirit must pass in order to come to the Idea are: the finite, the objective, and the Absolute Spirit. —

1) The finite spirit is the subjective concept, which contains the moments ideally before they have emerged (anthropology and psychology, which still do not consider the content).

2) The objective spirit, which has expressed itself in a universal system; its content is the state, which is an objective system produced by the spirit itself; it (the state) is the domain of morality. He has thus led us away from Kant's and Fichte's purely subjective consideration of the moral. But in its further development the state furnishes the concept of the world-historical, and with this the sphere of the objective spirit ends, and from here we must go over to the

3) Sphere of Absolute Spirit ([sphere] of the reconciliation)
    1) Art and poetry
    2) Religion
    3) Philosophy.
The spirit cannot find rest in the other spheres, the spirit must produce its own domain.

Not until this point is the spirit in its own element. Art is still linked to the pictorial, in religion, on the other hand, thought is the principle, the spirit cannot stop at the pictorial; but only in philosophy does the Idea (the truth) know itself. But herein there seems to be a pantheism, but that is not the subjective spirit, nor is it the objective spirit, the spirit in which all things move. In order to understand this we must consider Hegel's doctrine of the Trinity. The defect here is that only the Spirit is the perfect God, whereas the Scripture teaches that God is a personal God even before creation.

The basis for the pantheism (the weakness) in Hegel must be sought in the strength of the system (according to Hegel's own rule) which is the logical Idea, which he posits as the Absolute. But there is something higher than the logical Idea, and that is God; so that the logical Idea is indeed the Forms of God, but what is revealed in the logical Idea is the personal God. His mistake, then, is that he does not have existence itself or the personality itself but only the Idea. This one-sidedness emerged especially in Strauss, for whom the process of knowledge is the highest. A quite different position in the Hegelian school is the one that says that Hegel did not wish anything other than the system of personality, and the representative of this view is Göschel, who says that we must not only consider the thing we are dealing with when we begin with the abstract; for the last, namely, the Absolute Spirit, which in Hegel is defined as Science, is really the first, so that one should read the whole backwards, so that the logical Idea is the thought of the Absolute Spirit, which is the way God leads us to know Him. —

But at this point it must be noted that that would be a great defect in the system that pretends that it is the developed system that educates us. —Thus in Hegel's philosophy of nature there can be no talk of the creation at all, and that must logically be there, etc. We would then come to quite different conclusions. —Therefore, "the logical Idea was God's thought," but in such a way that God has still deeper thoughts than the logical Idea, and He has had them from eternity, and thus the logical Idea is not, then, as in Hegel, what really is evolving; here also Göschel is in discord with Hegel. The younger Fichte is the one who now polemicizes against Hegel. —

There are three great fundamental points which remain unclear, unanswered for Hegel:

1) the personal **God,**
2) the personal Christ,
3) the individual immortality.

The last question cannot be resolved from the purely logical standpoint, but [only on the level] of the personality. All of Hegel's opponents among the recent philosophers are at bottom his disciples since they slay him with his own weapons. —"[p]

Martensen's survey of Hegel follows the main lines of Hegel's *Encyclopedia.* Obviously Kierkegaard could not have read this presentation before Martensen himself had finished giving it, i.e., in the spring of 1838, more precisely, March 27, when the winter semester ended.

Meanwhile Kierkegaard was occupied with entirely different

[p] The full text of this summary of Martensen's lectures on the history of modern philosophy will be found in *Papirer,* II C 25 (2nd ed., vol. XII).

problems during this period. Poul Møller had just died (March 13), and Kierkegaard, understandably, had a great deal of difficulty in getting down to daily work.

It is important to go through his entries from the months of January, February, and March, 1838 (II A 682-710) however few and scattered they are. Only two, namely II A 697,[q] from January 17, and II A 701,[r] February 8, can be connected with Martensen,[s] and neither of them directly concerns Hegel. These two entries are only outbursts expressing contempt for the unoriginal people who claim to have gone beyond Hegel. Obviously Martensen's survey of Hegel was almost unimportant to him at this time.

Thus, at the end of March 1838 there is nothing that indicates that Kierkegaard had either studied Hegel himself or even made a start, an attempt, to do so. At most, we can speak only of a second-hand knowledge, and while he still had not, obviously not, any independent understanding of Hegel himself, still there is no doubt of his haughty contempt for the Hegelians in general and Martensen in particular.

Kierkegaard attended and summarized not only Martensen's lectures on the history of philosophy, at least in part, but also his lectures on the introduction to speculative dogmatics (II C 26),[t] where he confined himself to describing the main lines of the course and omitted the more precise explanations and references to sources and the literature that Martensen gave. Probably in order to prepare for his examinations Kierkegaard later borrowed or bought from another (unknown to us) student two neatly written notebooks (II C 27 and 28), the first of which contains, often almost verbatim, the same material Kierkegaard himself had summarized, and also Martensen's more detailed discussion of individual points and his references to sources and the literature. The second notebook (written by the same hand) contains the latter part of Martensen's series of lectures, which Kierkegaard did not attend. Probably there was another notebook, now lost, that contained paragraphs 24-59, which are missing both in Kierkegaard's own digest and in the summary he acquired. Martensen conducted his lectures on the "Prolegomena to Speculative Dogmatics," i.e., the introduction to the history of

q Hong, II, #1572.

r Hong, III, #3258.

s Who, however, is not named in either of them.

t Hong, V, #5299. This whole entry will be found in *Papirer*, XIII (2. Supplementbind).

philosophy just discussed, for the first time in the winter semester of 1837 and continued in the summer term of 1838 with "Speculative Dogmatics." He again took up his introduction to the history of philosophy, now under the title "Historia philosophiae recentioris (inde a Kantio ad Hegelium usque) ejusque ad theologiam relatio" [History of recent philosophy (from Kant to Hegel) and its relation to theology] in the winter semester of 1838 and continued with "Speculative Dogmatics" up to and including the summer semester of 1839. In the immediately following terms he lectured on symbolics and ethics.[7]

In the following, we shall give a brief account of what Kierkegaard himself found it worth taking note of, that is, the main introduction, which was supposed to delineate the program Martensen set for himself in the historical introduction previously described.

In his recollections *Af mit Levnet* [From My Life] (II, 1883, 4) Martensen relates how he came "into [his] own relation to Hegel." He had, he writes, to lead his hearers through Hegel. He had, if possible, to make them enthusiastic about Hegel, and yet he had to combat him, since he had to insist upon his own "theonomic" position as opposed to Hegel's "autonomic." Martensen sought only, he says, a thoughtful reflection on the given revelation, and therefore he could not align himself with a philosophy which would generate its own content. In this connection he explicitly notes that his position in the lectures was in agreement with what he had previously expressed in print (1837) in his thesis for the licentiate on human self-consciousness, and he explains why in the lectures on the history of philosophy he could not give his audience a coherent presentation of Schelling and Baader, "since Schelling's new system had still not appeared, and Baader's writings are aphoristic." Martensen evidently forgot in his old age that he had tried on the basis of Jacobi's still more aphoristic authorship to give such a presentation, which, moreover, was a quite successful sketch of the fundamental thoughts of Jacobi. For the reasons given, Martensen had to make Hegel the last great topic in the presentation.[8]

In line with his fundamental principles, Martensen begins his

[7] See Skat Arildsen's reproduction of the Catalogue of Lectures, *Martensen*, p. 156f.

[8] Kierkegaard's barbed comment in 1837 (II A 7; Hong, V, #5200) on Martensen, who played leap frog over his predecessors so as to advance into a vague infinity, he found no cause to revoke or even revise.

presentation of speculative dogmatics by stating that it "shows us the ultimate ground of Faith," a demonstration Martensen found necessary so that the theologians could again rise above the philosophers, and he would reconcile philosophy and theology by making the latter speculative, i.e., by applying the methods of philosophy to the received dogmas of the Church (§1). Then he elaborates on how the philosophy of religion has the entire domain of religion as its object, while the object of dogmatics is the ecclesiastical dogmas. Their truth, the implicit awareness of God in them can—it is said in good Hegelian fashion—also be found in art and is present in philosophy. Religion, and its content as formulated, is qualitatively distinct from art and philosophy by the fact that, apart from their objectivity, it contains the idea of God in the infinitely subjective and real existence in man (§3). In religion, Martensen says, man stands not only in an ideal but in an existential relation to the divine. This relation is more precisely defined (§4), as "one [which] through an infinite relation of opposition and dependence mediates the relation of identity and freedom." This relation cannot be established without a revelation in which God "objectivizes Himself for mankind," i.e., Faith does not produce its own content itself as speculative philosophy claims it does, but has a given content as a point of departure for speculative interpretation of it.

Religion and revelation again have their fundamental source (§5) in God's absolute personality, which is not only a substance, but a free subject, and which places itself in relation to mankind as personality and wishes to bring about unity between them. This unity is not immediately present, but must be produced through a historical development (§6) in heathendom, Judaism, and Christianity (§7), which is the "real system of personality," which is developed in more detail in the following paragraphs (as in II C 27 there is a much more complete presentation with explicit references to Jacob Böhme and Hegel's philosophy of religion).

Martensen's absorption in "the heathen manifestations of the divine" (§10 in II C 27) lead (in §§11-13) to a characterization of Judaism, which like the foregoing bears strong marks of influence from Hegel. Then in §14 he explains the Christian idea of God in which "the thought of the subjectless substance and the substanceless subject" is nullified in the dogma of the Trinity. The dogma of the Incarnation (§15) means the abrogation of the dualism between God and man, while (Strauss's) teaching on a mythical

Christ is explained as having its deeper foundation in an acosmism which is incompatible with Christianity. The Incarnation could take place only in the fullness of time (§16) i.e., the coming of Christ was mediated by the historical development of the human race and could not occur before "all relative and creaturely forms of the religious consciousness were exhausted," but the other aspect of this is that the coming of Christ is a miracle, so that the relation between Christ and the human race is a relation of infinite opposition and objectivity, and so the doctrine of Christ as the Savior of the world is the pivotal point in Christian preaching and the Christian message. The relation of opposition will transmute into a relation of identity (§17), which happens through the fact that the Holy Spirit is present in His Church, active in the Word and the Sacraments. Faith in God the Father, Son, and Holy Spirit, as generally recognized in the Church, is expressed in the Apostles' Creed (§18), whose content in the course of time has been more precisely developed and defined in relation to the heretical systems. Catholicism and Protestantism are the world-historical forms of the Christian consciousness and they have their necessary foundation in the development of the human spirit. The difference between them derives from their different definitions of the relation between the object of revelation and the human subject (§19), which is developed in more detail in the following paragraph where it is asserted that "only the Spirit itself in the form of free self-consciousness is the true principle of knowledge" and, in Martensen's view, the necessity of a speculative dogmatics has its foundation in this so-called reformist principle. Speculative dogmatics is neither supranaturalistic nor rationalistic (§21), but is a higher unity of these and other positions, and it "mediates itself its speculative insight" through the Scriptures, the Church, and the living faith, as it proceeds from the "infallible and original testimony of Christ" in Holy Scripture, which is the absolute norm and canon of knowledge (§22). Protestant, i.e., speculative dogmatics is not only Biblical, but also ecclesiastical (§23), which it demonstrates by its conformity with the canonical Scriptures and the universal creed of the Church. The third indispensable means for Christian knowledge is the living faith, "for what the intuition of the fact of the Incarnation is objectively, the same is the rebirth subjectively."

This is the last that Kierkegaard himself, generally speaking, heard and summarized from Martensen's lectures.

5. SIBBERN'S ANTI-HEGELIAN MONOGRAPH

Whereas Kierkegaard's reading of Erdmann caused him to become critically disposed against right-wing Hegelianism, without his having yet worked out an alternative to it, and while Fichte's article made him—at least for the moment—despondent, because its criticism of Hegel's and the right-wing Hegelians' views on the philosophy of religion in his opinion was better supported and worked out than he was then capable of himself, and while Martensen's lectures, as well as Martensen himself and those who thought the same way, rapidly became contemptible to him, something else was happening at the same time in the history of Hegelianism and philosophy in Denmark.

It is curious, and in this investigation it is important to emphasize this, that what was taking place was hardly discussed by Kierkegaard in any noteworthy degree at the time. As was said previously, what happened was that Heiberg published his periodical *Perseus, Journal for den speculative Idee*, whose first issue appeared in June 1837, and whose second and last issue came out in August 1838. Also in 1837 Poul Møller's article on immortality was published in *Maanedsskrift for Litteratur*,[9] in which he dissociated himself from Hegel. In April 1838, Sibbern finally began to publish in the same periodical his *Bemærkninger og Undersøgelser fornemmelig betreffende Hegels Philosophie* [Comments and Studies Chiefly Concerning Hegel's Philosophy].[10]

Sibbern's lengthy monograph, extremely critical of both Hegel and Heiberg, has previously been discussed in Kierkegaard research,[11] but we can hardly say that complete justice has been done to it. Although it is not necessary to go through every detail here, it will be useful to highlight several points in it:

Sibbern thinks that Heiberg takes philosophy rather casually, since he "rhapsodically concerns himself with elements from the more easily accessible and pleasant parts of the Hegelian sphere of

[9] On the importance of this article for Kierkegaard, especially later when he wrote *The Concept of Dread*, reference may be made especially to Gregor Malantschuk's perspicacious analysis in "Søren Kierkegaard og Poul M. Møller" in *Kierkegaardiana*, III (1959), 7-20.

[10] *Maanedsskrift for Litteratur* vols. 19, 20, various issues. Altogether the monograph totals 336 pages.

[11] See especially Victor Kuhr, *Modsigelsens Grundsætning*, [The Principle of Contradiction] (1915), 10f., and Jens Himmelstrup, *Sibbern* (1934), 82ff.; Morten Borup, *J. L. Heiberg*, II (1948), 187ff.

ideas; indeed, he shows himself . . . to be only a dilettante in philosophy. But [a] brilliant and lively dilettante" (vol. XIX, 290). Heiberg moves somewhat freely in Hegel, even begins to go beyond Hegel; but when that is the case Sibbern finds it deplorable that Heiberg criticizes Poul Møller's not being content to remain with Hegel (vol. XIX, 293). He further stresses that the doctrine of immortality in a philosophical system must be everywhere evident. It is found, Sibbern says, in Christianity and lies at the basis of all romantic poetry. In Hegel, on the contrary, this whole question is handled very unsatisfactorily. Nor does faith as emotion receive its due in Hegel (XIX, 294ff.). Sibbern claims (XIX, 298f.) that Hegel only carries out what Schelling established; and—as he looks back on what has just been considered—he asserts that "The Hegelian philosophy of Christianity does not correspond with what Hegel himself urged as a main requirement of all learning, that it should be immanent" (XIX, 300). Hegel approaches Christianity with his finished philosophy, although his philosophy is far more strongly influenced by Spinozistic ideas than by Christianity. The same is true of Hegel's philosophy of nature; it is significantly out of proportion with the conclusions of physics and physiology. Sibbern calls it "nebulous and tautologous" (XIX, 306). In his more detailed criticism of Hegel's philosophy of religion, Sibbern includes and emphasizes that of Heiberg, which so severely attacked Rothe and still more Steffens and Baader.

"Hegel would have philosophy begin with the first immediacy, so entirely pure, that there can be no assumption or postulate in it, so that there it is begun entirely without presuppositions" (XIX, 315); but, according to Sibbern, this claim depends on a mirage and contains within itself a very large assumption, which cannot be justified without going into the essence of philosophy, its whole course and manner. Certainly Hegel insists that philosophy should begin *"bittweise,"* but he nevertheless has his assumptions, which are clearly there, that he

> immediately without further ado sets off on a certain definite path in a certain definite direction, and lets his whole method infiltrate, in spite of the fact that according to his teaching . . . method completely coincides with the whole of philosophy itself, that with this method the fundamental insights of all philosophy are already given (XIX, 316).

The first definitions of concepts in Hegel (of *Seyn* and *Nichts*)

Sibbern finds "altogether flabby," and they really make no difference in understanding what follows. Actually, says Sibbern, Hegel lets philosophizing begin *ex ovo*, while it is supposed to appear to us that it begins *ex nihilo* or begins with a so-called spontaneous generation (XIX, 319). Sibbern also has critical objections to Hegel's moral philosophy: it belongs to "the most peculiarly handled, most neglected parts of his philosophy" (XIX, 322-323).

Sibbern notes furthermore that Hegel's intention that his whole philosophy should be cyclical has not come to fruition.

In this connection, Sibbern develops his own view of how the foundations of philosophy should be established.[12]

Sibbern also considers the dubious placement of *Phenomenology of the Spirit*, whether it belongs before or within the System.

A very important problem for Sibbern to clarify is philosophy's relation to faith. According to his view, the philosophy of Christianity can no more take the place of faith than the philosophy of love can replace love; but he finds that in Hegel just what would happen is that philosophy would replace faith.

Sibbern again returns to the question of the beginning of philosophy, and asserts contra Hegel (XIX, 346) that doubt cannot be the beginning of philosophy "for of such a mere doubt, which is only doubt and nothing else, one can say: from nothing nothing comes." But, he continues, the explanation is presumably that by doubt is meant a genuinely inquiring spirit, and it is not the philosophical system, but philosophizing that begins that way (XIX, 347); but furthermore, Sibbern thinks that "doubt surely has not presided when his [Hegel's] philosophy formed itself" (XIX, 352).

In the following section on the chief divisions of philosophy according to Hegel, two things in particular are important to note. In the first place in Hegel we encounter already in the so-called objective logic much "by which we find ourselves entirely immersed in a real sphere . . . where even space, but especially time have already entered" (XIX, 354). In the second place, Sibbern notes, Hegel has left out any discussion of the whole distinction between ideal and real being (XIX, 355).

Sibbern next discusses the principles of logic, and he immediately asserts against Hegel that the principle of contradiction "must hold completely throughout all thinking" (XIX, 425), and that "a denial

[12] "In this introduction to philosophy an all-embracing debate must prevail . . . [and it is] thus the foundation of the whole of philosophy itself, but in indirect form."

of the universal validity of the principle of contradiction consequently must lead to a denial of this denial itself, and thus reestablish it in its universal validity, and it is amazing that Hegel has
not seen this move" (XIX, 426). Sibbern insists on the principle of
identity and the principle of exclusion in a similar way.

In a longer section in which Sibbern criticizes "the excessively
heavy importance Hegel gives to thought, and the disproportion in
which he places feeling and the knowledge based on it," he uses
this opportunity to introduce a positive presentation of his own
theory of the three kinds of knowledge (XIX, 444ff.), viz., immediate intuition [den umiddelbare Anskuelse], conceptual knowledge [den begribende Erkenden] (according to Sibbern it was this
type of knowledge that Hegel had overemphasized), and finally,
knowledge based on harmonious resonance [Sympati], i.e., faith,
of which Sibbern says that "here we are grasped . . . , but we also
grasp" (XIX, 454).[u]

In harmony with Rothe and against Heiberg and his mentor
Hegel, Sibbern asserts the incomprehensibility of God. In support
of his position he refers to Jacobi and the elder Fichte, but curiously,
not to Schleiermacher.[v] Whereas Hegel ranks the speculative concept at the top, yet Sibbern thinks that the soul can culminate both
in poetry, art, love, religion, and philosophy and, moreover, in all
of them together (XIX, 546ff.).

Sibbern returns again to the structure and method of the system
in what follows (XIX, 554ff.). Here he stresses that Hegelian doctrine has no proper place for synthetic unities of the kind in which
two distinct elements that stand on a straight line meet each other
to form a unity. Sibbern characterizes the process in Hegel as a
spiral-shape ascending. By the trilogical path in Hegel, one is led
in a one-sided manner through the whole domain of philosophy,
but, says Sibbern, thereby it appears "very artificial" (XIX, 560);
and, what is for Sibbern very serious, in Hegel "life's many four-

[u] I have rendered the word "Sympati" by the two words "harmonious resonance" since that seems to come closer to Sibbern's meaning than the obvious English cognate. It would be interesting to compare similar classifications
of the various kinds of knowledge in Aquinas, à Kempis, Pascal, J. H. Newman, and William James with those of Sibbern and SK. Cf. George L. Stengren, "Connatural Knowledge in Aquinas and Kierkegaardian Subjectivity,"
Kierkegaardiana, X (1977), 182-189.

[v] He could also have referred to a great many Christian and Jewish thinkers in the Medieval period, e.g. Anselm and Maimonides, who also insisted on
this point.

nesses" (XIX, 562) are completely shunted aside. In this connection Sibbern himself explicitly refers to Baader's *Vierzahl des Lebens*.

Hegel's philosophy of religion, which Sibbern had touched on earlier, is the target of the sharpest criticism. This is especially true of the treatment of the doctrine of the Trinity in the system. Particularly characteristic is the following: "the Hegelian doctrine of the Trinity, in which much must astonish us, but perhaps nothing so much as the place it has received. That is, Hegel concludes his whole system under the heading "the Absolute Spirit" with the triad: Art, Revealed Religion, Philosophy; and if it may already be striking that revealed religion here takes its place in the middle, between art and philosophy, then it must be striking in the highest degree that now the whole Trinity is brought under this middle part in this trilogy. But think! The whole Trinity, hence that which is the supreme and most all-inclusive meaning of the world, the entire foundation of the totality, is constructed in the *middle* part of a Hegelian trilogy."

Concerning details, Sibbern remarks—correctly, by the way—that the idea of Fatherhood in particular has completely disappeared in Hegel, and in him there is really only a divine hypostasis, namely the Spirit, and in Hegel the actual humanity becomes what gets the middle place in the Trinity. Sibbern has hereby called attention to the point of connection with left-wing Hegelianism. (XIX, 573).[13]

6. OTHER FACTORS, ESPECIALLY SCHALLER'S CRITICISM OF STRAUSS

The situation of Hegelianism in Denmark in the spring of 1838 was such that its only important representative, Heiberg, had been severely attacked by Sibbern. Sibbern's philosophical colleague at the University, Poul Møller, in the last article he published before

[13] There is no need in this context to go into Sibbern's treatment of the state of philosophy in Denmark, his extensive countercriticism of Heiberg's review of Rothe's book *Læren om Treenighed og Forsoning* [The Doctrine of the Trinity and Redemption], his reflections on the concept of the bad infinite or his distinction between exemplar and individual and in connection with that his contribution to the debate on immortality. Nor is it necessary to speak about his review of Martensen's treatise on Faust and of [Henrik Hertz's play] *Svend Dyrings Huus*; but *later* the same question undeniably came up for Kierkegaard.

his early death, had also parted company with Hegel. Among the theologians who took a prominent position, Martensen was the only one who had been positively influenced by Hegel; but Baader was even more important for him.

It is worth noting what an insignificant role this whole philosophical ferment played for Kierkegaard. At this time he seems not even to have read Sibbern's large confrontation with Hegel and the Hegelians as it was published. It is true that he did not have a subscription to the periodical in which it was published; but he could very easily have had access to it, for example, in the Student Association. However, the main part of Sibbern's monograph was issued as an offprint, and Kierkegaard owned this (Ktl. 778) and read it some time or other, probably later. In any case, had Kierkegaard read Sibbern's monograph at the time there undoubtedly would have been indications of this in his *Papirer* entries; but we seek them in vain.

If we turn again to the *Papirer*, then so far as the present problem is concerned, there are very few notes from this and the immediately following period that we need pause over.

On April 17 Kierkegaard notes, as an addendum to an entry from June 3, 1837, a clarification from Carl Daub on humor (II A 79 [Hong, II, #1683]). Daub's *Vorlesungen über die philosophische Anthropologie* had just been published in 1838, and Kierkegaard had obviously quickly acquired this work and continued his subscription for the whole series of Daub's lectures, the last volume of which appeared in 1844 (Ktl. 472-472g).[14] The text before us is from Daub's Hegelian period. There is no index in the book, nor on the basis of §63 in the table of contents: *Die mittelbar beharrlichen Leidenschaften* [The Mediate Saving Passion] can Kierkegaard have been put on the track of the concept of humor and its treatment in Daub. We must assume then, either that he had got a reference to this passage in Daub and had procured his book and looked it up, or that by reading through this entire difficult work he had himself hit upon the expression. The first suggestion is the more likely one since there are no other indications at this point of his having read the whole work.

---

[14] The editors' (Marheineke and Dittenberger) preface, which is dated February 1838, indicates that as a textual basis for Daub's *Anthropology* they relied strongly on notebooks from two students who attended the author's last presentation in the winter semester of 1838 (p. V).

A few days later, on April 22, there is the brief, significant remark (II A 730 [Hong, V, #5313]) that "If Christ shall come to live in me, it must come to pass according to the heading for today's Gospel in the Almanac: Christ enters through closed doors"; scarcely a month later we find the noted entry (II A 228),[w] dated precisely at 10:30 A.M. May 19, about the indescribable joy.

As is well known, scholars do not agree on the interpretation of this and the immediately adjacent entries. But it is quite certain, in any case, that the entries have nothing to do with Hegel and Hegelianism.

In the fall of 1837 Kierkegaard had already moved out of home and was living in rented rooms on Løvstræde. It is reasonable to assume—with Sejer Kühle—that on Kierkegaard's twenty-fifth birthday, May 5, 1838, a reconciliation came about between him and his father. It is certain that we may speak of a religious experience here or, if you will, a religious awakening. His brother P. C. Kierkegaard wrote a few days later in his (unpublished) diary that "Søren begins now, God be praised, to come . . . closer to Christianity." On July 6 he went to Communion alone at the Cathedral. He had not done so since December 16, 1836, when he went with his father.[15] In the immediately succeeding days, several entries (II A 231ff.) testify to the crisis Kierkegaard was struggling through. The conclusion is: "I will strive to enter into a far more inward relation to Christianity" (II A 232).[x]

The experience, the crisis, meant Kierkegaard's Christian awakening. He had arrived at a crucial juncture. It is significant, and this has been stressed especially by Villads Christensen, that in this famous entry Kierkegaard was not expressing joy over something definite, such as salvation or grace; the experience indicated that his lengthy quest had received a definite direction toward Christianity.[16]

After having been reconciled with his father Kierkegaard moved back home again and curiously—or, better, significantly—enough

---

[w] Hong, V, #5324. This and the previous entry will also be found in Alexander Dru, ed., *The Journals of Kierkegaard* (New York: Harper Torchbooks, 1959), pp. 58-59.

[15] According to the Communion Book of Frue Kirke (unpublished, Royal Archives, Copenhagen), see Sejer Kühle, *SKs Barndom og Ungdom* (1950), 158ff. with notes.

[x] Hong, V, #5329; Dru, p. 59.

[16] Villads Christensen, *SKs Vej til Kristendommen* (1955), 29ff.

the first book he began to read and excerpt was Julius Schaller's *Der historische Christus und die Philosophie* (II C 54-58;ʸ Ktl. 759).

This book, published in 1838, is, as the subtitle indicates, a critique of the fundamental idea of D. F. Strauss's work *Das Leben Jesu*. The preface is dated April 1838, so obviously Kierkegaard obtained it soon after it appeared in the bookstores. The author could have been known to Kierkegaard through Bruno Bauer's *Zeitschrift für spekulative Theologie*, to which he had a subscription, and in the most recent issue Schaller had just written an article (pp. 263-328), *Zur Charakteristik der mythischen Erklärung der evangelischen Geschichte*.

Schaller, who like the slightly older Karl Rosenkranz belonged to the moderate center group of the early Hegelians, wished to establish in his work that the first one in whom the concept of the God-Man appeared could only be the real God-Man, hence, contra Strauss, he stresses the dogmatic importance of the historicity of Christ.

Kierkegaard summarizes and quotes (II C 54ff), partly in German but mostly in his own Danish translation, the major part of Schaller's objections to Strauss[17] and of his positive counterposition, that is, a theory about mankind's separation from God as the point of departure for redemption or reconciliation, which is elaborated with the help of the Hegelian dialectical method. Evidently Kierkegaard did not read Schaller's book all the way through and—as in other instances—had lost patience when it became clear to him that the problem of the speculative thinkers neither was nor could become his, and their explanations at most could have importance for him only as "prefatory studies" (II C 55, 56, 57). Although Kierkegaard, who was never prodigal with recognition, could find in Schaller something "said particularly splendidly" (II C 59), still he put the work aside; not until several years later, especially in *Philosophical Fragments* and *Concluding Unscientific Postscript*,

ʸ The excerpts will be found in vol. XIII. Kierkegaard's comments will be found in vol. II of the *Papirer*.

[17] "The mythical view [of Strauss] is also related negatively with the content of Christian doctrine, since the denial of the historical Christ's personal God-Humanity clearly has as a consequence the denial of personal God-Humanity altogether. . . . As soon as we employ the relation of type and individual consistently on the spirit, then the spirit above all and all spiritual interests, chiefly the personality becomes annihilated from the bottom." (II C 54; XIII, 167-168).

did he take up certain of its questions for renewed consideration.[18]

Kierkegaard seems not to have read Strauss's *Leben Jesu*, but contented himself with a secondhand knowledge of its epoch-making viewpoint through Schaller's work, among others.

Kierkegaard had indeed devoted a bit of time to Schaller's study; he worked on his summary of it in the period between July 23 and August 21, and it fills twenty-one tightly written small pages. It is painstaking, most complete at the beginning, where Kierkegaard literally adheres closely to the text; the second half is more abbreviated and more free in form. The synopsis is not printed in the *Papirer*, where only Kierkegaard's own observations in connection with the text are given *in extenso*.[z]

Since Kierkegaard's comments are understandable only with a background in Schaller's stream of thought, we shall first summarize concisely Schaller's theory of redemption, then give Kierkegaard's synopsis, and finally his observations.

By way of introduction, Schaller says that the critics of Strauss's work in general have not emphasized the author's statement that the innermost nucleus of Christian truth should not be disturbed by his critical investigation; they have, on the contrary, only grasped the designation "myth" and identified myth with falsehood (p. 1).

The scholarly criticism of sacred history and of the mythical position that emerges from this criticism generally tends to mediate and unite the positive datum of consciousness and traditional content of religion with the free self-consciousness of the spirit. This does not conflict with faith, for "this is essentially a living process, a free spiritual fact, in which the details of the positive content of religion encounter their unique essence and find expression" (p. 4). Faith is also knowledge, and there is no opposition between them. But on the other hand faith implies a rebirth of the spirit, which

---

[18] In his *Kierkegaard-Studien*, II (1933), 539-551, Emanuel Hirsch has maintained that in the summer of 1837 Kierkegaard was led into the problem of Faith and History through reading a periodical article by Karl Daub. But it can hardly be taken as proven that Daub had such radical and enduring importance for Kierkegaard as Hirsch maintains. In any case, the entries concerning Schaller's work show that in the late summer of 1838 he was significantly more occupied with this problem than he had been the year before.

[z] However, as has been pointed out in a previous note, the full text of Kierkegaard's digest of Schaller's work will be found in vol. XIII of the latest edition of the *Papirer*.

can happen only after it intuits the harmony (p. 5). On the whole it is true of philosophy that in relation to faith it is "only another way of taking possession of the objective truth" (p. 6). The author's Hegelian position is already clear in these introductory statements. Then he begins his sharp criticism of Strauss:

The person and life of Christ now belongs to the positive content of Christian doctrine; above all, what seems to be offensive to philosophical thought here is the immediate historical fact. This is what the mythical account wishes to reconcile: "The mythical view places the single person of the God-Man whose separate facts and events, which the Faith portrays as separate, i.e., as existing and actual, into the form of a universal ideal content, originally promulgated [*urgirt*] but even more, so that it leaves this content itself undisturbed, and recognizes it as the eternal absolute truth" (p. 7).

According to Schaller, the problem, then, is to get the immediate datum of consciousness [the historical] taken up in self-consciousness.

The mythical view hopes to solve this problem in the following way (p. 17ff.):

The necessary point of departure for this view is historical criticism, which religious faith cannot reject out of hand, since it is also historic faith. Historical criticism concerns itself initially with the conflicts in the various accounts, next with the impossibility [in principle] of even the factual [the eternal truth in historical form], finally with the impossibility of miracle. Behind historical criticism, then, there lies a definite philosophical view, namely one that denies miracles completely (p. 19). Strauss now takes, Schaller says, the further step of making Christ a symbolic figure, and he does this for philosophical and dogmatic reasons.

Even if the proponents of the mythical view should succeed in proving that the Biblical accounts are unhistorical, that does not automatically mean that they are mythical. For Strauss, the historical nucleus of the evangelical accounts is nothing but the occasion for the generative process of self-consciousness (p. 27). Schaller maintains, furthermore (p. 29), that the mythical interpretation must necessarily culminate in a critique of the doctrines of the Church. (This was done in Strauss's theory of faith, which was written before this but published later.)

In the next section ("The Estrangement of Man and God as Presupposition of Redemption," pp. 32-57), Schaller raises the critical question for the mythical interpretation, namely, is the immediate historical fact as unimportant as this interpretation maintains? Schaller holds, on the contrary, that it is relevant, and—throughout his work—he plainly tries to harmonize it with Hegel's *Lectures on the Philosophy of Religion.*

In Schaller's critique of Strauss's Christology (pp. 57-66), he claims that it is all too indefinite: "The idea of the God-Human should contain eternal truth, the reality of which should not be a single historical person alone, but be the human species" (p. 57). But in that way the correct relation between "species and exemplar" is distorted, for "it becomes irrefutably certain that the pure substantial participation of the knowing subject itself in the impersonal God-Human is not redemption but estrangement. In this way, the mythical view is also related negatively to the content of Christian doctrine because the denial of the personal God-Humanity of the historical Christ at the same time has the consequence of denying personal God-Humanity entirely" (p. 65).

Kierkegaard next summarizes Schaller's theory of redemption as follows:[19]

This redemption enters . . . only as mediation of the supreme opposition, not of the relation of substance [p. 18] to its accident, but of the relation of the subject to the subject. Therefore the basis of redemption on the side of mankind is precisely the certainty that even the atomic individuality of the subject does not absolutely divorce mankind from God; but that much more this summit of finitude is recognized and maintained in God. Thus it is not just another relation, not just another association and union between God and mankind which manages to resolve the essentially spiritual divorce to [bring about] redemption; but one and only one [relation, that of] personal unity.— The redemption is almost a new Faith, a new awareness, a new knowledge of God.—This new relation to God must, however, essentially proceed from the side of God; for without that it becomes an empty attempt within subjectivity's own limits, an insubstantial appearance, only a notion [*en blot Menen*]. On the whole, it lies within the concept of truth that in relation to subjective knowledge it exists as a *starting point*. For our knowledge the truth is the absolute "prius" which we do not invent, but discover, which we make ourselves conscious of and

[19] *Papirer*, II C 54; vol. XIII, 169-172.

by attentive reflection have to assimilate and reproduce. | The relation of error to the truth. | In the acknowledgment of redemption there also lies a deeper insight into sin.—The new knowledge also brings about *a new life* not only in relation to the earlier historical development, but also to every earlier manifestation within its own domain. It is here that the idea of redemption must be developed, in the pure element of knowledge, and disassociated from any reference to any historical phenomenon. But the idea of redemption leads us again by its own concretion and vitality, by its factual reality, over into historical appearances, and here our entire interest will be concentrated on the personality of Christ and its relation to the Idea, just as to the reality of redemption.

The speculative concept of redemption is the concept of the Spirit altogether, and here the relation between the finite and Absolute Spirit, or the finite self-consciousness and the Absolute Self-Consciousness, is handled excellently. The conclusion is: that *mankind's real knowledge of God is God's knowledge of Himself*. Kantian philosophy especially brought the contrast of subject and object, certainty and truth, to consciousness.—The perfect contrast of reflection is in its fundamental opposition between *subjective thought and objective being*. Knowledge becomes only self-knowledge. But precisely because this opposition shall be an absolutely insuperable one, because the subject is capable of holding itself immediately opposite the object, then in its first finitude it is also absolute, absolutely independent, *causa sui* [cause of itself], not just an ephemeral moment of the Absolute Substance, but I, self-conscious, self-knowing, self-determining [*Sigselvsætten*], infinite practical skill. But also the idealism of self-consciousness is only apparently peace with itself. The practical infinity always retains theoretical finitude as its condition, and the ego struggles out of its world of idealism to the unity of idea and reality, a unity that shall endure forever but that shall never be finished. Thus the subject, just as in the Jewish religion, is ineffective in its unsatisfied striving; but if in the Jewish religion it was the Absolute Subject that pushed the finite subject back into its finitude, so that in the absolute object of its consciousness it saw only the loss of itself, then in the system of subjective idealism it is the finite ego itself that breaks off every real relation, and thereby in spite of all its efforts and all its longing it becomes stuck in its first and insuperable finitude.—And so Spinoza grants the finite spirit, if not practical, then surely theoretical freedom, and this freedom consists in the individual's relinquishing all of its finite relations and interests: [i.e.] its modality, and the Absolute brings its immanent distinctionless unity and simplicity to consciousness, thus the substance ceases to be a foreign object, an alien necessity, and refers to itself in the thinking subject as self-love [refers] to itself. But just this consciousness is a contradicting moment [for] the substance itself, it is now actually no longer the immediate and only existing unity of being and thought, no longer a universality which annihilates the singular, but much more a power that expands and raises the singular to universality.—The substance is only *"an sich"* the unity of being and thought, does not itself think itself, but is only thought, [i.e.] is real, not in and for itself absolutely, but only [as] object for another, and thus [an] ephemeral, contingent moment. The subject which not only knows itself; but also in self-consciousness has recognized its essence can only place itself as finite over against the object, which also contains within itself the maintenance and strengthening of its own self-knowledge. . . ."

It was then that Kierkegaard arrived at the point at which he could no longer refrain from the critical comment which is formulated in *Papirer* II C 55. Against Schaller's speculative reflections, which he finds promising in and for themselves, he asserts that they do not concern the individual, existing, believing human. They are only "prefatory studies," as he puts it. Speculative thinkers busy themselves only with the possible, not with the real, not with the reality of the existent. Surely it is granted that these speculative reflections depend on necessary logical principles for allegiance; but when a relation of opposition between God and man is used as an example, then it is only *logical*, and the *real* relation of opposition, which derives from mankind's sin (II C 57), is hardly considered.

Just as was the case with the Hegelian writings previously discussed, it is apparent here, that Kierkegaard acquired through them a knowledge of Hegelian speculation and its view of various chief and present problems; but there is no indication that Kierkegaard's interest was aroused enough to tackle Hegel's own works. Rather, the general impression is that he studied these writings by the Hegelians carefully, but their problematic and their solutions did not satisfy him. Kierkegaard clearly expresses his fundamental disagreement; in the middle of reading Schaller's book he comes to the conclusion that he concisely formulates as follows:

> On the relation between Christianity and philosophy
> Motto: When a man meets a man on the path,
> and one man has a rake and one man has a spade
> can either man do the other any harm?— (II A 239)[aa]

In prosaic terms this means that Christianity, as Kierkegaard understands it at this point, and philosophy, which undoubtedly should be understood as speculative here, are completely heterogeneous quantities, which do not concern each other.[20]

Moreover, there can be no doubt that both external and internal events during the summer and late summer of 1838 had contributed to placing distance between Kierkegaard and Hegelian thought. His knowledge of Hegelian thought cannot be called either extensive or penetrating; but it was sufficient for him to dissociate himself from it.

7. DISCUSSION OF EARLIER RESEARCHERS AND CONCLUSION

Our discussion has shown that in the period we have been considering there is conclusive evidence of Kierkegaard's reading and knowledge of certain Hegelian and anti-Hegelian works and monographs. His synopses reveal Kierkegaard's understanding, his interests, and his reactions. However, we look in vain for convincing evidence that Kierkegaard had tackled Hegel's own works. That he had acquired some knowledge both of speculative philosophy in the wider sense and of Hegelianism in particular, there can be no remaining doubt after what has just been shown. His thoroughgoing critical attitude is obvious. Indeed, we observe how with care and interest he began to read and excerpt one or another speculative work, how he attended and summarized some lectures, and

---

[aa] Hong, vol. III #3259.

[20] Cf., among others N. H. Søe, "S.K. s lære om paradokset" in *Nordisk teologi: Idéer och Män* [festskrift] till Ragnar Bring (Lund, Sweden: C.W.K. Gleerups Förlag, 1955), pp. 102-122. [Cf. also Reidar Thomte, *Kierkegaard's Philosophy of Religion* (Princeton: Princeton University Press, 1948).]

how his disagreement and impatience grew until he simply could not restrain his critical attack. This is especially evident in the case of Schaller's work which we have just discussed, and here it is also particularly striking that Kierkegaard's critique is not directed against individual special points, even if they are the actual occasions, rather it is aimed at confrontation in principle and testifies to the fact that even in his youth Kierkegaard's problematic in the philosophy of religion was totally different from that of the Hegelian school.

Before taking up the investigation of the following period, it is useful to undertake a brief presentation of the most striking opinions and conclusions of previous scholars in order to clarify the relation between this study and earlier ones.

First, Reuter has made a penetrating attempt to explain Kierkegaard's relation to Hegel during this period.

Reuter is not entirely mistaken in calling the year 1837 a transitional year in Kierkegaard's youthful development as a thinker. It is also correct that at the end of the year (*Papirer*, II C 50)[bb] Kierkegaard had arrived at a clear insight into the untenability of Hegel's and especially of his adherents' thought, which cannot contain the possibility of the scandal which is given in Christianity, and which prohibits every attempt to subsume it under total schemes in the history of religion or the philosophy of religion. Nor can one deny Reuter's view that to a constantly increasing degree Kierkegaard became clear about the oppositions that cannot and should not be reconciled, while Hegel would do just that—reconcile all oppositions in a higher unity. However, what we can correctly object to Reuter's treatment of the whole complex historical problem is that he obviously did not devote sufficient time and care to the scrutiny of details. His conclusions therefore are expressed in vague generalities even on the points where it is not just the general, but the special relations that elicit interest. Furthermore, when Reuter (p. 42) maintains that even in the thought of putting oppositions together, which Kierkegaard constantly did, this should indicate that he never tried entirely to liberate himself from Hegel, then we must note two considerations about this claim. In the first place, dialectical thought taken on the whole was not Hegel's invention, but is of earlier origin. In the second place, the use of dialectical thought appears in Kierkegaard before there can be any question of his having had any real first-hand knowledge of Hegel.

[bb] Hong, V, #5286.

Kuhr's short topical study[cc] deals with a slightly later period in Kierkegaard's development as a thinker in relation to Hegelian speculation, and neither Bohlin, Himmelstrup, nor Geismar has undertaken and presented detailed analyses such as provided in the present chapter.

The only scholar who has produced a really thorough analytic work relevant to the issues in this study is Hirsch.

We have already discussed Hirsch's interpretation of Kierkegaard and Erdmann. Concerning his explication of I. H. Fichte's philosophy and Kierkegaard's relation to it, it must be said that, even if Hirsch is correct in claiming that Kierkegaard had read the younger Fichte's philosophy before he read Hegel, Hirsch has still not established how comprehensive and penetrating this reading was. When Hirsch says (p. 511) that Fichte had anticipated Kierkegaard's later "fundamental position opposite Hegel," while he has in other respects sketched what is peculiar to Kierkegaard, it may seem relevant that he has not quite accurately investigated the actual contact between Kierkegaard and Fichte. By way of example, we can point out that Hirsch refers (p. 509, note) to Fichte's *Beiträge zur Charakteristik der neueren Philosophie* in the first edition (1829) without mentioning that Kierkegaard owned not this edition, but the very significantly enlarged second edition, which appeared in 1841 (Ktl. 508), in which the presentation and critique of Hegel's philosophy takes up approximately a quarter of the whole book (pp. 782-1032).

As has been said above, Kierkegaard himself claimed to have only a cursory knowledge of I. H. Fichte, and actually that was only of the Prospectus, which reinforced his own still only incompletely developed and formulated views, and which we can confine ourselves to here. As far as the problem in this part of the study is concerned, there is no mistaking Kierkegaard's reading of this monograph and his reaction to it: they meant a critical predisposition.

Scholarship since Hirsch's work need not be further discussed. We can only emphasize that his conclusions are often taken to be definitive, although there is not sufficient basis for doing so.

[cc] Victor Kuhr, *Modsigelsens Grundsætning* (Copenhagen: Gyldendal, 1915).

CHAPTER IV

The Period from September 1838
to July 3, 1840

1. SCOPE

THE PERIOD to be dealt with in this chapter is bounded on the one side by the publication of Kierkegaard's literary debut, *Af en endnu Levendes Papirer* [From the Papers of One Still Living][a] on September 7, 1838, and on the other side by July 3, 1840, when Kierkegaard took his final examinations in theology. As has been the procedure in the previous pages, we shall study in detail Kierkegaard's contact with Hegel and Hegelianism in chronological order. Thus we turn first to *Af en endnu Levendes Papirer*, then to the entries II A 257-581 and 786-824 in the *Papirer*, third to the draft of the play *Striden mellem den gamle og den nye Sæbekielder*, fourth, *Papirer*, II C 4-10 and 60-62, and finally to Kierkegaard's examination petition and other sources.

2. *From the Papers of One Still Living*

Kierkegaard's first book, *Af en endnu Levendes Papirer*, appeared on September 7, 1838. Apparently he had originally considered publishing this review of Hans Christian Andersen's novel *Kun en Spillemand* [Only a Fiddler][b] (1837), in Heiberg's *Perseus*, but he abandoned that idea.[1]

---

[a] Unfortunately there is no English translation of this work.

[b] This together with another novel titled *O.T.* (1836) was published in English under the common title *Life in Denmark*. Cf. P. M. Mitchell, *A History of Danish Literature* (Copenhagen: Gyldendal, 1957), p. 152.

[1] Cf. *Breve og Aktstykker vedr. SK*, #9: A letter from SK to Heiberg dated July 28, 1838, is obviously connected with discussions between the author and the editor. H. P. Holst (1811-1893), Kierkegaard's former school chum, maintained later that he had been his confidant at the time he had submitted his articles to Heiberg's *Interimsblade*, and he relates that he had the manuscript for linguistic inspection and almost translated it from Latin into Danish (see *Kierkegaards Efterladte Papirer*, ed. H. P. Barfod, I [1869] li); Emil Boesen also knew the manuscript. See his letter of July 20, 1838 to

During these years Heiberg was indisputably Denmark's leading esthetician and esthetic critic, and his periodical was highly regarded. Certainly there was the colorless, the so-called "professor-periodical" *Maanedsskrift for Litteratur*,[2] smacking of conservative taste, but for an ambitious young man like Kierkegaard there would be quite enough prestige in launching his career as a literary critic in Heiberg's periodical rather than in the University professors' literary organ. On the other hand, it is extremely important to note in this connection the fact that Heiberg's periodical represented Hegelianism. Probably for the still young Kierkegaard the important thing was to express himself in a place where his debut would be noticed.

Whatever the reason may have been—the size of the manuscript alone could have been a factor, its form and content no less—the plan was abandoned, and Kierkegaard's analysis and estimate of Hans Christian Andersen as novelist appeared instead as a separate book.

If our task were to analyze Kierkegaard's first published work exhaustively, we should have to engage in various explorations; but our questions will be limited to what relationship this book has to Hegel and Hegelianism.

On the first page, Kierkegaard mentions with respect Hegel's "great attempt to begin with nothing," and on the next page he points out the difference on this point between Hegel and his followers, the Hegelians. Again, a page or so later Hegel is mentioned, and once more at the end of the introduction he refers to "the endless series of bricklayer's helpers, who from Hegel toss philosophical building stones from hand to hand." Kierkegaard asserts that H. C. Andersen has not been in contact with philosophical developments at all—which obviously was not to be expected either.

These are the only places where Hegel and the Hegelians are explicitly mentioned in the book; but apart from these we have tried to find contacts with Hegel in several respects, such as the purely verbal one in the expression "genuine wealth" [*gediegne Fylde*] which Kierkegaard himself put in quotation marks. It has a certain similarity with Hegel's expression in his introduction to

---

Martin Hammerich, quoted in Sejer Kühle, SK (1950), 125 [and in *Breve og Akstykker vedr. SK*, II, 30]

[2] On this see Morten Borup, *J. L. Heiberg*, II (1948), 132-138, cf. *Breve og Aktstykker vedr. SK*, #9, with commentary.

the *Lectures on the Philosophy of Fine Art*, the first volume of which H. G. Hotho published in the summer of 1835.

Thus there is not much reliable, concrete evidence of a relation to Hegel and the Hegelians in this first book; but the question is: what do these expressions really tell us? What knowledge of Hegel, what understanding, and what attitude toward Hegel do they indicate?

They can be analyzed in the same order in which they appear in the text.

"Hegel's great attempt to begin with nothing."

Kierkegaard mentions this as a phenomenon typical of the age; but neither he himself nor any of the many scholars who have commented on his first book have noted the discrepancy with Hegel himself. Kierkegaard obviously has read neither *Phenomenology of the Spirit* nor *Lectures on the History of Philosophy*, which Michelet edited beginning in 1833; but—as his note on the next page shows—he has obviously seen the table of contents of Hegel's *Science of Logic*. Had Kierkegaard only read Hegel's prefaces to the first and second editions of that work and the introductory section "With what must the science begin," he would hardly have written what he did here. For Hegel, logic begins chiefly with "being," and according to his own interpretation (and actual development) historically after the spirit has moved through all the stages described in *Phenomenology of the Spirit*. This is a process of development which with the same regularity runs through world history (the macrocosm) as in the single individual (the microcosm). What Kierkegaard has written is simply incorrect; in Hegel pure "being" turns out to be identical with pure "nothing," but it is not immediately understood that way.

Kierkegaard maintains that the tendency in the philosophical work of the time to wish to begin entirely from the beginning has found its most remarkable expression in Hegel's philosophy, and Kierkegaard incorrectly claims that it begins with nothing. His next comment, on the other hand, is partly correct, namely, that "the whole negation is only an effort within the System's own limits, undertaken just in the interest of recovering the 'genuine richness' of existence."

It is correct to say that Hegel wishes to take up or, more accurately, "to conceive" the totality of existence in his philosophical system, or, to express it better, to show its rationality; but that does not mean that we can say that Hegel succeeded. Kierkegaard says nothing about this either, he focuses here only, and correctly, on Hegel's philosophical intention.

Kierkegaard says next that "the beginning from nothing, which Hegel speaks of, was arranged by him into the system and was by no means a failure to appreciate the great richness reality has." To that he adjoins a footnote on the Hegelians and reality.

It is clear then, that the essay's first statement on Hegel himself indicates no more than the one on the previous page about Kierkegaard's knowledge of Hegel, and it frankly expresses a positive evaluation—considering Kierkegaard's quantitatively scanty knowledge of what he so definitely speaks of.

A few pages later, while discussing the political theorists of the age, Kierkegaard mentions "the negative moment, through which and in virtue of which all movements happen (Hegel's immanent negativity of the concept)," thus displaying a knowledge—which he could have received from Martensen's survey (II C 25)—of an important theme in the Hegelian notion of the character of the speculative concept, namely, that it contains within itself oppositions (which must never be understood as the contradictory opposites of traditional formal logic) which, according to Hegel, function as the driving force, the principle of movement, in the dialectical process. It was especially in *Science of Logic* (II, 43-70)[c] in the sections on "difference," "variety," "opposition," and "contradiction" that Hegel chiefly deals with this relation, while it is practiced everywhere in the system.

It is remarkable, even strange now, that while discussing the Hegelians' relation to reality in a footnote (*Samlede Værker*, 2nd ed., XIII, 58), Kierkegaard refers to Hegel's *Logic* and shows that he is quite well aware that it begins with "being," not immediately with "nothing." It is not unlikely that the disharmony between the text and the footnote can be explained by inferring that the note was added later. Kierkegaard, who could have written his other comments on the basis of a secondhand knowledge of Hegel, may have obtained Hegel's own work, and at least glanced at the table of contents, and possibly also read the first chapter of Book I, on "Being," whereas the third section of Book II "Actuality" had evidently not tempted him to make a closer study when he was writing *Af en endnu Levendes Papirer*. It can be noted that Heiberg, who in *Perseus* #2, which was published in August 1838, published the

[c] Trans. W. H. Johnston and L. G. Struthers (New York: Macmillan, 1929).

first (and all that appeared) 23 paragraphs of his own logical system, which was clearly influenced by Hegel. But he did not get to the concept "actuality" but only to "quantity," so that we can assume that Kierkegaard got his present understanding of Hegelian philosophy from this article. In any case Martensen's previously summarized lectures must be taken as the starting point for Kierkegaard's understanding of Hegel and Hegelianism.

When we ignore the play on words that Kierkegaard employs in the footnote, there can be no doubt that the word "actuality" here means a present, empirically demonstrable, given existence. It is of this that he maintains that, in the first place, Hegel takes as the given, while—in the second place—the Hegelians regard it as the product of a logical, i.e., speculative-logical, thought process. For Kierkegaard actuality is chiefly a determination of being, whereas for Hegel it is a determination of essence; i.e., actuality for Hegel is a concept, which belongs to the sphere of logic, not to the sphere of the philosophy of the real. This emerges clearly from the above-mentioned section of Hegel's *Logic*, which Kierkegaard thus obviously had not read at this time. For our present purposes, however, we need only to note an actual discrepancy in conception, and this is a discord about which Kierkegaard was not entirely aware. He did realize that it *was* Hegel who interpreted reality, or, more correctly, used the word "actuality" as a term for the product of a speculative thought process, while the Hegelians' various terminologies and definitions of concepts are of no special interest in this connection.

It is worth noting that, even at this early point in Kierkegaard's published work as a writer, he shows respect for Hegel, contempt for his adherents and followers, to whom he refers as "the endless series of bricklayer's helpers, who from Hegel toss philosophical building stones from hand to hand," and in the footnote just mentioned warns the reader not to believe their words.

In the statement "the whole younger generation . . . is so completely occupied with introducing and writing introductions," we find the same disrespectful estimate without looking for any particular target, perhaps apart from Martensen.

Kierkegaard's description and evaluation of the liberal political approach corresponds closely with his other earlier and contemporaneous statements, both public and private.[3]

[3] Cf. (among others) *Papirer*, I A 328 [Hong, V, #5181]; I B 2 (the lecture at the Student Association, Nov. 28, 1835; [Hong, V, #5116], II A 378

Hirsch (*Kierkegaard-Studien*, I, 7) thought he had found a relationship between Kierkegaard's attitude here and the one Hegel expresses in his famous Preface to *Philosophy of Right* (June 1820); but Hirsch has not noticed that the political conservatism that Kierkegaard gives expression to here and elsewhere, on the whole does not have the philosophical motivation that Hegel has given to his. Nor has Kierkegaard, either here or elsewhere, worked out anything that in any way can be thought of as a political program or interpreted as such, and there is in him, as distinct from Hegel, no real discussion of the state as a definite organizational structure, considered as "the objective Spirit."

After pointing out how contemporary philosophy wishes to begin with nothing, and how the same tendency manifests itself among the politicians, Kierkegaard turns to contemporary novel and short story literature, in which he can find the same tendency expressed: it begins with nothing, and "nothing" here means the familiar, the everyday.

As representative of the older generation he takes Thomasine Gyllembourg,[d] as a representative of the younger generation An-

---

(Hong, IV, #4092), 436 [#4093] 460 [#4094], 481 [#4096], 710 [#4085], 735 [#4086], 754 [4087], 774 [#4088], from which we can quote: "the liberals have, as it says in the folk tale, a tongue and an empty head, like the clapper of a church bell" and 783 [#4090]: "Precisely because the politicians ignore the continuous, therefore of the three indicators of the validity of the common spirit they consider only two . . . but entirely miss the third— antiquity." Also Kierkegaard's articles in Heiberg's *Interimsblad til Kjøbenhavns flyvende Post*, Dec. 17, 1834, Feb. 18, 1836, and March 15, 1836, and April 10, 1836, especially the last two, clearly show his political conservatism (these will be found in SV XIII 11-44; they have been omitted from the third edition and are unavailable in English). From a somewhat later period we may call attention to the correspondence with J.L.A. Kolderup-Rosenvinge beginning in July 1848 and continuing for a year (*Breve og Aktstykker vedr. SK*, #180, 184, 186, 188, 189, 190, 211, 214, 217) from which we can quote a typical statement from letter #184 (August 1848): "No, politics is not my field; to keep up with politics, even only the domestic, in these times is for me, at least, an impossibility. When something moves very quickly, one makes an attempt to keep up; when something moves very slowly one has to endure the boredom of following it. But when something moves back and forth, up and down and down and up, and stands still, and turns around and up and down and back again: then I am in no position to give it willing pursuit; if that should be the case, I would rather go as a "reluctant volunteer" in the war, than sit at home—and keep up."

[d] Countess Gyllembourg-Ehrensvärd (1773-1856) née Thomasine Buntzen, was married to Peter Andreas Heiberg. Their son, Johan Ludvig Heiberg,

dreas Nicolai de Saint-Aubain (Carl Bernhard),[e] while Steen Steensen Blicher[f] is treated separately.

There is no place for a critical discussion of Kierkegaard's description and estimate here. Suffice it to say that his evaluation, including that of H. C. Andersen as a novelist, is uncommonly sure, and that in our own day historians of literature and estheticians offer views that do not essentially diverge from those of Kierkegaard.[4]

Had Kierkegaard been a faithful adherent of Hegel at this time, he could have sketched the literary situation in Denmark somewhat like this: the older romantics, such as Oehlenschläger and Staffeldt,[g] were lost in reverie, in poetry (thesis); the prose writers got lost in

has, of course, already been discussed in this book and is familiar to students of Kierkegaard. She later married a Swedish nobleman who had been indirectly implicated in the assassination of King Gustav III of Sweden (the event which was the basis of Verdi's opera "A Masked Ball"). She began her literary career when she was nearly sixty, and at the age of seventy-two she published a novel titled *Two Ages* (1845). Kierkegaard wrote a lengthy appreciation of this, *En litterair Anmeldelse* [A Literary Notice], 1846. An English translation by Alexander Dru of the latter part of Kierkegaard's reflections on Fru Gyllembourg's book has been published under the title *The Present Age* (New York: Harper Torchbooks, 1962) and a complete trans. by Howard V. Hong and Edna H. Hong, *Two Ages*, has been published as vol. XIV, *Kierkegaard's Writings* (Princeton: Princeton University Press, 1978). On Fru Gyllembourg, see Peter Rohde. *Søren Kierkegaard*, trans. Alan Moray Williams (London: Allen & Unwin, 1963), pp. 108-113; P. M. Mitchell. *A History of Danish Literature* (Copenhagen: Gyldendal, 1957), pp. 101, 135, 139-140.

[e] A. N. de Saint-Aubain (1798-1865). Talented author of novels and short stories, etc. His mother, Anna Bolette Buntzen, was Fru Gyllembourg-Ehrensvärd's older sister. The latter was one of his literary models. His first cousin, Johan Ludvig Heiberg, gave him the nom-de-plume "Carl Bernhard." Cf. DBL, XX, 488-493.

[f] Steen Steensen Blicher (1782-1848), a Jutland clergyman, had a generally unhappy life. His verse and stories, however, have been widely read in Denmark from his own time to the present, so that he occupies a position in Danish Literature comparable to that of Charles Dickens in English. Cf. P. M. Mitchell, *A History of Danish Literature, passim.*

[4] Cf. among others, Vald. Vedel, *Guldalderen i dansk Digtning*, 1890 (2nd ed., 1948); Vilhelm Andersen in *Illustreret dansk Litteraturhistorie*, III (1924); F. J. Billeskov Jansen in *Danmarks Digtekunst*, III (1958). Oluf Friis in *Dansk Litteraturhistorie*, II (1965), is milder in his judgment.

[g] Adam Oehlenschläger (1779-1850) and Schack Staffeldt (1769-1826) are discussed in some detail in Mitchell, *History of Danish Literature*, pp. 105-117.

the humdrum (antithesis); whereas Heiberg, with his "vaude-villes," mediated and found poetry in prose (synthesis).[h]

Following his critical glance over the contemporary literary scene Kierkegaard then turns a severely critical eye toward H. C. Andersen. The introductory remarks are of the formal esthetic type. He says that Andersen "has leaped over his epic," for after his lyric period he must then "in an orderly fashion" run through the epic in order to end with the dramatic.

In these statements some have thought that they have discovered in Kierkegaard a Hegelian-Heibergian esthetician;[5] but how much weight and significance can we give to these expressions?

It is well known that Heiberg's schema is this: Lyric—Epic—Drama, which means, respectively, the immediate, the reflected, and the higher unity of these two stages,[6] while Hegel in his *Philosophy of Fine Art* (IV, 97-330) has the series Epic—Lyric—Drama. The original publication of the volume of Hegel's *Lectures on the Philosophy of Fine Art* containing this passage was in June 1838,[7] that is, long after Heiberg had presented his esthetics. Thus, so far as the sequence of *genres* is concerned, Keirkegaard is aligned with Heiberg rather than Hegel here.

What is germane to the understanding of the cited and the relevant subsequent statements of Kierkegaard now is that, unlike either Hegel or Heiberg, he puts the main emphasis on the development and maturation of the personality—in the case of H. C. Andersen. As determinists, neither Hegel nor Heiberg could have written as Kierkegaard does here, for consistency required them to regard a different development impossible under the given conditions of the individual concerned; whereas Kierkegaard presupposes the individual human's freedom and responsibility for his own personal development, in the present instance for the development of poetic abilities.

[h] This last phrase about Heiberg, could also be translated as: "found poetry in the prosaic."

[5] E. g., Frithiof Brandt, *Den unge S.K.* [The Young Søren Kierkegaard], 1929, 193.

[6] See, for example, Heiberg's *Prosaiske Skrifter*, III, 208, and *passim*. Kierkegaard had known this article from its original publication in *Kjøbenhavns flyvende Post*, 1838 (cf. *Papirer*, I C 59). Cf. further, Paul V. Rubow, *Dansk litterær Kritik indtil 1870* (1921), esp. p. 102ff, and Morten Borup, *J. L. Heiberg*, II (1948), 110ff.

[7] See *Allgemeine Bibliographie für Deutschland*, 22.6, 1838.

The most fundamental previous investigation of Kierkegaard's first published book in its relation to Hegel was undertaken by Hirsch, and he thinks that it can hardly be assumed that Kierkegaard had read Hegel's *Philosophy of Fine Art* before he wrote his own book, and that Kierkegaard surely "on individual points has learned much, or if you will, everything from Hegelianism, and is still on the whole no Hegelian."[8] This study and its conclusion is fully documented and convincing, and it may be taken to be supererogatory here to repeat or try to improve on what Hirsch has accomplished concerning the formal esthetic problems. That at this time Kierkegaard was not a Hegelian as an esthetician, moreover, can be seen simply by a comparison with reviews written by Heiberg —for example of Henrik Hertz' play *Svend Dyrings Huus*[i] in the first issue of *Perseus*. Reference could also be made to Kierkegaard's view of genius or his notion of what an attitude toward life is, and in both instances his divergence from both the romantic and the Hegelian view would be strikingly evident.

While a more precise investigation of Kierkegaard as a literary critic would belong to the history of esthetic criticism,[9] it can be noted here by way of conclusion that, while Kierkegaard's factual knowledge of Hegel and Hegelian esthetics and literary criticism is neither especially complete nor penetrating (that is, insofar as Kierkegaard did not understand Hegelian views from the total perspective that motivated them), he certainly appropriated the terminology and viewpoints of his time in individual instances. But Hirsch is correct, the predominant emphasis of the book is entirely un-Hegelian.

Vilhelm Andersen in his book on Poul Møller indirectly said the same thing, as the following quote illustrates:

It was [H. C.] Andersen's self-complacent nonsense, his theory of the pampered genius, which irritated Poul Møller's disciple. His reasoning can be summarized in the statement: Andersen

[8] *Kierkegaard-Studien*, p. 17-25. Excerpts from Hegel's *Philosophy of Fine Art* do not turn up until 1841-1842. See *Papirer*, III C 34 [Hong, V, #5545].

[i] Henrik Hertz (1798-1870), noted dramatist very closely associated with Heiberg, wrote some fifty plays, many of them for Heiberg's wife, the most famous actress in Denmark. Two of his plays, *The Savings Bank* (1836) and *Svend Dyring's House* (1837), are still produced occasionally in Denmark. Cf. Mitchell, *History of Danish Literature*, esp. pp. 140-142.

[9] Cf. Aage Henriksen, "Kierkegaard's Reviews of Literature" in *Symposion Kierkegaardianum*, 1955, 75-84.

has no attitude toward life, he is no true poet, because he is not
a true human. To put it briefly: It was the recently deceased
thinker who constitutes the content of the Papers of one still
living. Was not the unlikely title of this little work well chosen
indeed with respect to its circumstances?[10]

The last question can undoubtedly be answered negatively. Poul
Møller died on March 13, 1838; Kierkegaard's father on August 9.
The latter's death had the most profound significance.[j]

3. *Papirer*, II A 257-581 AND 786-824

If we turn now to the many entries Kierkegaard made during the
same period, the impression that was strengthened by reading *Af
en endnu Levendes Papirer* is only confirmed, namely that his
knowledge of Hegel's own and his disciples' writings was not extensive, nor was it especially penetrating. But on the other hand,
Kierkegaard's attitude toward Hegelian thought, and his evaluation of it is certain, and it is unsympathetic. He constantly speaks
of the Hegelians in the third person—which Frithiof Brandt long
ago noted—and without sympathy, not to mention respect.

Already on September 12, 1838, Kierkegaard remarks ironically
(II A 260)[k] that "certain people" confidently assure us that they
have gone beyond Hegel—an expression that closely corresponds
to the later one, so familiar in the Authorship, "to go further"—
but according to Kierkegaard's interpretation of the situation it
means only that they have rushed through Hegel's philosophy without having understood it completely. It is not unlikely that here,
as so often later, Kierkegaard was thinking of Martensen especially;
but no definite indicator for this assumption is to be found in the
entry cited.

---

[10] *Poul Møller* (3rd ed. 1944), 388. In his *Gaadefulde Stadier paa Kierkegaards Vej* [Mysterious Stages on Kierkegaard's Way] (Copenhagen: Rosenkilde og Baggers Forlag, 1974), pp. 39-51, H. P. Rohde has convincingly
shown that SK adapted the title from Prince Hermann Ludwig Heinrich
Pückler-Muskau's (1785-1871) book *Briefe eines Verstorbenen* [Letters from
One Deceased] (Munich: F. G. Franckh, 1830). SK had read this and other
writings of this now forgotten, odd writer who used the pseudonym Tutti
Frutti. See *Papirer* I A 41 (with note) [Hong, V, #5071].

[j] Cf. *Papirer*, II A 209, 243; Hong, V, #5302, 5335. These entries will also
be found in Dru, *Journals*, pp. 58, 59f.

[k] Hong, II, #1573.

In the entry II A 282[1], a marginal note to another marginal note
from November 2, 1838, occasioned by his reading in church history in anticipation of his examinations for the degree in theology,
Kierkegaard quotes (in German) from Hegel's *Lectures on the
Philosophy of History*. It should be noted that the reference is to the
second edition (1840) of these lectures, not to the first edition published by Eduard Gans and Karl Hegel in 1837. It is quite strange
that this work is not listed in the Auction Catalogue of Kierkegaard's library, and it must be assumed to be most likely that not
until later, while writing *On the Concept of Irony*, did Kierkegaard
become acquainted with his work and quoted an—otherwise quite
fortuitous—bit of historical information from it. This assumption
is made more likely by the fact that none of the other entries from
this period bears the mark of either this or other works of Hegel.

From the entry II A 305[m] it appears that Kierkegaard had attended one of Sibbern's—never published—*Forelæsninger over
Christendomsphilosophie*[11] [Lectures on the Philosophy of Chris-
tianity], which represented a position significantly divergent from
Hegel. Simply from the approval Kierkegaard gives to Sibbern's
views in this entry we obviously cannot conclude that there is an
overall relation between their opinions, or that Sibbern possibly ex-
erted some influence on Kierkegaard, although it is not unlikely
that an exchange of thought took place between the older and the
younger thinker, who were, indeed, personally acquainted.

About a month later, on January 20, 1839, in the entry II A
335[n] Kierkegaard remarks: "Hegel is a Johannes Climacus who
does not storm the heavens as do the giants, by setting mountain
upon mountain—but enters them by means of his syllogisms."
Kierkegaard encountered the name Johannes Climacus in C. E.
Scharling's Danish translation of de Wette's *Lærebog i den christelige Sædelære og sammes Historie* (1835) [Textbook of Christian
Ethics and its History] which he used while preparing for his examinations. The comparison does not testify to any particular knowledge of Hegel's philosophy in general or his dialectical method in
particular, mainly since Hegel just does *not* construct his arguments

[1] Not in Hong.

[m] Hong, I, #194.

[11] On Sibbern's views see Skat Arildsen, *H. L. Martensen*, I (1932), 42-45,
and Jens Himmelstrup, *Sibbern* (1934), 227ff.

[n] Hong, II, #1575.

as syllogisms.[12] The statement, in its generality, can hardly be connected with any definite passage in Hegel.

In the beginning of February Kierkegaard acquired Anton
Günther's *Die Juste-Milieus in der deutschen Philosophie gegen-
wärtiger Zeit* (Ktl. 522) [The Precise Context of Contemporary
German Philosophy]; but the odd title, which Kierkegaard called
"splendid," captivated him "to the degree . . . that I just never
got the book read; but remained stationary at the aphorism of the
title page" (II A 356).[o] There are also many entries from this period
connected with his preparation for his theology examination, but
we can hardly consider independent studies here.

On February 19 he speaks of "the abuses to which orthodox
Hegelians have pressed their master's categories" (II A 371),[p] and
again on March 12 he speaks in the third person of "the Hegelians,"
who are always hunting for "the category of the bad infinity" in life
(II A 381).[q] In the succeeding weeks he was constantly occupied
with studying for his examinations, which lay on Kierkegaard as a
burden he had taken upon himself as a Christian duty that strug-
gled against his natural inclination (cf. II A 422).[r] Then on May
22 we find the entry that is like a motto for the whole first half of
the Authorship: "But there is given a view of the world, according to which the paradox is higher than any system" (II A 439).[s]

On the same day in the next entry (II A 440)[t] Kierkegaard expresses his doubts about "the philosophers' "—he does not say which
ones—relation to Christianity, and he continues, presumably under
the influence of Schleiermacher, with the assertion that "every
dogma is nothing other than a more concrete extension of the
common human consciousness," a statement that has its parallel
in Schleiermacher's noted claim in *The Christian Faith* (§15) that
"Christian doctrines are accounts of the Christian religious affec-
tions set forth in speech." This viewpoint is elaborated a couple of

[12] Cf. especially *Science of Logic*, II, 301-342.

[o] Hong, III, #3271. Günther's book was published in Vienna in 1838. Anton Günther (1783-1863), Austrian theologian, felt called upon to combat
Pantheism of modern philosophy, especially in what he considered its most
insidious form, the Hegelian.

[p] Hong, II, #1576.

[q] Hong, II, #1577.

[r] Hong, V, #5385.

[s] Hong, III, #3071.

[t] Hong, III, #3273.

days later (II A 443)[u] in a way in which the concept of sin places
a basic split between Kierkegaard's and Hegel's (for example) interpretations. The same is the case with the entry II A 448,[v] the first
anticipation of the significant note at the beginning of *Philosophical
Fragments*.[13]

In the summer, on June 14, 1839, Kierkegaard again expresses
a view which is in complete opposition to Hegel's, namely, the
well-known statement:

> That relative opposites can be mediated, in truth we do not
> need Hegel [to tell us], since it is found in the ancients that
> they can be distinguished; that absolute opposites can be
> mediated, that will personality protest against for all eternity."[w]

In a note on this entry, the editors of the *Papirer* appropriately
refer to Mynster's article "Rationalisme. Supranaturalisme" and
to Sibbern's review of Heiberg's *Perseus*. It is known that both
Mynster and Sibbern repudiated Hegelian speculation and its adherents in Denmark, particularly Heiberg and Martensen, and
Kierkegaard is fundamentally at one with Sibbern's and Mynster's
philosophical objections here.[14] Again some time later in an undated
entry (II A 493)[x] Kierkegaard gives an interpretation of the
relation between philosophy and Christianity that is fundamentally
opposed to the Hegelian view: "Philosophy enters into Christianity as an object of inquiry, which faces its inquisitor with a history
which coincides in all essential moments and which is yet entirely
distinct." By philosophy Kierkegaard as usual probably means
speculative idealism. Possibly this entry is connected with Kierkegaard's reading of I. H. Fichte's article "Aphorismen über die
Zukunft der Theologie, in ihrem Verhältnisse zu Spekulation und
Mythologie,"[15] an article against the basic viewpoint of which

[u] Hong, I, #446.

[v] Hong, II, #2088.

[13] Page 12, note #1. Cf. my commentary on this text in the English translation (2nd ed.) of the *Philosophical Fragments*, pp. 174-180, and my article
"Die historische Methode in der Kierkegaard-Forschung durch ein Beispiel
beleuchtet" in *Symposion Kierkegaardianum*, 1955, 280-297.

[w] II A 454; Hong, II, #1578.

[14] Cf. my article "Kierkegaards Verhältnis zu Hegel" in *Theologische
Zeitschrift* (1957), 200-226, with references to sources and to the literature.

[x] Hong, III, #3274.

[15] *Zeitschrift für Philosophie und spekulative Theologie*, 1839, 199ff.

Kierkegaard reacted in a critical entry on July 28 (II A 517).[y] Here he explicitly rejects Fichte's speculative theism, which, according to his interpretation, weakens the Christian concept of revelation. We find the same tendency in an entry two days later (II A 523),[z] and again a week later (II A 529).[aa]

As the year wears on, the fewer the entries Kierkegaard makes in his Journal, until—in view of the demands made by his studying for his examinations—he completely stops keeping his Journal. There are not many separate papers from this parenthetical period either.

There is the question of the notes II A 786-824,[bb] where in many places he expresses himself on the relation between Christianity and philosophy. The motto[cc] expresses his fundamental view: they are incompatible (II A 786).[dd] Thus it is completely identical with the view expressed in the Journal entries from the same period.

The very few concrete allusions to particular philosophers and theologians in the entries from the whole period dealt with here only fortify the impression that this really was a parenthesis in Kierkegaard's life. This is not to say that it was an unimportant period. For even if he does not seem to have enlarged his knowledge of Hegelian philosophy, and had read only I. H. Fichte's article cited above, nonetheless his attitude was consolidated during this time, both positively in relation to Christianity, such as he understood it at the time, and negatively, not only toward Hegelianism, but also toward philosophical theism critical of Hegel. It can hardly be ruled out that this studying for the final examinations in theological textbooks and notebooks itself influenced his interpretation of Christianity, and, in that way indirectly influenced his attitude toward speculative philosophy.[16]

[y] Hong, III, #3276.

[z] Hong, II, #2266.

[aa] Hong, III, #3279.

[bb] Most of these entries will be found in various volumes of Hong.

[cc] This motto in II A 786 is the same one found in II A 239. See Chap. III, sect. 6 *supra*.

[dd] Hong, III, #3266.

[16] It can be pointed out here that there is no intention either in the present, the previous, or the subsequent chapters, of giving a complete account of the general assumptions which Kierkegaard—through examination requirements, etc.—had to share with his contemporaries. Such an account belongs to Church history, the history of philosophy, and the history of literature. Nor is there any intention of giving an account of all the especially Kierkegaardian

4. "The Conflict Between the Old and the New Soap-Cellar"[17]

This document shows Kierkegaard the student from an entirely unfamiliar aspect, in the role of a playwright. This is a draft of a play, the full title of which is:

"The Conflict Between the Old and the New Soap-Cellar, heroic-patriotic-cosmopolitan-philanthropic-fatalistic drama in several acts."

We are also informed that "this piece is quite merry in the beginning, very sad in the middle, but very happy at the end" (*Papirer*, II B 1).

The *dramatis personae* are:

Willibald, a young man
Echo, his friend
Mr. von Skipjack, a philosopher
Mr. Harry Rushjob, a makeshift genius
Mr. Phrase, an adventurer, member of several scholarly associations and contributor to manifold journals.

Skipjack, Rushjob, and Phrase "are maintained at public expense in the Prytaneum." These important personages are joined, moreover, by "a fly, which for several years has been known to spend the winter with the blessed Hegel, and which had the singular good fortune during the composition of his work: Phenomenology of the Spirit to have sat upon his immortal nose several times," and in addition, some not further identified "wholesalers, polytechnicians, pedestrians." Finally there enter a ventriloquist and a horn, which is the "organ of the public mind."

---

premises and their significance such as Valdemar Ammundsen and Emanuel Hirsch in particular, and others have done, and whose important works must be taken for granted here. Only the texts of Kierkegaard that probably or actually have a direct relation to Hegel are taken up for analysis. This is consciously one-sided, by which various intrinsically significant and interesting questions are not made the object of an independent discussion. Likewise, an explicit confrontation of the results and viewpoints of this investigation with those of earlier scholars is undertaken only where it is deemed natural do do so, while it has not been found necessary either to repeat what others have said well and correctly enough, or to mention or discuss a long series of scholars and authors who have had other purposes and who have employed other methods than the one practiced here.

[17] In a slightly different version, this section was published in the Japanese Kierkegaard Association's annual *Kierkegaard-Study*, 1965, but it is repeated here for the sake of completeness.

Frithiof Brandt was the first to have taken this student drama seriously. Earlier researchers passed over it in silence, embarrassed that the great thinker had descended to such things at all. But since Brandt, Emanuel Hirsch, Knud Jensenius, and lastly Carl Roos have concerned themselves with this text, which is in many respects tricky and difficult.[18]

First, and in the main in harmony with Carl Roos, we can give a summary of the content of the text with some individual remarks on it:

The chief character in the play, Willibald, after a short monologue (which is not written out) decides to go to a tea party. He meets Echo there, who has been the life of the party with his cleverness, wit, and jests borrowed from Willibald. When Willibald wants to leave the party, the hostess tries to detain him; but he slips out and returns home to his room.[ee] This gives us an indication of the date of this text, when we note that the young man did not have an apartment but only a single room, and compare that with the fact that Kierkegaard himself had moved out of home in his father's house (Nytorv 2) in September 1837, to rent a room at Løvstræde 7 in Copenhagen.

In the second scene Willibald is alone in his study, seated on his sofa with a pipe in his mouth and surrounded by many open books and scraps of paper on which he has made notes. He is reading Chamisso's *Peter Schlemihl*, the story of a man whose shadow went about independently. Upset by what he reads, he asks whether this story is not actually his own, whether he is not—like Aurora's husband[ff]—crumbling so as to end as a freak of nature under a bell

[18] Brandt, *Den unge SK,* 419ff., Hirsch, *Kierkegaard-Studien,* (1933), I, 432, and II, 556ff.; Jensenius: *Nogle Kierkegaard-Studier* [Some Kierkegaard-Studies], 1932, 70ff.; Carl Roos, *K. og Goethe* [Kierkegaard and Goethe], 1955, 130ff. [Walter Lowrie, in his *Short Life of Kierkegaard* (Princeton: Princeton University Press, 1942) p. 106, referring to Brandt's work identifies Willibald as representing SK, and Echo as the poet Hertz, a fellow student and friend of Kierkegaard.]

[ee] Again, on the basis of Brandt's work, Lowrie observes that this scene is based on an actual party at the home of J. L. Heiberg. Hertz, SK, and Poul Møller were among the guests. Furthermore, there is an entry in the *Papirer* (I A 161) Eng. trans. in Dru, p. 51; Hong, V #5141) which rather vividly reflects SK's feelings after this party. Cf. Lowrie, *Short Life,* pp. 106-107.

[ff] Tithonus, husband of Aurora (Dawn or Eos), turns up several times as a symbol in the *Papirer.* Cf. I A 302. Eos obtained the gift of immortality for Tithonus from Zeus, but she neglected to ask for eternal youth for him, so he grew older and shriveled, and finally his voice became shrill and he turned

jar, like a homunculus. Still, his reflections continue, if that is what he becomes, then in spite of that he will "during a noble and learned professor's lectures break the glass and my life's hyperbole will eclipse all his decimal and algebra computations," so that the bourgeois, the philistines, will be dumbfounded with horror.

While making these reflections he puffs on his pipe, and the smoke condenses into shapes. He wants to create a shadow of himself as a shadow, and the outcome is that his tormentor, Echo, appears. This raises a doubt within him about his self-identity; he comes to a hasty decision, grabs his sword to take Echo's life, "You overscrupulous bookkeeper of all my words," but the smoke figure is —nothing. He turns the sword against himself, but stops his attempt because of a cough: he has got a bit of quill in his throat. There is a knock on the door and the real Echo enters.—Roos (p. 134) interprets this thus: the feather in his throat explains what it means to him to be a shadow. He is the shadow of all the literature he has devoured, and that means that he is sick. The conversation between Willibald and Echo begins then with quotations from Bürger's *Lenore*.—Echo sees the sword and asks what it is for, and Willibald replies that he was just about "at the urging of a compassionate demon to slay a grasshopper, so that it could fall by the hand of its only friend." Naturally, Echo does not understand him. He doesn't understand the allusion to the grasshopper, which is Aurora's husband, who had dwindled away (Brandt, pp. 434-435 in connection with *Papirer*, I A 302 [Hong, II, #1189]). The compassionate demon, according to Brandt, is the young Kierkegaard's notorious demon wit, which could overpower him when he least desired it.

Echo wants an explanation of why Willibald left the party so early. Willibald puts him off with an ironic answer, which Echo does not understand, and the conversation turns to the relation of novels to reality. Willibald then returns, quite naturally, to his "feather," says that he was spitting blood and sends Echo for a physician. When Echo rushes out, Willibald sends a curse after him and wishes for himself only to become free of his worst affliction: friends.

Now Willibald fades out rapidly, and in the third scene Echo returns with the physician, for whom he describes Willibald as "a

---

into a cicada. Cf. Robert Graves, *The Greek Myths* (New York: George Braziller, 1955), 40 c. Cf. also SK, *The Concept of Irony*, "Irony after Fichte," p. 289.

most peculiar person, an eccentric, full of the most curious notions which flutter about, when like that goddess he writes upon a leaf which he lets the wind carry away," and which Echo has dealt with a great deal, in fact, he has taken a direct reckoning of it in his "double entry bookkeeping of ideas" as Willibald has put it. The physician is not interested in this chatter—which perhaps, as Brandt conjectures, refers to Henrik Hertz's (unprinted) books of studies and roman à clef *Stemninger og Tilstande* [Moods and Conditions], which appeared in 1839—and so the physician leaves.

Willibald has not realized his hope of finally escaping, for once, bothersome friends. He is halted in his flight by three Christian revivalists (probably SK is thinking here of Peter Christian Kierkegaard, Jacob Christian Lindberg, and A. G. Rudelbach—all three at the close of the 1830s were ardent followers of Grundtvig). The three want to wager on which one of them is the greatest sinner. Reciting aloud, Willibald succeeds in eluding the police, who had been sent "to apprehend some revivalists." (Lindberg held "Christian meetings" in his home without ecclesiastical permission, and various efforts were made to prevent him from doing so).[19] Willibald now vanishes from the face of the earth.

In the first scene of the second act we find ourselves in a fantastic setting, the Prytaneum, where everything is triangular, i.e., Hegelian. Ole Wadt (who was probably modeled on Kierkegaard's friend, the editor Giødvad), and the politician Harry Rushjob (surely Orla Lehmann) are having a discussion, which breaks up when both become angry.

These two remain on the stage; but now they are joined by the little, insignificant von Skipjack (probably J. L. Heiberg) and Phrase (most likely Martensen). Phrase wants to strive toward the realization of the "grandiose goal" of science, and also to make its result accessible to the people, so that "contemporary progress may gain in extensity what it loses in intensity." Von Skipjack is skeptical about popularizing. Modern philosophy, he says, which takes its point of departure from Descartes' *de omnibus dubitandum* [all things are to be doubted] (not his *cogito ergo sum* [I think, therefore I am] which Roos mistakenly writes on p. 135) begins precisely with an infinite doubt, and he is not even sure that he has himself doubted fundamentally enough.[gg] In any case, this kind of

[19] Cf. K. Baagø, *Magister Jacob Christian Lindberg* (1958), *passim*.

[gg] Aside from the rich irony here, it may be pointed out that these allusions to Descartes are debatable.

great scientific problem cannot be made understandable to the common man. Phrase quickly retreats: he was not thinking of the common herd, but of the cultured middle class. It should certainly be possible to make it comprehensible for the latter group if one only adjusts the style a bit. This notion immediately captivates Wadt: one must remove some of the sharply (tri-)angular, round off the structures somewhat, for it depends on the style, the presentation. Rushjob interrupts with his "Philosophy me here and philosophy me there. It does not depend on philosophy. It is a practical question, the questions of life—to put it briefly, life." Skipjack replies: "well, what is life" and Phrase answers with a well-known quote from Sibbern.[hh] Skipjack now explains why he replied with his question, and he goes into more detail about why it is so difficult to make philosophy popular, for it demands a fixed position that he

[hh] Well known, presumably, to SK's contemporaries. The quote (from II B 16) is: "Life is one going out of itself to return to itself." In Sibbern's own words:

"Life, what is first and constitutive of the organism, is emerging from an inner source, not just potentially, but actually manifesting itself and constantly maintaining activity in a totality of manifold parts or indeed in a certain external appearance, which appearance by the very activity of this life both is formed for that which it is, so and incessantly is maintained as a whole existing for itself. Thus the unity of the organism is by no means a collection or compound producing unity, but an original [unity], in which that which unites the manifold parts into a whole is the first, which forming itself has brought forth the whole manifoldness, in which it now lives and acts." F. C. Sibbern, *Menneskets aandelige Natur og Væsen. Et Udkast til en Psychologie* [The Spiritual Nature and Essence of Man. An Outline for a Psychology] (Copenhagen, 1819) first part, p. 14.

Some years later Sibbern defined life as follows: "Life indeed comes from an inner source, and with an inner force working itself forward, organizing and individualizing activity and the process of activity, which as it by a certain material or substrate constitutes itself as the one in this, its externally subsisting activity and effort, about which it still can be asked, whether a soul can be said to live and subsist therein, as the living essence in something manifesting such a life." F. C. Sibbern, *Psychologie* (Copenhagen, 1856), p. 15.

The Hegelian view was satirized by Fritz Jürgensen (1818-1863) in his book *Tegninger* [Drawings] (Copenhagen, 1860). Cartoon #13 has the following parody of a Hegelian definition of life as a caption: "It is obvious that being (the immediate) strides forward and becomes another self (a negation of the immediate) and thus its immanent (not designated from without) content. It stops, and becomes its negative self; but it resumes a development of becoming in itself, and this resumption is the definite origin of individuality, which is a product of the former, and becomes a primordial form for further development. This is life."

cannot find in the common sphere of reasoning. Rushjob answers
with the cheap shot that von Skipjack is lame and therefore has difficulty in getting a firm footing.

In the third scene, Willibald enters and prostrates himself with
joy at having been liberated from his previous life, kisses the earth,
respectfully goes to meet with Skipjack and says to him that he
still does not know just where he has actually arrived at this stage,
but the whole atmosphere gives him the impression that "here
wisdom may be found," and that here he can become cured of
"that abominable relativity I had yielded to before." Skipjack immediately gives the diagnosis: Willibald has to a severe degree suf-
fered from the Faustian, that is, the doubt, which has characterized
the whole of modern philosophy since Descartes. When the others
arrive von Skipjack discusses this, so all can hear it. Phrase inquires
whether this is the same theme that he had already appropriated a
large part of. Even if it is, he would still like to hear it repeated,
so that in that way he can be enabled "from speculation's Mount of
the Ascension to survey the incarnations of the great historical
ideas." Skipjack expresses his joy at having such an indefatigable
disciple who will soon be able to go into action, indeed not to the
same degree as his master, von Skipjack himself—but at least so
that he "will be able honorably to fill a docent's position in the
northern countries and chase away the hyperborean dark." Then
von Skipjack continues his discourse, regretting that "unworthy
individuals, ignorant people, have slipped into our Society, who [are
occupied with] the most subordinate interests" instead of [joining]
with the true philosophers "to celebrate the great, now imminent
holy day of the world-historical viewpoint, on which mankind, i.e.,
philosophy, after having passed from the immediate paradisiacal
state of innocence through the dialectic of life turns back to the immediate, just because there is no need to work with intuitive joy
to revive the already experienced drama of the world." He will not
even allow himself to be disturbed, in fact he is even prepared, in the
authentic speculative manner, to see the opposite viewpoint as a
"negligible moment." He returns to Descartes' fundamental principle of the doubt, which in every well-ordered speculative state
ought to be learned during instruction for Confirmation, and about
which no Bachelor of Theology ought to be ignorant, when in the
final analysis it is the scientific slogan of the state, and when it constantly "will remind us of the genesis of our intellectual life."

The chairman of the meeting tries to stop his harangue, but to no avail: von Skipjack maintains that ordinarily he can give his lecture on modern philosophy in a minute and a half and that is only out of consideration for "our catechumen," Willibald, that he has spoken a bit more extensively. He then continues, in spite of the chairman's repeated attempt to stop his chatter, to speak of Spinoza, Kant, and Fichte. At this point, on the order of the chairman, the attendants have come forward ready to seize him and throw him out. On seeing this, he complains that he has not been able to say what he wants to say about Schleiermacher, but he does manage to state the most important point, namely, that "it was Hegel who speculatively concentrated the previous systems, and therefore with him knowledge reached its authentic dogmatic pinnacle." With this he declares that he is finished and with Hegel the history of the world is over; nothing else now remains but mythology (Strauss!), and he becomes a mythological figure himself.

Now Phrase enters the proceedings again. He calls von Skipjack's last outburst an expression of an entirely one-sided position. Although he has gone beyond Hegel, "in what respect I still cannot say quite precisely; but I have gone beyond him." Indignant, von Skipjack calls him a traitor, a Judas against the eternal Idea incarnate in himself. When von Skipjack is taken away by the attendants, Phrase then begins in his own name precisely the same lecture on modern philosophy, Descartes, the principle of doubt, etc. Then he is interrupted by the chairman, who does not want tempers agitated again.

Willibald was not particularly edified by von Skipjack's philosophical lectures, and the members of the Prytaneum are not sure what should be done with him. Finally they decide to send him to an intellectual establishment the Prytaneum has set up under the name of "the World-historical College." To be sure, it was still not completed, but its Great Hall alone was so large that four professors could teach simultaneously without disturbing one another. Indeed, it was so large that the audience could never hear what they said.

"Here Willibald upon personal contact was now gradually won over to the views that were currently held in the Prytaneum," and he had thus far already regretted the remark, which in his irritation at von Skipjack he had passed on to the chairman, namely, why did the sun in the Prytaneum stand still, so that even time had stopped?

Scene 4: At a general meeting Harry Rushjob requests permission to speak, and declares that it is his understanding that the unique phenomenon of the stationary sun is a dawning, "that it is that solemn dawn which is the sun's battle against the final struggles of the dark" etc. with a tirade whose individual expressions are typically Grundtvigian. Von Skipjack begins again with his elegant speculative twaddle, and concludes with the comment that this speculative reflection can be compared with a snake that bites its own tail, or with an insight that is an outlook, which looks back into its own eye, which it also sees out of at the same time. Rushjob interrupts these ramblings "which are nothing other than Hegel's notorious perpetual motion thought." Of course, von Skipjack will not allow himself to be cut off by such objections, but maintains, contrary to Rushjob, that it is a dusk, for "philosophy is precisely the evening of life, and with Hegel, who speculatively concentrated the previous rational systems it [i.e., the dusk] has entered the world-historical." Phrase repeats his—phrase: I have gone beyond Hegel. Now they all begin shouting at one another. Rushjob wishes a vote on the question; but von Skipjack declares that by balloting one only enters into the bad infinity. The chairman also expresses doubt about whether the laws permit voting in such a case, and it is revealed that the Prytaneum, which Ole Wadt has just called "our ancient society," is only a yearling. The whole quarrel stops abruptly, however, when Willibald points out that the dispute turns on a misinterpretation of his question. He had not asked about the physical sun at all, but had only "wanted to suggest the poetic, philosophical, cosmo-political eternity, which in an intellectual sense already permeated the Prytaneum." The participants are pacified by this, and the general meeting breaks up.

Act III, *Scene 1*: Willibald strolls through a fantastic ambience in the neighborhood of the Prytaneum. He has been converted. He proclaims his enthusiasm for the Absolute Spirit, into which he has now obtained an insight, thanks to his immortal teacher von Skipjack. Now the light has dawned on him. A fly buzzes by, reciting Hegelian propositions. He realizes that now world-history is finished, time has stopped, the sun stands still, now when even nature is so permeated with the Concept, that a wretched fly can "maintain the Concept," i.e., the speculative Concept.

Scene 2: Ole Wadt has now arrived with von Skipjack, and Wadt asks Willibald to bring about a reconciliation within the Prytaneum. Willibald promises to do everything within his power. He proposes that, in order to indicate that peace has again descended, they should begin a new reckoning of time and give the association a new name "under which it would nevertheless otherwise remain the same. I suggest, therefore, that in the future we call it: The New-and the Old Prytaneum, written, mind you, with the hyphen." Rushjob is obviously indifferent to logical categories [*Bestemmelser*] of this kind; but yet he can approve of them only insofar as they might indicate a new development. On the contrary, von Skipjack cannot approve of their abolishing the old title [*Indskrift*] Prytaneum and then writing it anew, for that "would only be turning back to the Immediate, where the dialectical oppositions still have not developed themselves and speculatively penetrated one another." Thus it happens that the whole incident has cast light on a myth, which they all know, namely, the battle between the old and the new Soap-Cellar, of which also the speculative meaning of the myth taken as a whole becomes clear: it contains an anticipation of history.

Then, on the suggestion of Ole Wadt, they adjourn to erect a monument to the memory of that unforgettable day, and it is raised to the accompaniment of many enthusiastic toasts "especially to Willibald."

Most of the characters in this unique drama, Kierkegaard's only effort in this genre, have already been identified in connection with Brandt's, Hirsch's, and Roos's studies. The earlier editors of Kierkegaard's *Papirer* showed excessive discretion when in the foreword to this volume (p. xi) they write that "we have entirely refrained from indicating in the notes which particular persons and circumstances among S.K.'s contemporaries . . . have been taken into consideration there. . . ."

There can scarcely be any doubt that, among the incidental characters, Ole Wadt is modeled on Giødvad and Harry Rushjob [Holla Hastværksen] is a caricature of Orla Lehmann, with whom Kierkegaard is known to have engaged in polemics earlier. After Brandt's analysis, there can be no reason to deny that Henrik Hertz is the model for Echo. This is significant for an attempt to determine the date of composition of this play. Mr. Phrase is probably Martensen and von Skipjack is Heiberg. On this point it should be noted that Kierkegaard has somewhat changed the latter in particular and made him say things that historically would more properly belong to Martensen. We must grant Kierkegaard the right to this poetic license, and he has obviously made general use of it in his little drama.

In Martensen's lengthy review (1836) of Heiberg's *Introductory Lecture to the . . . Course in Logic* [*Indledningsforedrag til det . . . logiske Cursus*], in his theological dissertation *On the Autonomy of Human Self-Consciousness* [*Den menneskelige Selvbevidstheds Autonomie*], and in the—still unpublished—*Lectures on the Introduction to Speculative Dogmatics* [*Forelæsninger over Indledning til speculativ Dogmatik*], he gives brief or lengthy surveys or sketches of modern philosophy with emphasis on Descartes and his two axioms. The statement found in Kierkegaard's play (*Papirer,* II B 16, p. 296) and which is put in the mouth of von Skipjack: "Doubt is the specific [feature] of modern philosophy, which, speaking parenthetically, began with Descartes, who said *de omnibus disputandum est* [all things must be debated] whereby he completely annihilated the principle that previously went as a fundamental rule: *de gustibus non est disputandum* [there's no arguing tastes]" is thus nearly verbatim Martensen's summary in the above review. It is almost verbatim, for the change at the end (from *credo ut intelligam* [I believe so that I may understand: cf. Anselm, Augustine] to what is in the context ludicrous, *de gustibus non est disputandum*) is obviously made with full awareness on the part of Kierkegaard. In his play he wishes to give a caricature of a philosophic aesthete, not of a philosophizing theologian.

Phrase's repeated assurances that he has gone beyond Hegel, without his being able to say exactly where he has arrived, corresponds closely with Kierkegaard's remarks after having read Martensen's review (*Papirer,* II A 7) "After . . . having leap-frogged over all his predecessors he has advanced out into an indefinite infinity." The truth, which Kierkegaard could scarcely be thought to have had sufficient knowledge of at this point in time, is that during his long study trip abroad Martensen had been strongly influenced by the unique Franz von Baader in Munich, who, to a certain extent was opposed to Hegel, but in 1836 Martensen had still not formulated his position. Hence Kierkegaard's sarcastic remark is in and of itself quite correct.

Who, then, is the chief character, Willibald? Brandt (p. 421) identifies him with Kierkegaard himself, and Hirsch (p. 556) concurs with Brandt on this point. Roos, on the other hand, is inclined to interpret the whole draft as a parody on *Faust* (p. 141), and he thinks (pp. 145-146) that Willibald

is to a certain extent a caricature of the Kierkegaard, who kept a constant watch lest he himself should become a copy, a double, a self-parody. The similarity conflicts with the acceptance of the dogmas of the Prytaneum. The model then becomes rather Martensen. But yet the perspective is wider and independent of personal reference to an individual person: the model for Willibald, who changes about, is in the final analysis the members of the younger generation, who indeed have something of the Faust in themselves but who travel the same road as Goethe's Faust. It is they who are parodied. Seen in this way the sketch of the Soap-Cellar is interesting in a larger context than the relation to Hertz, the Academy, and Martensen, even if they were also present in [Kierkegaard's] thoughts.

Furthermore, Roos takes the position, in support of a suggestion by Hirsch, that Kierkegaard borrowed the name and character from Eichendorff's short story *Viel Lärmen um Nichts* [Much Noise about Nothing], which he has parodied at the same time.

If Roos is correct in his interpretation, then not much of Kierkegaard himself remains as a model for Willibald. To maintain this interpretation, we must assume that there are two different persons named Willibald in Kierkegaard's play, which is unlikely, since the personality of Willibald has identity and continuity through the changing scenes and acts. In whatever way Martensen might be the pattern for the Willibald who appears in the first act and who is clearly the same in the two following acts is not evident. For then we must assume either that Kierkegaard had knowledge of a disposition toward duplicity [*Dobbeltgængeri*] and split personality combined with suicidal tendencies in the young Martensen, or that Kierkegaard must have creatively endowed his chief character with traits that are quite unlikely in connection with Martensen, but that correctly understood—correspond precisely with those of Kierkegaard himself, as we know him both from his own remarks and those of others. Furthermore, contrary to Roos's suggestion that Martensen is a possible model for Willibald, the actual background must be understood quite otherwise than would be natural if Willibald is Martensen instead of Kierkegaard himself. It is simply impossible for Martensen to have left a party at the Heiberg's in annoyance on the evening of June 4, 1836—and Brandt (pp. 431f.) has conclusively shown that that must have been the party that is mentioned at the beginning of Kierkegaard's play. Martensen could hardly have been one of the guests, since he was in Paris at the time. Furthermore, it is unlikely that Martensen would have

an admirer, an Echo, who would have conscientiously kept an account of his witticisms [*Indfald*] for himself to use them to the
annoyance of Willibald. The truth of the matter is, that, on the
basis of what is known about Martensen at that time, he had no
original ideas (only didactic lectures, etc.) that one would have
found worthy to be preserved in writing for posterity. On the other
hand, that situation corresponds perfectly with Hertz' relation to
Kierkegaard during the period around the end of the 1830s. Willibald's irritation at Echo, moreover, corresponds to a high degree
to Kierkegaard's attitude toward Rasmus Nielsen a decade later,
when the controversy erupted over Martensen's just published *Dogmatics*. Even though he still did not exclude him from private conversation, Kierkegaard was terribly annoyed at Rasmus Nielsen for
putting into print—but without citing the source!—Kierkegaard's
criticism of Martensen's views. Finally, it would have been most
peculiar for Kierkegaard to have used Martensen as a model both
for the main character, Willibald, and for the secondary character,
Phrase, when these two characters have on the whole so little in
common. To take only a single example, it is said of Willibald
(*Papirer*, II B 19, p. 301) that he "by personal contact [was] gradually won over to the views which were currently held in the
Prytaneum;" he was thus converted to Hegelianism not by a study
trip abroad, for example, but by "personal contact," hence, chiefly
through conversations and discussions. Of Phrase, on the other
hand, we are given to understand that he had been a Hegelian—and
he constantly manifests his obsequious pupil's relation to the older
von Skipjack—but now he has gone further, he has transcended
Hegel. This can only match Martensen, but it also applies to him
perfectly. This is precisely the way we know him from his own
writings, from his lectures, and from his own memoires written at
the beginning of the 1880s.

Thus it must be taken as unlikely that Martensen should even in
the slightest way been the model for Willibald, whose traits in every
act of the play correspond closely to those of Kierkegaard himself.
To be sure, this is a caricaturing description, self-ironic, just as the
characteristics of the other *dramatis personae* are ironically carica-
tured. The story of the conversion is a clear indication of this. That
Willibald, alias Kierkegaard, had known and talked with the Danish Hegelians is so likely that there is no point in discussing it here.
But in reality he was never converted to Hegelianism either tempo-
rarily or over any extended period.

The decisive proof of the correctness of this interpretation, that Kierkegaard did not become a Hegelian, is simply the existence of the play itself. A convinced Hegelian could never have written a play such as Kierkegaard's since the system prohibited a position that Kierkegaard consciously embraced.

The supercilious attitude that emerges in ironic tones in the question about the sun's position that Willibald submits to the chairman, shows a decisive feature in Kierkegaard. Willibald actually regrets having submitted the question; but in the general meeting, when it comes up for debate, he nevertheless allows the whole assembly to discuss it at length before he reveals the essential point, that he actually had been thinking of something quite different from what the debaters believe in their naiveté, at which point the meaninglessness of the debate becomes apparent to all. He could, indeed, have clarified his meaning immediately; but instead lets the others argue [*vrøvle ud*], so that at the end he can show himself as the master of the situation with a single remark. It is precisely here that we have Kierkegaard himself.

So much for the persons and their models.

Now for the locales of the discussion. Brandt's interpretation of the places of the discussion is as follows: the actual background of the first act was an evening party at the Heiberg's on June 4, 1836, at which, among others Henrik Hertz and Poul Møller were present; the two last acts [are based on events that] actually took place at what was established in April 1839 as *Den Akademiske Læseforening* [The Academic Lecture Association], which soon became known as the Academy. To describe the atmosphere of this group, Brandt employs statements of both Fr. Nielsen and Carl Plough, its first president.[20]

What Plough wrote then is worth quoting here again:

> Some of the non-theologians also attended Martensen's lectures, from which they crowded into the adjacent Academy [Martensen's lectures took place on Wednesday and Friday from 5 to 6 p.m.] and the philosophical studies cultivated for a while by the older and younger people influenced by him during the first nine months the Academy existed furnished rich material for conversation, and the lecture rooms were disproportionately well supplied with the same fare. . . . The result of

[20] A major work on student life in Copenhagen in the eighteen thirties is H.C.A. Lund: *Studenter-foreningens Historie*, I (1896).

this was that nearly all conversations were conducted in Hegelian terminology; but these discussions used a jargon of unnecessary foreign words, which posited or negated, manifested or mediated everything possible, and soon elicited a satire, which surely contributed a great deal to getting them abolished.

Whether by "satire" Kierkegaard is referred to cannot be established with certainty; but it cannot be entirely excluded. Even if Kierkegaard's little play, existing only in rough draft, was never performed, it is not inconceivable that he could have shown his manuscript to one or several friends, who in such a case would not have hesitated to use some of its repartee—like Echo! This is only a conjecture which is presented here by way of supplementing Brandt's analysis.

When Hertz's roman à clef *Stemninger og Tilstande* [Moods and Conditions] first appeared in July 1839, and Echo, alias Hertz, used Kierkegaard as the model for the figure "the translator" there, which Brandt has convincingly demonstrated, then it is clear why Brandt thinks that the play can be dated immediately after *Stemninger og Tilstande*, i.e., that it must have been written down then —and in any case as far as the last two acts are concerned—also concerns events between July 1839 and the spring of 1840.

Hirsch (*Kierkegaard-Studien*, II, p. 556, note) has raised some objections to this attempt to establish the date of the play's composition.

Hirsch relies on the literary form, which he holds is that of the romantic, satirical comedy, with a concealed, tragic background. Hirsch finds the closest parallel in Eichendorff's *Krieg der Philister* [War of the Philistines]. When, in the first act, Echo adorns himself with borrowed feathers to Willibald's annoyance, Hirsch thinks that Kierkegaard had a precedent in Hoffmann's *Klein Zaches genannt Zinnober*.

Although it is natural to suggest that Kierkegaard, here as well as often later in his Authorship, used definite literary models, in this case there is an unfortunate discrepancy that argues against Hirsch's hypothesis about Hoffmann's novel.

In Hoffmann (Chap. 3), Student Balthasar himself recites his poem about the love of the nightingale for the red rose at a tea party at the home of Professor Mosch Terpin, and it is only the rest of the party, put under a spell by the fairy Rosabelverdes disguised as an old maid, which believes that it is the loathsome, conceited, and ridiculous gnome Zinnober who has written and recited the poem. In order to defend his opinion, Hirsch must adopt the view that Echo is not patterned on Hertz, but is Kierkegaard's own alter ego.

If this hypothesis were correct, then the first two scenes would become totally unlikely, thus: Willibald's alter ego Echo meets Willibald at a party, becomes annoyed at himself there, goes home —to himself—fantasizes about creating a man—who therefore also would be his alter ego. The cloud of pipe smoke then takes on the form of Echo, whose head he wants to chop off, "but which is nothing"—hence his alter ego, at whom he has just been annoyed, is nothing—and at the same instant Echo, again according to Hirsch's theory, this alter ego nothing, knocks on the door, then runs for the physician, while Willibald himself vanishes.

The theory that Hertz is the model for Echo is more immediately plausible than Hirsch's interpretation.

At the same time that Hirsch rejects Brandt's interpretation on this point, he likewise rejects Brandt's theory that the Prytaneum in the play corresponds to the Academy, and, with that, he offers an earlier dating (the winter of 1838-1839) than Brandt. He holds that the Prytaneum is the stronghold of the Danish Hegelians. He likewise identifies Ole Wadt as Giødvad, Phrase as Martensen, and the chairman as Heiberg, but thinks that he cannot express an opinion on who was the model for von Skipjack. Furthermore, he holds that the play contains an account of an internal dispute in this Prytaneum, and he interprets this disagreement, which nevertheless did not lead to a complete split, as a dispute between the Danish right-wing Hegelians and left-wing Hegelians. Furthermore, Hirsch agrees with Brandt's interpretation of Harry Rushjob [Holla Hastværksen] as Orla Lehmann, whom, consequently, Kierkegaard should have presented as a kind of left Hegelian, according to Hirsch's opinion, but for which there is practically no basis in reality.

We must assume that the play was written after December 2, 1837, as Roos (p. 131) maintains, and most likely also after Martensen's introductory lectures. According to Hirsch's analysis, it was written in the winter of 1838-1839, while Brandt thinks that it could not have been written before July 1839. Hirsch takes the latter to be unlikely: Kierkegaard had considered dedicating the play to "the four crazy brothers in Claudius" (Hirsch refers to *Papirer*, I C 5, which is incorrect; it should be II B 5). On October 26, 1838, Kierkegaard made a reference (II A 279) to Claudius, whose works he had just acquired in an 1838 edition (Ktl. #1631-1632), and Hirsch maintains that beginning in April 1839 Kierkegaard was so occupied with other problems—his engagement to Regine Olsen and studying for his final examinations—that he would hardly have had either the time or inclination [*Sans*] for the particular issues covered in the play. Thus, in Hirsch's opinion, it must have been written shortly after Kierkegaard's first published book, *Af en endnu Levendes Papirer* [From the Papers of One Still Living], which appeared on September 7, 1838.

Now there is the question of when the draft of the play was written down, and a second question of when the events occurred that apparently provided the actual background. There is no difficulty in assuming a shorter or longer interval, and what furnishes the background for the first scenes can, indeed, in the sphere of reality have taken place considerably earlier than what is sketched in the succeeding scenes.

If the identification of Echo with Hertz is correct, and if the Prytaneum is a caricature—evidently quite mild—of the actual Academy, then the date of composition can hardly be more definitely fixed than sometime after July 1839, when Hertz's *Stemninger og Tilstande* appeared, and prior to the summer of 1840. In this respect Brandt is correct. But Hirsch's suggestion that after April 1839 Kierkegaard was so occupied with other things and other problems that he could hardly have given thought to the problems contained in the draft of the play, and that consequently it must have been written earlier, does not have particular weight. In the first place, Hirsch has not taken into account the dimensions of this draft. If we bear in mind Kierkegaard's known rate of speed in working, we see that the whole thing could have been written in only a few days. In the second place, there is abundant evidence to show that Kierkegaard was often occupied by several—and far greater and more serious—problems at the same time. The story of his engagement to Regine Olsen and the dissertation, the *Edifying Discourses* and the contemporaneous extensive pseudonymous Authorship, the religious crisis at Easter in 1848, and the simultaneous aesthetical writing on Mrs. Heiberg as an actress, all show clearly that Kierkegaard could simultaneously master the most diverse topics and problems. Even though it is quite true that he was chiefly concerned with other matters beginning with the spring of 1839, neither internal nor external evidence decisively argues against such

a late date of composition as after July 1839, while the reasons
adduced by Brandt for this *terminus a quo* retain their weight.

The second question, on the actual background, no doubt has
greater topical interest. Here also Brandt has clarified a great deal
of the material, and only a single observation of Hirsch, namely on
the conflict between the right-wing and the left-wing Hegelians,
requires attention here.

It is well known that on his lengthy study tour of foreign universities (October 1834-autumn 1836) Martensen became acquainted
with this controversy, and he made some comments on it in his
introductory lectures. But he was not the only one to brief Danish
academicians on this topic. Already in 1836, the two slightly older
Danish theology professors Clausen and Hohlenberg in their important *Tidsskrift for Udenlandsk Theologisk Litteratur* [Journal of
Foreign Theological Literature] provided a translation of the chief
passages of Strauss's *Das Leben Jesu*, together with some critical
interjections against the author's left Hegelian viewpoints. The following year the Faculty of Theology at the University of Copenhagen sponsored a prize essay competition on the topic, which was
timely in this connection, and likewise in 1837 the above periodical
provided an extract from F. C. Baur's *Das christliche des Platonismus*. This book soon became quite important for Kierkegaard,
when he worked on his dissertation *On the Concept of Irony with
Constant Reference to Socrates*. Poul Møller published, also in 1837,
his last major treatise *Om Muligheden af Beviser for Menneskets
Udødelighed* [On the Possibility of Proofs of Human Immortality].
This work also took up an important issue, a point on which the
right-wing and left-wing Hegelians diverged.

We can also recall that H. N. Clausen's quite reliable *Optegnelser
om mit Levneds og min Tids Historie* [Reminiscences of the Story
of My Life and Times] (1877) recounts that:

> that genial lecture [i.e. Martensen's] here became supported by
> the novelty of the thing; for, while importantly modified, more
> than the Hegelian garb would make it appear, yet it could not
> be other than that the content of Christian Revelation came to
> be regarded as something hitherto unknown and unheard of,
> and the new sort of Gospel evoked the greatest interest among
> the students . . . many thought that by putting on a fake specu-
> lative costume they would be swiftly and easily raised to the
> pinnacle of knowledge where the laborious acquisition of posi-

tive cognitive skills becomes superfluous. It was understandable and easily explained that during these years interest in exegetical studies declined more and more while the majority of the students found a crude substitute in the philosophical terminology which played such a major role in the Hegelian schools. 'The popular philosophy of the age' soon became—to use a Kierkegaardian term,—'the philosophy of the youth of the time.'[ii] They found youthful pleasure in this fanfare, which itself became the object of some admiration when they heard themselves rattling around like empty barrels (pp. 211-213).

Although this account was written long after the events it describes, it can be substantiated in many ways. In this connection, a single clarification furnished[21] by Vilhelm Rode, is of interest, *viz.*:

This means that the members of the Academy, as well as others, were vulnerable to criticism. Just at the beginning of the Association, a major philosophical life emerged at the University; this indeed brought much good and much intellectual excitement with it, but then many contented themselves with a sort of philosophical shell, and many—particularly among the theologians—immersed themselves in Hegel, or more accurately: Hegelian jargon, to the degree that it was not always easy for laymen to understand them. Then these tendencies met their deserved opposition in the Academy itself, and declined rather swiftly among most of them after they were sufficiently ridiculed in speech, songs, nonsense papers, comedies, and wherever else they could be attacked.

On the basis of these clarifications, it is not unlikely, then, that Kierkegaard's draft was in fact intended by him to be a student comedy, and, according to what has been said, it fitted very well into the whole situation at the time. Yet obviously we cannot exclude the possibility that Kierkegaard freely both used [actual events and persons] and even supplemented a good deal [in his draft], without our being able, 125-130 years later, to clarify whether every detail is pure poetry or whether it has a concrete background

[ii] These two expressions involve a play on words in Danish which cannot be reproduced in English.

[21] "Bidrag til den danske Studenterforenings Historie" [Contribution to the History of the Danish Student Association] in *Nordisk Universitets-Tidsskrift* (1854), 142-143.

in historical reality. But in general, it holds true that the more we work with Kierkegaard, the more reality comes to light.

Kierkegaard had thought of calling his play "The All-Embracing Debate of All against All, or: the Crazier the Better, From the Papers of One Still Living Published Contrary to his Will by S. Kierkegaard" (*Papirer*, II B 3), the same title—in part—used for his first published book. This draft for the title makes it certainly unlikely that the date of composition can be placed as late as might otherwise be reasonable, since Kierkegaard can scarcely be thought to have wanted to employ the same title for two so different manuscripts. Since, however, the whole draft, including the different title pages (especially toward the end), is quite roughly developed, almost only sketched, its whole tendency is so definitely marked, moreover, that it seems probable that Kierkegaard had already made the first entries sometime after Martensen's introductory lectures had begun, then left the whole thing aside for a while before he took it up again and continued the work. It is, then, hardly possible to arrive at complete assurance on the question of dating. Kierkegaard used the same kind of paper for the whole manuscript and his handwriting is the same, quite neat throughout, so we can not utilize external criteria.

We may now attempt to answer the most important question here, namely, concerning the chief character Willibald and his attitude toward Hegelianism and its Danish representatives. Jensenius (pp. 71-72, note 14) has suggested a solution in these words:

> When Willibald comes to the Prytaneum, happy at being liberated from the life to which he had previously been enslaved, it is surely Kierkegaard who has turned expectantly from the aesthetic-despairing life (the romantic) to Hegel's philosophy (obviously now [in retrospect] seen with irony by Kierkegaard). . . .

This interpretation contains something that is quite important on the whole, but it lacks one crucial aspect.

In the first scene, which is quite fully developed, Willibald, i.e. Kierkegaard, is the despairing romantic who has fled from the aesthetic party to the solitude in which he falls into thoughts of suicide. Just as he fled from the party, here he tries to escape from himself. The attempt is impeded by the troublesome friend from whom he also flees "in hopes yet once more of escaping friends"

(*Papirer*, II B 13, p. 293). The attempted flight comes to naught, for
—as it is said—:

> In confusion he had run into a man who, as he now discovered,
> was strolling along immersed in conversation with two others.
> After having made his apology, he got the response that he
> need not have made any apology; for he was a great sinner as
> he well knew, and that should only make him happy, if the
> good fortune might befall him to suffer something for the sake
> of Christ.

He also flees from these three revivalist Christians. As the synopsis
above indicates, it is probable that the three persons spoken of here
are modeled on Kierkegaard's elder brother, the later Bishop P. C.
Kierkegaard, and his two friends, A. G. Rudelbach and J. C. Lindberg. Willibald also flees from the Grundtvigians—and takes refuge
among the Hegelians in the second act of the play.

Now it must be noted that Kierkegaard's description of the
Hegelians is a caricature, which clearly shows Kierkegaard's attitude toward their whole movement. But at the end of the play there
is no indication—as perhaps we might have expected in conjunction
with the play's otherwise pervasive flight motif—that the main character flees from the Hegelians, in spite of the superciliously ironical
attitude he has just shown. He remains with them—in the play.
Kierkegaard could hardly have written just this play were he not
actually an outsider who from a position other than that of the
Hegelians could pour out all his irony over them.

What was Kierkegaard's own position when he wrote his little
draft for a play? It was not entirely the same as his beloved teacher
Poul Møller adopted toward the end of his life and which Kierkegaard has sketched in an immortal note in *Concluding Unscientific
Postscript* (p. 34),

> it was remarkable that while everyone was Hegelian, P. M.
> judged quite otherwise, that at first [and] for a long time he
> spoke of Hegel almost indignantly until the sound humorous
> nature which was in him taught him to smile especially at
> Hegelianism, or, to recall P. M. still more accurately, to laugh
> quite heartily at them. For who has been enamored of P. M.
> and forgotten his humor; who has admired him and forgotten
> his soundness, who has known him and forgotten his laughter,

which did one good even when it was not entirely clear what he was laughing at; for his distraction was sometimes confusing.

Kierkegaard's own position at this time (1839-1840) was not entirely the same as that of Poul Møller. It was not fully clarified, except in the negative sense in the ridiculing of Hegelianism; but it was along the same lines as Poul Møller's as evidenced by the Journal entries cited above.

Kierkegaard's first encounter with Hegelianism as a student immediately produced a severely critical reaction in him. But since it came from such a complicated poetic nature as his, he did not set out to compose a lengthy prose refutation. With more secure instinct he chose another and more effective literary form than the academic treatise, namely, that of the play.

5. OTHER SOURCES FROM THIS PERIOD

Finally, if we turn our attention to the other sources extant from this period, it appears that they are mainly indirect contributions to the elucidation of the chief question of this investigation.

The entries II C 4-10 are purely exegetical, related to Kierkegaard's preparation for his examinations, and they contain—and this is worth noting in the present context—no indication that the exegetes Kierkegaard heard and read[22] had given him any impression of the then new viewpoints, redolent of Hegelian speculation, which were manifesting themselves in Germany with such names as Baur and Strauss as the most important.

While Kierkegaard's exegetical work, as well as his reading of church history had been a required chore,[jj] which nevertheless was reflected later on in the Authorship, his concern with systematic theology, and within that area dogmatics (and the history of dogma) especially and the philosophy of religion, was significant and went considerably beyond the requirements for his examinations.

Thus in December 1838 Kierkegaard was very much occupied

---

[22] He heard and read Clausen, Hohlenberg, and Scharling. He read the chiefly conservative commentaries of Olshausen, Tholuck, Rückert, and de Wette, while as a lexical aid he adhered to Bretschneider's noted work.

[jj] His lack of interest in these areas during the time under consideration was only temporary. Over the course of subsequent years his interest particularly in the forms and history of religious life grew quite strong.

with J. A. Möhler's *Athanasius* (*Papirer*, II C 29-31),[kk] and he particularly focused his attention on Möhler's not entirely impartial
accounts of the history of dogma concerning the early controversies
over Christology.[23] He also acquired F. C. Baur's great work in the
history of dogma published in 1838, *Die christliche Lehre von Versöhnung in ihrer geschichtlichen Entwicklung von der ältesten Zeit
bis auf die neueste* and made short notes while reading it, but only
concerning Baur's section on John Scotus Eriugena,[ll] the Hegel of
the early Middle Ages, precisely on the question that both at the
moment and later seriously concerned him (Christological issues,
especially the relation between the divine and the human, and the
meaning of the Passion and Death of Christ). In the addenda to his
earlier notes on Clausen's dogmatic lectures (I C 19), and which are
found in numbers II C 34, 35 and 36,[mm] there are various materials
in biblical theology and the history of dogma; but nothing there
indicates that Clausen's lectures induced him to tackle Hegel or
Hegelian theologians—which we should not expect either. Both in
his large work *Det Nye Testaments Hermeneutik*, 1840 (e.g., pp.
370ff.) and in his popular *Udvikling af de christelige Hovedlær-
domme* [Exposition of the Chief Christian Doctrines] (publ. 1844,
based on the lectures of the fall term 1841) Clausen explicitly dissociated himself from Hegelian speculation.[24] In treating the rela-

[kk] Kierkegaard's brief comments on his reading of Johan Adam Möhler's
Athanasius der Grosse und die Kirche seiner Zeit, I-II (Mainz, 1827), will be
found in vol. II of the *Papirer*. The text of his summary (in Danish) of this
work will be found in vol. XIII. Cf. Hong, V, #5357.

[23] H. Roos, in *Søren Kierkegaard and Catholicism*, trans. Richard M.
Brackett (Westminster, Maryland: The Newman Press, 1954), pp. xv-xviii,
has noted that in November 1837 Kierkegaard had read the lengthy selections
in translation from Möhler's *Symbolik*, brought out in Clausen and Hohlenberg's *Tidsskrift for udenlandsk teologisk Litteratur* in 1834. It must be
noted that Roos inadvertently takes this extract to be "a review" and thus
mistakenly claims that Kierkegaard seems not to have read this major work
of Möhler. In any case, the cited extract (*Symbolik*, pp. 108-208) contains
Möhler's treatment of "the most important and most disputed dogmas" (introductory comments on the translation).

[ll] On Eriugena (A.D. 810-877) cf. Bryar and Stengren, *The Rebirth of
Learning* (New York: Putnam, 1968), pp. 142-146.

[mm] II C 34, Hong, I, #36; II C 36, Hong, V, #5419. Portions of II C 34
will be found in the *Papirer*, vol. II, the remainder, and the full text of II
C 36, will be found in Vol. XIII. II C 35 will be found with I C 19 in
vol. XII.

[24] In the first book, p. 364ff, and in the latter book, especially p. 88ff, the
rejection is particularly sharply formulated.

tion between revelation and reason, Clausen, in terminology probably determined by that of Baur in *Die Christliche Gnosis oder die
christliche Religionsphilosophie in ihrer geschichtlichen Entwicklung* (1835), describes Hegelianism as a modern elaboration of
Gnosticism which betrays Christianity just as it pretends to defend
it and its truth, and Clausen maintains (just as, for example, Sibbern had in the article discussed above) that there is an unbroken
line from Hegel to left-wing Hegelianism.

Further, we may mention a few mutually quite dissimilar writings which from the end of July until the beginning of November
1838 Kierkegaard was deeply involved with.

After having finished Schaller's book (discussed *supra*) Kierkegaard set to work on the Schleiermacher disciple Karl Heinrich
Sack's *Christliche Polemik*, a companion piece to his previously
published apologetics, which Kierkegaard also owned (Ktl. 755 and
756). Kierkegaard's summaries of certain sections of this highly
structured work, a kind of pathology of Christianity, in which the
author describes and rejects one after the other naturalism, my-
thologism, literalism, ergism, orthodoxism, spiritualism, rationalism,
gnosticism, separatism, mysticism, pietism, theocratism, hierarchism,
and Caesaropapism, are particularly concise, but as in the case of
Schaller's correct enough. Kierkegaard quite rapidly became somewhat disappointed while reading and only found it worth taking
the trouble to express his limited approval of Sack's presentation of
indifferentism and gnosticism (II C 60).[nn]

The next work Kierkegaard read in the fall of 1838 was, like
Sack's, a textbook, namely, Rosenkranz's *Encyklopädie der theo-
logischen Wissenschaften* (1831, Ktl. 35), a Hegelian counterpart to
Schleiermacher's *Kurze Darstellung des theologischen Studiums*
[Short Exposition of Theological Studies].

Rosenkranz's well-disposed and clearly written work, divided into
the main sections, speculative, historical, and practical theology (an
arrangement that is not accidental for the author),[25] Kierkegaard

[nn] Hong, V, #5350. Again, portions of this entry are in vol. II of the
Papirer, and the rest will be found in vol. XIII.

[25] "Speculative theology developed the idea of the Christian religion as the
absolute religion as the knowledge of which, independent of the appearance
of the essence, in and for itself proceeds from the idea itself and is to that
degree the absolute self-knowledge of religion," while "Historical theology
is the knowledge which in space and time in finiteness relinquished the
idea of absolute religion; it grasps the essence in its appearance as empirically
given with the accidentally commingled fact," and "Practical theology is the

did not excerpt and summarize with very great attention beyond the three main sections. From the first, on speculative theology, he did not note much, and nothing of what was most characteristic of Rosenkranz as a Hegelian, his constant mediations and "abrogations" [*Ophævelser: Aufhebungen*] does Kierkegaard seem to have paid attention to in any considerable degree. Only the section (pp. 66ff.)[oo] on "the evil" did he summarize. From the second main section, on historical theology (pp. 103-329), Kierkegaard noted down considerably more, in the main with the result that he obtained an overall view of the distinctive features of the traditional theological disciplines and their mutual connections, followed by a number of notes on information and divisions of periods within the area of Church history proper. From the third and last main section, on practical theology, Kierkegaard only repeated a few definitions and noted the names of the various disciplines.

The most remarkable thing about this reading is the high degree to which Kierkegaard has confined himself to a simple summary of opinions and facts; only rarely does he manifest his appreciation or disapproval. We must assume that it was mainly in connection with the forthcoming examinations that Kierkegaard devoted himself to the study of this work. In a draft of a letter to Emil Boesen,[26] probably from the summer of 1838, he writes: "what is more unlikely than an *homme de lettres* who studies for a final university examination?" That was his own situation, but indeed described only from one aspect, since what he did not say, and perhaps did not realize at the time was that the studies required at the close of the 1830s in no small degree influenced his outlook and problematic especially in the first period of the Authorship. Kierkegaard scholarship has by and large been concerned with his particular background and interests, the unique atmosphere of his childhood home, "the earthquake," the story of the engagement, and other standard topics; but the general principles that he shared with contemporary students also have their significance which should neither be overemphasized nor underestimated.

Nor do the letters from this period contain anything of importance in this context, and his Petition for Examination (*Breve og*

knowledge of the form, in which absolute religion immediately exists, and in whose dialetical explication it has its individual vitality . . ." (p. xxxiv).

[oo] Kierkegaard's summary of this will be found in the *Papirer*, vol. XIII, p. 185.

[26] *Breve og Aktstykker,* #8.

Aktstykker, #XI) is noteworthy only for the fact that it indicates that during this period he entirely ceased studying theology in order to study philosophy. As might be expected, Professor Engelstoft's report on the examination (*Breve og Aktstykker*, #XII) contains nothing other than the traditional topics.

6. THE PERIOD FROM JULY 3, 1840, TO SEPTEMBER 29, 1841

In the time between the completion of the final examinations in theology and the defense of the Master's thesis *On the Concept of Irony*, Kierkegaard was chiefly occupied with three different things, namely, the engagement, the Pastoral Seminary, and the intensive work on the manuscript of *On the Concept of Irony*, which was submitted at the beginning of June, 1841,[27] accepted July 16, printed September 16, and defended September 29.

Relatively few of the great many entries from this period (III A 1-146, 210-226, together with III B 1 and III C 1-25) have direct relation to the topic here.

The first book Kierkegaard tackled after his examinations was the later famous A. P. Adler's quite new *Den isolerede Subjectivitet i dens vigtigste Skikkelser* [Isolated Subjectivity in its Most Important Forms] (defended June 24, 1840), which provided the occasion for a few critical remarks (III A 1 and 11).[pp]

Adler's thought process begins as follows: Thought is born with man, just as is the body and the outer nature, being. Originally there is no opposition between thought and being, but a relation of interdependence, and "a thought abstracted from being is a nonentity, a vacuity" (p. 2). On the other hand, being has thought as its necessary presupposition, since being without thought would only be chaos.

Philosophy begins with thought, which takes a stand against being and begins with doubt, which negates and annihilates everything—so as subsequently to give birth to it anew (p. 4). Philosophy can doubt about everything except "the general concept of being," which thus is the necessary and ultimate point of departure for philosophy. The philosophy that takes thought to be the principle of existence is one-sided and subjective, and therefore existence

---

[27] Sibbern reports this in his account of June 16, 1841, printed in *Kirkehistoriske Samlinger*, 6th ser., vol. VI (1949), 291.

[pp] Hong, II #1587; III, #3281.

must be simultaneously maintained to be the principle of thought, so that philosophy becomes subjective-objective (p. 6), and Adler finds the characteristic of "modern philosophy," i.e., Hegel's, to be that it is not only a realm of thought, but also one of reality. The harmonious relation between thought and being thus assumes, Adler maintains, various forms in the different stages from that of nature to that of the revealed religion. In nature there is no conflict between thought and being (p. 7), nor is there in the animal world, where instinct represents the categories of thinking. On the lowest human level there is also an immediate unity, where thought and experience work together, while Adler finds an example of their detachment from each other in Indian philosophy. Taken unilaterally, thought and experience are empty abstractions (p. 11), and the truth consists in the fact that one is given with the other and they cannot be separated. Invoking Hegel, Adler maintains that this point of view is one of the most essential fruits of modern philosophy, and he maintains further that just as little as thought and being can be separated in reality, just so little can they be separated in consciousness, they are "correlates" (p. 13). The thought and being of the whole universe has its unity in the concept; but this unity is still only an ideal unity, it is the subjective aspect of the truth and of the world spirit, wherefore it negates itself from ideal, subjective unity to real, independent unity, i.e., to Idea (p. 16), which happens through reality and the phenomenon, i.e., the manifoldness of the world, historical reality, the particulars, whereupon the concept will rediscover itself in the Idea's unity of subjectivity and objectivity. Isolated, objectivity produces pantheism and pancosmism (p. 19), while an isolation of subjectivity results in the positions that the rest of the treatise describes and illustrates with examples largely drawn from Hegel. Just as subjectivity is partly a detail of being, partly a detail of thought, partly both in the form of the particular, of the consciousness, thus it is said (p. 25) that the isolated subjectivity is partly an isolated (abstract-infinite) subjectivity with respect to being, partly an isolated subjectivity with respect to thought, partly an isolated subjectivity with respect to both (the consciousness).

It cannot be said with certainty whether Kierkegaard had read Adler's book all the way through; but it is not likely. The two entries cited are linked only with the exposition of Adler summarized here, and Kierkegaard's criticism in the first entry is directed against Adler's, and therewith the Hegelians', neglect of the problem of the relation between metaphysical reality and historical reality as well as their failure to understand that historical reality is a unity of the metaphysical (here = the necessary) and the accidental, thus failing to understand that the task of the individual, of the personality is to make itself aware of both its "eternal validity" and its "accidental finitude" together with realizing its individual task precisely in finitude and not in a fantastic place outside of it. Here Kierkegaard raises questions that he takes up for more ample response later in the Authorship.

In the second critical note against Adler (III A 11), written a couple of weeks after the first, Kierkegaard mentions something else, namely the language, which "the philosophers," i.e., the Hegelians, have overlooked in their talk about presuppositionless thought, which Adler also adopts by way of introduction—which he obviously only thinks is free of prejudice. Perhaps, as the editors indicate in their note, Kierkegaard was also thinking of Heiberg's *Det logiske System*, the first (and last) twenty-three paragraphs of which were published in *Perseus*, #2, which appeared in August 1838 and in which Heiberg gives his interpretation of philosophy's absolute beginning. This is likewise a question Kierkegaard takes up for critical treatment in the Authorship, especially in the *Postscript*.

Probably with Martensen's prolegomena (emphasizing the history of philosophy) to speculative dogmatics in mind, in the entry III A 3[qq] (July 5, 1840), with explicit reference to the entry (II C 55)[rr] concerning Schaller discussed *supra*, Kierkegaard repeats his earlier (August 1838) objection to modern philosophy and to that of Hegel in particular. In the later entry he says of modern philosophy that it is "really only . . . an introduction to making it possible to philosophize." It does not go into a genuine "anthropological contemplation," which means, as it is developed more precisely in the next entry, III A 4,[ss] written on the same day, that it has not undertaken a responsible consideration of the question of what mankind's sinfulness means as a possible obstacle for the recovery of the original unity between the divine and the human. The doubt in speculative philosophy of religion is not taken to be an important obstacle, only as a necessary transitional link in the recovery of the original unity, and therefore the doubt is not radical but basically harmless. Yet,

[qq] Hong, I, #37.
[rr] Hong, III, #3261.
[ss] Hong, I, #773.

Kierkegaard says, there must be raised not an impersonal, but an existential doubt, even a passionate concern about the condition on which not knowledge's, but faith's unity between the divine and the human shall be obtained, when sin is taken seriously. With this, Kierkegaard suggests that there is not any continuous transition from mankind's actual sinful stage to that of Faith but, on the contrary, a passionate transition (or as he calls it later), a leap.

Again we see here in embryo a fundamental incompatibility between Kierkegaard and Hegelian thought, anticipations of the later thoroughgoing clash, both the indirect and the direct attack on Hegel and his adherents, with its pointing out of inconsistencies and of its failure to consider relevant questions.

In the following entry (III A 5),[tt] which like the others discussed here was written during the composition of *On the Concept of Irony*, we get the first striking comparison of the Platonic teaching on recollection (anamnesis) as the source of knowledge and the Hegelian (Heibergian) theory of philosophy as a reflection on what is present in the consciousness, as a consequence of which self-knowledge properly is knowledge of God, as Heiberg maintained in his Prospectus (1833). Even if Kierkegaard had objections, he does not yet say that self-knowledge seen from the Christian perspective is not knowledge of God but the awareness of sin. He refers to his earlier entries, from 1838 (II A 301, 302, 523-528)[uu] which are related to Sibbern's *Forelæsninger over Christendomsphilosophie.*

On the same day (July 10, 1840) an entry occurs (III A 6)[vv] in which Kierkegaard expresses his misgivings about Hegel's unsympathetic attitude toward the edifying. There is no reference to any definite passage, rather it is said that Hegel's hate for the edifying "emerges everywhere." The observation is not incorrect, although somewhat exaggerated and universalized. Hegel's clearest, most direct statement on the topic is found in his letter dated August 2, 1816 to Fr. von Raumer *Ueber den Vortrag der Philosophie auf Universitäten* [About Lectures on Philosophy in the University] (S. W. Jubilaumsäusgabe, III, 317ff.), in which he speaks very critically of Franz von Baader's and especially Fr. Schlegel's way of lecturing on philosophy: they do it more like propagandists and revivalists than like philosophers. This does not mean, however, any total rejection on the part of Hegel of the "edifying" function of

[tt] Hong, II, #2274.
[uu] Hong, II, #2257, 2258, 2266-2271.
[vv] Hong, II, #1588.

philosophy: "I mentioned just now the edification, which is often expected from philosophy; I should think also that if youth are instructed, it is never for edification. But they have to satisfy a need related to it. . . ." In other places too, as for example in the programmatic preface to the *Phenomenology of the Spirit*, where Hegel rejects Schelling and generally refines his position in relation to other contemporary thinkers, and in the large critical treatise on Kant, Jacobi, and Fichte (*Glauben und Wissen*, S. W. Jubiläumsausgabe, I, 277-433) could have given Kierkegaard cause for his statement, which—characteristically enough—is accompanied by a rejoinder, which points to the final words in the "Ultimatum" in *Either/Or* (II, 356), to the *Edifying Discourses* in the first period of the Authorship, and to the significant comment IV A 42[ww] (February 1843). The rejoinder says significantly that the edifying is "the finite spirit's Amen," i.e., man's submission to the truth about it, and that is "an aspect of knowledge [*Erkjendelsen*] which ought not to be overlooked," and it probably means either that here Kierkegaard finds himself close to Baader's (and Martensen's) position, which is characterized by the Anselmian *credo ut intelligam*, or that, as in the "Ultimatum," as against God man is always in the wrong.

Kierkegaard obviously had books by and about Hegel with him on his trip to Jutland (July 19-August 6, 1840). The brief comment (III A 34)[xx] on Hegel as a parenthesis in Schelling, which we only wait to be closed, indicates an awareness of the expectations that were initially entertained for Schelling's positive philosophy (which Martensen had heard a bit of, cf. *supra*, chapter III, section 4), and which Kierkegaard also shared for a while. An unusual acknowledgement of Hegel on the part of Kierkegaard must also be noted. It is III A 37,[yy] where it is said that Hegel, as distinct from earlier philosophers shows "that language has thought immanent in itself." It is impossible to establish with certainty which passage in Hegel Kierkegaard was thinking of when he wrote this comment. The closest we can come to suggesting a source is to assume that Kierkegaard had been reading the first part of the *Encyclopedia of the Philosophical Sciences* (in the section on the "Preliminary Notion" of logic),[zz] where it is said, in part, that "language is the work of thought: . . . Logic is the study of thought pure and simple, or of

[ww] Hong, IV, #4847.   [xx] Hong, II, #1589.   [yy] Hong, II, #1590.

[zz] *The Logic of Hegel* (from *The Encyclopedia of the Philosophical Sciences*) trans. by William Wallace (Oxford: The Clarendon Press, 1892). The quoted passages which follow are from pp. 38, 49, 50f.

the pure thought-forms. . . . Logic is the all-animating spirit of all the sciences, and its categories the spiritual hierarchy. They are the heart and centre of things: and yet they are always on our lips. . . . Language is the main depository of these types of thought. . . ."[28]

Finally we should discuss briefly a series of entries which, without direct relation to Hegel, show how Kierkegaard's independent interpretation of various central topics in the philosophy of religion got their provisional formulation and thus contribute further to understanding how he took an unsympathetic attitude toward Hegel himself as well as toward the Hegelians.

In *Papirer*, III A 39,[aaa] also from the trip to Jutland, Kierkegaard repeats his earlier reflections on the relation between doubt-knowledge on the one hand and consciousness of sin-assurance of the forgiveness of sin on the other hand.[29] Just as in III A 3, it is maintained that there is no parallel between the two situations (such as the Hegelian position would maintain): knowledge emerges from doubt "with an inner consistency," i.e., there is a continuous transition, whereas assurance of forgiveness of sin cannot result as a matter of course from consciousness of sin. Another difference between the two relations is that whereas doubt must be understood as the result of an act of the will on the part of man (one can decide to doubt, as Descartes did by making doubt his one methodical principle, or one can decide not to doubt), consciousness of sin is an "objective act," i.e., not caused by man himself, not proceeding from man alone, but from God in the consciousness. A third difference is that whereas knowledge (speculatively understood) does not have a necessary connection with anything historical, awareness of the forgiveness of sin is inseparably linked with something definitely historical, namely "the whole manifestation of Christ." The entry points toward *Philosophical Fragments* and *The Concept of Dread* with their sharp distinctions between the pairs of concepts doubt-knowledge and despair (= consciousness of sin in the entry here)-faith, and the incompatibility with the Speculative philosophy of religion is insurmountable.

A slightly later entry (III A 48),[bbb] which deals with the same

[28] Kierkegaard's and Hegel's theories of language will not be discussed further here. Lars Bejerholm treats them thoroughly in his *Meddelelsens Dialektik* [Dialectic of Communication] (1962), esp. pp. 28-119.

[aaa] Hong, II, #1100.

[29] Cf. II A 63 [Hong, IV, #3994]; III A 3 [I, #37], together with III A 215, 216 [II, #1201, 1101] (loose *Papirer* from 1840), as well as others.

[bbb] Hong, II, #1240.

topics as III A 11,[ccc] polemically asserts against the Hegelians, who would begin philosophy without presuppositions, that philosophy cannot begin without a presupposition, indeed it plainly should begin with one. In a later entry, III A 107,[ddd] written while he was reading K. F. Hermann's *Geschichte und System der Platonischen Philosophie*, which plays a not insignificant role in *On the Concept of Irony*, Kierkegaard repeats (from Hermann) a quote from Aristotle (I Metaphysics, 2 982b 10-20) in which it is held that philosophy begins with wonder, which Kierkegaard finds to be a positive point of departure in contrast with the "modern" claim that philosophy begins with doubt.

There is also in this entry a line leading back to Kierkegaard's concern with the figure of Faust as the doubter personified, and pointing forward to the draft of *Johannes Climacus, or De omnibus dubitandum est*, while contemporary skeptics are sharply criticized for never having seriously doubted, so that their so-called doubt is "pandering," a frivolous way of speaking.

As a motto for the whole subsequent Authorship in the area of the philosophy of religion up to and including the *Postscript*, Kierkegaard then says briefly and to the point in the following entry (III A 108)[eee] that "Philosophy's Idea is mediation—Christianity's [is] the paradox," which implies that speculative philosophy, for that is what is meant here, is incompatible with Christianity, and that its attempt to understand Christianity by incorporating it into the system is a mistake.

As with the previously discussed entries a line also leads back from this one to II A 102 and 608, III A 211 (June 14, 1840),[fff] where Kierkegaard still used the expression "a speculative Christian theory of knowledge" in a positive sense, which he soon stopped.

Then we may mention the entry (III A 118),[ggg] the interpretation of which, partly because of Kierkegaard's distinctive terminology, has been disputed.[30] We shall not take a stand here on the question

[ccc] Hong, III, #3281.

[ddd] Hong, III, #3284.

[eee] Hong, III, #3072.

[fff] Hong, II, #1690, 1711, 2277.

[ggg] Hong, IV, #4004.

[30] See Valter Lindström, *Stadiernas teologi* [Theology of the Stages] (1943), 351-356, with references to Heinrich Barth's article "Kierkegaard, der Denker" (in *Zwischen den Zeiten*, 1926), to Herman Diem's *Philosophie und Christentum bei Sören Kierkegaard* (1929), and last but not least Hirsch's *Kierkegaard-Studien*.

of whether Kierkegaard was orthodox or not in his adherence to synergism (in the sense of responsibility) as a Christian principle. It should only be pointed out that the assertion at the end of the entry that there is in sin an element of freedom is in opposition to the Hegelian view, according to which it appears with necessity. The Fall, Hegel says, is "the eternal, necessary history of mankind" (*Lectures on the Philosophy of Religion*, I, 276).

A very important expression of Kierkegaard's desire not to be considered a Hegelian is found in the draft III B 1[hhh] directed against H. C. Andersen's *En Comedie i det Grønne* [A Comedy in the Garden]. In this play Andersen retaliated against Kierkegaard's *Af en endnu Levendes Papirer* by putting "in the mouth of one of the characters a whole long tirade from my [SK] little piece." This character, played by Phister, "should now be a twaddling Hegelian," which Kierkegaard considers a stupid remark by Andersen, "who has monopolized negative ownership of all philosophy and of all higher scholarship." Andersen has simply not grasped the concept of what a Hegelian is as a type; thus Kierkegaard takes the opportunity to explain what he understands by a Hegelian: it may be either a man who has "comprehended this theory's view of the world, assimilated it, found rest in it, and now with a certain true pride [can say] of himself: I too have had the honor to serve under Hegel," or it may be a man who "fleetingly touched by this thought, has now been captivated by a conclusion he has not grasped." In neither of these two senses was Kierkegaard himself a Hegelian, but he sees it is a hopeless task to make Andersen realize that.

Several things in Kierkegaard's trial sermon in the Pastoral Seminary and the various literary exercises from his studies there (III C 1-25)[iii] point toward the "Ultimatum" in *Either/Or, Fear and Trembling* and the first *Edifying Discourses.*

7. Conclusion

With regard to the main problem of this investigation, it has been shown that during the whole period under consideration here Kierkegaard had had various forms of contact with Hegelianism, sufficient for him to adopt a not particularly penetrating nor detailed

[hhh] Unfortunately this delightful piece will not be included in Hong's edition of the *Journals and Papers.*

[iii] Most of these will be found in various volumes of Hong's *Journals and Papers.*

comprehensive position. When he wrote his first book, he had only a mediocre knowledge of Hegel himself. On the other hand, his own problems, attempts to resolve them, and attitudes, especially on the relation between Christianity and philosophy, as well as questions concerning the philosophy of religion in general, were so entirely different from those of Hegel and his followers that it would be a complete misrepresentation to describe him as a Hegelian. Rather he was an anti-Hegelian, just as Sibbern was, as Poul Møller became at the end, as Clausen was. The many extant, most often brief, notes from this period, as well as "The Battle Between the Old and the New Soap-Cellar" and excerpts and summaries from his reading, bear no evidence of any significant concern either with Hegel himself or with the views of the Hegelians and their attempt to employ the dialectical method. Kierkegaard was not particularly impressed with Hegelianism, on the contrary, he treated its adherents ironically and devoted neither enduring nor more penetrating attention to the whole matter at this time. That would come later.

CHAPTER V

On the Concept of Irony

1. THE PROBLEM

On the Concept of Irony is a most difficult work to study, so ambiguous, even equivocal is it on crucial points.[1] Like every investigator of Socrates, Kierkegaard had his difficulties in getting a clear focus on this Athenian sage. He explains it himself thus:

> If we say now that that which constituted the substantial in his [i.e., Socrates'] existence was irony . . . [and] if we postulate further that irony is a negative concept, then we easily see how difficult it becomes to fix an image of him, yes, it seems impossible or at least as hard as to depict an elf with a hat which makes him invisible (*On the Concept of Irony*, p. 50).

No less difficult is it for us, on similar and other grounds, to establish a definite, unequivocal interpretation of Kierkegaard's own position in this work. This is true both of his understanding of Socrates as ironist and of his evaluation of Socratic irony just as it is the case with his interpretation and judgment on romantic irony.

In *On the Concept of Irony*, Socrates is presented as the chief character, the object of the study; Fr. Schlegel, Tieck, and Solger as secondary characters. The decisive impulse both for a correct understanding and for evaluation of these thinkers' and poets' attitude toward life, their ironic point of view, came from Hegel; but from the way Kierkegaard stresses this, one gets "a little asthmatic doubt" about whether this is also meant seriously.

We can doubt a little the seriousness of Kierkegaard's assertions about Hegel's influence on his understanding and evaluation of irony in its two chief forms, when we have solid grounds for maintaining that, prior to publishing *On the Concept of Irony* Kierkegaard was not an adherent of Hegel's philosophy, and when we know that he began his genuine Authorship after (in *Either/*

---

[1] In a somewhat different form this chapter was published in *Tijdschrift voor Filosofie*, 1965, 521ff., but is repeated here for the sake of completeness.

Or) with a clash with Hegel. We can also, as several scholars and interpreters have done, doubt the correctness of Kierkegaard's self-proclaimed discipleship of Hegel in this book on the basis of the stream of moral and psychological reflections we find there and because we cannot imagine that such a shrewd genius as Kierkegaard could possibly have let himself be taken in by Hegel.

The question here is not what position toward Hegel Kierkegaard adopted before and after *On the Concept of Irony* but what directly and indirectly emerges from the book itself in all its subtlety.

As is generally known, the first—and larger—main part of Kierkegaard's dissertation aims at proving that Socrates' position was irony understood as infinite, absolute negativity. Thus he analyzes Socrates' personality, teaching, and fate and ends every point in the first, long chapter, "The Conception Made Possible," with a question: now what sort of thing is this? Let us call it irony. It is possibly irony. In the next chapter, "The Conception Made Actual," from a consideration of Socrates' "daimon" and of his conviction by the Athenians, Kierkegaard shows that Socrates' position was not only possibly but actually irony, and in the third chapter, "The Conception Made Necessary," he maintains that his notion of Socrates as an ironist is the only correct one. Socratic irony so understood is judged as "world-historically justified" (p. 288). In the second main portion of the dissertation, he wants to demonstrate that the irony of the romantics, the theoretical basis of which he maintains is Fichte's philosophy, was, unlike Socratic irony, not "in the service of the world-spirit," for, as he goes on to say, "It was not [as in the case of Socrates] a moment of the given reality that was to be negated and replaced with a new moment; but it was all historical reality that it negated so as to make room for a self-created reality" (p. 292). Romantic irony is then judged to be not only relatively but absolutely unjustified.[2]

We can, then, raise the same question as Kierkegaard: What sort of thing is this? It does indeed look like a Hegelian history of philosophy, philosophy of history, and ethics rolled into one. Possibly it is. Was the writer of *On the Concept of Irony* really a disciple of Hegel? Are we to believe that it is plainly necessary to classify

---

[2] It has not been deemed necessary to give a more ample summary here. P. Mesnard has done so in *Le vrai visage de Kierkegaard*, 1948, 117-180. The sketch here follows closely the one given by Himmelstrup in his *Terminologisk Ordbog* . . . (2nd ed., 1964), 104f., naturally because I do not think myself capable of giving a more apt one.

On the Concept of Irony, and perhaps even its author, the 28-year-old Candidate in Theology Severinus Aabye Kierkegaard, as Hegelian?[3]

To answer these questions, we can for the present experimentally disregard Kierkegaard's personal, private position and simply consider Kierkegaard's name on the title page a pseudonym that represents a particular point of view on the basis of which the book was written, a pseudonym that plays a role as a Hegelian historian of philosophy.[a]

What must be looked into first, then, is what this "Kierkegaard" actually knew of Hegel and what this knowledge meant for the development of *On the Concept of Irony* in its details and as a literary whole.

2. KIERKEGAARD'S KNOWLEDGE OF HEGEL IN *On the Concept of Irony*

In *On the Concept of Irony* Kierkegaard refers quite frequently to Hegel. Somewhat evenly distributed throughout the various sections of the work, but with the majority in the later sections, there are approximately thirty quotations and references, several closely connected, to Hegel's works. These *loci* may provide the basis for a determination of Kierkegaard's relation to Hegal *in toto* and in detail in this work.

Taking due note of what the topic of the work required, or at least made desirable, it is important to see which works of Hegel Kierkegaard used and which he left out of his discussion. Naturally we cannot, simply because nothing is said, conclude with certainty that the author did not know any other writings of Hegel beyond the ones he expressly employed. But since Kierkegaard almost always reacted to every stimulus from his reading or other type of information, it is reasonable to assume that during the composition

---

[3] As late as 1850 Kierkegaard wrote the following in his *Journal*: "Influenced as I was by Hegel and all that was fashionable, without sufficient maturity rightly to grasp the great, somewhere in my dissertation I have not been able to avoid presenting it as an imperfection in Socrates that he had no eye for the totality but saw the individual only numerically. Oh, I was a Hegelian fool, this is exactly a great proof of how great an ethician Socrates was." (*Papier*, X 3 A 477 [Hong, IV, #4281].)

[a] Lee M. Capel makes a similar suggestion in the notes (p. 357) to his translation of *On the Concept of Irony*. Prof. Thulstrup informs me that he discussed this point thoroughly with Capel when he studied in Copenhagen.

of *On the Concept of Irony* he did not concern himself with the writings of Hegel other than the ones he explicitly identifies.

Only a single book and a single article, which Hegel published himself, are identified and used by Kierkegaard, namely, *Philosophy of Right* and the long review of Solger's writings.

On the other hand, he used much more extensively Hegel's posthumously published lectures, *Philosophy of History, Fine Art* and *History of Philosophy*. In our own day these first editions of Hegel's lectures have been severely criticized for their unreliability, and rightly so. As an example of this we need only mention Johannes Hoffmeister's detailed account of the deficiencies in Michelet's edition of the *History of Philosophy*,[4] and in this connection it can be noted that in a few places Kierkegaard himself makes critical remarks about these first editions. Thus he says on the treatment of the Sophists in Michelet's edition of Hegel's *History of Philosophy*:

> The extensive treatment . . . is . . . so it seems to me, not always in harmony with itself and sometimes bears the character of a collection of scattered remarks, which often show a lack of subordination to the classification suggested by the divisions (p. 225, note).

Concerning the chapter on Socrates he says that:

> there is often so much brought together, that it is difficult to find the context (p. 246).

So in what way did Kierkegaard read these Hegel texts?

This question can be answered only by going through each of these works by itself and each passage used in them by itself.

The obvious sequence for taking these works up must be Hegel's own, as it appears from his *Encyclopedia of the Philosophical Sciences* (§§487-572),[b] i.e., the *Philosophy of Right* must come first,

---

[4] In the preface to Hoffmeister's edition of *System und Geschichte der Philosophie* (1944), pp. i-xliv. Cf. also Julius Stenzel's *Hegels Auffassung der griechischen Philosophie* (in his *Kleine Schriften zur griechischen Philosophie* [1956], p. 310), and K.H.E. de Jong in *Hegel und Plotin* (1916), p. 33; de Jong also directs attention, in a reference to O. Apelt's *Die Behandlung der Geschichte der Philosophie bei Fries und bei Hegel* (1912), to the fact that it was Fries, not Hegel who first wished to describe the history of philosophy as a developing system.

[b] English translation of the third part of the *Encyclopedia* under the title, Hegel's *Philosophy of Mind*, by William Wallace (Oxford: The Clarendon Press, 1894), pp. 106-181.

then the *Philosophy of History, Fine Art*, the review of Solger, and finally the *History of Philosophy*. It was these books, lectures, and articles that Kierkegaard demonstrably used either in whole or in part.

a. Kierkegaard's Use of Hegel's
Philosophy of Right

There are not many traces of direct use of Hegel's *Philosophy of Right* in *On the Concept of Irony*.

On page 189, Kierkegaard mentions Hegel's quite brief discussion of Socrates in the *Philosophy of Right* §279 (p. 184); but Kierkegaard does not mention that Hegel refers there to his discussion of Socrates in §138, where in a "Zusatz" it is said that Socrates "lived in the time of the corruption of the Athenian democracy; he sublimated the present, and retired within himself, there to seek the right and the good" (p. 255).

In the paragraph cited by Kierkegaard (§279 from the section on "the internal aspect of the constitution"), Hegel maintains that monarchy is the correct form of government:—"It is only as a person, the monarch, that the personality of the state is actual" (p. 182) —and the monarch has divine sovereignty. Hegel rejects the theory of the sovereignty of the people in favor of the monarchical. Thus when we must answer the question of how we begin to discover which person ought to be the monarch, then, Hegel says, we come to the origin of the need for oracles, daimons, and the like. It is in this connection that Socrates' daimon is identified by Hegel as "the beginning of self-knowing and thus of true freedom" (p. 184).

On page 248 Kierkegaard discusses, without providing any definite references, Hegel's renowned distinction between morality and ethics in the *Philosophy of Right*.

In the passage under discussion, Kierkegaard considers the question of the sense in which Socrates can be called the founder of morality. His answer is that Socrates "universalized subjectivity," and he employs mostly Hegelian categories both in his interpretation and in his evaluation.

Kierkegaard does not take account of the fact that Hegel's *Philosophy of Right* as a totality does not occupy a large place within the whole Hegelian system, and thus the uniquely Hegelian element does not receive full justice in Kierkegaard.

As is well known, within the context of the Hegelian system the *Philosophy of Right* is a description of the Objective Spirit, the world of freedom, in which the transindividual will becomes "in-and-for-itself free."[5] Its first expression is abstract, formal right, for which the discrete individual, a juridical person, is the subject of right. The external sphere of freedom of the subject of right derives from the concept of the thing as possession and property. The negation is thus the violation of, e.g., property rights through injustice, deceit, and crime. The negation is negated by punishment, through which right is restored. The relative opposition to the abstract right as the outer thus becomes morality as the inner, the disposition that wills the right; but morality can become immobilized and remain at the purpose alone, the pure intention and conscience as a simply formal relation to the good (§§129-141). If the conscience is not determined by something higher than itself, it determines itself purely subjectively and thereby becomes a form of the evil, a form that, according to Hegel, can appear as an individualistic ethics, or as moral hypocrisy, or as probabilism, or finally as the purely ironical life style, which places itself entirely beyond the moral. Finally, the higher unity of the two relative opposites, abstract right and morality, is then "the ethical," which contains both the objective and the subjective, in which freedom has become nature, and in which the Objective Spirit has obtained actuality, so that there is no room for subjective capriciousness. This higher unity, the ethical, unfolds itself in the family, civil society, and in the state as its highest expression, "the actuality of the ethical Ideal" (§257). Since every state by its very nature claims to be absolute, a possibility of conflict thus arises, in which results and verdicts are identical in world history, which Hegel treats in the next work: the *Philosophy of History*.

b. Kierkegard's Use of Hegel's
Lectures on the Philosophy of History

The first point at which Kierkegaard quotes from this work of Hegel is on page 189, midway into *On the Concept of Irony* in the first part of Chapter II, in which he discusses "The Daimon of Socrates," where Hegel's explanation of the daimonic in Socrates is quoted with approval.[c] It should be noted that Kierkegaard explicitly refers to the second edition of Hegel's work, produced by

---

[5] Cf. what was said earlier about Hegel's *Philosophy of Right* [*supra*, Chap. II, sect. 2].

[c] The passage quoted by Kierkegaard will be found in J. Sibree's translation of Hegel's *Philosophy of History* (New York: Dover Publications, 1956), pp. 269-270.

Eduard Gans and Karl Hegel, the preface of which is dated May 16, 1840. Thus the relevant chapter in Kierkegaard's thesis cannot, at the earliest, have been definitely composed until several weeks after this date, when this new edition of Hegel's work would have been available in the bookstores.[6] Immediately following this quotation from Hegel, Kierkegaard quotes Rötscher's similar description of Socrates in *Aristophanes und sein Zeitalter* (1827, p. 254), and then he quotes from Hegel's *Philosophy of Right* and *History of Philosophy*.

Kierkegaard's procedure is one in which he first considers the daimon of Socrates as a philological problem [*crux filologorum*], identifies what are in his judgment a few quite improbable interpretations of the phenomenon, then refers to the comment of the Schleiermacher disciple, Fr. Ast (*Platons Leben und Schriften*, 1816, p. 483) on the word "τὸ δαιμόνιον," disagrees with Ast's notion of the Socratic daimon as both restraining and prompting, prefers Plato as a source rather than Xenophon, and concludes with an interpretation of the daimon as an entirely abstract, admonishing factor, which in the final analysis only lets its voice be heard by Socrates and his friends in their quite private concerns. This interpretation is the one Kierkegaard presents in connection with Hegel and Rötscher, but it is worth noting that he does it in such a way as to place considerable emphasis on the negative function of the daimon and uses this interpretation as a key theme in his argument for his renowned thesis about Socrates as representative of negativity who only touches subjectivity in its full richness.

The next place where Kierkegaard quotes this work of Hegel is in a note (p. 223) in which an episode from *Mahabharata*, summarized by Hegel, is quoted. The expression Kierkegaard uses to show how he does not want to present Socrates is a superfluous adornment that demonstrates only that Kierkegaard had read, at least in part, the section on India in Hegel's *Philosophy of History* (p. 151).

The third and last place is of considerable importance. As background for "making necessary" the conception of Socrates as total ironist, Kierkegaard wishes to give a short description of the Sophists and of Athens in its period of intellectual decadence. In this description he first supports his position by reference to Rötscher's work and asserts that "the evil principle in the Greek

---

[6] Cf. Emanuel Hirsch's introduction to his translation *Über den Begriff der Ironie* (1961), pp. vii-xi, on the time of composition.

[city-]state was the capriciousness of finite subjectivity (i.e., un-justified subjectivity)" (p. 224), thus one of a random individual's haphazard private opinions and decisions, and this—for him un-justifiable—principle found expression among the Sophists. Before he goes on to develop how Socrates "must have been constituted" so as to be able to annihilate the reprehensible Sophists, he wishes to amplify his concept of them, and therefore he quotes in a note (which could mean that this is a later addition, since the references to Rötscher are given in the text) Hegel's abbreviated description of the Sophists in the *Philosophy of History* (pp. 268, 269; *On the Concept of Irony*, pp. 225f.), a description, we would have to agree with Kierkegaard, which is particularly apt and lucid. It is evident from his notes (SW, XVIII, 5-42) that Hegel's sources are Plato's *Protagoras* especially, and then, of course, the *Gorgias, Meno, Euthydemus,* and *Theaetetus,* as well as Diogenes Laertius and Sextus Empiricus.

While Kierkegaard quotes only these passages from Hegel's *Philosophy of History,* the question naturally arises whether, with agreement or rejection, he had in another way utilized this work as a whole, and thus whether its main lines of thought were important for Kierkegaard during the composition of *On the Concept of Irony.*

In the literature on Kierkegaard, this question has been answered in the affirmative by Jens Himmelstrup,[7] who maintains that Kierkegaard's consideration of Socrates' irony is relatively legiti-mate, since its negativity was a necessary conduit toward the positiv-ity of Platonic philosophy, and the irony of the romantics is absolute-ly unjustified, since positivity in the world historical development had already been attained with Hegel, "is correctly seen only against the background of Kierkegaard's Hegelian-tinged conception of history, just as his whole position would be able to find its justifica-tion only in such a conception of history."

Is it, I wonder, so certain that, in *On the Concept of Irony,* Kierkegaard had a conception of history that is tinged with Hegel? Just the talk of an unjustified form of appearance of irony must raise doubts, since for Hegel's metaphysically based, deterministic

---

[7] *Søren Kierkegaards Opfattelse af Sokrates,* 1924, 45, and *passim*; the de-scription given here is essentially in agreement with Nicolai Hartmann's in-terpretation *Philosophie des deutschen Idealismus* (2nd ed., 1960), 539ff. Johannes Witt-Hansen has contributed a valuable chapter to the scanty Danish research into Hegel on this point in *Om Generalisation og Generalisations-problemer i de matematiske og historiske Videnskaber* (1963), 97ff.

philosophy of history there can be no discussion of anything as entirely unjustified.

It is a commonplace that Hegel's philosophy of history constitutes, in continuation of *Philosophy of Right* in his finite system the doctrine of "the Objective Spirit," i.e., the Transindividual Spirit, the Idea of reason in its dialectical unfolding in time, as nature is its unfolding in space.

Hegel's philosophy of history is purely teleological. For him, history is a teleologically determined process of development, and his philosophy of history is permeated with an optimistic attitude about the providential omnipotence and final victory of reason, in comparison with which Leibniz's *Theodicy* seems anemic. For Hegel, to conceive the historical development means to apprehend it in its inner necessity to the exclusion of all contingencies, i.e., to conceive the free unfolding of the Spirit concretely in the dimension of time, corresponding to "the logic" where, according to Hegel, it unfolds itself abstractly outside of the dimension of time, as pure thought, and historical consciousness is the Spirit's knowledge of itself as free, in its total independence from anything else.[8] For Hegel, necessity and freedom are essentially synonyms. The spirit of history is concrete for Hegel, it is not the spirit of a person but of a people. The various nations are the individuals of history, which qualitatively differentiate themselves reciprocally, and which individually have a necessary place in the development, but also only a relative legitimacy, namely as manifestations of the World Spirit and as conduits for the unfolding of freedom and of mankind's knowledge of its freedom. The Oriental people were unaware of freedom. Among them there was only one, the despot, who was free. The Greeks knew that not just one individual, but that *some* were free. Only with the Christian interpretation of man did the knowledge slowly triumph that all men are free, since man as such is free. Since the course of history, its dialectical unfolding, is described by Hegel as determined, it is thus illegitimate and doomed to failure if an individual people or a single individual wishes to anticipate or forestall the march of events by asserting private will against the general, divine Will, which has concretized itself in every age in the established social order, its laws and

---

[8] "God is the absolutely perfect Being, and can, therefore, will nothing other than himself—his own Will. The Nature of his Will—that is, His Nature itself—is what we here call the Idea of Freedom; translating the language of Religion into that of Thought." *Philosophy of History*, p. 20.

administration. Seen from the other side, there is no sacrifice too great for the altar of rational freedom, and it is precisely "the cunning of the Idea" to use apparently destructive means for its positive goals. Neither an individual nor a people is a norm in itself, they are only means for the self-realization of divine reason in time, in history, and their subjective freedom is an illusion.

It is characteristic of Hegel's *Philosophy of History* that it is not divided into three parts as we might expect, but into four, comprising the Oriental world, the Greek world, the Roman world, and the Germanic world. This is, indeed, evidently an inconsistency, probably motivated in part by the tradition of philosophical history deriving from the prophecies in the Book of Daniel concerning the kingdoms of the world, partly from the subsidiary motive of rendering a justification from the perspective of the philosophy of history for what prevailed in his own time and place. It is also inconsistent for Hegel to work with a concept of subjective freedom at all, when it is only freedom to realize its bondage, and when this realization is said to emerge with necessity. It is furthermore inconsistent of Hegel to pass moral judgments on behalf of divine reason on events of the past, as for example, the condemnation of Socrates and its possible legitimacy, when according to his own account these events could not have happened any other way or with any other outcome than what they actually had. It is entirely devoid of meaning in this connection to speak of guilt and responsibility, when every such assertion proceeds from a concept of freedom totally different from Hegel's and hence follows a philosophical anthropology completely different from Hegel's.

With respect to Socrates in particular and the interpretation of him in Hegel's *Philosophy of History*, we may take as the most typical the identification of Socrates as a "chief pivotal point of the Spirit in itself," as Hegel puts it in his *Lectures on the History of Philosophy* I, 384), namely for "interiority," and his world historical function was the dissolution of the old and the discovery of the new. At that time the highest form of government in Greece was democracy, the possibility of which is contingent on the citizens being "ethical individuals," but Socrates was a disrupter of the immediate equilibrium, for he was only "moral" not "ethical," i.e., he adhered to his private conscience and conviction and opposed his private views to the prevailing ones of society. He was thus a revolutionary who was rightly condemned to death as the absolute enemy of the Athenian people. Also inherent in the conviction of Socrates—according to Hegel's evaluation—was the profound tragedy that the Athenians would have to discover that what they had condemned in Socrates had already taken firm root in themselves and that they were just as culpable as the one condemned and just as innocent as he. Socrates' irony was only the subjective figure of the dialectic, a way of behaving, a form.

What is relevant here is that Socrates is described as a necessary, and therefore relatively justified, moment in the Spirit's dialectical unfolding in time, in the history of the world.

If we then read the pertinent chapter in this connection in Kierkegaard's *On the Concept of Irony*, namely the chapter entitled "The world historical validity of irony" (pp. 276-288), it gives the undeniably very strong impression of having been written on the basis of a view of the philosophy of history derived from Hegel both in conception and in evaluation.

In that text Kierkegaard first repeats his general definition of irony as "the infinitely absolute negativity" (p. 276), and then asserts that, for the ironist, reality has lost its validity. Thus there are two types of ironists, one for whom the invalidated reality is the historically actualized Idea in any time and place, and the other for whom the invalidated reality is any or all reality, including the ironist's own.

The development of the world occurs, Kierkegaard says, through a contradiction, as the Idea can become concrete only through a people and individuals, and

> The given actuality of a certain age is valid for a people and the individuals constituting that people. To the extent that one does not wish to say that this development is past, however, this actuality must be displaced by another actuality, and this must take place through this people and these individuals (p. 277).

This means that the world historical development consists of a series of collisions between the old and the new, between the one reality and another. The individual in whom the collision occurs can now relate himself differentially to the actuality, both to the old and the new. The individual can become a victim, or a prophet, or a tragic hero, or finally the individual can show himself to be an ironist, for whom the given actuality is inconvenient inasmuch as it has lost its validity, while the ironist does not possess the new actuality that should replace the old as a more perfect concretation of the Idea, and the ironist thereby in a negative sense stands free in relation to reality and is himself conscious of his own irony.

To that extent we can indeed, with Himmelstrup, speak of an interpretation of history redolent of Hegel in Kierkegaard. But as soon as Kierkegaard interprets Socrates' essential standpoint as irony, and as soon as he introduces a distinction between legitimate and illegitimate irony, he is independent of Hegel's philosophy of history, in fact, he is in opposition to it. If the Hegelian philosophy of history is to be carried out consistently, the distinction between legitimate and illegitimate irony in the way Kierkegaard develops it is in the proper sense meaningless, since whatever actually appears in history must have a relative legitimacy according to Hegel's interpretation. Thus it is only by an inconsistency that Hegel—and Kierkegaard with him—rejects, not Socratic, but romantic irony as illegitimate in an absolute, and not just in a relative sense. With considerable severity Kierkegaard turns against Hegel's one-sided notion of irony as romantic irony, his deficient understanding of the truth of irony, that is, its justification in a given situation, and his consequent misunderstanding of Socrates. On this point, not much Hegelianism remains in Kierkegaard, and there is still a most important difference that has not been mentioned, namely, that according to Hegel the single individual really has no freedom himself to choose his position in the case of the ironic, but is only a more or less perfect bearer of the unfolding of the Idea in time, whereas according to Kierkegaard, the individual has freedom to choose, with the possibility of choosing wrongly and reprehensibly —as the romantics.

c. Kierkegaard's Use of Hegel's
Lectures on the Philosophy of Fine Art

Quite early in *On the Concept of Irony* (p. 83) some have thought that they have found a trace of Kierkegaard's use of Hegel's esthetics, namely in the expression "the infinite subjectivizing of love." The editors [of the Danish edition of SK's *Complete Works*] refer to Hegel (SW, XIII, 178ff.),[d] the section on "Love"; but the expression itself is not to be found there, in the second part of *Philosophy of Fine Art*.

[d] Hegel, *The Philosophy of Fine Art*, trans. F.P.B. Osmaston (New York: Hacker Art Books, 1975), 4 vols. The section referred to here begins on II, 309. References will be to this English translation.

Emanuel Hirsch calls attention[9] to the fact that when Hegel discusses the romantic type of art he constantly speaks of the infinite principle of subjectivity and also of love, in which the Spirit's movement from the substantial through the subjective turns back to itself in concrete form. This brief summary is quite correct; but Kierkegaard does not quote Hegel at this point.

In Kierkegaard the connection is this: he asserts that "The Abstract in the early Platonic Dialogues culminates in Irony" (p. 78), and in the course of his analysis of the *Symposium*, which he sees under this rubric, he discusses Diotima, Phaedrus, Pausanias, Eryximachus, Aristophanes, Agathon, and—as the last—Socrates.

Concerning Socrates' discourse on Eros, Kierkegaard asserts that Socrates does not "peel off the shell to get at the nut, but hollows out the kernel," i.e., empties the concept "eros" of content by defining it only as longing for something that one lacks. This longing is what Kierkegaard—alluding to Hegel—calls the infinite subjectivizing of love, i.e., Socrates goes from the concrete to the abstract, which is rendered entirely devoid of content, and there he stops, just where the investigation really should begin.

Just as in the above instance, the editors of the Danish edition of SK's *Complete Works* trace the expression "the pantheism of the imagination" (*On the Concept of Irony*, pp. 132-133) to Hegel's *Philosophy of Fine Art*. In the first part of that work (II, 89) Hegel does indeed use the expression "the pantheism of art." But again Hirsch (*Uber den Begriff der Ironie*, note 140, p. 349) has given the correct reference, namely to Hegel's *Philosophy of History* (p. 141) in the section on India, where it is said that "the Indian view is a total, universal pantheism, and is, however, a pantheism of imagination, not of thought."

The situation is not much better in the next place (p. 216) where the Greek individuality is described as "beautiful individuality," an expression Kierkegaard attributes to Hegel. This expression is, indeed, used in the *Philosophy of Fine Art*, but only in the table of contents, not in the corresponding place in the text.[e]

In the relevant passage in Kierkegaard, the discussion is about

[9] Note 65 on p. 342 of his previously mentioned translation of Kierkegaard's thesis.

[e] But this phrase is not used in the table of contents in the Osmaston translation. The editors of the third Danish edition of the *Complete Works* of SK and Capel in his translation of *On the Concept of Irony* correctly cite Hegel's *Philosophy of History*, p. 238, where the expression "*Individuality conditioned by Beauty*" occurs.

the intellectual love that Socrates had for young men, and Kierkegaard interprets this as a "consuming enthusiasm in the service of possibility," the enthusiasm of the ironist, which accomplishes nothing because it never gets beyond possibility. Kierkegaard does not precisely speak of Socrates there as a "beautiful individuality."

Again, Hirsch has given a more accurate reference, namely to Hegel's *Philosophy of History* (pp. 238-240), where Hegel describes the Greek spirit as the free, beautiful individuality that transforms nature into culture, into works of art, namely "the subjective work of art, that is, the culture of man himself;—the objective work of art, that is the shaping of the world of divinities; finally, the political work of art, the nature of the constitution and of the individuals under it."

Finally, beginning on p. 282, Kierkegaard discusses Hegel's treatment of the concept of irony, both the Socratic and the romantic— particularly the latter.

Kierkegaard gives a description here of the Hegelian understanding of the concept of irony on the basis of statements in the *Lectures on the History of Philosophy*, the *Philosophy of Right*, and last but not least, *Lectures on the Philosophy of Fine Art* (especially I, 88ff.).

We will look at Hegel's treatment of the question first. The context in his *Fine Art* is this, that in the long Introduction Hegel treats of:

   I The provisional definition of Aesthetics and its place in the system
  II Scientific methods for dealing with the beautiful and art
 III The concept of the beauty of art
  IV Historical deduction of the true concept of art
   V Division of the subject

It is under the third point of the penultimate section (Historical deduction of the true concept of art) that Hegel finally considers irony, and for him that chiefly means romantic irony.

Hegel follows the development from Kant, continues with Schiller, Winckelman, and Schelling, and concludes with "irony."

In this connection he identifies first August Wilhelm and Friedrich von Schlegel as talented critics but not really philosophical minds, so that neither of them deserves the reputation of being speculative thinkers. Since their critical standard was not based on fundamental philosophical principles, their critical judgment was insecure (*Phil. of Fine Art*, I, 87).

Friedrich von Schlegel in particular, according to Hegel, developed on this basis "the so-called irony," which derived from Fichtean philosophy, whose principles were applied to art. Hegel says that for Fichte the point of departure was the ego "and, indeed, the ego remains throughout abstract and formal." This ego is sovereign, and can produce and again annihilate all (*Fine Art*, I, 88). If this is correct nothing at all is valuable in and for itself, but something is valuable only insofar as the ego regards it as such. Thus being-in-and-for itself is an appearance, an illusion. For this ego treats being artistically, not seriously, with an assumed divine genius and a consequent contempt for the bourgeois, the philistine.

Furthermore, Hegel emphasizes the "vanity" of irony (p. 90f.) concerning all that is factual, ethical, valuable, right, objectively valid, apart from subjectivity itself in its self-centeredness.

The romantic work of art is treated in a similar way. It is without form and character.

Finally, Hegel mentions that it was especially Solger and Ludwig Tieck who had adopted irony as the supreme principle of art. While Hegel does not much care for Tieck, he grants Solger some recognition.

Concerning the above passage, Kierkergaard wishes to illustrate a weakness in Hegel's whole interpretation of irony. With language so strongly appreciative that it can easily be interpreted as ironic (although naturally that is not the only possible interpretation), Kierkegaard says that Hegel wished to stop the prodigal sons of speculation on their road to perdition "but he did not always use the gentlest means for this," and by focusing his attention only on the—illegitimate—romantic irony, Hegel has, in Kierkegaard's opinion, overlooked the truth of irony, i.e. its relative legitimacy in a given historical situation (*On the Concept of Irony*, p. 282).

A few pages later (pp. 289ff., in the chapter on "Irony after Fichte") Kierkegaard gives a summary that shows a very strong dependence on the passage from Hegel just discussed.

The last place in his dissertation where Kierkegaard quotes Hegel's *Fine Art* is on page 323. It is the quite appreciative statement about Solger from the section cited in the Introduction to the *Philosophy of Fine Art* (I, 93).

Kierkegaard made only very cursory reference to the main themes of the *Philosophy of Right*, although to a somewhat greater degree he worked with the chief thoughts in Hegel's *Philosophy of History*. It is characteristic, thus, of his use of the *Philosophy of Fine Art* that it is only a series of items and opinions on particular phenomena that Kierkegaard has taken notice of, and his treatment lacks the needed perspective.

As is well known, the *Philosophy of Fine Art* is for Hegel the first link in the doctrine of the Absolute Spirit, so that the Absolute Spirit is the manifestation of the Idea for sensory contemplation in the work of art, the individual work of art. The Idea unfolds itself first in the symbolic, most closely corresponding to Oriental art, where the bond between the spiritual (*aandelige*) and the sensual is loosely knit, while the second stage, the classical, corresponds to ancient art, where the spiritual is completely absorbed in the sensual, where there is harmony between content (*Stof*) and form. The third stage of the Idea is the romantic, most closely corresponding to the poetry of the modern period, where the abundance of the spirit overcomes the sensual content and cannot find adequate expression in the form. In this classification Hegel was inconsistent with his general speculative conceptual development, which should have been formulated: symbolic, romantic, classical. If we adhere to Hegel's own systematic structure, we would have to say that the objective spirit in world history has triumphed over the Absolute by allowing works of art to emerge in the various eras in conceptually incorrect sequence. Hence Hegel's criticism of the romantics and of their romantic irony for appearing at an unjustified point in time is a symptom of his own inconsistency. The historical development defied the system's dialectical conceptual development, which in Hegel's judgment was deplorable, not for the System, but for historical reality.

In his teaching on the various arts, Hegel arrives at the conclusion that the symbolic art form obtains its actualization in architecture, the classical in sculpture, and the romantic in painting, music, and poetry. The principle of classification is, as in his *Phenomenology of the Spirit*, the relation of the spiritual (*Aandelige*) to the sensual (*Sanselige*). Thus architecture is given the lowest position, since in architecture the spiritual does not get any adequate expression, whereas there is harmony in sculpture, and the spiritual is dominant in painting, music, and poetry, which are arranged in the triad epic-lyric-dramatic. The further subdivisions have no particular significance in this context. It should only be noted that both in the

Introduction to the work and whenever the opportunity arises in the body of the work Hegel strongly rejects romantic esthetics in general and its concept of irony in particular, and it was chiefly these sections that Kierkegaard employed.[10]

d. Kierkegaard's Use of Hegel's Critique of Solger's *nachgelassene Schriften und Briefwechsel* (SW, XX, 132-202)

The last great work from Hegel's hand which Kierkegaard utilized during the composition of *On the Concept of Irony* is the long critique of Solger's correspondence and posthumous writings which Hegel published in 1828 in *Jahrbücher für wissenschaftliche Kritik*.

The first place Kierkegaard quotes this review is in the beginning of Part II of *On the Concept of Irony* (p. 261, note) in the passage in which he wanted to deal with "the second potentiality of sub-jectivity" (p. 260) i.e., romantic irony. Kierkegaard points out that Friedrich Schlegel tried to assert irony in relation to actuality, while Tieck sought to assert it in poetry, and Solger became estheti-cally and philosophically aware of it. Then he says that "finally, irony here met its master in Hegel," who annihilated it as unjusti-fied (*On the Concept of Irony*, p. 260).

Kierkegaard then turns his attention to a difficulty in the develop-ment of the concept in its second phase, the fact that it is without a history: Solger complains that A. W. von Schlegel only touches on it, and Hegel complains that the same thing is also true of Solger and Tieck.

For his part Kierkegaard complains that Hegel has not elaborated the concept satisfactorily either, and as support of this opinion Kierkegaard offers a quotation from Hegel's review of Solger, a passage from the end of the lengthy critical treatment.

On the immediately preceding pages, Hegel had, not without jus-tification, severely criticized Solger's many loose or only loosely defined concepts. He says, among other things, of Solger's use of the term "incomprehensibility" that "this is likewise one of the many words used vaguely and without any understanding" (SW

---

[10] Max Schasler's *Kritische Geschichte der Aesthetik*, I-II (1872), continues to have its value, even with regard to the chapter on Hegel, along with more recent presentations such as Kuno Fischer's and Nicolai Hartmann's and—from the Danish side—Paul V. Rubow's clear exposition in *Dansk litterær Kritik i det nittende Aarhundrede* [Danish Literary Criticism in the 19th Century] (1921), 81ff., to which the above brief sketch is essentially indebted.

XX, 179) and claims that Solger has scarcely made clear either to himself or to the reader what he personally means by "thought," "knowledge," etc. (p. 180).

Hegel then proceeds to discuss irony according to Solger (p. 182). Hegel says that we should expect to find an explanation in Solger. The foundation is the Fichtean ego-philosophy, the correctness of which, however, Hegel finds not established by any compelling philosophic argument, but asserted only axiomatically, that is, without proof. Fichte himself ultimately reformed; but Friedrich von Schlegel without further ado simply adopted Fichte's point of departure and thus, for instance, did not do justice to the "innocent" Socratic irony (p. 184). In Solger there is, according to Hegel, a vagueness in the concept of irony: on the one hand he denies that irony means "the scornful indifference to everything" (p. 185), but on the other hand he contradicts this assertion with all his other explanations, which Hegel illustrates with the help of quotations, in which Solger chiefly speaks of divine irony. Hegel then says, immediately before the passage Kierkegaard quotes, that it is almost comical, a kind of unconscious irony, that Solger complains that only in a single place does Tieck explicitly discuss irony.

Somewhat further on (p. 285) Kierkegaard quotes and paraphrases Hegel's statements in the review (SW XX, 184-185) concerning the difference between the Socratic and the Schlegelian ironies.

In this context Kierkegaard says nothing more about Schlegelian irony. But with regard to Socratic irony, he repeats here his objection to Hegel's interpretation: Socrates' irony was not, as Hegel maintained, only a form of expression, but his position. His ignorance was total and he was conscious of it. Hegel did not understand this, Kierkegaard says, just as he was not entirely consistent in his understanding of Socrates either.

In the chapter "Irony after Fichte" Kierkegaard again refers to the review of Solger.

In this context Kierkegaard gives a general description of romantic irony, a description that is at the same time a critique: it was always superior to reality, always judging and condemning without providing anything positive, and, Kierkegaard continues, "this judging and condemning behavior is what Hegel especially reproaches in Friedrich von Schlegel" (*On the Concept of Irony*, p. 295; cf. Hegel, SW XX, 161).

In the place referred to, Hegel says of Schlegel that

he has always been quick to pass judgment, without considering the philosophical content, the philosophical propositions, or the sequence of ideas arising from them, and even less did he attempt to prove them either right or wrong.

Similarly quite in tandem with Hegel's attitude here is Kierkegaard's next use of Hegel, namely in his criticism of Tieck. Tieck is reproached for having lived in "nothing but feelings," in which boredom is the only continuity (pp. 301-302). Insofar as we can detect it, Kierkegaard's understanding here was essentially developed from the passages from Tieck's *Correspondence* quoted by Hegel, but the designation "boredom" is Kierkegaard's, not Hegel's.

Finally, there are a few places toward the end of *On the Concept of Irony* where Kierkegaard quotes Hegel's review of Solger.

On p. 323 Kierkegaard quotes only a comment from Hegel (SW XX, 182), where he says that in Solger one can find irony treated as a principle [but we look in vain for it]. Kierkegaard then goes on to say that it is most difficult to give an account of Solger's position, because he "has gotten himself completely lost in the negative," indeed, he is "the metaphysical knight of the negative," who instead of giving a strictly philosophical [*videnskabelig*] account only provides aphoristic outbursts so that his terminology is more poetic than philosophic. Kierkegaard relies on Hegel here, so that Hegel's statements are a point of departure for him. We encounter the same sort of thing on pages 328ff., where Solger's speculative-dogmatic considerations are discussed. Kierkegaard refers to the same passages in Solger that Hegel quotes (SW XX, 165), and criticizes Solger along the same lines as Hegel, although more sharply, and—as distinct from Hegel, whose critique is purely philosophical—here Kierkegaard criticizes Solger from a theological perspective.

Finally, in the last place (pp. 330f.) where Kierkegaard quotes this article by Hegel, he approvingly employs a critical comment from Hegel on Solger's confused statements on the meaning of negation.

e. Kierkegaard's Use of Hegel's
Lectures on the History of Philosophy

The first place in *On the Concept of Irony* where Kierkegaard quotes K. L. Michelet's edition of Hegel's *Lectures on the History of Philosophy* is in a note (p. 165).

The context in Kierkegaard is this: In a—possibly ironically in-tended—unreserved agreement with Rötscher (*Aristophanes und sein Zeitalter*, 1827) he wishes to give a brief synopsis of Aristoph-anes' *The Clouds*, and first dwells on the role of the chorus as rep-resenting "nothingness,"[11] also called "the purely negative dialectic." In this connection he quotes, also with approval, a statement from Hegel (*History of Philosophy*, I, 406) where it is said that we ought not reproach the Sophists for not having taken the Good as a principle, since the fault lay in the overall aimlessness of the time. Socrates was the first, says Hegel, to have discovered that the Good is the end in itself, and—in accordance with the dialectical unfold-ing of the Idea in the dimension of time—this discovery could not have taken place at an earlier point in time: "every discovery has its time."

Kierkegaard's note gives the impression of having been a later addition, and it is worth remarking that he does not identify here Hegel's speculative foundation for the evaluation of the Sophists.

The next place is on page 181 of *On the Concept of Irony*, where, also in a footnote, Kierkegaard refers to Hegel's *History of Philoso-phy* (I, 426ff). Hegel says there that it conflicts with German serious-ness to see a morally upright man such as Socrates was in actual life presented in a comedy; but in the other hand Aristophanes was quite correct in presenting Socrates as the negative in a comical vein.

While Hegel, according to his comprehensive viewpoint, neces-sarily had to find a positive element in Socrates, as he had to find it in every philosopher, Kierkegaard parts company with Hegel by interpreting Socrates, or at least presenting him, as totally negative without Hegel's reservation concerning Aristophanes' description, in line with the main point of view governing the evaluation of sources for knowledge about Socrates in *On the Concept of Irony*. As is well known, in this work Kierkegaard wishes to maintain that whereas Xenophon makes Socrates banal and Plato idealizes him, Aristophanes' caricature comes closest to the historical reality.[12]

[11] There is no intention here of answering the question of the correctness of Kierkegaard's (or Hegel's) interpretation of historical phenomena, as for example, the role of the chorus. On this point reference may be made to F. M. Cornford's *The Origin of Attic Comedy*, ed. Th. H. Gaster (1961) or to the relevant chapters in A. Lesky's *Geschichte der griechischen Literatur* (2nd ed., 1963).

[12] It should be emphasized here that in his estimate of Aristophanes' comedy as a source for understanding Socrates, Kierkegaard could find significant

The next place where Kierkegaard employed Hegel's *History of Philosophy* is on pages 189-190, where he considers the question of what Socrates' daimon was, and in this connection he refers to and quotes the *History of Philosophy*, I, 421ff., 431ff.[f]

Kierkegaard asserts here that the upshot of Hegel's analyses is that Socrates' position is conceived (speculatively) as that of subjectivity, interiority, or, in the expression of the Danish Hegelian A. P. Adler, that of isolated subjectivity. Instead of the oracle, Socrates had his daimon, who unlike the oracle that spoke of the universally valid, spoke only of what concerned Socrates as a private person (his

---

support not only in Hegel (*History of Philosophy*, I, 426ff.), but also in Th. A. Rötscher, who was strongly influenced by Hegel, and whose work (*Aristophanes und sein Zeitalter*) Kierkegaard used and which he frequently quoted and referred to, most often with complete agreement in *On the Concept of Irony* (cf. p. 159ff., 165ff., 172f., 174, 178, 181, 189, 199, and 224) as has been stressed by Aage Kabell in *Kierkegaardstudiet i Norden* (1948), p. 232f. Rötscher's main theme (*Aristophanes und sein Zeitalter*, pp. 247-258) is that Socrates consistently accentuated the principle of subjectivity, thereby—gratuitously—turning himself against "the ordinary ethics," represented by the Athenian state and its citizens, and was therefore—justifiably—ridiculed by Aristophanes and then, also justifiably, condemned and executed, since he represented the corrupting principle, whereas (in *The Clouds*) Strepsiades represented the older Athenian generation, attached to tradition, and Pheidippides represented the younger generation. Conservatism triumphed over Socrates' new depravity, which is indicated in the comedy by the Thinkery's burning down at the end. It may be noted that, curiously, while important classical philologists and historians of philosophy in the twentieth century (such as Wilamowitz-Moellendorff, *Platon*, I [1919], 98-99, and W. Norvin, *Sokrates* [1934], 17) have completely rejected Aristophanes' comedy as a historical source, yet in recent years various scholars (Wolfgang Schmid, *Das Sokrates bild der Wolken* in *Philologus* [1948], 209ff.), Rudolf Stark, *Sokratisches in den "Vögeln" des Aristophanes* (in *Rheinisches Museum* N.F. [1953], 77-89) and especially Hartmut Erbse, *Sokrates in Schatten der aristophanischen Wolken* (in *Hermes* [1954], 385-420) maintain that there may be found in Aristophanes a long series of reliable historical traits for a description of Socrates in youth and middle age, his attitude toward the philosophy of nature, toward the Sophists, and his maieutic as well as his irony (which, however, is not understood by these scholars in the same way as Kierkegaard understood it). See also Povl Johs. Jensen, *Sokrates* (Copenhagen: G.E.C. Gad, 1969).

[f] It is probably worth noting again that the English translation of Hegel's *Lectures on the History of Philosophy* cited here (and throughout the present translation) was made from the later, expanded edition of Michelet, whereas Thulstrup correctly cites the *Jubiläumsausgabe*, which reprints only the earlier text used by Kierkegaard.

"particular situation," p. 191). In agreement with Hegel Kierkegaard points out that Socrates' daimon should not be called or understood as conscience, and it is noteworthy that Kierkegaard goes
further than Hegel in that he uses this interpretation of the daimon
as a point of departure for his own striking interpretation of Socrates. Hegel emphasizes in the places cited that Socrates' daimon
cannot be presented as an exemplar of a "protective spirit, angel, and
such-like, nor even of conscience" and—with most references to
Xenophon's *Memorabilia, Apology* and some to Plato's *Apology*—
Hegel arrives at the same conclusion given by Kierkegaard, that
Socrates' daimon expresses itself only about "particular issues" not
about anything general in art and knowledge: "The daimon stands
. . . midway between the externality of the Oracle and the pure
interiority of the Spirit" (*History of Philosophy*, I, 425). It is thus
on the basis of this understanding of the daimon that Hegel, while
dealing with the first charge against Socrates—that he did not believe in the gods, but introduced new deities—concludes that Socrates was justifiably accused.

A little further on (p. 195) Kierkegaard maintains that Socrates'
ignorance was not empirical but philosophical or metaphysical, and
then he says that this can also be expressed thus, that he had the
Idea as a limit, i.e., there was nothing positive in him, he only arrived at, but did not enter into the new positivity, that of Plato.

To substantiate the correctness of this interpretation, Kierkegaard
then explores what are for him the relevant passages in Plato's
Apology, and accordingly, he goes into the function of the oracle in
various periods in Greece: previously, the Delphic Oracle spoke
with divine authority; at a later time (that of Plato) it posed scientific (geometrical) problems.

This conception, which according to a modern view of the oracle
is undeniably very peculiar,[13] is one the correctness of which Kierkegaard wishes to substantiate with a quote from Hegel (*History of
Philosophy*, II, 4), the context of which is as follows:

Hegel asserts (II, 1) that the third division of the first period
in the history of philosophy, consisting of Plato and Aristotle, is
"The expansion of knowledge, and more precisely from the Socratic position to the scientific. With Plato, philosophic science as
science began," and Hegel goes on to assert that "the right of self-

[13] Cf. for example, Martin P. Nilsson, *Geschichte der griechischen Religion*,
I (2nd ed., 1955), 216ff. and *passim*.

conscious thought, which Socrates had raised to a principle,—this purely abstract right Plato expanded into the sphere of science" (II, 1f).

Thus it is in this rather broad biographical introduction that Hegel speaks of Plato's formation, technical skills and knowledge, including mathematics, and in this connection he mentions the story about the oracle's having posed a mathematical problem for Plato, which Hegel interprets in this way: "it is a change in the spirit of the oracle, which is most noteworthy" (II, 5). Hegel does not expand this theme, but only mentions it as support for his previously given thesis that with Plato philosophy was raised to science.

Following up these themes, Kierkegaard observes (p. 198) that it was Socrates' divine vocation that in the first place, restrained him from immersing himself speculatively, and in the second place, urged him to convince every individual of the same thing: "He had not come to save the world, but to condemn it"; but in that way Socrates became only a "transitional moment," the prerequisite for a deeper relationship (p. 199).

Kierkegaard supports this interpretation first with a quotation from Rötscher (*Aristophanes*, p. 273) and then with a statement by Hegel (*History of Philosophy*, I, 399) on which he does not comment. The quotation is from the beginning of Hegel's lengthy section on Socrates.

The next place is on page 209, where the charge against Socrates as a seducer, that is, that he led the youth astray, is treated.

Here again Kierkegaard takes as his point of departure Hegel's treatment of the question (*History of Philosophy*, I, 435ff.). Kierkegaard mentions that in evaluating Socrates' conduct Hegel says that it was unjustifiable for Socrates to have intruded into the relationship between parents and children. Kierkegaard's summary of Hegel is correct. In the relevant section Hegel confines himself chiefly to Xenophon's *Apology* and in only one place refers to Plato's *Apology*, and he comes to the conclusion that the accusation was justified (I, 438). Socrates must be acknowledged to be guilty, for without authority for doing so, he interfered in the relationship between parents and children.

Kierkegaard concurs in this evaluation, but adds that surely the Athenian state could agree with Socrates that in education the wisest should be preferred to the less wise; but the crucial issue of who in a particular instance is the more perspicacious cannot be settled by the individual himself (pp. 209f.) since the family stands over the individual, and the state over the family. For Socrates, however, neither family life nor public life had any importance. For him the state and the family were aggregates of individuals, and he related to them only as individuals. It was precisely this, Kierkegaard asserts, that was reprehensible in Socrates. When someone claimed that it is to be reckoned as something praiseworthy in him that he would not take payment for his instruction, Kierkegaard considers his refusal of payment quite proper: since Socrates correctly maintained that he knew nothing, in all decency he could certainly not take payment for communicating *this* wisdom (p. 212).

After having thus taken a position concerning the two charges against Socrates, Kierkegaard discusses (pp. 217ff.) the question of the alternative punishment after the question of guilt had been determined by the court.[14]

---

[14] Peter Wilhelm Forchhammer published in 1837 *Die Athener und Sokrates*, the subtitle of which declares his point of view: *Die Gesetzlichen und der Revolutionär*. This little publication was used by Kierkegaard, just as that of Rötscher, usually with almost demonstrative force (cf. *On the Concept of Irony*, pp. 194, 204, 207, 216, and 217). This was reviewed by Rötscher in the Hegelian-oriented *Jahrbücher für wissenschaftliche Kritik* (Jahrg, 1838, Sp. 139-149) and evoked a rejoinder, which Kierkegaard also knew (*On the Concept of Irony*, pp. 186 and 204), by Th. Heinsius, *Sokrates nach dem Grade seiner Schuld* (1839) (cf. Kabell, *Kierkegaardstudiet*, pp. 232f.).

Forchhammer first quotes the written charge against Socrates with its two points: (1) Socrates committed a crime against the State, in that he did not believe in the gods of the State, and (2) Socrates committed a crime against the State by corrupting the youth. Thus, there was a religious and a moral complaint. As far as the first is concerned, Forchhammer immediately (p. 3) asserts that the complaint was justified. Socrates had not kept the oath that every Athenian man had to take when he reached eighteen and became registered in the list of citizens with all the rights and duties thereof, but on the contrary acted against the State with his new wisdom, claiming that his daimon had dissuaded him from busying himself with the affairs of State, which it was the religiously based duty of every Athenian citizen to take an active part in (p. 7). On the following pages Forchhammer then refutes Xenophon's and Plato's orations in defense of Socrates, after which (p. 12) he takes up the second charge, the moral one, first sketching the political and constitutional situation in Athens at the time of Socrates. He (p. 23) asserts that Socrates was undemocratic. Supporters of the established order at the time were democrats, the opponents of the oligarchy, i.e. destructive aristocrats. Socrates and his political disciple Alcibiades were, according to Forchhammer, not nearly so clever as Aristophanes in *The Clouds*. Forchhammer then tells of Socrates' political activity (p. 26), that three years be-

Here he also first follows Hegel in the opinion that Socrates was rightly condemned to death, because by the alternative punishment he suggested he would still set his individual will up against the general will.

It must be noted here that Hegel (*History of Philosophy*, I, 446) holds that Socrates was also a tragic hero, who had an individual, absolute right on his side, so that a conflict arose between the individual and the general right.

Kierkegaard follows Hegel, but unlike Hegel he does not explain Socrates' situation as that of a tragic hero, but as that of a total ironist: Socrates did not see the verdict of the state as an objectively valid decision, since the state "to a certain degree" (p. 219) did not even exist for him. He dwelt only on the numerical, and it seems not to have occurred to him that a quantitative determination can pass over into a qualitative one.

If this remark should be understood literally and not ironically, then on this one point Kierkegaard should be described as a Hegelian, since it was Hegel himself who maintained in *Science of Logic* not only the possibility but the necessity of a transition from quantity to a new quality. It can also be noted in passing that it was precisely on this point in the *Logic* that Kierkegaard later concentrated in his critique of Hegel, e.g., in *Philosophical Fragments* (pp. 53-54 with note on Chryssipus, pp. 217-218).

On page 223 of *Concept of Irony* Kierkegaard quotes a general remark from Hegel's *History of Philosophy* (I, 384) that "Socrates

---

fore his death the democracy was restored, and none thought to accuse Socrates for his earlier political activity; but since he continued his subversive activity and influenced anti-democrats such as Alcibiades and Xenophon, Forchhammer says, we can establish that the second charge was also justified. The conclusion is that Socrates actually incited revolution (p. 61).

Forchhammer maintains that in his defense statement Socrates—according to Plato—does not answer the politically motivated accusations at all, but carries the whole thing over to a different level and, with his own suggested punishment, virtually compelled the judges to choose that of the accusers instead. The deeper basis for Socrates' guilt lay, in Forchhammer's interpretation, "in the 'unethics' of his ethics, in the immorality of his moral [theory], in the subservience to logic instead of to love of country, of wife and children, of kin and fellow citizens" (p. 72). Indeed Forchhammer maintains that Plato and Xenophon were perhaps insane, and his final conclusion (p. 74) is that never has a court of law rendered a sentence that was more in harmony with the law than the sentence that was passed on Socrates in Athens.

In a short postscript Forchhammer appeals to Hegel as support for his position, and he expresses himself in such a way that his work would surely have won the approval of Niebuhr.

did not spring out of the earth like a toadstool, but stood in a determinate continuity with his time."

Kierkegaard attaches an addendum to this, that even if the statement is correct, we cannot understand and explain Socrates entirely in terms of his antecedents and milieu.

When Hegel says that he was a "chief pivotal point of the Spirit in itself" Kierkegaard does not deny this not peculiarly Hegelian interpretation, but adds that not only was Socrates, so to speak, a conclusion of historical premises but there was more to him than was contained in the premises. He was, in Plato's expression (*Apology* 30D) a divine gift.

In a footnote (*Concept of Irony*, pp. 225f.) Hegel's treatment of the Sophists is discussed. Kierkegaard finds the treatment there not always consistent and sometimes disorganized. However correct this observation may be, it must be pointed out that it is surprising that Kierkegaard did not notice in what a defective way Michelet had edited Hegel's lectures (cf. *supra,* Chapter V, section 2).

On p. 229 Kierkegaard quotes a longer passage from Hegel's chapter on the Sophists (*History of Philosophy*, I, 352), and here it is worth noting that Kierkegaard renders a technically strong criticism against Hegel's understanding of the Sophists and their significance. Kierkegaard even uses the expression here, that we must entertain "reservations about the correctness of his presentation" and he supports this dissenting estimate partly, as in the note mentioned above, by calling attention to the self-contradictory aspects of Hegel's description, partly by pointing out that if Hegel's interpretation were correct, then we would have to identify Socrates with the Sophists (p. 229).

In the note on page 230 he considers Protagoras' famous dictum that "Man is the measure of all things," and Kierkegaard reproaches Hegel (*History of Philosophy*, I, 373, 374) here for an audacious interpretation (as if the dictum had had *telos* instead of *metron*) just as he takes sharp exception to "many Hegelians" who are said to have propagated the misinterpretation.[15]

On page 237 Kierkegaard speaks of the many philosophical schools other than that of Plato which derived from Socrates. In this connection, Kierkegaard asserts, it could seem necessary in order to explain this fact to assume a high degree of positivity in Socrates; but Kierkegaard gives as his own view, that in Socrates

[15] Cf. my commentary on the *Philosophical Fragments* (Princeton: Princeton University Press, 1962), pp. 210-211.

there was not a fullness but, on the contrary, an emptiness, total irony, and that this is the correct explanation of the phenomenon of several Socratic schools.

Kierkegaard links individual statements (*History of Philosophy*, I, 449, 452) in which Hegel explains this situation by claiming that Socrates' position was so indefinite and abstract that it permitted several strongly divergent schools, each of which could appeal to Socrates on its own behalf.

What is noteworthy here is that only with great reservations Kierkegaard concedes that Hegel was right, in that he maintains that not only did Socrates have no positive philosophical system, but he had no positivity at all. To this qualification of Hegel's notion Kierkegaard adjoins an expansion on another point, that is, he maintains that Socrates' position contains an "enormous elasticity," which entailed a stimulus for positivity.

In the note on page 238f. he again reproaches Hegel's lack of consistency (*History of Philosophy*, I, 449).

In a supplement on Hegel's conception of Socrates beginning on page 241, Kierkegaard discusses in some detail Hegel's relation to the ancient sources and maintains that we find in Hegel nothing to illuminate the relation between the three contemporaneous accounts beyond a quite general comment (*History of Philosophy*, I, 406) in which Hegel uses Xenophon's *Memorabilia* and *Apology* as well as Plato's *Apology* "entirely as a matter of course" (p. 243).

After such introductory remarks, Kierkegaard goes on to a summary account of Hegel's "main presentation of Socrates" (pp. 245ff.) about which he says that it begins and ends with Socrates' person.

Kierkegaard then raises the question, in what sense can Socrates be said to be the founder of morality? He repeats Hegel's interpretation, and thereupon (pp. 245ff.) renders a criticism of Hegel revolving on two points: in the first place, Hegel had not paid attention to Socrates' divine mission and in the second place, Hegel interprets—in Kierkegaard's view, mistakenly—the Socratic irony as a form, a restrained moment, as a way of dealing with people, not as an essential determination [*Væsensbestemmelse*].

On page 279, in the chapter on the world historical validity of irony, Kierkegaard again quotes Hegel's *History of Philosophy* (I, 400), from the section on Socratic irony.

Kierkegaard begins here to sketch a philosophy of history:

For the absolute ironist, being [*Tilværelsen*], in the sense of historical reality ("the historically actualized Idea") has lost its significance. Being [*Tilværelsen*] and the ironist have become totally alienated from each other. Now if on the one hand the development of the world is the unfolding of the Idea in time, independent of individuals, then on the other hand, this can transpire only through generations and individuals (cf. *supra*, section 2b). Furthermore, the given of any time, the actual historical reality must, necessarily, be superseded by a new one, through individuals. Thus an individual can become a tragic sacrifice, as the old reality shows its legitimacy by demanding a sacrifice in order to be overcome, while the new reality shows its right by placing a sacrifice on the altar of victory. At the turning points of history prophetic individuals also emerge, who do not possess but have a presentiment of the future, and further, one encounters the tragic hero, who fights for the actualization of the new, and finally, one encounters the ironic subject (p. 278), for whom the given reality has lost its validity, while on the other hand he does not possess the new. The ironist is also a sacrifice demanded by the development.

What is noteworthy now is that Kierkegaard maintains that irony in its historical reality corresponds to the negative in Hegel's system (p. 279), i.e., it is the mainspring of the development. The ironist, who does not possess the new, annihilates the given reality through itself and thereby enters into the service of the irony of the world.

Then Kierkegaard adjoins to this exposition without any transition a quotation from Hegel's *History of Philosophy* (I, 400), a quotation that should confirm or at least support the interpretation already given, and Kierkegaard continues his thought process by speaking of John the Baptist as a world historical parallel to Socrates.

In Hegel this is merely a parenthetical comment. Hegel confines the discussion of Socratic irony before the parenthesis and then turns to the irony of the romantics, especially Friedrich Schlegel's supposed expansion of the concept of irony: "people have wanted to make this irony [of Socrates] into something quite different, they have expanded it into a universal principle" (*History of Philosophy*, I, 400) which Hegel takes to be unjustified.

Kierkegaard does not touch on this point here at all; instead he focuses his attention only on Hegel's subsequent discussion of the irony of the world, i.e., the irony that comes from without, which affects the individual. Kierkegaard goes on to develop the point that irony is "the first and abstract determination of subjectivity" (p. 281) and as such manifests itself for the first time in world history in Socrates. On this point he comments that concerning the important question of whether in any individual instance irony is justified or unjustified "only history can judge" (p. 280).

It is just after this that Kierkegaard (pp. 282ff.) renders a very powerful criticism of Hegel, under two headings, first, that Hegel's interpretation of irony is one-sidedly dominated by the romantic concept of irony so that Hegel has "overlooked the truth of irony"; second, that Hegel refuses to understand Socrates' position, not just his mode of expression, as irony. Kierkegaard expands on these two points in more detail in what follows.

In the same section (pp. 283ff.) Kierkegaard quotes several passages from Hegel (*History of Philosophy*, I, 397-406).

In his treatment of Socratic irony, Hegel comes to the conclusion that it is "a way of interacting in society" (*History of Philosophy*, I, 398), which Kierkegaard regards as a quite inadequate definition. He then objects to Hegel's claim that, by his attempt "to make the abstract concrete," Socrates only let the abstract idea become visible. Kierkegaard explains what is, according to his own interpretation, Hegel's mistaken description by calling it a confusion of the Socratic and the Platonic irony (which again has two forms), as well as asserting that Hegel has not got clear the fact that, in his life, Socrates did not proceed from the abstract to the concrete, but the other way around. He also objects to Hegel's treatment of Socrates' maieutic method, that he understood it in an all too banal way, since Hegel did not distinguish between the two essentially distinct ways of asking questions, namely, questioning in order to get an answer, and questioning so as to shame and ridicule—which, according to Kierkegaard's interpretation, was Socrates' way of questioning.

Hegel's *History of Philosophy*, which concludes the doctrine of the Absolute Spirit, is written from the perspective "that the sequence of the systems of philosophy in history is itself like the sequence in the logical deduction of the conceptual determinations of the Idea" (I, 30). Thus, the atemporal and the temporally determined dialectical development are asserted to be identical, and we can, assuming that Hegel is consistent, simply from the placement of individual philosophers in the scheme of the history of philosophy infer his evaluation of them.

On the whole, then, it was not necessary for Kierkegaard to study the entire work. The famous speculative structure is also found in Hegel's exposition of Greek philosophy, in which the pre-Socratic philosophy is treated in the first chapter (thesis), the Sophists, Socrates, and the Socratics in the second chapter (antithesis), and Plato and Aristotle in the third chapter. But as always in Hegel, the "negative" philosophers are understood in the words of Goethe, as "a part of every Power/which constantly wants to do evil and constantly produces the good" (*Faust*, I, 1336-1337).

As is evident from what has been said above, Kierkegaard knew and, with some reservations, agreed with this point of view in *On the Concept of Irony*.

3. Kierkegaard's Understanding of, and Attitude Toward, Hegel in *On the Concept of Irony*

a. The preceding account of Kierkegaard's actual knowledge of various works of Hegel has shown that he had a rather complete knowledge of the third part of the system, the philosophy of Spirit, in general, and particularly in the places and sections of it which especially dealt with Socratic and romantic irony.

Furthermore, it has been shown that, generally speaking, there were a great many instances of agreement on particular points both in interpretation and evaluation between Hegel and Kierkegaard. So also it has been shown that there were important differences. The most important of the latter is that Kierkegaard takes it as a misunderstanding on the part of Hegel to ascribe to Socrates a certain positivity, in that according to Kierkegaard Socrates was not only in mode of expression but also in essence an ironist, i.e. totally negative over against a given historical reality, so that he was rightly condemned to death. It has also been shown that both in understanding and in the evaluation of romantic irony, the points of agreement between Kierkegaard and Hegel outnumber by far the few disagreements.

In these circumstances it is easy to understand that the first Kierkegaard scholar who has analyzed in depth the interpretation of Socrates in *On the Concept of Irony*, namely Jens Himmelstrup,[16]

[16] *Søren Kierkegaards Oppattelse af Sokrates* (1924), p. 309, and *passim*. In this chapter we have mainly taken into consideration Himmelstrup's important work, which—in spite of differences of opinion and criticisms—remains the chief work on Kierkegaard's disputation. But we should also mention that both before and after his work there appeared a number of sharply divergent interpretations of Kierkegaard's relation to Hegel in this limited

area. Harald Høffding did not devote much space to *On the Concept of Irony* in his book *Søren Kierkegaard som Filosof* (1892, 2nd ed., 1919, p. 55), saying only that there were indications of a criticism of speculative philosophy. Vilhelm Andersen, in his book on *Poul Møller* (1894, 3rd ed., 1944, 388ff.), asserts that on, so to speak, all the relevant points, *On the Concept of Irony* is a continuation of Poul Møller's characteristic (and anti-Hegelian) thought process. In his thoughtful major work *Tider og Typer af dansk Aands Historie*, with the subtitle *Goethe II*, 1916, Vilhelm Andersen identified himself with the view that Kierkegaard had described Socrates on the basis of Hegel's interpretation (pp. 86f.). Criticisms against Himmelstrup's conclusions have been rendered, especially by R. Schottländer (in *Philosophischer Anzeiger*, IV, 1930, 27-41, with Himmelstrup's rejoinder, pp. 42-50); by Hermann Diem (among others, in his *Philosophie und Christentum bei Sören Kierkegaard*, 1929 [cf. also his *Kierkegaard's Dialectic of Existence*, 1959, and his *Kierkegaard: An Introduction*, 1966]; by Eduard Geismar (*Søren Kierkegaard*, I [1926], 95-103). While W. Ruttenbeck (*Sören Kierkegaard* [1929], 158-159), for example, criticizes both Himmelstrup and Geismar. Emanuel Hirsch (In *Kierkegaard-Studien*, esp. II [1933], 568-601) stresses Kierkegaard's quite significant dependence on Hegel in choice of material and framing of problems, but notes at the same time that this does not mean that Kierkegaard was a Hegelian in the disputation, but on the other hand was in the line of the German speculative anti-Hegelian theists (especially I. H. Fichte as the most important). In the translation of Kierkegaard's work (1960) mentioned earlier, and for which he wrote an introduction and commentary, Hirsch adheres to his interpretation of 1933, and adds to that his significant observations and hypotheses concerning the circumstances of the work's composition. Of the many overall presentations of Kierkegaard's world of thought we must single out here P. Mesnard's *Le vrai visage de Kierkegaard* (1948, esp. pp. 117-180 on *On the Concept of Irony*). Van Munster (in "Een analyse van Kierkegaards proefschrift" in *Tijdschrift voor Philosophie* [1956], 347-380) arrives at the conclusion that Kierkegaard's disputation is neither romantic nor Hegelian, but rather in it he works with the same categories as in the Authorship proper, an interpretation with which I can agree in principle. The Germanic philologist I. Strohschneider-Kohrs maintains (in *Die romantische Ironie in Theorie und Gestaltung* [1960], esp. pp. 220-222) that in Kierkegaard's conception and judgment of romantic irony Hegel's position is repeated and made more precise, while E. Pivčević (in *Ironie als Daseinsform bei Søren Kierkegaard*, 1960)—under a certain influence of W. Rehm's views in *Kierkegaard und der Verführer* (1949)—defends the thesis that Kierkegaard, in his understanding and estimate of Socrates and Socratic irony as well as in other respects, was in the main determined by the romantic attitude toward life, so that the dissertation is to be understood as a not entirely successful self-confrontation from Kierkegaard's side. None of the scholars mentioned expresses as comprehensive an understanding of Hegel, as I have presented, nor of an interpretation of Kierkegaard as set forth in the present book. My disagreement with them, thus, in spite of agreement on many particular points, is fundamental, which does not eliminate a significant debt of gratitude to their learned and perspicacious investigations. Lee M. Capel's English translation *On the Concept of Irony* (1966), to which he came to the conclusion that Kierkegaard's position at the time was "essentially Hegelian," a conclusion Himmelstrup also maintains in his latest work, the second edition of his *Terminologisk Ordbog til Søren Kierkegaards Værker* (1964), e.g., page 105.

The question of whether Kierkegaard's position in *On the Concept of Irony* actually can be said to have been essentially Hegelian, however, cannot be completely answered just from analyses such as the foregoing or the one that Himmelstrup has undertaken in his pioneering work, since one would also have to investigate the problem of whether Kierkegaard's understanding of Hegel not only in the individual points mentioned but also as a totality can be said to be adequate or inadequate, correct or deficient. If it turns out to be deficient, then we cannot justify describing Kierkegaard's position as essentially Hegelian. The possibility opens up that Kierkegaard intended to play the role of a Hegelian historian of philosophy, that he made an experiment.

---

wrote an introduction and commentary, is a valuable work, which faithfully summarizes and at times expands upon what has hitherto appeared in the scholarly literature, especially that of Hirsch. In his introduction Capel gives a good sketch of the historical background in a more restricted sense with particular reference to the relationship with Martensen, Heiberg, and Hegel himself, while in the translator's notes (pp. 351-429) he gives a very clear summary of the previous research (pp. 351-357), in which, among other things, he mentions "the suspicion that Kierkegaard was perhaps performing as his own pseudonym when writing the essay on irony" (p. 357) and says (p. 428) that "Kierkegaard was never a Hegelian . . . was ever an opponent of the system." Capel's historical information is precise and carefully developed, as were his interpretations of individual points.

It should be noted that it lies outside the limits of the analysis presented here to take a position concerning questions about the correctness or incorrectness of Kierkegaard's interpretation of Socratic and romantic irony. In order to answer these questions even somewhat completely, we would need a separate treatise that would have to take into account, *inter alia*, O. Ribbeck's analysis of the classical concept of irony (*Rheinisches Museum für Philologie*, N. F., vol. 31, 1876, 381-400), Vilh. Buchner's more penetrating study of the same topic (in *Hermes, Zeitschrift f. klass. Philol.*, vol. 76, 1941, 339-358), the modern discussion of the problems of Socrates, such as it has been most precisely formulated by Olof Gigon (*Sokrates, sein Bild in Dichtung und Geschichte*, 1947), and as discussed with unsurpassed scholarship by V. de Magelhães-Vilhena (in *Le Problème de Socrate*, 1952), and the scholarship on romantic irony, which in Germany received its fundamental work in Rud. Haym's *Die romantische Schule* (1870), and which has been extended in Robert Minder's book on *Ludwig Tieck* (1936), Max Kommerell's monograph on *Jean Paul* (1933, 3rd ed., 1957), among others, and as treated—in my opinion, more extensively than penetratingly—in Strohschneider-Kohrs' above-mentioned work.

b. It will have been noticed that in all essential respects Kierkegaard knew and utilized the historical sections within the various works of Hegel that belong to the philosophy of Spirit. In *On the Concept of Irony* we find neither the *Phenomenology of Spirit* nor the *Science of Logic* nor the *Encyclopedia of the Philosophical Sciences* mentioned, that is, none of the major systematic works published by Hegel himself. The most natural assumption is, then, that while writing his book Kierkegaard did not have firsthand knowledge of these works, and his understanding of Hegel's philosophy as a whole, as system, was correspondingly deficient.

There is a generally unbroken tradition among historians of philosophy, who are chiefly interested in and oriented toward the theory of knowledge, according to which Hegel's philosophy[17] is

[17] With regard to the following description of the intention and method of Hegel's philosophy cf. my introduction to Kierkegaard's *Postscript*, II (1962), 59ff., and the references to the sources and literature recounted there. Concerning the understanding of intention and structure in Hegel's philosophy, I owe most to Iwan Iljin's *Die Philosophie Hegels als kontemplative Gotteslehre* (1946), and after this work I stand in the greatest debt to Hans Leisegang's *Denkformen* (2nd ed., 1951), while on the other hand, for example, Robert Heiss's two books, *Wesen und Formen der Dialektik* (1959) and *Die grossen Dialektiker des 19. Jahrhunderts* (1963) have not been particularly useful to me. It can, indeed, be explicitly emphasized here that Kierkegaard and his contemporaries had only limited possibilities for a complete understanding of Hegel in his connection with the earlier speculative tradition in European intellectual life and his development up to the *Phenomenology of Spirit*. Certainly, in 1844 Karl Rosenkranz's *Hegel's Leben* appeared, in which a number of documents from Hegel's youth were published (pp. 431ff.); but Dilthey (*Die Jugendgeschichte Hegels*, 1905), and Anton Thomsen (*Hegel, Udvikling af hans Filosofi til 1806*, 1905) first marked an epoch in Hegel research with their analyses of manuscripts of Hegel, which at that time had not yet been published. The most important book in this connection, *Hegels Theologische Jugendschriften*, was published in 1907 by Hermann Nohl (cf. his preface from 1959, to his republication of Dilthey's work in Dilthey's *Gesammelte Schriften*, IV) [T. M. Knox's translation of Hegel's *Early Theological Writings* (Chicago: University of Chicago Press, 1948; reprinted, University of Pennsylvania Press, 1971) does not include all of the texts in Nohl, but in a prefatory note the work of Nohl and Dilthey is briefly discussed]. During the succeeding years, there followed Ehrenberg and Link's, Lasson's, Hoffmeister's, and other editions, which made possible, *inter alia*, works such as that of Haerings' conceptual analysis and Glockner's synthesis (in *Hegel*, I: *Schwierigkeiten und Voraussetzungen der Hegelschen Philosophie*, 3rd ed. ("Endgültige Fassung") 1954; II: *Entwicklung und Schicksal der Hegelschen Philosophie*, 2nd ed., 1958), and, for example, Jean Hyppolite's monograph on the *Phenomenology of Spirit*. An extremely critical and very one-sided

understood as the concluding highwater mark of German speculative idealism. Kant is taken as the first, Hegel as the last, within the philosophical development from 1781, when the *Critique of Pure Reason* appeared, to 1831, when Hegel died, in the following way: Fichte sought to overcome the Kantian dualism between things in themselves and as they appear to human knowledge by entirely eliminating the notion of "the thing in itself" and tracing everything back to the productive ego, and thus elaborated subjective idealism; Schelling had in mind the demonstration of an absolute identity between the ideal and the real, between mind [Aand] and nature, and would thereby produce objective idealism; finally Hegel, by adopting a duality in the Absolute, in which the negative element was understood as the mainspring, as it were, of being [*Tilværelsen*], would show the Absolute's unfolding of itself as Spirit, and in that way Hegel established absolute idealism.

This view goes back to Hegel himself, who in the concluding section of his *Lectures on the History of Philosophy* (III, 409-554) synthesizes the most recent development in philosophy in such a way that the dialectical process of the Idea must with metaphysical necessity lead from Kant through Fichte and Schelling to his own philosophy, there to stop, since the conclusion, namely,

> the thought which is at home with itself, and at the same time embraces the universe therein, and transforms it into an intelligent world

is achieved in Hegel's own system, which crowns "the strivings of the Spirit through twenty-five hundred years" (III, 546).

However, if we wish to understand how Hegel can utter such proud words, the following are the most germane principles—although correct in their parameters—but perhaps not sufficient to justify this boast.

It is well known that Hegel's *Phenomenology of the Spirit* is not only his first outstanding (*helstøbte*) large work after the course of several years and endeavors in various directions; but it is qualitatively distinct from the preceding in that it not only presupposes studies and philosophical considerations but is also an experience, a vision of the divine universe of thought. The work can first and foremost be understood as a description of this vision, while the whole authorship following upon it, "the System" itself can be un-

account of the shifting trends of Hegel's philosophy is W. R. Beyer's *Hegel-Bilder, Kritik der Hegel-Deutungen*, 1964.

derstood chiefly as a reasoning process built out of that vision. In this authorship there is incorporated an extraordinarily comprehensive empirical content, including views of the earlier philosophers, molded in such a way as to prove the correctness of Hegel's chief comprehensive philosophical view, which was grounded neither empirically nor rationally.

In *Phenomenology of the Spirit* it was Hegel's intention to describe how the individual spirit develops itself from immediacy, over several stages, with inevitable necessity to the speculative spirit in a dialectical process, which at the same time is a description of the way by which the universal Spirit has penetrated world history.

If this is the case, then we eliminate the old dilemma of Hegel scholarship, whether *Phenomenology of the Spirit* is an introduction to the system or the system itself under a particular aspect, as well as the question of whether this work is a peculiar theory of knowledge or a philosophy of history. The work can be correctly read under all these aspects, in that it describes both how the individual and how the universal Spirit—which is identified with a philosophical pantheism, which already in his youth Hegel had praised in the poem *Eleusis*[18]—develops itself through relative oppositions, from "sense certainty" through various stages to "absolute knowledge." This series of levels corresponds in a peculiar way to a philosopher of religion such as Plotinus' description of the ascending way toward the One, while the descending way and the attempt of the divine to return to itself is sketched in Hegel's subsequent works, systematically incorporated in the tripartite *Encyclopedia of the Philosophical Sciences*.

In *Phenomenology of the Spirit*—considered apart from the polemical preface "On Scientific Knowledge," directed especially against Schelling and which was written last—Hegel utilizes the so-called dialectical method, the fundamental characteristics of which can be mentioned here:

The dialectical in Hegel's understanding of it—as it was expressed by Høffding—in the first place was a property of all human thoughts, which gives rise to the fact that individual thoughts, formulated in individual concepts, with an immanent, inexorable necessity lead to other thoughts, and the dialectical is in the second place a property of the objects of the thought, which means that they—just as the subject of the thought—necessarily belong together,

[18] Printed in Johs. Hoffmeister's *Dokumente zu Hegels Entwicklung* (1936), 380-383.

which thus means that thought and being are at bottom identical and both are an expression of the divine Spirit.

Since every concept is limited and determined by the sole fact that its content (definition) is different from that of all other concepts, according to Hegel, by consistently thinking it through it leads to its contradiction, its negation. Every concept, and especially the fundamental concepts, the categories, aims to give expression to the whole of reality, since—according to Hegel's view—only being [*Tilværelsen*] as an organic whole can be unconditionally real. But when this intention is realized, it shows the limit of every concept. This limit in the positive concept is the negative, which is constantly implied in the positive. As the negation enters in, "it spills over" into a new thesis, for what is negated is only the defined content of the earlier thesis, not all, only some content. Then a new concept is produced, which includes the old within itself, takes it up in a larger context, abrogates [*ophæver*] it, as it is called with an—from Hegel's side conscious—ambiguous expression.[g] The first concept and the second, its contradiction, are both taken up [*hæves derpaa begge op*] then into a higher unity, which again functions as the first concept (thesis) in a new, corresponding dialectical movement to a higher plane—and so on.

A typical example can show better than lengthy explanations how this dialectical thought process proceeds according to Hegel.

The most elementary concept is the concept of being [*Væren*], that is, not some particular existing thing [*noget værende*], but only being without content, without any definite character. This "pure" concept of being "spills over" into its dialectical opposite, i.e., into nothing. If both concepts, Being and Nothing, are sublimated [*ophæves*] into a higher concept, we then have Becoming [*Vorden*], a coming-into-being [*Tilblivelse*], after which the dialectical movement goes on to the concept "something," which comes into being [*bliver til*], is developed and disappears again by being sublimated into "something else"—and so forth.

This dialectic of thought, in which the speculative concept's negative element is above all the mainspring, the progressive thrusting force of the movement, is for Hegel the expression of, indeed, at bottom is identical with the dialectic of being, of existence (the

[g] The ambiguity exists in both the German verb (*aufheben*) used by Hegel and the Danish equivalent used by Kierkegaard and Thulstrup (*ophæve*). See, for example, the illuminating discussion of this point in Lee M. Capel's translation of *On the Concept of Irony*, p. 430.

terms *being* and *existence* are used here in the ordinary sense, not with a specially Hegelian force), and Hegel's system, including *Phenomenology of Spirit*, is an unfolding of the dialectic of both thought and of existence as two sides of the same coin.

Every finite, limited phenomenon, by the very fact of its limitation, points beyond itself to that which quite simply lies beyond its limits, and it is, then, only a moment in the totality of existence, which is conceived as a living organism by Hegel.

It seems, now, in the first instance through simple observations and experiences, that the opposites—in the sphere of both thought and being—merge into each other precisely through the power of the relation of opposition; thus it is, for example with life-death, light-dark, or in the conceptual pair right-wrong, or in the relation master-slave.

Hegel would understand both the development of nature and the course of history as controlled by this objective dialectic of existence, and—what is important there in order to understand his system in harmony with his own intention: the earlier stages passed through have determined the development of the later ones.

An example from Hegel's history of philosophy can illustrate his thought process: ancient Greece represented the immediate harmony, the positivity, in the dialectic of thought: the thesis. The Sophists and also Socrates represented the destructive force, the negativity. This negation of the immediate thesis was, furthermore, a necessary transitional stage for a new higher thesis, philosophically represented by Plato, who was conditioned by the previous dialectical development, and so on until Hegel's own speculative idealism incorporated the whole previous development into itself, conceived in its limited validity.

This basic view of the dialectic of thought and existence, which obviously has as its presupposition a particular anthropology—in which the human intellect is emphasized rather than feeling and will (which the animals also have)—dominates *Phenomenology of the Spirit*.

The human's, the finite spirit's, knowledge of the Absolute Spirit and the Absolute Spirit's knowledge of itself are, in Hegel's view, two aspects of the same thing; but not every type of knowledge results in adequate knowledge of the Absolute, although the lower types of knowledge are steps on the way to the absolute knowledge of the Absolute.

Hegel begins with the natural, immediate, unscientific knowledge of consciousness and shows its dialectical development, as he wishes to demonstrate how the lower stages are taken up in the higher, with the absolutely more adequate forms of consciousness, until absolute knowledge is reached.

Phenomenology of Spirit is divided into three main sections corresponding to the three chief phases of consciousness. The first of these is consciousness of an object as an empirical datum over against a knowing subject. This phase Hegel calls consciousness (*Bewusstseyn*). The next phase is the one in which consciousness makes itself an object, that is, the phase of self-consciousness; and the third phase is consciousness and self-consciousness in the synthesis of reason, the higher unity of objectivity and subjectivity.

Hegel begins with what he calls sense-certainty, the naïve, uncritical sensory observation, which for the immediate consciousness seems to be the most secure and content-filled type of knowledge. It soon becomes evident, Hegel says, that a description of particular objects can take place only by resort to universal terms that can just as well be applied to other particular objects beside the one a person wishes to describe at the moment. It thus becomes evident that knowledge through immediate sensory observation far from being a secure and content-filled type of knowledge is rather an insecure and, all things considered, empty one.

The consciousness then raises the question of why this is the case, and now turns its glance on itself, becoming self-consciousness.

The first form of self-consciousness is the desire by which the self still has to do with an external object, an object the self wishes to dominate. Now if this object is also a self, there the self-consciousness first becomes truly conscious of itself as a self. The one self is confronted with the other and craves recognition, which, when obtained, results in the master-slave relation. This relation, like the preceding and the following—except for the last of all—contains inner opposites, which drives the dialectical development further. First comes the Stoic consciousness, which flees to its own interior, by which both become masters or both become slaves, where inner freedom and self-sufficiency dominate. In this way the development is driven further to the skeptical consciousness, for which only the self itself remains unchallenged, while everything else is doubted and denied.

However, the skeptical consciousness contains an implicit self-contradiction, since it is impossible for the skeptic to eliminate natural consciousness. Confirmation and denial are found side by side in the same consciousness, which thus becomes divided and unhappy thereby (the unhappy consciousness), it becomes alienated from itself.

The contradictions and inner-dividedness of the unhappy self-consciousness are overcome in the third phase, in which the finite spirit raises itself to the common, universal self-consciousness on the stage of reason.

This third phase is the synthesis of consciousness and self-consciousness. On this stage of reason nature is conceived as the objective expression of the Infinite Spirit, with which the finite spirit itself is united.

This insight, this rational concept, can assume different forms:

In the developed religious consciousness, nature is regarded as God's creation and self-manifestation, and the consciousness regards itself as united with God and with other creatures; but this religious consideration expresses itself in inadequate images and representations, whereas the absolute science [*Viden*] expresses the same truth in adequate philosophical concepts.

In the stages of reason (which, according to Hegel, also contain logic, psychology, and ethics, which may be left out of the discussion here), the Absolute, Infinite Spirit comes to explicit consciousness of itself in constantly ascending degrees, so that nearest to the goal stands religion, whose culmination is Christianity, and the goal, absolute knowledge of the Absolute, is reached in the concluding chapter of *Phenomenology of the Spirit*.

The content of the Absolute's knowledge of itself, pure thought, which is the same as pure being, is elaborated in the succeeding system, beginning with the Logic, which deals with the inner Trinitarian life of the divine prior to the visible (and thus temporally and spatially determined) creation of the world, and it continues with the philosophy of nature, which concerns the withdrawal of the divine from its proper and right condition. This is completed in the philosophy of spirit, which treats the appearance of the divine in the subjective, the objective, and the absolute Spirit, which—threefold like each of the previous stages—comprises art, revealed religion, and philosophy, the highest and thus definitive form of which, Hegel's own, contains the knowledge of God in the speculative concept's completely adequate form, and that is a knowledge of God that is identical with human self-knowledge.

This whole cosmic and individual process is thought by Hegel to proceed with absolute metaphysical necessity, in a dialectical development, which is conceived rationally with the help of the dialectical method, the function of which in Hegel corresponds to the Intellectual Intuition in Schelling.

Thus it is Hegel's intention to fuse—to reconcile, as Hegel himself most frequently puts it, or mediate, as the Danish Hegelians and Kierkegaard usually said—two traditions in the philosophy of religion: one, which can briefly be characterized by names such as Poseidonios, Plotinus, John Scotus Erigena, Nicolas of Cusa, Jacob Böhme, and Schelling; and the other, which is characterized by the chief names in rationalist thought from Aristotle to Spinoza. The experience, the vision of the divine universe, its hierarchical structure and life, is what is primary for Hegel, whereas the working out, the description, the reasoning out of this is what is secondary, although—on a first reading of Hegel—this is what is most conspicuous.[19]

The goal of Hegel's philosophical endeavors was adequate knowledge of God, which he wanted to obtain by conceiving the Absolute as self-active Spirit, which on the way upward develops itself in constantly progressive self-determination, from a unity full of difference, over manifoldness to a new, higher unity. Human thought, which should follow this dialectical process, must therefore remain "fluid" as Hegel puts it, i.e., concepts as the instruments of thought must not be static, but, like the contrast-filled objects of thought, dynamic. The problem of the pre-Socratics, of Plato, and of Aristotle about the world of change and the relation of thought to it is taken up in a new way by Hegel, with a certain connection with Fichte's dialectic.

Thus in an original way Hegel wished to create a synthesis of Heraclitus' and Parmenides' contributions, at the cost of relinquishing the principle of contradiction and the principle of identity in the speculative logic, since he maintained that, while the simple view has its object as a whole before it (the immediate concrete), this is

[19] In the Introduction to my edition of the *Postscript* I have presented in more detail my interpretation of Hegel and the two lines of tradition (§§1-4). As far as I am aware, I am the only one to have set forth this interpretation. Neither in the general histories of philosophy that have appeared from the eighteen-thirties, after Hegel's death, to our own days, that is, from Michelet's to Chevalier's and Copleston's, nor in the comprehensive Hegel scholarship from Haym to Findlay, to name only an early and a modern scholar, do we find this. As a rule they have emphasized one or the other line without having understood that Hegel attempted to fuse them together.

divided by the philosophy of reflection (the philosophy of under-standing, under which, in Hegel's view, Kant belongs), which can-not retain the totality, whereas the speculative philosophy overcomes both empiricism and rationalism, conceives the unity in the opposites and formulates this unity in the concrete concept, which at the same time is the means and goal of thought, since the highest thought is being and the highest being is thought, which is precisely what is formulated in the concept.

The source of this unique form of thought in Hegel can probably be found in his early concern with the Johannine writings in the New Testament and the allegorical and mystical tradition in the interpretation of them.[20] In the Johannine teaching of the Logos and in the identification of God, Spirit, truth, the life and the way, Hegel found an expression of his fundamental thought about the divine Idea, which was in the beginning, is Spirit and is God, which endowed Itself with fleshly form, is light and life, and Who will conduct the whole world back to God. In accordance with this, Hegel's logic should be understood as actually the doctrine of the Logos, in that he wishes to unite the Greek Logos speculation with the Biblical world of thought, and his logic should, then, be under-stood as

the system of pure reason . . . the domain of pure thought . . . this domain is the truth, as it is, without concealment in-and-for-itself. One can therefore express it that this content is the repre-sentation of God, as He is in His eternal essence [*Wesen*] prior to the creation of nature and a finite spirit.[h]

After the creation, according to Hegel's interpretation, the dialec-tical development in time and history had arrived at the point he called the speculative Good Friday, where his own task as philosopher was to let the divine rise from the dead. In his view, it lay in the nature [*Væsen*] of the divine to die and to become living again, and it was the resurrected, living deity he wished to know

[20] Through such a work as H. N. Clausen's *Det Nye Testaments Her-meneutik* (1840) (Ktl. 468), to mention only one possible source, Kierke-gaard could have acquired an insight into this tradition and thereby could have had the possibility of understanding Hegel's main intention better than he gives any indication of—at least in 1840-1841; but nothing shows that Kierkegaard grasped this connection clearly.

[h] Hegel's *Science of Logic*, trans. W. H. Johnston and H. Struthers (Lon-don: Allen & Unwin, 1929) I, 60. Hegel's *Science of Logic*, trans. A. V. Miller (London: Allen & Unwin, 1969), p. 50.

and describe in his philosophy. According to Hegel's interpretation, the world is a divine emanation, which is like a living organism, and thought, which should conceive this totality from its origin, in its unfolding, and in its return to the source from which it came must conform to its object,[1] which unfolds itself in an eternally repeated cycle, like the cycle of life, which is first concentrated in the seed, which grows and develops itself into a plant with stem, leaves, and flowers, which sets fruit with seeds, which fall to the ground, whereupon the process begins again. Since for Hegel the Spirit is identical with life, its highest reality, thought, must unfold itself precisely like the living organism, which will be expressed in thought through thesis, antithesis, and synthesis. The pure thought, Logos, turns back to itself after having produced the world and made it intelligible in Hegel's own philosophical system, which incorporates all science [Viden].

We can, then, with a good deal of justification describe the Hegelian system, constructed as it is on these principles [Forudsætninger] and elaborated with the aid of the dialectical method, as panlogism and pantheism, as rationalism and irrationalism. In relation to the "atemporal" system builders as, for example, Plotinus and Spinoza, the unique thing about Hegel is the incorporation of history, the course of time, which he attempted, and the dialectical method—and thus, what Kierkegaard in his Authorship called "the [introduction of] movement into logic"—which is inseparable from the system.

c. If the understanding of Hegel's philosophy, its principles, its method, and its goal sketched here is in the main correct, in harmony with Hegel's understanding of himself as a philosopher, then there is no difficulty in seeing that the understanding of Hegel that is directly and indirectly stated in Kierkegaard's *On the Concept of Irony* must be described as being not incorrect, but incomplete.

To substantiate the accuracy of this description of Kierkegaard's relation to Hegel at this point, we can look into his understanding of the three relevant points, Hegel's principles, Hegel's methods, and Hegel's goal, and we will find that a perusal of *On the Concept of Irony*, undertaken with a view to clarifying Kierkegaard's understanding of these three points shows that on the whole, he has nothing to say about Hegel's principles, nor anything about Hegel's

[1] Cf. John Scotus Erigena, *De Divisione Naturae*, Books I & II where a similar (dialectical) process of emanation and return is described.

purpose. On Hegel's method we find only scattered comments, and on that point we can only say that in a very limited sense Kierkegaard imitated Hegel as, for example, in the arrangement of the first part of the work.

Not surprisingly, this conclusion is seen against the background of the investigation of Kierkegaard's notorious reading of Hegel, which was essentially confined to sections containing historical matters and conceptual analyses, in which there was no particular occasion for Hegel to give major accounts of the points mentioned, which indeed he treated elsewhere in the system.

Nor is the conclusion surprising when we peruse Kierkegaard's work to determine where references and quotations of Hegel appear. Neither in Kierkegaard's Introduction nor in the first large chapter ("The Conception Made Possible" pp. 51-184, more than a third of the whole work) do we find anything other than scattered comments in relation to Hegel on special points, and furthermore, these comments are found chiefly in the notes. This supports the theory advanced by Emanuel Hirsch that the work was composed in two periods, in 1838 and 1840-1841, with preparation for the final examinations and the engagement to Regine as termini, and his assertion that not until the winter of 1838-1839 is it demonstrable that Kierkegaard had read Hegel himself.[21] Not until page 159 is "a Hegelian," i.e. Rötscher mentioned, and we must go from here to Kierkegaard's second chapter (p. 189) before Hegel rightly comes into the picture—as the one who in any case for the present apparently solves the difficulties. Kierkegaard's approval of Hegel there—just as his approval of Hegelians such as Rötscher (e.g., p. 159) and Forchhammer (e.g., p. 204)—is so strongly put that we may well ask whether it is meant sincerely or ironically. In the second half of the book we find, as it appeared in the account of Kierkegaard's knowledge of Hegel, the most quotations and other points of contact; but none of them contain any discussion of Hegel's principles, method, and purpose.

This conclusion, that Kierkegaard's understanding of Hegel, such as it appears in *On the Concept of Irony*, is not incorrect but incomplete is a simple statement of fact, not a value judgment.

We can, then, as a matter of curiosity, ask whether Kierkegaard's thesis on Socrates and Socratic irony and on the romantics and romantic irony would have been developed differently if while

[21] Hirsch in his "Geschichtliche Einleitung" to his translation of the work *Über den Begriff der Ironie* (1961), pp. vii-xi.

working on it he had had a fuller and more penetrating knowledge of Hegel's philosophy, its principles, its dialectical method, and its high purpose. The answer, just as hypothetically, must be that it is not likely. As far as either Hegel or other authors and philosophers are concerned, Kierkegaard used only what he found relevant in them to the definite aim he had in each one of his writings. With regard to *On the Concept of Irony* we can only regret that at the time he composed it Kierkegaard evidently did not know the important section in *Phenomenology of Spirit* where Hegel characterizes and evaluates the romantic attitude toward life (pp. 611-679).[22]

However, it is not only Kierkegaard's terminology in *On the Concept of Irony* that is to a great extent redolent of Hegel and the Hegelians, which needs no further proof than that it is conspicuous everywhere in the text,[23] but also his arrangement with its threefold division in the first part (the conception made possible, made actual, made necessary) and in the second part, the chapter on the romantic ironists—Schlegel, Tieck, and Solger (Schlegel, who "sought to maintain it [irony] in relation to reality, . . . Tieck, who sought to maintain it in poetry, . . . Solger, who became conscious of this esthetically and philosophically" [p. 260])—is evidently formed according to the pattern of Hegel.

More important than these external features, which are clearly designed to give the reader the impression that he has a Hegelian book before him, are obviously the precise points of agreement with Hegel we have adduced.

The various points of agreement in the conception of historical individuals (as, for example, Aristophanes as a source for the interpretation of Socrates, the Sophists, Socrates' condemnation, his world historical role, Fichte's significance for the romantics, etc.) have been shown in the preceding section, as have the most important points of disagreement also. The points of agreement, apparent and real, are also so obvious that there is nothing surprising in the fact that Kierkegaard's position has been understood as es-

---

[22] On this point cf. especially Emanuel Hirsch's article in *Die idealistische Philosophie und das Christentum* (1926), 117-139.

[23] Concepts such as the abstract, the concrete, consciousness, dialectic, negative dialectic, Idea, inner-outer, moment, morality, negativity, phenomenon, reflection, speculation, subjectivity, ethics, appearance, immediacy, world history, essence [*Væsen*], and various others are used as familiar elements everywhere in Kierkegaard.

sentially Hegelian. The conception of Socrates is described in the book itself (p. 246) as a modification of Hegel's and in the conception of romantic irony his solidarity with Hegel is just as conspicuous.

Then there is, as the most important, the evaluation placed upon irony, both the Socratic and the romantic, which Himmelstrup (*Terminologisk Ordbog*, pp. 61 and 71), among others, has understood as positively influenced by Hegel's ethics and philosophy of history.

It actually seems as if Kierkegaard's ethical attitudes here are Hegelian, and he clearly took exceedingly great care that the reader could get a strong impression that that was the case. The evaluation appears, as was mentioned earlier, especially in the judgment of Socratic irony as relatively justified over against a given historical reality and of the romantic irony as unjustified, since it would annul any historically given reality. With regard to this understanding of Kierkegaard's ethical criteria as Hegelian, it must at the same time be noted that a partial or total rejection of irony as an attitude toward life can very well proceed from ethical viewpoints other than that of Hegel, even if the result, rejection, is the same.

The next question is whether there can be quite definite views identified in *On the Concept of Irony* that show that Kierkegaard's own proper position is not Hegelian. If such can be demonstrated, then it is accordingly likely that the Hegelian traits—formal and real agreements—are only to be understood as a mask, so that we may suggest that in his text Kierkegaard used his own name as a pseudonym, he played a role, he wanted the reader to believe that he had before him one of the books influenced and dominated by Hegel that were so common at that time. If these attitudes furthermore turn out to be in harmony with the ones Kierkegaard manifested in his private notes, not intended for publication, written before, after, and contemporaneous with *On the Concept of Irony*, then the presumption is strengthened that in that book he wished to appear in the role of a Hegelian historian of philosophy, although in reality he was not.

Certainly also from features that will be mentioned below, we can draw another conclusion, which indeed must be taken to be less plausible, namely that Kierkegaard, as a matter of fact, during the definitive editing of *On the Concept of Irony* in a period from 1840 to 1841, had been seriously convinced of the correctness of Hegel's philosophy at least on certain points.

Various attitudes and features in *On the Concept of Irony* can be identified as typically non-Hegelian. There are such as even the choice of the topic of the dissertation and the treatment of it, varying from humorous tolerance to strong moral condemnation, and a treatment in which antipathetic sympathy is just as unmistakable as sympathetic antipathy. Further, there is the attempt in the first half to interpret Socrates through two "combined accounts" (p. 50 and *passim*). We look in vain for anything comparable in Hegel, and Kierkegaard himself remarks critically that

> in his [Hegel's] presentation of Socrates in the *History of Philosophy* there is found, in spite of the fact that he notes it himself, that with respect to Socrates there is not so much a discussion of philosophy as of individual life, absolutely nothing to illuminate the relation between the three distinct contemporary conceptions of Socrates (p. 243).

The "individual life" was precisely Kierkegaard's interest not Hegel's.

As important as such features are for illuminating the differences in Kierkegaard's actual position and that of Hegel, still there are others, which not only show discrepancies and differences but also show the incompatibility of the proper positions of the two thinkers.

We can take as our point of departure the Latin theses that Kierkegaard elaborated for his book.

He put this one first: "The similarity between Christ and Socrates consists essentially in dissimilarity" (p. 349).

In the first place, this thesis is quite in harmony with entries in Kierkegaard's *Papirer* contemporaneous with *On the Concept of Irony* (among others, III A 108, 211, 216)[j] and with later, more thoroughly developed viewpoints (most important here, naturally, *Philosophical Fragments*, which could have had this thesis as a motto). In the second place it developed polemically against a thesis adduced by F. C. Baur, who was influenced by Hegel, and it implies a fundamental conflict with Hegel's own philosophy.

In his important work *Das Christliche des Platonismus oder Sokrates und Christus* (1837), which is the first book Kierkegaard mentions in *On the Concept of Irony* (p. 51), F. C. Baur had certainly pointed out various differences,[24] but he had put much more

---

[j] Hong, III, #3072; II, #2277, #1101.

[24] For example, p. 24: "Socratic philosophy and Christianity are related . . . to each other as self-knowledge and knowledge of sin" and p. 152,

emphasis on analogies (the anamnesis doctrine—the doctrine of the image of God, thoughts on redemption, the doctrine of the soul's fall, preexistence, the doctrine of immortality), and is, on the whole, significantly influenced by Hegel.

In *On the Concept of Irony*, Kierkegaard speaks of Baur with great appreciation, whether that is to be taken at face value or ironically, but he immediately adds in a note (p. 52) these significant words:

> I could wish, were this wish not already outside the limits of the present essay, that it were permitted to me within the confines of this study to go into the relation between Socrates and Christ, on which Baur, in the above-mentioned book has said so much that is noteworthy. I say this in spite of the fact that there still always remains for me a modest little asthmatic doubt that the similarity consists in dissimilarity, and that there is an analogy only because there is an opposition."

This point of view is later expanded upon in a note (p. 242) where it is emphasized (as in the first note quoted) that Christ was the Truth—and Socrates neither was that nor did he know of it and that the relation of Christ to the historically given reality was "absolutely real," while that of the ironist Socrates was indifferent or negative.

Such an attitude in Kierkegaard is not only in disharmony with F. C. Baur's but is also in its foundation and consequences—consequences that lay beyond the limits of *On the Concept of Irony*, and which Kierkegaard expressly did not wish to deal with in this work, but would later—totally incompatible with Hegel's philosophy, in which it is the fundamental postulate that Christ brought no other message and did no other work than what speculative philosophy in Hegel's own version taught and accomplished.

Kierkegaard consciously and explicitly left these significant questions out of *On the Concept of Irony*. In this work, which was not theological but philosophical, he confined himself within the limits he himself had established. Within those limits it was possible for him on some points to be in agreement with Hegel, give Hegel his assent, declare himself inspired by Hegel, to play the role of a Hegelian historian of philosophy—and in spite of this indicate that

---

where Baur maintains that the important difference between Platonism and Christianity is that according to Christianity "the human cannot raise itself to the divine unless the divine has descended to the human."

he had another and categorically different standard of irony than that of Hegel.

This is clearly stated in thesis 8, where he says that "Irony, as infinite and absolute negativity, is the lightest and weakest meaning of subjectivity," which immediately suggests that subjectivity has other and higher possibilities than the ironic position. This corresponds quite closely with Kierkegaard's later (especially in *Concluding Unscientific Postscript*) fully developed theory of the stages, according to which an individual is never directly, immediately, what it was created for, planned to be, but chooses among certain possibilities, of which the ironist is only one. This theory of stages, which is only suggested in *On the Concept of Irony*, is also in total discord with Hegel's philosophy, in which the norm for personality was speculative insight, not as for Kierkegaard an ethical position toward one's self and to the self's given reality as a task.

Kierkegaard, with such opinions, which (motivated by *On the Concept of Irony*'s whole, chosen limits and function as a philosophical thesis) are only hinted at in that work, was not a Hegelian, but one who as an experimenter chose the indirect method, chose to appear as a wolf in sheep's clothing, to play the role of a Hegelian historian of philosophy. This looked so artless and harmless—and in the course of time some have allowed themselves to be deceived by the costume, have in complete seriousness believed of Kierkegaard, the master of irony, that his outside, the academic dissertation *On the Concept of Irony*, full of scholarship and perspicacity, was also his inside. That is a strange misunderstanding of a thinker who could not only write a book about irony but who could also use irony himself.

It is a curious misconception that Kierkegaard should have been a Hegelian in earnest when he wrote *On the Concept of Irony*. He wasn't before and he did not become one later. It is an odd misunderstanding when the first thesis of the work says clearly enough that he was not, and when the last statement in the work says the same thing with all desirable clarity, thus:

> Finally, insofar as there can be any question of the "eternal validity" of irony, then this question can only find its answer through an investigation of the domain of humor. Humor contains a far deeper skepticism than irony; for here it is not finitude, but sinfulness, that everything turns upon; The skepticism [of humor] is related to [the skepticism] of irony as ignorance to the old

thesis: *credo quia absurdum*;[k] but it also contains a far deeper positivity [than irony]; for it does not occupy itself with the human, but with theoanthropic determinations, it does not find rest in making man human, but by making man God-Man. But all this lies beyond the confines of this investigation, and insofar as one should wish matter for afterthought, then I shall refer to Prof. Martensen's review of Heiberg's *New Poems* (pp. 341-342).

Kierkegaard does not say that we can find the solutions to these questions in Martensen's review, but only that there is material for reflection there. Perhaps Kierkegaard's concluding lines, which Martensen could read first in the manuscript, since as University Professor he got Kierkegaard's treatise for judgment, and then in print in the elegant copy that Kierkegaard sent him with a nice dedication, had given Martensen a little material for reflection—but on that we know nothing.

4. CONCLUSION

The conclusion of the investigation in this chapter can be presented quite briefly: Kierkegaard's understanding of Hegel's philosophy as a totality, as well as its solidarity with two earlier philosophical traditions, is in *On the Concept of Irony* not directly wrong, but must be characterized as incomplete.

On the basis of a partial knowledge of the dialectical method and of certain parts of Hegel's works, the historical, not the systematic, Kierkegaard as an experiment wished to try his hand at the role of a Hegelian historian of philosophy.

Kierkegaard's own position, which is not formulated directly or fully thought out in this work, cannot correctly be designated as Hegelian.

[k] "I believe because it is absurd," attributed to Tertullian.

CHAPTER VI

From *On the Concept of Irony*
to *Either/Or*

1. INTRODUCTORY COMMENT

AFTER the defense of his thesis on September 29, 1841, and the final break with Regine Olsen on October 11 of the same year, Kierkegaard was a free man. Two weeks after the break he journeyed to Berlin, from which he returned March 6, 1842, completed the manuscript of *Either/Or* in November of the same year, and published this work on February 20, 1843.

During this period, from October 1841 to February 1843 Kierkegaard continued his study of Hegel, the Hegelians, and a decidedly anti-Hegelian thinker, Schelling. We must, then, undertake a study of this in the following section. First, the Journal entries (III A 146-209, together with III A 227-246, IV A 1-43, as well as IV A 194-197)[a] and *Papers* and *Letters* from the same period, then his summaries of Marheineke's lectures on dogmatics in Berlin (III C 26).[b] After this we will take up the comprehensive summaries of Schelling, then his entries from Werder, and finally, his reading of Hegel as well as other entries relevant to this investigation.

2. *Papirer*, III A 146-209, III A 227-246, IV A 1-43, IV A 194-197, AND LETTERS FROM THE SAME PERIOD

Up to November 20, 1842, when he completed the manuscript of *Either/Or*, Kierkegaard's *Journal*, as might be expected, is essentially occupied with reflections concerning his broken engagement. The same is true of various letters he wrote to different people in Copenhagen from Berlin.[1] In only a single place does he quote

---

[a] Reference to the Hong translation of the *Journal* entries will be made as they occur in what follows.

[b] Hong, V, #5514.

[1] *Breve og Aktstykker vedr. SK* No. 49-70. [*Letters and Documents Con-*

Hegel favorably, and only in a single entry (III A 179),[c] written after November 22, 1841, does he mention Schelling: "Now I have placed all my hope in Schelling,—but if only I knew that I could make her happy, I would travel this very evening. . . ."

This entry, written after Kierkegaard had heard Schelling's second lecture, on the relation of philosophy to reality, is best treated in connection with Kierkegaard's summaries. Here we should only bear in mind the great expectations he brought with him. As is well known, these expectations were not fulfilled.

In the beginning of December Kierkegaard read a part of Hegel's *Lectures on the Philosophy of Fine Art*, thus—according to P. A. Heiberg's dating[2]—at the same time that he was about to finish the composition of *The Equilibrium Between the Esthetic and the Ethical in the Composition of the Personality*, and was writing *The Diary of the Seducer, The First Love, Rotation*, and last but not least, *The Reflections of Classical Tragedy in Modern Tragedy*, for which Hegel's *Philosophy of Fine Art* has considerable significance.

This renewed study of Hegel's *Philosophy of Fine Art*, which Kierkegaard had read portions of during the composition of *On the Concept of Irony* (cf. *supra*, Chapter V, section 2c) gave him the occasion to quote a passage from Hegel's section on "the individual epic action" (IV, 134-135).

The context in Kierkegaard is this: he asserts that passion is the genuine standard for humans. Without passion one is wretched—passion gives greatness. He then happens to think about Regine Olsen's brother, Jonas Christian Olsen, who after the engagement was broken wrote in a letter (now lost) to Kierkegaard that he would hate SK "as no one before has hated." Were the good Jonas really capable of hating according to the standard, then indeed Kierkegaard would count himself lucky, for being contemporaneous with such a passionately great man.

In connection with these observations on passion, of essential significance for understanding of *Either/Or* (cf. the motto from Young on the title page of Vol. I), a quotation from Hegel is given.

This quotation is detached from the context of thought in Hegel,

cerning *Søren Kierkegaard*, trans. Henrik Rosenmeier, *Kierkegaard's Writings*, vol. XXV (Princeton: Princeton University Press, 1978).]

[c] Hong, V, #5535.

[2] *Nogle Bidrag til Enten-Ellers Tilblivelseshistorie* [Some Contributions to the History of the Genesis of *Either/Or*], 1910, 32-33.

but not misconceived. Kierkegaard himself claims (III C 31)[d] that "one often grasps Hegel best in his casual remarks." In Kierkegaard what is involved at this point (as is so often the case) is not at all to understand Hegel in and for himself, but to illustrate a particular phenomenon with the help of a quotation, and it quite clearly does not matter that it just happens to be Hegel's statement and not, for example, Sibbern's or Heiberg's. What was of fundamental importance for Hegel, as indicated by the placement of the statement in the systematic context: the third part of *Philosophy of Fine Art*, third chapter, first main heading, second point under the second subpoint—thus representing the negation in the dialectical development, did not concern Kierkegaard at all.

If we now turn from Kierkegaard's *Papirer* dating from this period to the letters he wrote from Berlin, we find a few items of interest.

Kierkegaard began to attend Marheineke's lectures, he writes to Boesen (October 31, 1841, *Letter* no. 49), and initially he was quite satisfied with them, although they contained nothing new to him. Schelling had not yet begun. In the middle of November Kierkegaard had, with great dissatisfaction, heard Steffens (mentioned in *Letter* no. 51, November 18, to Spang), and Schelling had begun to lecture to a packed auditorium. Kierkegaard became annoyed at the crowd and hubbub (from the ones who could not get in because of lack of space), but he had put his trust in Schelling and he attended faithfully. On December 14 (*Letter* no. 54) he again tells Boesen about Schelling's many listeners and briefly informs his friend about Schelling's negative and positive philosophy and about his description of Hegel's as "sophisticated Spinozism." The next day he writes at some length to Sibbern (*Letter* no. 55): he has heard Steffens lecture several times on anthropology, but he has become disappointed, although he had with "immense enthusiasm" read, among others, *Caricaturen des Heiligsten* (which he had already bought in January 1836. Cf. I A 250[e]). He calls Werder a virtuoso and almost a psychological phenomenon, for whom "his [own] life, his thought, the manifoldness of the outside world almost seems to get meaning for him only by being referred to Hegel's logic." In the letter to Sibbern, Schelling gets almost verbatim the same description as in the previous one to Boesen. On January 8,

[d] Hong, II, #1592.

[e] Hong, III, #2304.

1842, Kierkegaard again writes to Spang (*Letter* no. 61) that the second volume of Hegel's *Encyclopedia*, i.e., the lectures on the philosophy of nature, had been published by Michelet, who had allowed himself

> without showing the Association [of Hegel disciples, for the publication of Hegel's works] it, to write a preface, in which he somewhat severely attacks Schelling.

Schelling's posture was not exactly pleasing, and Kierkegaard says that "he looks as fierce as a vinegar maker." In the same letter he tells with restrained admiration of the brilliant Werder, who plays with the categories the way the strong man in Dyrehaven[f] plays with heavy balls: "it is frightening to look at, and as in Dyrehaven one is tempted sometimes to believe that they are paper balls." This may be compared with Kierkegaard's critical remarks on December 1, 1841 (III C 30)[g] against Werder. Kierkegaard became increasingly more critical of Schelling. He writes to Boesen on January 16, 1842 (*Letter* no. 62), that his later lectures unfortunately do not have a great deal of importance, and on February 6, also to Boesen (*Letter* no. 68), of his disappointed hopes with respect to Schelling as well as "confusion in my philosophical ideas." Schelling, he has "entirely given up, I only listen to him, write nothing, neither there nor at home," which was quite different from the beginning, then he wrote the lectures down in detail. Scarcely three weeks later Kierkegaard had completely lost patience with Schelling: he "twaddles boundlessly both in the extensive and the intensive sense" even "quite intolerably," as he writes in letters (no. 69 and 70) to Boesen and his brother, Peter Kierkegaard, who got the very plausible explanation that Kierkegaard "is too old to attend lectures, just as Schelling is too old to give them."

3. MARHEINEKE'S LECTURES ON DOGMATIC THEOLOGY

Marheineke was, after Daub's death in 1836, the most important theological right-wing Hegelian.[3] In a little text, published in May

---

[f] A park just outside of Copenhagen.

[g] Hong, I, #257.

[3] No major presentation of these two theologians' views is available. Barth has a quite scholarly essay on this "tragic figure" in *Die protestantische Theologie im 19. Jahrhundert* (1947, pp. 442-449), just as Hirsch devotes some pages to him in his *Geschichte der neuern evangelischen*

1842, entitled *Einleitung in die öffentlichen Vorlesungen über die Bedeutung der Hegelschen Philosophie in der christlichen Theologie*[h] he gave a clear account of his position after having, in a polemical introduction, separated himself from pietists and atheists, obscurantists in general, rationalists and supranaturalists, Schelling, Schleiermacher as well as Strauss, Feuerbach, Bruno Bauer, and the other left-wing Hegelians.

For Marheineke, Hegel's philosophy is simply philosophy itself:

It contains everything at least in the principles which the Spirit itself has worked on in thought for more than three thousand years (p. 51).

This cannot be evaded or ignored by any theologian, since this philosophy alone is in a position not only to prove the agreement of the truths of faith with reason but to raise Faith from the lower sphere of representation to absolute science [*Viden*] (pp. 52-53).

The lectures Kierkegaard attended (III C 26)[i] were an attempt to carry out this position. Hegel's method and system were for Marheineke so obviously correct that he sought to employ the method without further foundation and to assume the system, especially the *Encyclopedia* and the *Philosophy of Religion*, of course, as known and recognized. If we compare Marheineke's lectures with Martensen's, as Kierkegaard knew them, we may characterize Martensen's as formally far more elegant than Marheineke's whereas Marheineke has on his side greater weight of learning. As far as the dogmatic position is concerned, the lectures were given "with special reference to Daub's system," and they represent in the formulation a stage between the extensively revised second edition of *Die Grundlehren der christlichen Dogmatik*, which was kept to a rather concise style, and the broader, posthumously published presentation *System Der christlichen Dogmatik* (1847). While Martensen was under the positive influence of Baader, Marheineke parted company from that thinker in his speculative interpretation of the predominantly Lutheran-influenced dogmatics traditional at that time.

Theologie 1954, V, 366ff.), and Martin Schmidt gives a rather brief description in his revised edition of Horst Stephan's *Geschichte der deutschen evangelischen Theologie seit dem deutschen Idealismus* (1960, pp. 80-83).

[h] [Introduction to the public lectures on the importance of Hegelian philosophy in Christian theology].

[i] Hong, V, #5514.

Although after hearing Marheineke's first lecture, which he was very satisfied with, Kierkegaard wrote to Boesen (*Letter* no. 49, October 31, 1841) that it "contained nothing new," yet it was for him "quite pleasant to hear orally much of what one is accustomed to see printed," and he continued for a longer time to listen to Marheineke and to write down a rather lengthy but not especially careful summary.

No immediate reaction came from Kierkegaard, which probably can be explained by the fact that during these months he was far more occupied with other questions, privately, mostly with his engagement, and in the literary arena with the completion of *Either/Or*. But when, during the first six months of 1844, he wrote *Philosophical Fragments* and the *Concept of Dread* he also had Marheineke's presentation of "the origin of evil" and of Christology, among others, in his thoughts.

4. Schelling's Lectures on the Philosophy of Revelation

Unfortunately it is impossible to determine with certainty how Kierkegaard came to set such high expectations of Schelling as he had at first. There is a rare element of immediacy in Journal entry III A 179[j]:

> I am so happy to have heard Schelling's second lecture—indescribably. Long enough have I sighed and thoughts sighed in me; when he mentioned the word "reality" concerning the relation of philosophy to reality then the fetus of thought leaped with joy in me as in Elizabeth. I remember almost every word he said from that moment on. Here perhaps clarity can arrive. This one word, which reminded me of all my philosophical sufferings and pangs.—

Why did Kierkegaard's enthusiasm soon collapse, to be replaced in the end with indifference and contempt for Schelling?

This question must be answered under two headings, on Kierkegaard's problematic and on Schelling's.

It has been shown above how Kierkegaard first acquired a secondhand and then in the course of a very brief time, a not particularly complete firsthand knowledge of Hegel's philosophy as a whole and in certain details. From Martensen's survey of the system (*supra*, Chapter III, section 4), he could know that Hegel's concept of real-

[j] Hong, V, #5535.

ity as well as his concept of philosophy was not the ordinary one, but strongly divergent from it, from Heiberg's presentation of *The Speculative Logic* (1831-1832) which Kierkegaard apparently concerned himself with in 1837 (cf. II C 37),[k] as well as from Heiberg's Prospectus *On the Significance of Philosophy for the Present Time* (1833; cf. *supra*, Chapter I, section 2) he knew what a convinced Hegelian understood by reality and what he understood by philosophy, and he knew something of the sort from Adler's *The Isolated Subjectivity*, discussed earlier (*supra*, Chapter IV, section 6).

An account has also been given showing that the knowledge Kierkegaard acquired of the Hegelians' and of Hegel's own writings did not convince him of the correctness of their views; on the contrary, he became steadily more critical of them without yet having clearly formulated his own religious-philosophical position. In general, the most we can say is that his notion of Christianity excluded a basic agreement with Hegel's system and simultaneously opened up to him the possibility of another, still not clearly defined notion of the function and scope of philosophy, as well as a concept of "reality" which (unlike the Hegelian, which was primarily characterized by a speculative-logical constitution), instead, speaking completely provisionally, was characterized as the individual, presently existing [*forhaandenværende*] human reality as ethical task, a task that man theoretically as well as practically can relate himself to differently. In *On the Concept of Irony* Kierkegaard evaluated both Socrates' and the romantics' (the esthetes') irony negatively, because they did not relate themselves in the proper way to the presently existing reality as ethical task, and Kierkegaard's later explicit reproaches of the speculative thinker (especially in the *Postscript*) that he absent-mindedly lost himself in, for example, world-historical reflections instead of existing in the reality he is situated in, has the same motivation, only more fully set forth and founded on the earlier Authorship, both the pseudonymous, with its indirect communication, and the "official," with its direct preaching.

An important motive for Kierkegaard's trip to Berlin to hear Schelling, then, as we can infer from the statement quoted above, must have been that he had not found satisfactory solutions to his problems among the Hegelians or in Hegel himself, but now expected to find help in Schelling, who was anti-Hegelian, and who, with his "positive" philosophy which he had been so long preparing,

[k] Hong, I, #193.

intended both to provide the desired completion of his earlier "negative" philosophy and at the same time deliver a critique of Hegel's system.[4]

According to Kierkegaard's summary of Schelling's lectures, the following was said:[5] Schelling spoke of "philosophy and reality" in his second lecture as follows:

> Everything that is real has a double side: quid sit (what it is) quod sit (that it is). Thus philosophy can stand in a double relation thereto, one can have a concept without knowledge— a concept is an expression of quid sit, but it does not follow from

[4] This "positive" philosophy of Schelling has been interpreted—and particularly—evaluated in a great variety of ways. For example, such mutually and extremely different thinkers as the rationalist H.E.G. Paulus in *Die endlich offenbar gewordene positive Philosophie der Offenbarung* etc. (1843); Kierkegaard himself; the historian of philosophy Eduard Zeller in *Geschichte der deutschen Philosophie seit Leibniz* (1872); Høffding in *Philosophie i Tydskland efter Hegel* (1872) and in *The History of Modern Philosophy*, II; and Karl Jaspers in *Schelling* (1955) are united in the negative evaluation to which Jaspers has given expression by calling it a "Gnosis, which stupefied us with the vision of a seeming knowledge" (p. 9). Kuno Fischer in *Geschichte der neuern Philosophie* VII: *Schellings Leben, Werke und Lehre*, 3rd ed., 1902) is as always in his comprehensive work more faithfully documented than characterizing and evaluative, just as Nicolai Hartmann in *Die Philosophie des deutschen Idealismus* (2nd ed., 1960, an unaltered reprint of the first edition of 1923). H. Knittermeyer in *Schelling und die romantische Schule*, (1929) after his sympathetic but not uncritical presentation of Schelling, gives expression to a cautious positive evaluation —just as C. I. Scharling in *Grundtvig og Romantikken belyst ved Grundtvigs Forhold til Schelling* (1947), esp. pp. 213ff. A noteworthy attempt at rehabilitation is Walter Schulz's *Die Vollendung des deutschen Idealismus in der Spätphilosophie Schellings* (1955); while the contemporary debate on Schelling is expressed in *Verhandlungen der Schelling-Tagung in Bad Ragaz* (1954). Not without connection to the latter two works is the fact that two quite recent historians of philosophy, Jacques Chevalier's *Histoire de la Pensée*, III (1961), and Frederick Copleston's *History of Philosophy*, VII (1963) devote space to the "positive" philosophy, as, for example, Emile Bréhier *History of Philosophy*, VI, *The Nineteenth Century* (1968) only grants a few comments, while Nicola Abbagnano in *Storia della Filosofia*, 2nd ed., III (1963) takes some notice of it.

[5] III C 27 (Hong, V, #5536). In what follows we will only summarize what is significant for the chief topic of this investigation, i.e., Schelling's critique of Hegel, while Schelling's exposition of his "positive" philosophy, its teaching on potency and theory of demythologizing, can be touched upon only insofar as they relate to his position concerning Hegel. A more detailed summary of Schelling's lectures is given in Paulus' work (cited in the previous note) pp. 212ff.

that that I know: quod sit—but there is no knowledge without the concept. In knowledge, then, there is the double, whereby it is recollection. When I see a plant, I remember it and include it within the universal, so that I recognize it as a plant.

In line with that distinction, Schelling differentiates (beginning with the third lecture) between philosophy as teaching about essence (later called the pure philosophy of reason or speculative philosophy = the negative philosophy) and philosophy as teaching about being [or "Existence, as some moderns put it"]. The existing can be known in experience, wherefore it must be in the reason, whose content is "the infinite potency of being" [i.e., its possibility, not its actuality], its "potential being" [Seynkönnen] which passes over into "being" [Seyn] and thus into thought, "but the whole movement is in the direction of essence [quidditas] not of existence [quodditas] and this actuality is only possibility in another sense," to which Kierkegaard adds this marginal note as clarification: "This he illustrated also therefore by appealing to geometry, which has hardly any interest at all in any individual triangle." The immediate content of reason, it is said in the fourth lecture, is "not something actual, the opposite of the actual is its content" by which is probably meant the possible "potentia," which can, but need not pass over into the real, to "Seyn" and "first when the real has passed over, it excludes the other from itself, but establishes it just by that fact, for to exclude it is aussersich-setzen [to place it outside of itself]." Schelling develops this further in the last part of the fourth lecture, while in the fifth lecture he maintains that potency is opposed to actual being, and that pure being is just as little "the actual being as potency is." By the actual is meant that "which has passed from potency to act; otherwise it would not be pure being. But it is not potency. No, it is not immediate potency, but it can be mediate potency." These potencies are developed in a definite process, in nature and in the spirit, and correspondingly there are two philosophies, philosophy of nature and philosophy of spirit.

Science as treated up to this point, Schelling says in the sixth lecture, is "an exclusion of everything there is of reason's alien content, that which must be left to experience, which goes beyond the reason," which means—to put it briefly—that the philosophy of reason is philosophy of essence, the philosophy of experience is philosophy of being. Schelling's distinctions between various potencies of being can be left out of the account here. The pure philosophy of reason is called hereafter the negative philosophy, and Schelling claims that when it has come to its limits, it must then undergo an "inversion," so that its object becomes experience, which again means that the content of the a priori science of reason is all reality "but only what it is, not that it is" (seventh lecture). This science of reason is now the philosophy of identity, whose point of departure is indifference, and whose conclusion is the identity of subject and object. Historically this is linked with Fichte, whose point of departure was Kant's philosophy. This has nothing to do with existence (ninth lecture); but not until the science of reason under discussion

is brought to know itself as negative is it finished, but that is impossible, without having the positive outside itself at least as possibility. But if the positive does not come soon, then the negative easily becomes obscured, and one takes the logical for the real

[as in Hegel]. According to Schelling, Spinoza is guilty of this confusion and Hegel represents only a "sophisticated Spinozism" (ninth lecture; cf. Kierkegaard's expression in the letter to Boesen dated December 14, 1841, mentioned above).

Beginning with the tenth lecture, Schelling undertakes an explicit confrontation with Hegel. Hegel took his point of departure in the philosophy of identity, but mistakenly thought that this philosophy was a system of existence, with the development of which one made a mistake in appealing to intellectual intuition, which according to his interpretation one "knew nothing about, which perhaps was something accidental, subjective, a private matter for the chosen few." Schelling maintains, over against the alleged misconception on the part of Hegel, that the expression "intellectual intuition" does not come from him at all, but from Fichte, who chose it in contrast to sensory intuition, in which subject and object are distinct—whereas in intellectual intuition they are identical (and thus the designation: philosophy of identity). Instead of intellectual intuition Hegel had then posited the logic "as the science which shall prove the existence of the Absolute, and thereby he moves to another science," which Schelling finds dubious. Science of the Absolute must thus be proven twice, first in the logic and then in the following, second science. Now if for Hegel "Seyn" meant essence, not being, potency, not act, then his philosophy would not have been confused; but he meant being, and from that he passed straight to the Idea "as the really actualized Idea" (eleventh lecture) that in Hegel is defined approximately like the Absolute in his philosophy of identity. With this the logical concludes and with that "the pure rational, not to say negative, philosophy," and with that philosophy was made into a system, "into an asserted, dogmatic system" which in the end became too heavy for Hegel himself. He excluded nature from the logic, and logic is thought about thought, which in Schelling's eyes ultimately excluded real thought, i.e. thought with a real content. Thus, according to Schelling, this is precisely the mistake in Hegel's logic, that it did not go further, that it left nature and the philosophy of spirit outside of itself (twelfth lecture). The transition from logic to nature, which Hegel maintained proceded with necessity, is not necessary at all:

> In the Idea lies no necessity for movement, still less for a movement by which it breaks out of itself. The Idea is ideality and reality and does not need any other mode to become real. In the Idea lies no necessity for nature, possibility is difficult [enough] to intuit, necessity still more difficult.

Instead Schelling inclines toward the theory that one should hardly speak at all of the existence of nature as a necessary product of logic, one should only presuppose its presence [forudsætte dens Tilstedeværelse] in an a priori fashion and defer it to another science, namely the positive philosophy. Schelling then takes up Hegel's theory hypothetically:

> now allow that the Idea has immersed itself in nature so as in this way again to come to Spirit as man, where it can shed [afstryge] all determinations of subjectivity and become object —God. This is indeed the second main problem [,] let us now see, what Hegel thinks he has produced here.

Hegel maintained, according to Schelling's summary, that earlier philosophy had God only as substance, not as Spirit; but—Schelling says—Hegel was hardly the discoverer of the definition of God as Spirit. Christianity already taught that, as everyone knows from the Catechism. In addition, Hegel's God as Spirit comes about only when the whole development is completed, *post festum*. God is for Hegel, mistakenly, a conclusion, not a point of departure, and even if one would maintain that for Hegel God is both beginning and end, then in any case there can be no mention of absolute identity, since in such a case there would be no movement at all, i.e., no dialectical unfolding, which Hegel definitely wishes to insist upon (thirteenth lecture). In the second edition of Hegel's *Logic* Schelling thinks that there is "an extraordinary passage" that could have become the point of departure for Hegel for the correct, positive philosophy; but Hegel did not make anything of it. The most he obtained was a notion of the Absolute as "Final Cause, since everything tended toward it." Now if everything is turned around, so that the ultimate "Final Cause" [*causa finalis*] becomes creative, then all intermediary causes must also become freely creative, which Hegel made no attempt to assert. Schelling thinks that that passage in Hegel, moreover, acquired a certain significance in his philosophy of religion, where, in particular, the doctrine of the Trinity should be reformed in line with Hegel's theory that God [necessarily] must reveal Himself, because His nature [*Væsen*] is process. This revelation is the world, and its essence [*Væsen*] is the Son, who must turn back to Himself through mankind, and that happens, according to Hegel, through art, religion, and philosophy. On the contrary, Schelling maintains, this is neither satisfying philosophy nor religion: it cannot possibly satisfy Christ, and it must offend the philosophers that it sought to merge itself with Christianity. Schelling emphatically asserts that the chief mistake in Hegel's philosophy is that it wants to be Christian, "for it did not need to go to that trouble, since a purely rational science as little needs to be that as geometry needs to be" (thirteenth lecture). The three instances—art, religion, and philosophy—which Hegel set up do not satisfy Schelling: rational science, i.e. Hegel's philosophy as it should rightly be understood, not as Hegel himself misconstrued it, knows nothing about religion, which it does not even contain as a possibility; of philosophy, which in Hegel's system occupied the third place, Schelling says (fourteenth lecture) that "it obviously is the one he took for granted, and thus [was] not a new philosophy." If the science of reason with art and religion has overstepped a limit, then Hegel leaves unanswered the question of how they can then fall back into themselves. Hegel should instead have left the third place vacant—namely for Schelling's positive philosophy—because he really did not have anything to fill it with. If, like the Hegelians, one would use Hegel's philosophy to grasp the positive, Schelling maintains (fifteenth lecture), then one was displaying a complete misunderstanding of Hegel, "for this it has already done and therein lies . . . precisely his mistake." In the efforts on behalf of the propagation of Hegel's philosophy special emphasis was put on grasping "God's personality within the rational science" where, according to Hegel's interpretation, it obviously had not been present before, although Hegel let the Absolute Spirit, which was not personal, freely determine itself to create, which was an inconsistency.

In contrast, Schelling then presents his own theory of positive and negative philosophy. Each is just as necessary as the other; but the positive philosophy has an entirely new method, and it does not need to be based on the negative philosophy, even though the latter has "a desire for the positive" (fifteenth lecture).

Although Kierkegaard continued to attend Schelling's lectures and to write out his rather complete summaries for a while, it is quite clear that his main interest was Schelling's criticisms of Hegel, that is, the negative aspect of Schelling's positive philosophy. Certainly, as he indicated in the letters written before his arrival and just at the beginning of the lectures, he entertained very great expectations for Schelling's counterpart to Hegel's system; but these hopes did not come to fruition. On the contrary, Schelling's later lectures were such a great disappointment to him that he did not attend them to the end. He went home to Copenhagen. There is scarcely any need for a profound explanation for this disappointment. The fact was simply that he was fully occupied with work on his own, for the time being mainly indirect, critique of Hegel, and at the same time his own positive counterpart. Now, although Kierkegaard's critical attitude toward Hegel—and the Hegelians—was in all likelihood confirmed by learning of Schelling's objections, then, to mention only a single item here, the theory of the stages of life that he was developing in *Either/Or*, was not compatible with Schelling's positive philosophy, such as Kierkegaard had the opportunity to know it, nor was his concept of the relation between reason and revelation in harmony with Schelling's either. Kierkegaard had sought help for the solution of his problem from Schelling; but he found only a new attempt at system-building, for which he could find no rational use.

5. Werder's Lectures on "Logic and Metaphysics, with Special Reference to Outstanding Systems in Ancient and Modern Philosophy"

In addition to the lectures of Marheineke and Schelling, Kierke-

gaard attended for a while in Berlin those of the Hegelian philosopher Karl Werder (III C 28, 29,[1] 30[m]—from December 1841); but
he did not record much from them. He already knew something
about Hegel's logic, especially from Heiberg, although he still does
not seem to have concerned himself much with Hegel's own presentation, neither the greater *Logic* nor the lesser, in the *Encyclopedia*.
Classical formal logic Kierkegaard knew mainly from Sibbern's
Logic as Doctrine of Thinking (*Logik som Tænkelære*, 2nd ed.,
1835, Ktl. 777).[n]

III C 28 and 29 contain only summary surveys, tables, and particular definitions, while III C 30 clearly shows that Kierkegaard was
by no means an uncritical listener.

Werder's logic, which in its published version, *Logik, als Com-
mentar und Ergänzgung zu Hegels Wissenschaft der Logik* (1841,
Ktl. 867), contains only the teaching on quality, i.e., only a ninth
of the whole speculative logic, contains no noteworthy divergencies
from Hegel, but emphasizes as the two important axioms, that the
laws of being and thought are identical, and that concepts are filled
with opposites, which is the basis for the alleged movement in
logic.[6]

Kierkegaard is critical of the speculative developments of the
concept in Werder. To his way of thinking they contain "a sheer
play" (III C 30), just as, in connection with this critique, he inter-
poses a similar objection against Marheineke ("this confusion"
III C 32[o]), while he still at this time lets Hegel, whose *Philosophy
of Fine Art* he was beginning to read, get off scot free.[7] The familiar

[1] Hong, V, #5537.   [m] Hong, I, #257.

[n] As far as I can discover, there is no English translation of this work.

[6] The logic of Hegel and of the Hegelians may be rightly understood as
onto-logic. In the history of logic they are, therefore, generally passed over.
Cf., among others, Jørgen Jørgensen's *A Treatise of Formal Logic*, I (1931)
("Historical Development"), and I. M. Bochenski's presentation of the history of the discipline in *A History of Formal Logic* (1961), where Hegel
is summarily dismissed (p. 258) as a logician, and the Hegelians are not
even mentioned.

[o] Hong, III, #3285.

[7] The most important article on Kierkegaard's understanding of Logic is
Paul L. Holmer's "Kierkegaard and Logic" (in *Kierkegaardiana*, II, 1957,
25-42). Several of Gregor Malantschuk's articles, such as, "Begrebet Fordoblelse hos S.K." (*Ibid.*, p. 43-53), "Frihedens Dialektik hos SK" (in
DTT, 1949, 193ff.) and not least his "Das Verhältnis zwischen Wahrheit
und Wirklichkeit . . ." (in *Orbis Litterarum*, 1955, 166ff.) treat the question in a wider context.

objections of Kierkegaard against Hegel's Logic in the *Postscript* and elsewhere, that he developed after he had studied Trendelenburg and Aristotle, he did not yet set forth in detail; but the tendency in the entries noted here is the same as later, when the critique is levied against precisely these two axioms.

6. KIERKEGAARD'S READING OF HEGEL'S *Philosophy of Fine Art*

As was said in the discussion of *On the Concept of Irony*, during the composition of that work Kierkegaard had already read at least certain sections of Hegel's *Philosophy of Fine Art* in Hotho's edition, the third volume of which appeared in 1838.

At the end of 1841 he had again occupied himself with this work, and this time exclusively with the third chapter of the Third Part, "On Poetry," and he had, quite concisely, made a note of a survey of the sections on epic, lyric, and dramatic poetry (III C 34).[p] Kierkegaard evidently did not concern himself with the introduction to the chapter (IV, 3-18). While his survey of the sections on epic and dramatic poetry contains individual critical remarks, the notes from the reading of Hegel's section on lyric poetry, rather typical of Kierkegaard, are as schematic as can be.

The result of this reading of Hegel's *Philosophy of Fine Art* first appears in *Either/Or*, especially in the section "The Ancient Tragical Motif as Reflected in the Modern" (I, 135-162). Both the notes here and *Either/Or* as a whole show that, although Kierkegaard was writing on theoretical esthetics, it was not his main interest or intention to work out an esthetic system, but on the contrary—in contrast to Hegel—in a poetic style of presentation to give expression to the point of view which is briefly and precisely formulated in III C 33[q] as follows:

> A passage where Hegel himself seems to suggest the imperfection of thought alone, that not even philosophy alone is the satisfactory expression of human life, or that thus personal life does not fulfill itself in thought alone, but in a totality of kinds of existence [*Existents-Arter*] and modes of expression. Cf. *Philosophy of Fine Art*, IV, 212-213.[r]

[p] Hong, V, #5545.   [q] Hong, II, #1593.

[r] I have taken the liberty of changing Kierkegaard's references to the volume and page of the German edition he used to the corresponding volume and page of the English translation.

In the passage referred to, in the section on the general character of the lyric, Hegel says that there is a form of Spirit[s] which in a certain respect stands higher than the imagination of emotion and conception, because it—i.e., philosophical thought—is able to bring the content to universal validity and necessary coherence; but, Hegel concedes (and it is this concession Kierkegaard took note of),

On the other hand, however, this form [of philosophy] is linked with abstraction, only developed in the element of thought as purely ideal universality, so that the concrete man can find himself constrained also to express the content and results of his philosophical consciousness in concrete fashion, as permeated with soul [Gemüth] and perception [Anschauung], imagination and feeling, so as thus to have and to give a total expression of the whole interior (IV, 212).

Kierkegaard's interest was precisely the concrete man Hegel speaks of, and the actuality of concrete man in existence. The actuality with which Hegel and his disciples were chiefly concerned was for Kierkegaard an abstraction, which one was in a position to be concerned about only in distraction from the existential.

Here in embryo lies the whole difference between Kierkegaard's thought, its principles [Forudsætninger], its method, and its conclusions, in its incompatibility and in its conflict [Modsætning] with Hegel's.

Kierkegaard has concisely indicated a relevant perspective in one of the Dispsalmata in Either/Or (I, 31):

What the philosophers say about reality is often as disappointing as a sign you see in a shop window, which reads: Pressing Done Here. If you brought your clothes to be pressed, you would be fooled; for the sign is only for sale.

Shortly after this Kierkegaard left Berlin's philosophical retail shop and acted like a soldier who bought a cannon and started his own private war.

7. Conclusion

The previously unpublished Journal entries of Kierkegaard discussed in this chapter, with a single exception, have not been used

---

[s] Osmaston translates Hegel's word Geist as "intelligence" here.

in the earlier Kierkegaard scholarship.[8] Thus we cannot speak of discussion and confrontation with other writers on Kierkegaard in this area; we can only briefly summarize the conclusion of this aspect of our study.

It appears that Kierkegaard could certainly still with positive interest concern himself with one or another detail in Hegel; but he found neither time nor occasion to deepen his study of Hegel or extend it to parts of the System that during the composition of *On the Concept of Irony* he had not demonstrably concerned himself with.

The situation was not much different with his more comprehensive concern with Marheineke and especially with Schelling. He lost patience with the one because he by and large repeated things that were familiar to Kierkegaard, and with the other because he simply talked nonsense. He was just as critical of the Hegelian logician Werder.

There is hardly any need to seek a profound explanation for Kierkegaard's attitude: he found no positive help for the solution of his own problematic, already sketched in the summer of 1835 (cf. *supra*, Chapter I, section 8), either in Hegelians such as Marheineke and Werder or in an anti-Hegelian such as Schelling. Moreover, as far as anti-Hegelianism is concerned, it would soon become evident that Kierkegaard worked most freely and best on his own.

[8] A. M. Koktanek in *Schellings Seinslehre und Kierkegaard* [Schelling's Doctrine of Being and Kierkegaard], 1962, where it is said in the Introduction (p. 15) that Kierkegaard misunderstood Hegel, and where it is said, as a concise description of Schelling's significance for Kierkegaard (p. 21), that Schelling delivered his brain-child.

CHAPTER VII

Hegel in Kierkegaard's *Papirer* from November 1842 to December 1845

1. INTRODUCTORY COMMENT

HEIBERG and Kuhr have already pointed out in their edition of Kierkegaard's *Papirer* that the period from the completion of the manuscript of *Either/Or* to the completion of the manuscript of *Concluding Unscientific Postscript*, that is, the three years indicated in the title of this chapter, were for Kierkegaard an unbroken period of work. "For this time period it has not been easy . . . to find a suitable place to make divisions," they say in their preface to volume IV (p. vii).

Although for external reasons the editors had to divide the entries into several volumes (IV, V, and VI), in the present study there is no compelling reason not to handle them together. Everyone familiar with Kierkegaard's *Papirer* knows that during the periods when his works flowed forth, there are relatively few entries in groups A and C. This is true of the period 1842-1846. In the time following that period there is a somewhat evenly balanced relation, quantitatively considered, between the *Papirer* and the *Works*. In the great publication pause from the fall of 1851 till the end of 1854, when Kierkegaard opened the public battle with the Church, the Journals swelled accordingly.

In addition to these external circumstances there are intrinsic reasons for studying the entries in *Papirer* IV-VI together. The individual questions and whole sets of problems Kierkegaard dealt with during this period both privately and publicly come up in connection with very few major themes, such as "Regine," which is left out of the present account, the romantic (the esthetic stage), which is only touched on here, and speculation, which became the object of Kierkegaard's indefatigable polemic, direct and indirect, precisely during the years 1842-1845 in the *Papirer* and in the *Works*. The point of attack and the tactics varied from book to book, but the purpose, the destruction of Hegelian speculation was everywhere the same.

Hence, it is reasonable in what follows first to go through all the relevant A entries, then the corresponding C entries, while the B entries are most naturally studied with the works to which they relate. B entries concerning unpublished works, as, for example, *Johannes Climacus; or, De Omnibus Dubitandum Est*, must, then, be discussed in this chapter rather than in the following one on the individual published works.

While on the basis of extant booksellers' records and various notes in several instances we can say with certainty when Kierkegaard had acquired a particular book from a bookstore in Copenhagen,[1] when he began to read it and from what point in time his reaction arises, then it is probable that during his first, quite extended stay in Berlin he bought both new and second-hand books. This presumption is supported by the many Journal entries from the fall of 1842 and thereafter where Kierkegaard quotes and refers to several thinkers whose names had not previously played a prominent role in his entries. Thus we find Descartes mentioned several times (IV A 1 and subsequently), whose works he used in the Amsterdam edition of 1678, which he had probably acquired second-hand, and Aristotle too, whom he began to read in the older German translations (e.g. Chr. Garve's translation of the *Ethics* and the *Politics*) as well as the newer ones (e.g., Roth's translation of the *Rhetoric*). We also find Leibniz more frequently cited, quoted, and discussed, as Kierkegaard read *Theodicy* in Gottsched's German translation of 1763. Also during this period Kierkegaard acquired and studied Trendelenburg's various logical and anti-Hegelian writings, just as he worked his way through a large part of Tennemann's *History*

---

[1] It would require a special study of the particular cases to clarify or make a probable determination of how Kierkegaard became aware of new books. As far as Danish works are concerned, it is not difficult to find out. He often first became aware of German theological and philosophical literature especially through the two periodicals he subscribed to for several years, namely, Clausen and Hohlenberg's well edited *Tidsskrift for udenlandsk theologisk Litteratur* and I. H. Fichte's anti-Hegelian *Zeitschrift für Philosophie and speculative Theologie*, which was an organ for speculative theism, with, among others, Carus, Chalybäus, Erdmann, C. Ph. Fischer, Günther, Lücke, Jul. Müller, Neander, Nitzsch, Rothe, Stahl, Staudenmaier, Steffens, Twesten, and Weisse as contributors, until this movement broke up with the years and died out. Under changing editors and titles, the periodical continued to appear until 1917, although it did not come out between 1848-1852. T. K. Oesterreich gives a general description of this periodical in Ueberweg's *Grundriss d. Gesch. d. Philos.* (IV, 13th ed., 1951, 233).

of Philosophy (which he had acquired in Copenhagen in May 1841) as well as Ritter's and Marbach's. We can also mention other, more scattered reading of various writers such as Flavius Philostratus, Herodotus, Bossuet's *History of the World*, and Hieronymus Cardanus.

Thus Kierkegaard broadened his horizons quite considerably at the same time he was writing his own books, and naturally, that is not without significance for his attitude toward Hegel and the Hegelians. Even if it is hardly possible to fix a completely firm pattern for his reading during these years, nevertheless it does permit us to discover a definite perspective there, which to a great degree helped to determine what he read and what he left aside. This must be constantly kept in mind in what follows, even if it is not explicitly mentioned with every point. If we were to characterize briefly the purpose of Kierkegaard's reading during these years, we could say that it was to construct his own position as a thinker on certain points and at the same time to equip his arsenal with aggressive weapons for his unrelenting battle against speculation in general and Hegel in particular.

2. *Papirer*, IV A 1-256 AND IV C 2-127

From November 20 on, under the heading "Esthetica," Kierkegaard has a series of entries (IV C 102-27)[a] made in connection with the reading of ancient and modern esthetic literature. He began to read Curtius's translation (done in 1753) of Aristotle's *Poetics* together with the translator's detailed notes and appended articles.[2] He concerned himself a bit with Lessing's *Hamburgische Dramaturgie* (IV C 110),[b] with Kant (114),[c] Boethius (117),[d] and others, chiefly in connection with Curtius's notes. Hegel, whose *Philosophy of Fine Art*, some parts of which as has been previously mentioned, he had studied quite deeply, is discussed only in passing (IV C 108),[e] and together with Martensen is described as a parrot in the notion of the concept of the comic. Hegel maintains (*Philosophy of Fine*

---

[a] Most of these will be found in Hong, vols. I and IV. The reader is advised to consult the "Collation of Entries" at the end of each volume to locate specific entries other than the ones identified here.

[2] On M. C. Curtius see, for example, *Nouv. Biog. Gen.*, 12, 648f.

[b] Hong, IV, #4826.

[c] Hong, IV, #4830.

[d] Hong, IV, #4833.

[e] Hong, II, #1738.

Art, IV, 301-302) that while every contrast between the real and the apparent [*mellem det Indre og det Ydre*] can be ridiculous, yet the contrast certainly belongs to the concept of the comic, but this also implies "infinite geniality and confidence, capable of rising above its own contradiction, and experiencing therein no taint of bitterness or sense of misfortune whatsoever." Corresponding to this is Kierkegaard's definition of the comic as a metaphysical concept that provides a reconciliation.

The remaining esthetic entries are only indirectly relevant to the elucidation of Kierkegaard's relation to Hegel insofar as they contribute to the development of Kierkegaard's own esthetic theory in its distinctive character as contrasted with that of Hegel; but we shall not give an account of Kierkegaard's esthetics in this work.

In the A entries from the end of November 1842 and the following months Kierkegaard only occasionally discusses Hegel directly, and then as a rule quite briefly. On the other hand he expanded his horizons in the history of philosophy considerably.

Although in the scholarly literature up to the present Kierkegaard's whole relation to Aristotle has not received an independent treatment, as desirable as that is, nor has his relation to Descartes,[3] yet his study of Leibniz has been treated.[4] It was especially these three thinkers, typical rationalists, that he concerned himself with during this period, at the same time as he was working through nearly half of Tennemann's history of philosophy. Occasionally there are a few entries on Spinoza, Hamann, and other original minds.

Thus, if we investigate the individual texts in the A entries, we see that as a rule Kierkegaard paid attention only to individual items, at times only curiosities, in these philosophers. He did not become an Aristotelian, nor a Cartesian, nor a Leibnizian from his reading. The most we can say is that he appropriated certain viewpoints and elements from his reading, generally in reconstructed form, in the world of thought he was himself constructing, and

[3] In my article "Kierkegaard og den filosofiske Idealisme" in *Kierkegaardiana* (1962), 88ff., as well as in my Introduction to *Afsluttende uvidenskabelige Efterskrift*, the essential relation on individual points has been illustrated.

[4] By Kalle Sorainen in *Eripainos Ajatus*, XVII (1952), 177-186. This article was not cited by L. Nedergaard-Hansen in *Bayle og Leibniz' Drøftelse af Theodicé-Problemet*, 1965, where Kierkegaard is briefly mentioned in various places.

especially such contributions as he found he could use in his clash with Hegelian speculation.

From Martensen's lectures on modern philosophy Kierkegaard certainly knew Descartes and his central position, at least by reputation; but it was not until the end of 1842 that he tackled the reading of Descartes himself and remarked (IV C 14)[f] naturally enough, that "one gets quite a different impression of Descartes by reading him oneself [rather than by just hearing or reading about him]." The first two entries (IV A 1 and 2)[g] contain only a quotation from Descartes and the comment that "one does not always need to write systems, then," occasioned by Descartes' *Meditations*, while an entry some time later (IV A 72)[h] quite concisely reveals that Kierkegaard's problematic was entirely different from that of Descartes; existential, not epistemological. In this entry he reproaches the skeptics, among whom he includes Descartes because of his principle of the methodic doubt, with the charge that while they recklessly raise an epistemological doubt, they do not do so ethically. They dare not say that they know anything with certainty; but they presume to act ethically, with responsibility, and the premise for daring to do that must indeed be a certainty about what constitutes correct behavior. If it is possible to cast doubt on this ethical certainty, then the skeptics are caught in an area where they thought they were safe.[5]

This was Kierkegaard's initial reaction to his reading of Descartes. Later followed the unfinished draft of *Johannes Climacus, or De Omnibus Dubitandum Est* (IV B 1-17),[i] and Kierkegaard's final judgment is found in the pseudonymous Authorship.[6]

The next philosopher mentioned in Kierkegaard's Journals is Aristotle (IV A 5, 8, 9, 10, 36, 63, 157, 205, and 207). As has been mentioned, Kierkegaard acquired Garve's translation of the *Nico-*

---

[f] Hong, I, #736. [g] Hong, V, #5573, 5574. [h] Hong, I, #774.

[5] In more recent works on this topic, e.g., Sven Eduard Rohde's *Zweifel und Erkenntnis* (*Lunds Univ. Årsskrift*, N.F., Avd. 1, vol. 41, No. 4, 1945), Konrad Marc-Wogau's "Der Zweifel Descartes" etc. (*Theoria*, XX, 1954, 128ff.) either no notice at all is taken, or only passing reference is made to Kierkegaard, and the same is true of G. Schnurr's *Skeptizismus als theologisches Problem* (1964).

[i] Trans. T. H. Croxall (Stanford: Stanford University Press, 1958). Some of these entries will also be found in Hong, vols. I, III, and V.

[6] Echoes are found in *Papirer* V A 30 [Hong, I, #1033], V B 15:11, and VIII² B 89, p. 186 (from 1847-1848) [Hong, I, #657].

machean Ethics and the *Politics*, as well as Roth's translation of the *Rhetoric*. The painstaking Garve had written a very complete introduction to his translation of the *Ethics*, containing a presentation of the history of ethics from Aristotle to Kant (I, 1798, pp. 1-395); but this evidently did not stimulate Kierkegaard to engage in a closer study of the history of ethics. From Aristotle himself, and also from Tennemann's presentation of Aristotle, which he was reading at the same time, Kierkegaard noted a series of historical points and examples. In the present context there is nothing of particular interest in these individual A entries. Only a single entry should be pointed out, namely, IV A 157,[j] in which the Aristotelian concept of God as the Unmoved Mover is characterized and rejected as rationalistic superstition. However, this did not prevent Kierkegaard later, in his "Experiment," *Philosophical Fragments* (p. 30), from letting his experimenter Johannes Climacus employ the Aristotelian definition as a point of departure for his own non-Aristotelian thought project or from letting it play a certain role again in the *Concluding Unscientific Postscript* (p. 277).

Kierkegaard had also acquired both Erdmann's edition of Leibniz's *Opera philosophica* (I-II, 1839-1840), which was followed by that of Gerhardt (1875ff.), and Gottsched's translation of *Theodicy* (1763), which contained Fontenelle's eulogy of Leibniz, together with notes by the translator, who did not in this work, as in his translation of Bayle's *Dictionary* (which Kierkegaard also owned), find occasion to announce on the title page that notes were especially provided "for offensive passages."

Kierkegaard had heard Leibniz briefly discussed by Martensen, just as he obviously—as in the case of Descartes and others—could have read about him in the various treatments of the history of modern philosophy that he gradually acquired. While reading Leibniz's main work, Kierkegaard made some *Journal* entries (IV A 11, 12, 14-18, 22, and 25).[k7] Only one of these is of interest in the present context, namely the first,[1] on freedom and necessity.

In the A entries Kierkegaard occasionally discusses other think-

[j] Hong, II, #1332.

[k] These will be found in Hong, vols. III, IV, and V.

[7] Kierkegaard's concern with Leibniz was not long lasting. He is mentioned a couple of times in 1844 (V B 15 and 56) and after that only in 1850 (X² A 403 [Hong, IV #4027]), when Kierkegaard was reading the "most worthy" Julius Müller's *Die Christliche Lehre von der Sünde*, which he owned in the third edition (1849, Ktl. 689-690).

[1] Hong, III, #2360.

ers, in most instances on the basis of his reading of Tennemann's and Marbach's histories of philosophy, in individual cases against the background of the reading of their own works.

Thus, for example, when he briefly mentions Heraclitus (IV A 20)[m] and the Pythagoreans (IV A 38)[n] it is in connection with reading Tennemann, while the discussion of the Platonic and Plotinian triad—music, love, philosophy—juxtaposed with the Hegelian art, religion, philosophy (IV A 159)[o] is taken up on the basis of Marbach's sketch, which the editors of the *Papirer* have quite correctly pointed out in a note on this entry. From February 1843 until May 1844 Kierkegaard had acquired the most important writings of Adolf Trendelenburg (whom he generally calls Trendlenburg) and gradually worked his way through them (IV A 40). In this Aristotelian he found sharp weapons that he could turn against speculative logic in Werder's, Heiberg's, and Hegel's development. We also find in a single instance a discussion of Hamann (IV A 39);[p] we find Rosenkranz's book on Schelling referred to (IV A 185);[q] Kant is mentioned briefly (IV A 176),[r] also Spinoza (IV A 190)[s]—with criticism. To this is added diverse, rather scattered reading.

Of those mentioned above, the most significant individual for this study is undoubtedly Trendelenburg; but the entries in group C from this period are so much more complete that it is more appropriate to discuss his influence on Kierkegaard under a later heading.

It is worth pointing out that the A entries contain a long series of notes in which Kierkegaard gives significant indications of the development of concepts and attitudes that a little later will find a place especially in the pseudonymous Authorship, and which imply a constantly growing opposition to Hegel and his disciples. These indications are both temporally and topically formulated in close connection with the studies in the history of philosophy discussed here, the significance of which for Kierkegaard's world of thought is thereby given in principle.

A series of typical examples can show this:

On the philosophical level we find, in connection with Kierkegaard's studies in the history of philosophy, entries on motion (IV A 20, Heraclitus; 38: the Pythagoreans; 54), on repetition (IV A 156 and 169). On the domain of the philosophy of religion we find

[m] Hong, III, #3290.   [n] Hong, I, #198.   [o] Hong, III, #3325.
[p] Hong, II, #1549.   [q] Hong, II, #1604.   [r] Hong, V, #5702.
[s] Hong, II, #1333.

among others an entry on the criterion for truth (IV A 42), and various entries on the paradox (IV A 47, 62, 103, 108, 191 on faith and reason) just as there are—in close connection with the last mentioned—important entries on Christology (IV A 24, 33, 103, 112, 183, 189).[t]

While studying Tennemann's *Geschichte der Philosophie* (I, 1798) Kierkegaard first read the lengthy chapter on the Eleatics (pp. 150-209) and then the following one on Heraclitus (pp. 209-240). When at the same time he read Fr. Jakob's translation of Flavius Philostratus (*Leben des Apollonius von Tyana*), he encountered there what we can call a typical "Verschlimmbesserung"[u] of a philosophical principle ("know thyself"). Then in Tennemann's discussion of one of Heraclitus's students he finds a satisfactory example of such a mistake: if one exaggerates the theory that all things are incessantly changing, then it passes over into its opposite and results in the Eleatic denial of change. The problem of change (in the realm of being, not that of thought—where Hegel created a stir by introducing it) Tennemann also treated in his discussion of the Pythagoreans, which Kierkegaard also noted (IV A 38), whereupon, after further studies (among them Trendelenburg's chapter on this in *Logische Untersuchungen*, I, 1840, 110-123) he presented his anti-Hegelian view of the problem especially in *Repetition* and later in the *Concluding Unscientific Postscript*.

It is somewhat similar in Kierkegaard's observations concerning the tricky concept of repetition. The entry IV A 156[v] shows how, while reading Marbach's compendious treatment of the history of philosophy in antiquity and the middle ages, Kierkegaard paused at a couple of places (I, 1838, 247f. on Aristotle's *Metaphysics* II, 1841, 4-5, in his retrospective glance at Greek philosophy), stopped by what he called "the Aristotelian categories: Das—Was—War—Seyn." One is tempted to say that here—as usual—Kierkegaard was

---

[t] All of the entries cited in this paragraph will be found in the various volumes of the Hong edition of the *Journals and Papers* under the appropriate topics. The "Collation of Entries" at the end of each volume should be consulted for the precise Hong numbers.

[u] This unusual German word has no English equivalent. It conveys the notion of ruining something by trying to improve it, roughly equivalent to "too much of a good thing," or if one spoonful of sugar in a cup of coffee is good, two will be twice as good, and so on until so much sugar has been added that the coffee is undrinkable—that would be *Verschlimmbesserung*.

[v] Hong, III, #3793.

not interested in Aristotle's metaphysics in general or his doctrine of categories in particular, but only in items that he could adapt to his own use. In a later entry (IV A 169)[w] there is a categorical statement, which points toward *The Concept of Dread* (esp. pp. 16-17, note), that "repetition is a religious category." If the concept of repetition should be understood in this way, then this understanding implies a dissociation from Hegel, for whom repetition in this sense plays no role.

The important entry (IV A 42)[x] in which Kierkegaard regrets that there are probably only a few who saw what perspective is expressed in the last statement of volume II of *Either/Or* (p. 356): "only the truth which edifies is true for you," is best read in conjunction with IV C 50,[y] where Kierkegaard on the basis of his reading in Tennemann (*Geschichte*, V, 1805, 302) about Sextus Empiricus and his doubt about the criteria of truth remarks that "the Christian statement [cf. especially I Corinthians 13 : 12] that I know to the same degree as I am known, is also of great importance here." This must be understood positively as meaning that God's knowledge of man is a prerequisite for man's knowledge of God, and negatively as meaning that man's self-knowledge is not—as it is maintained in idealistic (speculative) philosophy—knowledge of God, but on the contrary, knowledge of God (the condition for which is set by God, cf. esp. *Philosophical Fragments*) is the prerequisite for genuine self-knowledge, and therein is the truth, which can edify or build up existence in actuality.

The various entries on the paradox are also material for the development of Kierkegaard's own philosophy of religion and at the same time indirectly polemical against Hegel.

In the entry IV A 47[z] the appearance of Christ is called a paradox, at one and the same time God and man. But Kierkegaard distinguishes between the immediate contemporaries of Christ, who "had the worst paradox" to be scandalized at, and the later generations for whom it is easier to represent Him as the Son of God. The notion of contemporaneity, such as it is developed in the *Philosophical Fragments*, is not found here. In a slightly later entry (IV A 62)[aa] Kierkegaard goes to work deductively. On the basis of a theory of what a paradox must be in order to be a complete paradox, he asserts that the Incarnation is "surely" [i.e., entirely unquestionable] the

[w] Hong, III, #3794.
[y] Hong, I, #42.
[aa] Hong, III, #3076.

[x] Hong, IV, #4847.
[z] Hong, III, #3075.

highest metaphysical and religious paradox, but it is still not the deepest ethical paradox, which would not be polemical against the given existence [*Tilværelse*] as human, such as the historical life of Christ was, but (resigned?) in harmony with it, so that Christ should have bent Himself "under its whole triviality." This theory is developed a little more precisely in IV A 103,[bb] where the paradox, as it is said (IV C 84)[cc] "is to be developed solely out of the idea, and yet with constant reference to the appearance of Christ so as to see whether this is sufficiently paradoxical." There is no indication that Kierkegaard wishes to utilize the traditional historical (source-critical) method on the accounts of the Evangelists to discover "the historical Jesus," so as to develop a Christological theory on that basis; but there is an indication of correcting these accounts on the basis of a purely theoretical definition of the paradox.[8] That the paradox theory presented was developed as an indirect polemic against Hegel and the Hegelians, among whom nothing of the sort is found, should not require any further demonstration, much the less so, since Kierkegaard says (IV A 103)[dd] without precise identification that if his

> most worthy contemporary theologians and philosophers had four cents worth of thoughts in their heads [which, according to Kierkegaard they did not have], then they would have discovered long ago

the possibility of the Son of God's absolute incognito as human.

The same indirect anti-Hegelian tendency occurs in various other entries, of which a couple of examples will suffice:

The statement in IV A 24[ee] against taking faith as a purely historical faith, as Luther put it, probably should be understood in connection with Kierkegaard's reading of Leibniz, while IV A 33,[ff] which explains the Incarnation not as an expression of compassion or of (Hegelian) necessity, but as an expression of divine love (unmotivated *Agape* in the terminology of Anders Nygren), a thought that is further developed IV A 183[gg] implies a dissociation from

[bb] *Ibid.*, #3077.

[cc] *Ibid.*, #3074.

[8] On this point, cf. K. E. Løgstrup, "Christentum ohne den historischen Jesus" in *Orbis Litterarum*, XVIII (1963), 101ff.

[dd] Hong, III, #3077.

[ee] Hong, II, #1105.

[ff] Hong, I, #301.

[gg] Hong, III, #2402.

Hegel, for whom the world historical, divine self-unfolding must with immanent necessity result in the Incarnation (cf. among others, his *Philosophy of Religion*, III, 33-100, in the chapter on "The Kingdom of the Son").

If we turn from this to the relatively few entries from this period in which Hegel and/or the Hegelians are directly mentioned, their paucity can be understood partly on the basis of Kierkegaard's concern with his own thought processes and their development both in the Journals and in the Authorship, and partly on the basis of his reading in the history of philosophy, which on the whole fortified him in his critical attitude toward Hegel and related thinkers.

We have already discussed the first entry (IV A 159) in which the (Hegelian) triad—art, religion, philosophy—is mentioned in connection with that of Plato and especially that of Plotinus. In the entry IV A 162,[hh] which must have been written after March 1, 1843, Kierkegaard is sarcastic about "Heiberg and Associates" among whom he rarely, if ever, finds a single primitive, i.e. original, thought: "What they know, they have borrowed from Hegel. And Hegel is indeed profound,—therefore what Prof. Heiberg says is also profound." After April 30, 1843, when Kierkegaard got Rosenkranz's book on Schelling, it is put neatly and to the point that the system in the Hegelian school is a fiction just like Schelling's "infinite epos."

Finally, a single item in the A entries is of decisive importance for the understanding of the fundamental difference between Hegel's and Kierkegaard's conception of the goal of philosophy. This is IV A 192,[ii] which contains an allusion to Hegel's *Lectures on the History of Philosophy*.

Kierkegaard claims, probably with Spinoza in mind, that there is a monistic philosophy that struggles toward unity. Over against that ideal (which was Hegel's too) he then maintains that the thinker (like himself) who

> sees life's duplicity (dualism) is higher and deeper than the one who seeks after unity ... the one who sees eternity as *telos*, and above all the theological reflection is higher than all immanence ...,

which means a dissociation both from an atemporal philosophical monistic immanence like Spinoza's and from a philosophy like

[hh] Hong, V, #5697.
[ii] Hong, I, #704.

Hegel's, in which time (the course of history) is supposed to be conceived in its immanent evolution, and in which eternity is not seen as a transcendent goal (Ideal).

The C entries from this period contain, as has been briefly indicated in the examination of the A entries, various items of significance for the elucidation of Kierkegaard's knowledge of and position on Hegel.

While in IV C 2[jj] there is a schematic survey of Stoic logic, in this context it is of interest only in that it shows how Kierkegaard concerned himself with classical logic. The following entry (IV C 3) shows what attracted his attention in his reading of the first volume of Tennemann's history of philosophy. This entry has almost the character of a somewhat complete table of contents. Kierkegaard remarked that the Eleatics "discovered the difficulty of thinking a becoming [*Vordelse*]" which is exactly what Hegel proposed to incorporate into his logic, and when Kierkegaard reports Parmenides' view (via Tennemann) thus, that "to think nothing is the same as not to think at all,"[kk] he could also have used this argument against Hegel's doctrine of "nothing," just as Parmenides' following statement that "Being [*Væren*] is identical" could have been adopted and used polemically against Hegel's concept of being [*Væren*] as full of oppositions. In line with this, Kierkegaard carefully noted Zeno's four proofs against motion, just as he noted Empedocles' idealistic disposition toward an epistemological principle in the assertion that "All knowledge depends on the identity of the known and the knower."

The first C entry in which Descartes is mentioned (IV C 10)[ll] contains items that Kierkegaard could use in the development of his theory of dread, while the next entry[mm] is more significant in the present context. It must be noted in the first place that Kierkegaard juxtaposes Descartes with the greatest name in subjective idealism, Fichte, an association that was hardly accidental on Kierkegaard's part. In the second place, it should be pointed out that Kierkegaard was startled at the fact that according to Descartes "freedom in man [has] predominance over thought," i.e., the ethical ego has prece-

---

[jj] Hong, V, #5572.

[kk] Malebranche uses this principle as the basic premise of his distinctive version of the ontological argument. See George L. Stengren, "Malebranche's Version of the Ontological Argument" *Analecta Anselmiana*, IV (1975), pp. 231-237.

[ll] Hong, V, #5588.

[mm] Hong, III, #2338.

dence over the knowing ego, which Kierkegaard in a later marginal note[nn] explains by his later well known distinction between a pathos-filled transition (here from the realm of thought to that of the will) and a dialectical transition. While a dialectical (i.e. a thought-filled) transition in his view can occur only by a logical conclusion, a pathos-filled transition proceeds by an ethical decision, a choice, a leap. The same theory enters into several other entries, of which we must refer especially to IV C 60[oo] and 96,[pp] and this indicates a rejection of Hegel, in whose philosophy there are only transitions that in Kierkegaard's terminology must be described as dialectical.

On Aristotle, the next philosopher Kierkegaard began to study at this time, there are many C entries; but not many can be given particular significance in the present investigation.[9]

It is very important that Kierkegaard noted (IV C 23)[qq] that Aristotle maintains (*Nicomachean Ethics*, 1139b) that "the objects of science are things that can be only in a single way; what is scientifically knowable is therefore the necessary, the eternal." If this notion is adhered to strictly,[10] then scientific knowledge of human existence is thereby excluded. But according to Kierkegaard's theory, human existence is defined by freedom, not by necessity, and thus there is an additional rejection of the whole Hegelian philosophy, the object of which, the unfolding of the divine Spirit in the various forms, is precisely not immutable, but is held to be subject to the dialectical law of development.

Kierkegaard was not an uncritical reader of Aristotle, as is evident from his objections in IV C 26,[rr] where he reproaches Aristotle for his mistaken concept of God, and his unsatisfactory notion of the self and the spirit, just as a little later (IV C 65)[ss] he regrets that Aristotle has given no definition of category.

[nn] *Ibid.*, #2339.
[oo] Hong, II, #1244.
[pp] Hong, I, #896.
[9] In connection with the reading of Garve's translation of the *Ethics* there is a long series of entries (IV C 15-27), while IV C 28 is related to Aristotle's *Politics* and IV C 103ff. concerned with the *Poetics*, in Curtius's translation.
[qq] Hong, II, #2281.
[10] On this point cf. Søren Holm, *Søren Kierkegaards Historiefilosofi*, 1952, esp. chap. II: "Væren Som Evighedskategori" [Being as Category of Eternity].
[rr] Hong, IV, #3892.
[ss] Hong, II, #1597.

The entries IV C 47, 48,[tt] and 49 are chiefly connected with the reading of Tennemann's presentation of Aristotle (*Geschichte*), especially the account of the Aristotelian concept *kinesis* (change, movement), which Tennemann translated as "change": "The transition . . . from potentiality [*Möglichkeit*] to actuality is change κίνησις" (III, 1801, 127). Kierkegaard finds this of the greatest importance with respect to the movements in logic, and they belong with his anti-Hegelian comments on the dialectical and the pathos-filled transitions and on the leap, the discontinuous transition. Already while reading the first volume of Tennemann (IV A 54)[uu] Kierkegaard was involved in the same problems, and in several entries (esp. IV C 80, 87,[vv] and 97[ww]) he finds that Hegel has never done justice to the category of transition, since the transition from a quantitative to a qualitative determination can happen only by a leap, and one of the most difficult problems in all philosophy, the problem of change, has received a new designation in modern philosophy (i.e., the Hegelian), namely, transition and mediation. The Journal entry (IV A 54)[xx] says plainly that modern philosophy has never accounted for change.

While Kierkegaard's studies in the history of ancient philosophy, as is evident from above, clearly sharpened his critical attitude toward Hegel, particularly his logic, which Kierkegaard had not especially concerned himself with earlier, we may also pose the question of what significance his reading of Leibniz had at this time.

It is quite surprising to note Kierkegaard's sympathy for the wide-ranging and, in questions related to the philosophy of religion, irenic and optimistic Leibniz.

In his previously mentioned article, Sorainen arrives at conclusions there is no reason to dispute, only to emphasize. Kierkegaard finds a striking agreement (IV C 29)[yy] between his own thinking and Leibniz's assertion of "a concatenation of truths [in Leibniz: enchainement inviolable des vérités; Kierkegaard omits "inviolable"], a conclusion from causes." Leibniz says this of the truths of reason, not of the truths of faith. They lack precisely the link that would make a concatenation possible, and Kierkegaard then says "what else does this say than that it [i.e. the indemonstrable faith] is a paradox . . . which lacks continuity." Sorainen also correctly men-

[tt] Hong, I, #258, 259.
[vv] Hong, I, #260, 261.
[xx] Hong, III, #3294.

[uu] Hong, III, #3294.
[ww] Hong, V, #5601.
[yy] Hong, III, #3073.

tions at this point in his study (p. 180) that immediately after this Kierkegaard took the opportunity to attack Hegel for not having understood what it was all about, and he remarks that Leibniz (*Theodicy*, §185) was just not fond of paradoxes, unlike Bayle.

On another point too, Sorainen emphasizes Kierkegaard's kinship with Leibniz (at this time, of course) namely in the conception of evil as something only negative and imperfect, as well as on a third point, namely the rejection of "indifferentia æquilibrii [the indifference of equipoise]" (IV C 31 and 36).[zz]

It can be emphasized even more strongly than Sorainen does, that, as a reader of Leibniz, Kierkegaard was a severely critical reader. He finds a weakness in all the answers Leibniz gives Bayle (IV C 33),[aaa] and against his argument (*Theodicy* §181) he asserts that it proves nothing (IV C 35).[bbb] In connection with this he outlines a major question in the *Philosophical Fragments*, how Christianity can be the absolute truth when it has appeared historically, and this historical aspect of Christianity is not incidental to it (as it is for "the other ideas") but precisely what is essential to it. It can also be stressed that in his pursuit of a definition of the concept of the real (IV C 71)[ccc] and his observation of how the contingent belongs with it, he mentions the scholastics' and Leibniz's emphasis on the role of the contingent in voluntary action, and that Kierkegaard summarily asserts that Hegel could only arrive at the point where Leibniz began (IV C 73).[ddd]

Against this background it is not surprising that Kierkegaard's comments on Hegel himself during this period are few and altogether predominantly critical.

Most of these entries are without reference to any definite passage or work of Hegel; but even if it is thus difficult to determine with assurance in every single instance which of them Kierkegaard had in mind (or perhaps, in his hands), yet there are individual entries in which it appears certain that at this time Kierkegaard was occupied with works with which he had not previously concerned himself in a noteworthy way. They are: *Phenomenology of the Spirit*, *Philosophische Propädeutik*, and the *Encyclopedia of the Philosophical Sciences* (see IV C 62, 64, 66, 79, and 101).[eee]

[zz] Hong, III, #2365, 2366. [aaa] Hong, I, #41.
[bbb] Hong, II, #1635. [ccc] Hong, III, #3652.
[ddd] Hong, II, #1601.

[eee] All but the last of these will be found in Hong, vol. II. IV C 101 will be found in Hong, V, #5603.

In the entry IV C 59,[fff] on motion, Kierkegaard says that Hegel explains it "easily enough," i.e. he does not explain it at all, but only asserts in the *Phenomenology of the Spirit* (Introduction, p. 144) that

> the origination of the new object, which offers itself to consciousness without consciousness knowing how it acquires it, that to us who witness the process seems to be going on behind its back,

and Kierkegaard parallels, on the basis of reading Marbach's history of philosophy, this "explanation," which really says nothing, with Plotinus's statement about the unity of reason (nous) becoming a plurality inconspicuously.

In a similar way Hegel's teaching on the possible is criticized (IV C 62).[ggg] Kierkegaard mentions first that Hegel gives his teaching on the possible in the logic (*Science of Logic*, I, Book 2)[hhh] in the doctrine of essence, and, Kierkegaard says, "here we get the explanation that the possible is the actual, the actual is the possible." Hegel does not express himself in exactly that way, and it is most likely that Kierkegaard has given a highly simplified version on the basis of the more abbreviated presentation given by Hegel in his *Encyclopedia* §143,[iii] where he says "actuality . . . as identity in general . . . possibility." The entry in Kierkegaard, which is preliminary to the Interlude in *Philosophical Fragments*, shows, incidentally, only how his concept of logic has now become dominated by that of Aristotle, just as we get an inkling of Kierkegaard's philosophy of history, in which it became an axiom that the past has not transpired with any greater necessity than the future will take place, since freedom is decisive in both cases. In this respect, a definite contrary position is taken against the Hegelian philosophy of history, in which it is maintained that this happens with necessity.

In an entry (IV C 63)[jjj] that raises the question of what a category is, Kierkegaard asserts that "the modern [philosophers] have, as far as is known, not given any definition, at least not Hegel." In a

[fff] Hong, II, #1594.

[ggg] *Ibid.*, #1245.

[hhh] In the English translation, II, 15ff.

[iii] This portion of Hegel's *Encyclopedia* has been translated as *The Logic of Hegel* by William Wallace (Oxford: The Clarendon Press, 1892). The quotation will be found on p. 259 of this translation.

[jjj] Hong, II, #1595.

later addendum (IV C 64)[kkk] Kierkegaard remarks that the only place in Hegel where he has found anything "is in the little encyclopedia published by Rosenkrantz, p. 93." It is Hegel's *Philosophische Propädeutik*[lll] that Kierkegaard identifies in this way. In this work (SW III, 115) it is only said that

> Thought is threefold: 1) the categories; 2) the determinations of reflection; 3) concepts. The doctrine of both of the first constitutes the objective logic in metaphysics; the doctrine of concepts the proper or subjective logic.

Kierkegaard criticizes Hegel here for arbitrariness in terminology and for having put the category in a position it should not have; but he says nothing about what he understands by a category himself, nor about the fact that in various other places Hegel explicitly states what he means by category. An example of this is in the *Encyclopedia* §42,[mmm] "If we consider what we have before us first of all, it is chiefly a manifold; the categories are simplicities toward which this manifold converges." We might also suppose that Kierkegaard might have examined what such a trustworthy Hegelian logician as Erdmann had to say on the point in *Grundriss der Logik und Metaphysik* (publ. 1841; Ktl. 483), in which in a considerably clearer and better arranged fashion than Hegel himself he presents the speculative logic; but Kierkegaard evidently did not examine this. On the other hand, he read a little further in Hegel's *Propädeutik,* and in a later marginal note poses the question of whether being [*Væren*] is a category, which he answers negatively. He can indeed grant that Hegel is right in holding that unqualified being is the same as nothing, whereas quality, which Kierkegaard explains as being [*Væren*] determined by itself, is not nothing. This notion of Kierkegaard is so different from that of Hegel that he concludes by saying that in Hegel "the whole doctrine about being is a fatuous prelude to the doctrine of quality" (IV C 66).[nnn] Here Kierkegaard arrives at a conclusion similar to the one reached by Sibbern in the anti-Hegelian treatise (1838) discussed earlier (*supra,* Chapter III), apparently without direct dependence on the part of Kierkegaard.

In a couple of the following entries (IV C 67 and 79)[ooo] Kierkegaard's posture of opposition toward Hegel emerges even more

kkk *Ibid.,* #1596.
mmm *The Logic of Hegel,* p. 88.
ooo *Ibid.,* #1599, 1602.

lll No English translation of this work.
nnn Hong, II, #1598.

clearly. Kierkegaard asserts that it is meaningless to determine being quantitatively, for it either is or is not (IV C 67), and in the second of these two entries he categorically asserts that being does not belong to logic at all, i.e., that being, as he understands it is not just being and logic, is not ontology as Hegel thought (clearly expressed, e.g., in the *Propädeutik*, SW III, 172, where it is called "ontological logic"). In the same way Hegel is criticized (IV C 80)[ppp] for never having done justice to the category of transition.

The conclusion of this point in our study can now be summarized as follows: even though we frequently found very critical remarks earlier, by Kierkegaard against Hegel, they occur predominantly against the interpretation of historical phenomena, or esthetic, ethical, or religious concepts, and rarely against concepts and problems of logic and metaphysics. Only after Kierkegaard had read Aristotle, the history of ancient philosophy, Descartes, and Leibniz, did he concentrate his attention on Hegel's logic. Certainly he had previously had a secondhand knowledge of it, just as in Berlin he had summarized Werder's lectures (III C 28, 29, 30);[qqq] but the familiarity with it now was not happy: Kierkegaard immediately states on every relevant point his fundamental disagreement with Hegel. This was not just a discord on more or less significant items. They were only occasions for Kierkegaard to indicate, although still only sketchily, his completely different understanding of logic, and thus of metaphysics, which in his later work as a thinker developed into a theory that not only with respect to logic and metaphysics, but also concerning the philosophy of history, ethics, the philosophy of religion, and other subject areas, was quite different from that of Hegel and his disciples.

3. *Papirer* IV B 1-17: *Johannes Climacus, or, De Omnibus Dubitandum Est*[rrr]

The unfinished story, *Johannes Climacus, or, De Omnibus Dubitandum Est*, an autobiographical sketch that evolves into a philosophical analysis of the concept of doubt, was written during the same period as the *Papirer* entries just examined. We notice here, to a much greater degree than in both the A entries and the C entries, how Kierkegaard's new studies in the history of philosophy and

[ppp] Hong, I, #260.
[qqq] Hong, V, #5537; I, #257.
[rrr] Page references will be to the English translation by T. H. Croxall.

philosophical observations begin to bear fruit. In spite of the peaceful character of the beginning of the story, as a whole it bears a strong mark of opposition toward prevailing opinions, especially among the Hegelians. Kierkegaard has quite precisely described himself when in a Journal entry (IV A 83)[sss] he writes that it strikes him as extraordinarily difficult to abandon himself so peacefully that a polemical contrast is not clearly present.

Before turning our attention to certain points in the philosophical part of the story, it will be worth looking at the significance of the autobiographical section.

Three character traits of the Johannes Climacus of the story have been correctly emphasized, namely, his passion for thought, regardless of its content, the important development of his imagination, and his strong will. In addition, neither for his father nor for the very young Johannes Climacus was there any opposition between thought and being, between life in "ideality," as it is called, and in "reality." Their theoretical thinking and the practical conduct of their lives were in harmony,[11] just as Kierkegaard in the Preface to *Fear and Trembling* (p. 22) said of Descartes, that he "did what he said, and said what he did. Alas, alack, that is a great rarity in our times!" Among the modern philosophers—and not less among their yes men—he found, on the other hand, nothing but ill-considered phrases, inconsistencies, and discords between doctrine and life.

The plan of this unfinished short story was (IV B 16)[ttt] to strike at philosophy by sketching a young man who really acts according to what philosophy tells him to do, a person who begins by doubting about everything—and ends by despairing.[uuu] His life is thrown away for the sake of philosophy, and he finds the philosophers worse than the Pharisees, who impose heavy burdens and do not themselves lift them. The burdens of the Pharisees, at least, can be lifted; those of the philosophers cannot. They demand the impossible, and

> if there is, then, a young person who thinks that philosophizing is not talking or writing, but earnestly doing exactly what philosophy says one should do, then they let him waste several years of his life, and when it appears that it was impossible, then

[sss] Hong, V, #5644.
[11] Billeskov-Jansen in *SK's Værker i Udvalg*, IV (1950), 229.
[ttt] Croxall, p. 101.
[uuu] It may be useful to point out that in Danish *at tvivle* = to doubt, *at fortvivle* = to despair.

it has grasped him so deeply that perhaps his salvation becomes impossible (IV B 17).ᵛᵛᵛ

The existential interest is dominant, just as the motto of the story indicates.

This plan was not entirely fulfilled. In the first part of the story we get an (autobiographically) appropriate and clear description of the hero, Johannes Climacus alias Kierkegaard, at home, in school, at the university among those of the same age but not of the same mind.

The polemical tendency in the story is expressed at the beginning in "A Satisfaction to Note," where it is said that by the form alone (the novelistic, as distinct from the traditional form of the monograph) the author wishes to counteract

the abominable falsity which is the mark of modern philosophy, which is thus especially distinguished from older philosophy by its discovery that it was ridiculous to do what one said one did or had done (IV B 1; Croxall, pp. 102f.).

In the biographical section (pp. 112ff.), which describes how the hero "begins to philosophize with the help of traditional presentations," we get the first account of Johannes Climacus's reading that is relevant in the present context.

It is said that, although he had been at the University for a few years, Johannes had "read comparatively little." This describes Kierkegaard himself quite well until the fall of 1835, when he began to put theological textbooks aside to walk his own path, as has been shown in the initial chapters of the present study. It is said furthermore that he was particularly well informed about the classics he had learned to know in preparatory school, and that he returned to them now and then; but he did not really engage in classical studies. He did not read historical works. Both bits of information describe the young student Kierkegaard quite accurately; but what follows is even more interesting in the present context.

"If he encountered a book of modern philosophy," Kierkegaard says, "he did not put it aside until he had read it, but when he had read it, he was often dissatisfied and discouraged." Kierkegaard's many critical remarks which have already been mentioned or quoted in connection with his summaries of books, articles in periodicals, and lectures (which he rarely summarized entirely from beginning

ᵛᵛᵛ Croxall, p. 101f.

to end) reinforce the correctness of this concealed self-description. A typical example was his growing impatience with Schelling, whom he had approached with such great expectations. Just as striking, he goes on to say that his whole outlook did not make him feel like reading. The explanation was that he did not always find in what he read the strong logical consistency that was the passion of his own thought. When he devoted himself to his own thoughts again, they "did not lead him to anything." This is another revealing comment, since we saw in Kierkegaard's many entries from his student years a host of problems formulated, suggestions and tendencies that he later took up, but that he very rarely worked up into a comprehensive view in the usual sense. Rather we can say that the comment is the germination of an existential basic attitude that little by little gets its distinctive character and that is developing positively at the same time as a constantly growing negative position toward contemporary philosophy and theology.

Next it is said in the gently melancholic tone of ironic understatement [*Underdrivelses*] that pervades the whole story, that he refrained from any hasty judgment of the works he had read, since he heard others assess them quite differently, so that he inferred that the fault was in him, since he knew that he was not like other people, and since his upbringing had probably been imperfect.

Then Climacus began to get clear about his shame. By respecting other people's talk (and it is hardly an entirely unfounded suspicion to suggest that by "others" Kierkegaard alluded to Martensen after his return home from his study tour), he had hitherto learned to know only the minor prophets, not the great writers, i.e. "the great thinkers among the modern philosophers." He did not dare to try to read them "because he heard that they were so difficult that the study of them required a long time."

Climacus found himself in the unhappy situation that the works he knew were unsatisfactory to him. Those he did not know except through hearing about them, he dared not tackle. The only escape he could discover was to act like a soldier who bought a cannon and began for himself, i.e. he followed his inclination for silence to be busy with thoughts. He became, in the words of the *Postscript*, a private thinker, who listened carefully to what "others" said.

One definite principle in particular he heard repeated again and again, namely: "de omnibus dubitandum est."

This one principle became a task for his thought.

It had sounded in Martensen's lectures on the introduction to speculative dogmatics, which Kierkegaard had attended in the fall of 1837, and from which he had summarized the following:

> Descartes (d. 1650) said cogito ergo sum and de omnibus dubitandum est and thereby furnished the principle of modern Protestant subjectivity.[12] By the latter principle, de omnibus dubitandum est, he really gave the solution, for by no means did he denote by it a doubt about this or that, but about all, everything should be shaken, not to remain in this fluctuating state; but so that in this way certainty might ultimately remain (II C 18; November 29, 1837).[www]

This matches closely what Hegel said by way of introduction to Descartes in his *Lectures on the History of Philosophy*, III, 224-225:[xxx]

> He has begun at the beginning, with thought as such; and this is an absolute beginning. And that the beginning must only be from thought, he expressed in such a way that one must doubt about everything. Descartes made it the first requirement of philosophy that one must doubt everything, i.e., all presuppositions must be abandoned. *De omnibus dubitandum est* was the first principle of Descartes. . . . However, it does not have the same meaning [*Sinn*] as Skepticism, which set no other goal before itself than doubt itself . . . but it has rather the meaning that one must renounce every prejudgment. . . . This is not the case with the Skeptics; there doubt is the conclusion.

Quite clearly Hegel also says of Descartes that "he has taken an entirely new direction: with Descartes the new epoch in philosophy begins . . ." (III, 223).

We can recall "The Battle between the old and the new Soap Cellar" (cf. *supra* Chapter IV, section 4), especially von Skipjack's replies, when it is said then that their, i.e. the Hegelians', thought process in general was very short. That was surely remarkable for Johannes Climacus, who could not answer questions off-hand, "but

---

[12] Cf. Martensen's *De autonomia* etc., 1837, 19.

[www] Hong, V, #5277, gives only the title and dates of these lectures.

[xxx] The translation of the quote that follows, which is taken from the *Jubiläumsausgabe* of Hegel's *Sämtliche Werke* differs in some details from the English translation by Haldane and Simson, for which the above volume and page reference is given. This is because the Haldane and Simson translation is somewhat freer than mine, which tries to remain close to the original German style and arrangement.

he only saw therein a new advantage among them." Naturally
advantage [*Fortrin*] means mistake [*Fejltrin*] here.

Now Climacus had heard three main versions of this principle's
relation to philosophy, and he proceeds to analyze them (IV B 1;
Croxall, p. 116):

1) Philosophy begins with doubt.
2) One must have doubted in order to come to philosophize.
   and
3) Modern philosophy begins with doubt.

In this context it is particularly important to clarify how Kierkegaard's posing of problems and solutions relate to Hegel's (and thus
also to Martensen's and the thus far anonymous Danish Hegelians').

Climacus (Kierkegaard) takes the last version first. His reasoning
can be summarized as follows:

He takes it on authority that the principle is true in the sense
that something that people called modern philosophy as a matter
of fact began with doubt, as distinct from older philosophy, which
had another point of departure. Now if this beginning with doubt
should mean not only a fortuitous historical beginning but an
absolute one, then it must follow from that that only modern
philosophy that began with doubt could be philosophy properly so
called, which would mean the historical beginning was identical
with the absolute beginning. This strikes Climacus as a confusion
of "historical and eternal determinations," a confusion he did not
want to reject out of hand, but only had misgivings about. He
understood that it had caused great difficulties for philosophy that
Christianity claimed that it had come into the world with a beginning that was simultaneously historical and eternal. Now philosophy
would assert the same thing about itself.

We see here a reflection of the problem of *Philosophical Fragments*. If we do not in *De Omnibus Dubitandum Est* get any
solution of the question raised, it is sufficiently clear that even the
distinction between historical and eternal truths is un-Hegelian,
since these two kinds of truths are identical in Hegel's opinion.[13]

It is also possible, Climacus continues, that by this principle people
wanted to state that beginning with doubt is essential for all philosophy, not only the modern, since it is not said that a particular
modern philosophy, but just modern philosophy as such began with

---

[13] Cf. my description of Hegel's theory in the Introduction (and Commentary) to the *Philosophical Fragments* (2nd ed., 1962).

doubt. For the present he would assume that the principle is an historical principle; but that only raises a new problem, namely the question of how it came about that modern philosophy began with doubt. Did it happen accidentally or necessarily?

If modern philosophy had begun as a genuine case of chance, nothing could be inferred from that concerning either previous or succeeding philosophy and thus the principle would contain nothing but an historical account of how modern philosophy happened to begin; but if the statement is only historical, then it is inconsistent with the first principle given, that philosophy as such begins with doubt.

On the other hand, if modern philosophy began in this way only by an apparent coincidence, i.e. an occult necessity, then this necessity in an eternal sense would not be intuited until, in an unknown and uncertain future, modern philosophy has been completed, so that it would be available as a filled out and conceivable totality.

Here again we see the difference between Climacus's point of departure and conclusion and Hegel's interpretation. For Hegel, only by a lack of consistency is there room for a genuine chance event in history in general and in philosophy in particular. His metaphysically based determinism can in principle hardly contain even the possibility of anything accidental in the course of time and its content, since this is altogether a type of divine revelation, and if one would exempt anything at all in history from this necessity, then we must seek, according to Hegel's qualitative yardstick, for the exception without being able to get an answer. On this point there is Climacus's question—which is repeated and answered in *Concluding Unscientific Postscript*—about modern philosophy's culmination after the doubtful beginning. As far as Hegel was concerned the matter was clear. According to his conception, philosophy as such was completed with his own system, which contained the full and absolute truth in a form that completely covered the content:

The result [of the history of philosophy] is the thought which is at home with itself, and at the same time embraces the whole universe therein, and transforms it into an intelligent world,

as Hegel himself puts it in the conclusion of his *Lectures on the History of Philosophy* (III, 546). But why would Hegel write several, mutually somewhat diverse editions of the absolute, divine truth and its progress through world history? The Hegelians were not all satisfied with merely repeating it. In any event, Martensen wanted to go further, and the reason for this must be either that Hegel's *Encyclopedia* (in one of the editions, perhaps the last supervised by the author himself) did not contain the requisite divine truth at all, or—in the best case—only some of the truth, so that Martensen must have felt called upon to carry out a most needed supplemental work.

If now, Climacus continues his reflections, modern philosophy actually begins with doubt out of genuine necessity, then we must ask how there could have been philosophy previously, since it was so necessary to begin with doubt. Further, how had this previous philosophy begun—and ended in such a way that it was necessary for modern philosophy to begin with doubt, that is, begin with a total break with the previous by a leap?

Thus, if modern philosophy began with a relation of discontinuity vis-à-vis the previous, then in that respect this invalidates the Hegelian notion of the history of philosophy as a continuous dialectical advance toward perfection in his own *Encyclopedia*, the final revised edition. We could continue Climacus's reasoning in this way.

The tragicomic result of Climacus's reflections up to this point is that he has not advanced an inch beyond where he began. If, instead of asserting that "modern philosophy" or "philosophy" began with doubt, one says that Descartes began with doubt and others followed his example, then the statement would be essentially unproblematic. As the matter stands now, he hopes in vain that by listening to the talk of others he will get the requisite correct information about the real meaning of the statement. The explanation fails to appear. It then occurs to him that the secret is perhaps that

> modern philosophy is at one and the same time the historical and the eternal, and what is more, it is conscious of this itself. It is, then, a union, just like the union of the two natures in Christ.

But it is not clear to him how he should imagine such a combination, since the philosopher is confronted with the enormous task of having to encompass in his consciousness the most tremendous conflicts, namely, on the one side his own personality, and on the other side all the philosophy of the world as an unfolding of the eternal philosophy (IV B 1; Croxall, p. 124). Climacus faints just from trying to imagine this combination, and when he comes to he is dejected because it seems that this absolutist view is fundamentally a relativism, a skepticism, as he calls it, because "the individual's knowledge is forever only a knowledge of himself as a moment and of his significance as a moment." If this notion were to be thought through consistently, then the result would be that every individual moment should become aware of its own eternal validity as a moment in the totality, and since the whole is still not completed, simply because time has not run out, so the individual moment must conceive itself as a moment not only in relation to the past but also in relation to the future. Thus the individual would have to be omniscient and the world be finished, and finally an explanation must be given as to what moment in time could one grasp his own role as moment and therewith regard himself as completed, about which Climacus has not got any explanation either. If a previous development had proceeded with necessity, it must also be held consistently that future development proceeds with the same necessity, which must be predictable, foreseen. At bottom, Climacus thinks, it is not something human, but reserved to the divine to have such insight into the individual moment and such a comprehensive view of the unfolding of the history of the world.

Climacus does not solve here the problems he raises; but they are taken up again in the published writings of Climacus, *Philosophical Fragments* and *Concluding Unscientific Postscript*, for resolution. As before, and quite clearly here, even to raise such issues indicates a philosophical position different from Hegel's, and it indicates a logic quite different from Hegel's, and it suggests a goal quite different from that of Hegel. Climacus starts from the position of a private thinker, the logic is classical, the goal is self-understanding. For Hegel the starting position (as sketched in the chapter on *On the Concept of Irony*) is the experience of the divine, speculative-logical constructed universe, and his method is that of dialectical logic, and his goal adequate conceptualization of this universe as an all-inclusive system.

Yet, Climacus has still not finished trying to philosophize with the help of traditional representations, even though he has arrived at the conclusion he does not have the courage to believe, that the first statement he analyzed really contained an impossibility (IV B 1; Croxall, p. 126).

Then he tackles the statement "philosophy begins with doubt" to find out, if possible, what that can be thought to mean.

In the first place, he finds it curious for philosophy to begin with a negative concept such as doubt, which must presuppose something about which there ought to be doubt. The Greeks, on the contrary, taught "as far as he knew" that philosophy begins with wonder, an immediate determination that does not contain any polemic against the past. In the second place, he discovers that the statement as asserted by its spokesmen was not a philosophical proposition at all, but a historical one, just like the third one, and so he is back where he started.

Next, he asks "how does the individual relate himself to this proposition?" Then one day he heard

> one of the philosophizers maintain that this proposition belonged to "the eternal philosophy to which everyone who wishes to belong to philosophy must align himself."

But how could this happen, that the eternal, i.e. the atemporal, philosophy without beginning or end, still had a beginning, namely with doubt? He receives no explanation from the enthusiastic supporters of this proposition, no, "those inspiring and powerful words were so treacherous!" But Climacus still believes that he will be able to discover a rational meaning in the latter part of the inspiring speech, namely that everyone who wishes to adhere to philosophy must align himself with this eternal philosophy. To be sure, neither does he learn how he was to go about aligning himself with it; but if he cannot immediately understand it himself, perhaps it could be explained by the fact that he himself stands, and should begin, where the others had already ended. Before he can find out any more about that, he hears an astonishing new explanation, namely, that the beginning of philosophy is threefold: the absolute, the objective, and the subjective.[14] This sounds very good. But how is there doubt now from these three beginnings? Was there perhaps a fourth beginning? The explanation was, then, an explanation of everything except what Climacus wanted explained.

He must try again, then, and so he asks "how does the individual who proposes this statement relate himself to it?" (IV B 1; Croxall, p. 134), a quite un-Hegelian question insofar as the individual is an unimportant factor in Hegel's philosophy.

[14] Cf. the editors' [of the *Papirer*] reference to P. M. Stilling's *Philosophiske Betragtninger over den Speculative Logiks Betydning for Videnskaben* (1842), 9ff., 19ff., and 68ff., and on the absolute beginning, Heiberg's "Recension over Rothes Treenigheds-og Forsoningslære" in *Perseus*, I (1837), 35ff and 39ff.

The question he poses is whether the stated principle is in the same class as atemporal and impersonal mathematical principles or in a class with religious and ethical principles, where the personality of the one speaking has an important significance. He comes to the conclusion that it belongs to talk about the subjective beginning of philosophy, thus is classified with ethical and religious principles, and "the one who should present it must discover it, must have talent, must have authority."[15]

The next question, then, must concern the relation between disciple and teacher with regard to the stated principle, a question that points toward the distinction in *Philosophical Fragments* between the teacher whose person is essentially unimportant for the disciple and the teacher whose person is entirely decisive.

The final question for Climacus in this context is whether the stated principle should be taken on faith by the disciple in such a way that he should do what it says or whether he could only proceed from the fact that the teacher had doubted so profoundly about all things, that now one only needs to repeat his doubt?

For every new question to which he does not get an answer, or at least not a reasonable one, it becomes more and more clear to Climacus that "along this path one does not enter into philosophy; for this principle just annihilates the connection." However, new obstacles turn up constantly. If he should really doubt about all things, then as a consequence he must also doubt the validity of this assertion, and so again he is back where he started. He is still not quite sure whether it is something to laugh or cry about. He chooses for the present to smile through the tears and continues to be himself rather than be a philosopher on these terms.

But is there still a possibility for understanding that famous expression in a rational way?

One could perhaps tentatively suggest that the main assertion, *de omnibus dubitandum*, lies outside of philosophy and is only a preamble. By means of such a preparation one could possibly make himself worthy to begin philosophy later. Certainly it appears strange to Climacus that it should follow a negative direction. While a positive command makes it easy for the disciple to follow it, because in that way the teacher assumes the responsibility, a negative command detaches the disciple from the relation to the teacher.

[15] On this point cf. especially Lars Bejerholm's *Meddelelsens Dialektik* (1962).

Climacus decides in spite of these misgivings, to follow the direction about doubting everything:

> Come what will: let it bring me everything or nothing, let it make me wise or foolish, I will risk everything, but not give up thinking (IV B 1; Croxall, p. 142).

Climacus now seeks to think on his own account and risk, and so in his isolation he tries to remember one or another helpful, instructive statement from the philosophers who had gone through the trial of doubting, but in vain. The first thing he is able to think of is a statement that one should not waste time in doubting at all, but begin boldly to philosophize. The audience was enthusiastic, but Johannes Climacus, on the contrary, is ashamed on behalf of the speaker. Next he hears from "one of the philosophizers in whose statements people had special confidence," that a speculative doubt, not about this or that, but about everything, is by no means an easy matter. But wherein the difficulty of the matter consisted nothing is said.

Eventually, Climacus has had enough. He parts company forever from "the philosophizers," i.e., the Danish Hegelians. To be sure, he occasionally hears an isolated comment from them; but he determines not to act on it since he has had so many trying experiences of how deceitful their words were.

Climacus then asked, as simply as possible, what it was to doubt. The first thing that must be clarified seemed to be, how must existence [*Existensen*] be constituted, so that doubt can be possible (IV B 1; Croxall, p. 146).

An empirical answer would result only in a confused multiplicity (cf. IV C 75:[yyy] "What do I learn from experience? Nothing, or only numerical knowledge."). Therefore he inquires into the ideal possibility of doubt in the consciousness.

The consciousness of the child has doubt outside itself, its consciousness is immediate, that is, indefinite, and immediately everything is true, nothing is doubtful;[16] but in the next moment every-

---

[yyy] Hong, I, #1072.

[16] In a later note he refers to various theories, including that of Schleiermacher on feeling (*The Christian Faith*, 2nd ed., §5), and Hirsch points out in a note on this passage (in his German translation of Kierkegaard's *Gesammelte Werke*, 10. Abth., 1952, 192) that Climacus's description of the immediate stage corresponds almost verbatim to Schleiermacher's in *On Religion: Speeches to its Cultured Despisers*.

thing is untrue. If consciousness can remain in immediacy then the question of truth is moot.

The question of truth also forces the question of untruth, for at the same instant we ask about truth we have already asked about untruth [that is, as that which lies outside of truth, according to the rule: every determination is a negation]. We could now raise the question of whether the consciousness could not be thought to remain in immediacy; but this is declared a foolish question, since it is maintained that the consciousness would not be consciousness at all if it could do that. Immediacy is canceled by mediacy, which presupposes immediacy. Immediacy is described as reality, mediacy as ideality, expressed in language, in the word. After this, the consciousness is defined as the contradiction that appears at the very moment reality is stated [*udsiges*], since the statement as word, language, is ideality. With that, the possibility of doubt in consciousness is established [*fastlagt*], and the consciousness is defined as "a duplicity," which necessarily has two expressions. It is said that the duplicity is reality and ideality, and the consciousness is the connection. We can, then, either bring reality into relation with ideality or bring ideality into relation with reality. In reality alone there is no possibility for doubt, nor is there in ideality alone. The possibility of doubt first arises at the moment when they are juxtaposed in the consciousness.[17]

Climacus then remarks—just as does Vigilius Haufniensis in *The Concept of Dread* "Introduction" pp. 9-13—that "the terminology of modern [i.e. Hegelian] philosophy is often confused."

---

[17] Climacus's philosophical sketch here is a preparatory work for the later fully developed theories in the pseudonymous Authorship, which in the most recent research, especially by Gregor Malantschuk (e.g., in the article "Begrebet Fordoblelse hos Søren Kierkegaard" in *Kierkegaardiana*, 1957, 43ff.), Arild Christensen (e.g., in the article on "Søren Kierkegaards Inddelingsprincip" in *Kierkegaardiana* 1959, 21ff.) and by Johannes Sløk (especially in *Die Anthropologie Kierkegaards*, 1954) has concerned itself with. Among them, Sløk has with the greatest clarity and consistency made himself the spokesman for the view that Kierkegaard certainly to a very great degree employed the terminology and thought categories of speculative idealism, but not so as to adopt their content, on the contrary, to combat "speculation," "the system," with its own weapons. I agree in principle with this view as correct, but without following Sløk in every detail and without agreeing in every respect with his interpretation of Kierkegaard as a whole. On Kierkegaard's critique of the speculative confusion of langauge reference is made especially to Lars Bejerholm's *Meddelelsens Dialektik* (1962), particularly pp. 48ff.

He mentions some examples of this from Hegel's *Phenomenology of the Spirit*, just as he criticizes Hegel for not having explained how the transition between the different stages takes place: "if the transition consists only of a heading, then it is easy enough" (Croxall, p. 150, note 2).

Before he continued, Climacus then remarks, he asked himself whether what he had hitherto called consciousness was not "what one otherwise would call reflection"—thus in Hegelian usage a concept of reduplication [*Fordoblelsesbegreb*], which belongs to the second part of the *Logic*, the logic of essence, since "the classifications made by reflection are always dichotomatic," i.e., they make possible a relation, that can be made actual only in the consciousness, which is divided trichotomatically. If this is correct, it follows that the possibility of doubt can become an actuality only when the consciousness (which is now identified as spirit) is present. This means that doubt is not a pure determination of the understanding (a possibility within the realm of reflection), which is disinterested or, to use a more modern term, detached, can be replaced by something about which no doubt can prevail, as, for example, mathematical, esthetic, or metaphysical knowledge, which as a product of objective thought is only a presupposition for doubt, not (as in different ways maintained by Descartes and Hegel) its positive resolution (the indubitably certain knowledge). Only with consciousness can the possibility of doubt become actual, which means that doubt is far from being the presupposition or beginning of philosophy and the objective sciences. On the contrary, doubt has both this kind of philosophy and the special sciences that can be classified with it as a presupposition. Doubt does not lie within the sphere of the disinterested, but within that of the consciousness, that is, within the realm of the interested. In other words, doubt is not just intellectual, detached; correctly understood, it is existential. Therefore, if doubt is to be overcome (if there is to be a repetition, as Climacus puts it here), this cannot happen only through a (logical) inference, as Descartes and the speculative philosophers, who followed him on this point, thought. It must happen through a decision of the will, through a choice, a leap. If this decision is not made, repetition cannot take place and doubt appears, when seen from a higher stage, to be a type of despair (cf. IV B 13 and 16)[zzz] which can be overcome only by faith.

[zzz] Unfortunately, neither Croxall nor Hong includes the relevant passages

On the last point, the question of overcoming doubt, the interpretation is carried a little further than Climacus's thought process in IV B 1, namely toward its continuation in Kierkegaard's Authorship, especially the Climacus[aaaa] and Anti-Climacus[bbbb] writings (e.g., *Training in Christianity*, p. 83, note), so that it immediately becomes clear that in this uncompleted little autobiographical and philosophical work and its subsequent continuation we find a decisive foundation for the statement that from here on Kierkegaard abandoned any serious concern with the domestic Hegelians, and henceforth only in a restricted way, which will be investigated in what follows, did he continue to be occupied with Hegel's own system in its totality as well as in a series of details.[18]

4. *Papirer*, V A 1-113 AND V C 1-13

While Kierkegaard's trial sermon on February 24, 1844 (IV C 1; Croxall, pp. 159-173), on I Corinthians 2:6-9, as might be expected,

---

in their English translations. It may be appropriate to call attention again to the parallel in Danish between *tvivle* (doubt) and *fortvivlelse* (despair).

[aaaa] *Philosophical Fragments* and *Concluding Unscientific Postscript*.

[bbbb] *Sickness unto Death* and *Training in Christianity*.

[18] In the drafts for *De omnibus dubitandum est* (IV B 2-17) we find a series of items which only support the above summary and thus it does not seem necessary to go through this draft in detail here. It can be mentioned, for example, that Kierkegaard speaks of Hegel directly more frequently than in IV B 1; it is particularly obvious that he has studied the *Phenomenology of Spirit* and the section on Descartes in the *History of Philosophy* while composing this—but without anywhere speaking of anything but individual items in those two works. Martensen is also mentioned by name (IV B2, 7). As in the later works published by Kierkegaard himself, especially the *Postscript*, in the first draft he mentioned his opponents by name, whereas in the final version he only discusses their views, he speaks on principle.

In the drafts there are several striking formulations ("Doubt can never be stopped in itself," IV B 2, 12; "to go beyond Hegel—that was a serious matter, he feared that it might make him like Apollonius of Tyana, who also went beyond Pythagoras . . ." IV B 8, 11: "The skeptics doubted about everything, but that was not a finished result, on the contrary, it was the task of a lifetime . . . it is different when doubting about everything should be a beginning" IV B 13, 11; "Doubt is not overcome by the system but by faith," IV B 13, 18).

It can also be mentioned that several times Kierkegaard emphasized the ancient skeptics, about whom he had read in Tennemann particularly, to the disadvantage of the modern doubters. Finally, it can be noted that Kierkegaard does not, as in the entries from his youth, identify Faust as the doubter personified.

contains nothing directly related to the main topic of this investigation, so also in the A entries from March to December 1844 there are not many passages where Hegel and his disciples are directly discussed. The words of young Johannes Climacus (IV B 1; Croxall, p. 145) that he

> parted company forever from the philosophizers; even though now and again he heard a stray remark from them, he decided to pay no more attention to them, since he had had so many trying experiences of how deceitful their words were

certainly comes from Kierkegaard himself.

In what follows we shall sketch how Kierkegaard indeed parted company with both the great and the minor speculative thinkers, but nevertheless gave them some well meant parting advice, both in his *Papirer* and in the published works.

In the first A entry, as usual undated, but probably from March 1844, V A 1,[cccc] Kierkegaard summarily asserts that there are only three positions on the relation between faith and knowledge, and in all of them knowledge is something subsequent to faith. He does not expand upon his thought at this point, but returns to this question rather frequently. On the other hand, in V A 8[dddd] we get the first indication of the subsequently very important distinction between the first and the second immediacy. The first immediate God-consciousness (the humanistic, later in the *Postscript* comprising the stages up to and including religiousness A) can appear through the contemplation of nature, whereas the second immediate God-consciousness is determined by the consciousness of sin, since it presupposes revelation (in traditional terminology: the special revelation of Christ). He then says polemically that "this is where the battle should take place," that is, the Christian God-consciousness, faith in the strict sense, should not be made probable, since making something probable is possible only in, and belongs to the sphere of, knowledge: but on the other hand, a theory and a psychology of revelation should be worked out that can explain faith and sin in their natural relation. This development takes place in the companion works, *Philosophical Fragments* and *The Concept of Dread*.

In an entry shortly after this (V A 16)[eeee] Christianity is identified as the absolute religion. Such is also Hegel's description in his *Philosophy of Religion* (II, 327f.); but Hegel and Kierkegaard base their similar sounding descriptions on irreconcilably different

[cccc] Hong, II, #1111.   [dddd] Hong, II, #1335.   [eeee] Hong, I, #46.

grounds. Kierkegaard calls Christianity the absolute religion "because it has conceived of men as sinners," by which the difference between mankind and God is marked in the clearest possible way, whereas Hegel's conception is that Christianity is the absolute religion because God is such that

> He distinguishes Himself from Himself, and is an object for Himself, but in this distinction He is purely identical with Himself, is in fact Spirit. This concept is now realized, consciousness knows this content and knows that it is itself absolutely interwoven with this content; in the concept which is the process of God, it is itself a moment. The finite consciousness knows God only insofar as God knows Himself in it; thus God is Spirit, the Spirit of His Church, i.e., of those who worship Him. This is the perfect religion, the concept become objective to itself (Hegel, *Lectures on the Philosophy of Religion*, II, 327f.).

Since "consciousness," "Spirit," and "Concept" in Hegel's philosophy are at one and the same time both human and divine, this means then, that for Hegel it is this likeness of mankind to God which is the basis for the description of Christianity as the absolute religion, because in Christianity, according to his conception, the likeness is perfectly manifested. We could put it this way, that "consciousness of God" in Hegel's thought contains both a subjective and an objective genitive.

The differences from Hegel and the Hegelians in Kierkegaard's entries from this point on are everywhere evident, although he does not explicitly comment on it very often.

Thus it appears in the scale he presents in V A 28:[ffff] first, the immediate, then reflection, then faith. Certainly he does not explicitly say here that the scale is a counterpart of Hegel's, especially in *Phenomenology of Spirit*, with its sequence from "consciousness" to "absolute knowledge"—criticized by Kierkegaard in *De Omnibus Dubitandum Est*—; but the fact is clear enough, especially when we consider the rashness with which Hegel in his *Philosophische Propädeutik* (SW, III, 97) joins the immediate and faith, and says that

> this absolute Essence [the eternal law of reason] is present in our pure consciousness and reveals itself to us therein. The

[ffff] Hong, I, #49.

knowledge of it [absolute knowledge] as mediated through it [i.e., through being known] in us, is immediate for us and can to that extent be called faith.

Probably Kierkegaard had not only Hegel in mind here but also Jacobi, since just at this time he was occupied with the latter's writings.[19]

The target is clearer in V A 46,[gggg] on Danish philosophy, "if there ever comes to be such a thing." This, according to Kierkegaard's opinion, will be different from German philosophy in this respect, that

it definitely will not begin with nothing or without any pre-suppositions, or explain everything by mediating, because, on the contrary, it begins with the proposition that there are many things between heaven and earth which no philosopher has explained.

More important than this rejection for our present investigation is an entry such as V A 68[hhhh] on the principles of logic and their area of validity.[20]

Hegel wished to incorporate classical logic with its axioms in modified form as a subordinate division of speculative logic. Its area of validity was not only limited by Hegel to the sphere of pure thought; he also restricted it to include only the domain of the understanding (or: reflection, or: abstraction), while on the other hand, according to Hegel, speculative logic is valid in the qualitatively higher and quantitatively more inclusive realm of reason,

---

[19] See, for instance V A 21 (Hong, V, #5728), 30 (I, #1033), 31 (III, #3298), 33 (I, #745), 35 (I, #810), 40 (II, #113), 47 (I, #624), B 157 (not in Hong), 207 (not in Hong); C 7 (III, #2349), 13 (especially on his concept of faith; Hong, V, #5733).

[gggg] Hong, III, #3299.

[hhhh] Hong, I, #705.

[20] The entry was first basically analyzed by Kuhr in *Modsigelsens Grundsætning* [The Principle of Contradiction], 1915; reference should also be made to Paul Holmer's article "Kierkegaard and Logic," in *Kierkegaardiana*, II (1957), 25-42, and G. Malantschuk's "Søren Kierkegaards Teori om Springet og hans Virkelighedsbegreb" [Søren Kierkegaard's Theory of the Leap and his Concept of Reality] in *Kierkegaardiana*, I (1955), 7-15. A thought-provoking witness to the fact that speculative logic is not a bygone factor can be found in Bela Fogorasi's *Logik* (1955), where, for example, the validity of the principle of identity in its classical formulation is rejected because "mankind does not think according to this law" (p. 36).

including man's existence [*Tilværelse*] (especially as philosophizing essence). Kierkegaard, on the contrary, maintains (in consonance with Sibbern and Mynster) that classical logic, to be sure, has a limited area of validity (the world of pure thought and abstraction); but that does not mean that speculative logic should prevail over and above it. In Kierkegaard's opinion, speculative logic by and large has no validity, but is purely a creature of the imagination (cf. V A 73).[iiii] In the human actuality [*Tilværelse*], in existence [*Existensen*], it holds true that there are and there must be, so long as it is such, contradictions: "On the one side I have the eternal truth, on the other side manifold existence [*Tilværelse*], which man as such cannot penetrate, for thus he would have to be omniscient[jjjj] as God is—and which, consequently, Hegel had to maintain that he himself was. Thus Hegel wished to abolish the contradictions of existence with the aid of his special logic, while Kierkegaard, on the contrary, would maintain them in their paradoxicality.

While Kierkegaard's criticism of speculative logic strongly increased after he had begun his studies in ancient philosophy, beginning in May 1844 it gets a further reinforcement from his reading of Trendelenburg's various anti-Hegelian (and pro-Aristotelian) writings. Kierkegaard acquired his *Logische Untersuchungen* [Logical Investigations] (1840) on January 15, 1844 (see the note on IV A 40[kkkk]) and the two short controversial writings *Die logische Frage in Hegel's System* [The Logical Question in Hegel's System] (1843) as early as May 1843. In the spring of 1844 Kierkegaard had studied Trendelenburg's *Elementa logices Aristoteleae*,[21] [The Elements of Aristotelian Logic], his *Erläuterungen zu den Elementen der aristotelischen Logik* [Explanations of the Elements of Aristotelian Logic], and his anti-Hegelian books just mentioned.

There can hardly be any doubt that Trendelenburg, both positively, through his presentation of Aristotelian logic, and negatively, through his profound and sharp criticism of Hegelian logic, had great importance for Kierkegaard. On the other hand we must not overlook the fact that Kierkegaard had failed to find in Trendelenburg certain items of significance to him for the development of his own theories, especially in this opposed position to Hegel. To be sure, he praises Trendelenburg (e.g. V A 74) for maintaining

[iiii] Hong, II, #1605.　　[jjjj] Hong, I, #705.　　[kkkk] Not in Hong.

[21] One of the rare printing errors in Heiberg and Kuhr's edition of the *Papirer* is found in the note on V A 74 [Hong, III, #2341], where this is given as "Aristoteli*c*ae."

that basic principles can only be proven indirectly;[22] but in the same entry he says—perhaps with a certain regret—that Trendelenburg "seems not to be at all aware of the leap." Correspondingly, he says (IV C 12)[llll] that Trendelenburg adheres too much to examples from mathematics and the natural sciences, while Kierkegaard himself chiefly devotes himself to what belongs within "the sphere of freedom," i.e., existence [*Existensen*] and thus the areas of the problems of ethics and the philosophy of religion. To this sphere of freedom, Kierkegaard's theory of the leap also essentially belongs (and therewith the pathos-filled transitions) although this theory "ideally should be suggested in logic" (the dialectical transitions) and above all the leap must "not be explained away by lying, as Hegel does."

In connection with this reading of Trendelenburg there is V A 75[mmmm] on Hegel's arbitrary use of the concept of immediacy, and V A 90,[nnnn] where all speculative-Hegelian talk of "a higher unity, which is supposed to unite absolute disparities" is rejected as only a metaphysical attack on ethics, whose absolute opposites, good and evil, cannot be mediated into a higher unity.

Whether Kierkegaard's objections against Hegel are correct or not, which we need not decide at this point, these short entries show that Kierkegaard's study of Hegel had actually been concluded. The disharmony was fundamental and it appears at any point that Kierkegaard pounced on in Hegel. To an increasing degree and in a constantly growing literary development, Kierkegaard at the same time formulated and made precise his own original thought, in the private entries and in the published works in the first phase of the Authorship up to and including the *Postscript*.

The Greeks became his consolation against

> the confounded mendacity which entered into philosophy with Hegel, the endless insinuating and betraying, and the parading and spinning out of one or another single passage from the Greek.—"Praised be Trendelenburg ..." (V A 98).[oooo]

At one point in 1844 Kierkegaard outlined a plan for an anti-

---

[22] *Logische Untersuchungen*, II (1840), 330, the question is raised (and answered): "How does it happen ... that even the principles of the System, on which all solidity depend, are mostly left to an indirect proof?"

[llll] Hong, III, #2352.

[mmmm] Hong, II, #1941.

[nnnn] *Ibid.*, #1247.

[oooo] Hong, III, #3300.

Hegelian periodical (V A 100-101).[pppp] It remained only a plan, in which he immediately made note of some questions he would address to Martensen and Heiberg. *Forord* (Prefaces)[qqqq] was, however, published (cf. Chapter VIII, section 6 *infra*).

There are not many C entries from March to December 1844 (V C 1-13).[rrrr]

The first C entries are a schematic formulation of the problem of the leap and the various kinds of transitions,[23] where Hegel is briefly mentioned several times. Kierkegaard refers there to *Phenomenology of Spirit* and to *Science of Logic*, just as he has examined what the Hegelians A. P. Adler,[ssss] Karl Werder (*Logik* etc., 1841), and Heiberg[tttt] have said on the question. He notes Schelling as an anti-Hegelian and refers to some passages in Rosenkranz's book on Schelling, which he had acquired the previous year on April 30, 1843 (see the note on IV A 185),[uuuu] and he comments that "the way Hegel cuts off the bad infinity is a leap" (V C 7)[vvvv] to which he adjoined several other kinds of leap, and noted what he later used in the *Postscript*, that Lessing used the word "leap" itself, which Kierkegaard discovered while he was reading Jacobi.

The following C entries show Kierkegaard's reading of Trendelenburg's above-mentioned presentation of Aristotelian logic (V C 11)[wwww] and of the first part of the fourth volume of Jacobi's works, the last Jacobi himself had written, that is, his "Preliminary Report" [*Vorbericht*]. He read Trendelenburg as a logician, Jacobi as philosopher of faith, but without reading either of them as a wholehearted adherent. Through the reading of Jacobi's *Ueber die Lehre des Spinoza, in Briefen an Herrn Moses Mendelssohn* Kierkegaard

---

[pppp] Hong, V, #5712, 5713.

[qqqq] There is, as yet, no English translation of this work.

[rrrr] Hong, III, #2345-2352; V C II, V, #5742; V C 13, V, #5733; V C 13:4, II, #1114.

[23] On this point cf. especially Malantschuk's articles "Begrebet Fordoblelse," "Frihedens Dialektik," "Das Verhältnis zwischen Wahrheit und Wirklichkeit."

[ssss] *Populaire Foredrag over Hegels objective Logik* [Popular Lectures on Hegel's Objective Logic] (1842), which Kierkegaard mentioned in V B 49 (not in Hong).

[tttt] "Det logiske System . . . Paragrapherne 1-23," *Perseus*, #2, which appeared in August 1838.

[uuuu] Hong, II, #1604.

[vvvv] Hong, III, #2349. Cf., for example, Hegel, *Science of Logic* I, 164ff.

[wwww] Hong, V, #5742.

became seriously interested in Lessing, whom he put in a place of honor in the *Postscript*.

5. *Papirer*, VI A 1-156 and C 1-5

The constantly increasing rift between Kierkegaard and Hegel, which is the more evident the further we read in the *Papirer*, is seen in the entries in the Journal and in the loose papers until the end of the year 1845, when he submitted the manuscript of *Concluding Unscientific Postscript* to the printer.

Quite characteristically Kierkegaard returns a work on Hegel's *Philosophy of Fine Art*, which Reitzel had sent him for inspection, and only noted its title (VI A 4).[xxxx] Just as characteristically, he praises Socrates for his consistency in his assertion of ignorance while at the same time he deprecates Hegel (VI A 15.)[yyyy] Public opinion is called by the philosophers, i.e., the Hegelians, "the objective spirit" (VI A26),[zzzz] and the philosophers themselves, now called "the speculators" (VI A 63, cf. 64),[aaaaa] are called "foolishly objective" because they have, so to speak, completely forgotten to include the thinker in their thought. Even if the system were to be so obliging as to show Kierkegaard a little place ("a guest room in the attic"), still he would prefer to be a free thinker ("like a bird on a twig," VI A 66).[bbbbb] A review of *Philosophical Fragments* in a German theological publication gave Kierkegaard occasion to remark (VI A 84)[ccccc] that his procedure in this work, namely

> to allow Christianity to be, as it were, an invention of Johannes Climacus is precisely a biting satire on the impudence of philosophy against it. And so again the orthodox types emerge in the experiment . . . that is the irony. But the seriousness lies precisely in the same thing, in this way to want to do justice to Christianity—before someone mediates it.

Martensen's *Grundrids til Moralphilosophiens System* [Fundamentals of a System of Moral Philosophy], to a great degree in-

[xxxx] Hong, V, #5768.
[yyyy] Hong, III, #3303.
[zzzz] Hong, IV, #4108.
[aaaaa] *Ibid.*, #4538, 4539. Hong translates "Spekulanterne" as "theorizers."
[bbbbb] Hong, III, #3304.
[ccccc] Hong, V, #5827.

fluenced by Hegel,[24] receives an especially sharp remark (VI A 92)[ddddd] precisely for its Hegelianism, and once more Kierkegaard mentions Hegel himself, in a loose entry (VI A 145),[eeeee] a draft for a dialogue between Socrates and Hegel on Kierkegaard's old problem: the dialectic of beginning. That for Kierkegaard, Socrates is the master of the conversation is evident. Trendelenburg is also mentioned.

The remaining A entries generally bear a slightly different character from the two previous volumes. There are certainly various indications of new trends of thought, such as for a presentation of "a new science [*Videnskab*]: the Christian art of speaking," which Kierkegaard considered writing with Aristotle's *Rhetoric* as a model[25] (VI A 17[fffff] and *passim*, as well as VI C 2-5[ggggg]); and for the interpretation of religious suffering. There are, however, relatively numerous entries, which only show individual observations from his reading, his strolls, from the short trip to Berlin in May 1845, just as there are several entries in connection with the reception of the published writings. He was in the main, finished with Hegel and the Hegelians, and not until A. P. Adler aroused a certain notice with his story of conversion and his distracted writings did Kierkegaard, under a particular perspective, take up Hegelian speculation for renewed treatment.

6. CONCLUSION

The groups of Kierkegaard's entries studied here have not previously been treated independently with reference to an understanding of Kierkegaard's relation to Hegel, although naturally they have been studied and used by everyone who has undertaken to work with this period. It seems to me that there is no compelling reason to engage in a discussion of the general approach and particulars in the entries with regard to the other Kierkegaard scholars, a discussion that would have to go beyond the few remarks and references given along the way here.

[24] Cf. Skat Arildsen's *H. L. Martensen* (1932), 199ff.
[ddddd] Hong, I, #921.
[eeeee] Hong, III, #3306.
[25] On this point cf. especially Lars Bejerholm's *Meddelelsens Dialektik* (1962), 192.
[fffff] Hong, I, #627.
[ggggg] Hong, V, #5779-5782.

The results of the investigation in this chapter can be summarized as follows.

Kierkegaard's studies in the history of philosophy, including, among others, Aristotle, Descartes, and Leibniz, were undertaken chiefly to obtain viewpoints and ingredients to use in the elaboration of his own world of thought and—ancillary to that—to use in the confrontation with speculative idealism. The uncompleted *Johannes Climacus* shows as clearly as can be imagined Kierkegaard's essential break with speculation. The last entries from this period show that Kierkegaard was essentially finished with speculation, which was totally rejected. What remained for him was only to develop in detail what in his entries he had remarked on individual, decisive points and sketched in broad outlines. The entries show that as far as Kierkegaard was concerned, he was completely clear about his relation to Hegelian speculation, and that he was cured of any inclination to walk its broad path.

The next question is, then, what is the situation in the first period of the Authorship, up to and including *Concluding Unscientific Postscript*, in the series of works he published, among other reasons, to evoke in others, if possible, the same clarity he had himself worked up to.

CHAPTER VIII

Kierkegaard's Indirect and Direct Clash with Hegel in the Authorship from *Either/Or* to *Concluding Unscientific Postscript*

1. INTRODUCTORY COMMENT

JUST AS KIERKEGAARD's private jottings from November 1842 to December 1845 bear clear indications of having been done during an uninterrupted period of work, so also the Authorship during these three years manifests a coherent but complicated totality.

It would not be unreasonable in this connection to look for an answer to the question of Kierkegaard's clash with Hegel through an analysis that would ignore the works as separate productions and read them as if they were chapters of a single book. This approach could be defended with particularly good reason, and it would, in a way, correspond to the purely systematic presentations of Kierkegaard's world of thought such as Malantschuk's renowned *Kierkegaard's Way to the Truth* (Minneapolis, Minnesota: Augsburg Publishing House, 1963) or Sløk's *Die Anthropologie Kierkegaards*. If we approach the task in this way, however, we will not adequately take into account the fact that Kierkegaard did not publish his thoughts during this period as a multivolume work. He wrote and published the works as separate entities, and each of them is in itself a totality, a whole, a globe, as it has been correctly said, "which turns on its own axis," and just as correctly: "But as a globe it has a fixed connection with other globes; Kierkegaard's works are related to each other as globes in a planetary system."[1] To a higher degree than the purely systematic presentations, the many works on the Authorship that are arranged with somewhat equal attention to the temporal and conceptual [*tankemæssige*] sequences, such as Lindström's *Stadiernas teologi* [Theology of the Stages], or Anna Paulsen's *Sören Kierkegaard, Deuter unserer Existenz* [SK, Interpreter of Our Existence], or Knud Hansen's *Sören Kierkegaard, Ideens Digter* [SK, Poet of the Idea], respect Kierke-

---

[1] F. J. Billeskov Jansen in the Introduction (p. xvii) to *Kierkegaards Værker i Udvalg* [Selections from Kierkegaard's Works], I (1950).

gaard's own approach, which simply cannot be called haphazard.

In these and similar presentations, in various ways and with diverse results it becomes clear that in Kierkegaard's Authorship there is a close connection between the chronological sequence in which different questions are taken up and the systematic rank order of the thoughts. Thus, if we follow the presentation of the stages, for example, it is clear that chronology and method converge. This elementary observation can then lead us, in connection with statements in the later Kierkegaard, to try to interpret the Authorship as having come about according to a pedagogically deliberate and precisely arranged plan that Kierkegaard must have established quite early. This interpretation provides a significant counterpart to Schleiermacher's noted presentation of the mutual relation of the Platonic dialogues. If we apply a similar hermeneutic principle to Kierkegaard's Authorship, it can be systematized, and we can with its aid answer the main question of this investigation concerning Kierkegaard's relation to Hegel with particular clarity and conciseness, namely by situating Hegel in his definitive place in a thus constructed Kierkegaardian system. Placement and evaluation would then, in Hegel's case and in that of others, become identical.

This approach would undeniably simplify a complex issue; but if one were to employ it consistently, there would be a not inconsiderable risk of either ignoring entirely or at least trivializing facts and problems that have had significance for the question of Kierkegaard's relation to Hegel. Thus, for example, it has been evident in the previous chapters of this investigation that Kierkegaard's relation to Hegel, both as concerns his secondhand and later firsthand knowledge and understanding, and as concerns his position thereto, went through a development, which in this investigation is seen as a process of enlightenment, in which various factors, such as Kierkegaard's studies in ancient philosophy, for example, demonstrably had influence. Even if Kierkegaard was a genius, he was certainly neither a saint, apostle, nor endowed with divine foreknowledge and omniscience so that he could a priori take a definitive position toward a philosophy before he had at least penetrated it somewhat through study. Despite his totally undeniable genius and originality in certain respects, in various other respects Kierkegaard was not much different from others[2] for whom reading,

[2] Cf. for example, Frithiof Brandt's concluding statement in *Søren Kierkegaard og Pengene* [SK and Money] (1935), 159.

thought, and writing went together as far as possible. Thus it was in Kierkegaard's private notes as well as in his published works, which are "stages" on the way to enlightenment. P. A. Heiberg has maintained that Kierkegaard's story was not the story of a sickness, but rather the history of a cure.[3] This thesis can also be utilized concerning Kierkegaard's relation to Hegel, provided, of course, that we emphasize equally the two elements "cure" and "history." If he was never himself especially severely attacked by the sickness, viz., speculative philosophy particularly in the version of Hegel, if he was at most exposed to its attack during a brief period in his youth and quite superficially infected here and there in his world of thought, then at least he cured himself with harsh medications of his own and others' devising, and sought through his writings to give his worthy contemporaries a drastic remedy against Hegel. In his Authorship demolition and construction [*Opbygning*] went together, and if we wish to understand this, the most relevant approach will be to follow the process step by step; that is, we must take each work individually before we can even speak of a systematic synthesis.

Since in this section of the investigation there is no intention of giving a complete presentation (either historically or systematically arranged) of Kierkegaard's world of thought, so, as in the previous chapters, in what follows a considerable amount of material in the works of Kierkegaard must be left out of the discussion. The parameters are set by the object of this study; the method is the same as has been used up to this point. The arrangement is as far as possible Kierkegaard's own, as the works are examined in the sequence in which they appeared.[4]

2. Judge William's Direct and Indirect Criticism of "Speculation" in *Either/Or* II

Even in the choice of the literary form of *Either/Or* there is a clear

---

[3] Especially in his major work: *Søren Kierkegaards religiøse Udvikling* [SK's Religious Development] (1925), particularly on the last page (377), where Heiberg sums up his study with the single word *Helbredelseshistorie* —"the history of a cure."

[4] That the edifying and poetic works receive a less prominent place in this study than in, e.g., Geismar's, Hirsch's, Mesnard's, Anna Paulsen's, and other complete presentations of Kierkegaard's life and thought must be considered an arrangement that requires no further justification.

opposition to Hegel and his speculative disciples' predilection for the direct, pedagogical approach in monographs or textbooks. By means of this poetic work to confront the reader with an alternative between the esthetic and the ethical attitude toward life, there is a clear indication of the rejection of the speculative mode of development in which individual choice is illusory because the process originates and continues with necessity, not freedom, for the individual as well as for world history. Certainly the pseudonymity of the work—apart from much else which is significant—is a manifestation of the fact that the author did not want to appear as a professorial or other authority. Although these frequently emphasized indicators are obvious, this does not answer every question about *Either/Or* and its relation to Hegel.

The presentation of the esthetic stage (which manifests itself in several ways) in the first part of *Either/Or* closely matches the interpretation (and evaluation) of romantic irony in *On the Concept of Irony*. It is more subtle and, directly as well as indirectly, more precisely described than in Kierkegaard's thesis. With regard to the main question of the present study, the relation to Hegel, the first part of *Either/Or* is not especially problematical. The most important thing to be noted in this respect is that in his theoretical esthetics Kierkegaard rather extensively took into account the Hegelian H. G. Hotho's *Vorstudien für Leben und Kunst* [Preliminary Studies for Life and Art] (1835) and Hegel's own *Lectures on the Philosophy of Fine Art*,[5] so that he freely took what he could find use for, and he criticized where, as a theoretical esthetician, he found it called for, and left the remainder alone. Kierkegaard did not give, and had no intention of giving, a completely developed esthetic system as a counterpart of Hegel's (or J. L. Heiberg's) in *Either/Or*.

On the other hand, in the second part of *Either/Or* a few questions occur on the relation to Hegel that require treatment.

In Judge William's first essay, "The Aesthetic Validity of Marriage" (*Either/Or*, II, 5-157), his intention is to convince the young esthete that the esthetic attitude toward life must be made into a

---

[5] On this point the reader is referred to F. J. Billeskov Jansen's commentary volume, *Kierkegaards Værker i Udvalg*, IV (1950), 21 (on Hotho) and pp. 24-28 (on Hegel). In my commentary on H. Fauteck's German translation *Entweder-Oder* (*Kierkegaards ästhetisch-philosophische Schriften*, hrsgg. v. Hermann Diem u. Walter Rest), 1960, pp. 937-1025, notes will be found on the individual passages where Hegel and others are quoted or discussed.

mastered moment, as it is called in *On the Concept of Irony* (pp. 240, 256, 340, and esp. 337), i.e., the immediate, romantic infatuation with the instant must enter into a harmonious union with the enduring love of marriage and its ethical obligations.

This could appear to exemplify what Kierkegaard frequently speaks of in deprecatory terms, Hegelian reconciliation ("mediation," as Kierkegaard often puts it) of seeming opposites; and Høffding, for example, thinks that the ethical stage in Kierkegaard's poetic presentations has Hegel's concept as its most immediate basis.[6] However there is much in Judge William's first essay which decisively speaks against such a notion.

If we leave out of consideration the systematic foundation of Hegel's concept of marriage, which he has most thoroughly treated in *Philosophy of Right* (pp. 110-122), then we can find a series of parallels and particular agreements or similarities between his and Judge William's views. However a demonstration of such parallels would not solve the problem of Judge William's possible Hegelian background or sympathies, since the specifically Hegelian and what is specifically Judge William does not consist in a panegyric of marital love, its fidelity, perseverance, etc., for we would probably have no difficulty in finding parallels both in older and more recent textbooks on Christian ethics and in literature, which there is no need to illustrate here. The difference between Hegel and the Judge consists in the foundation, which in Hegel lies in the placement of the discussion of marriage within the system as a totality, and which in Judge William is given in another way.

Hegel's *Philosophy of Right*, its purpose and its place in the system (as the doctrine of the objective spirit) has already been briefly, but in this connection sufficiently, described (Chapter I, section 2). On his treatment of marriage we need only add his statement that:

> Marriage contains, as the immediate type of ethical relationship, first the moment of physical vitality in its totality, namely as the actuality of the species and its process. But, secondly, in self-consciousness the natural sexual union—a union purely internal or being-in-itself [*an sich seyende*] and for that very reason only an external unity in its existence—is changed into a spiritual, a self-conscious love (p. 111).

In the following paragraphs Hegel continues with a discussion of

[6] *Danske Filosofer* (1909), p. 158; cf. *Søren Kierkegaard som Filosof*, 2nd ed. (1919), pp. 92ff.

the subjective conditions of marriage in the special disposition of two persons for each other, and its objective condition in their free agreement to constitute one person (i.e., person juridically understood). The ethical in marriage consists in the consciousness of this unity as a substantial goal, a unity obtained by entering into marriage in compliance with existing legal and ecclesiastical rules and ceremonies (§164). Through its rationality the natural condition of the two sexes obtains its intellectual and ethical significance in monogamy, the foundation of the family, whose external reality as a juridical person is its property, its assets. Hegel discusses the family's property right in the following paragraphs, then the questions of the rearing of children and the dissolution of the family, after which he goes on to treat of civil society as a transitional stage for the perfect speculative state.

Certainly in these paragraphs Hegel rejects Kant's view of marriage as only a civil contractual relationship (§161, additions, p. 262) and Friedrich von Schlegel's encomium of free love in *Lucinda* (§164, additions, p. 263); but in Hegel there is at most only passing mention of the establishment of ethical attitudes and no mention at all of choice of personality or the personality's choice in the same sense as in Judge William in *Either/Or*.

The whole section on marriage in Hegel's *Philosophy of Right* should be correctly understood, that is, in harmony with Hegel's intention, as a necessary link in the speculative development of the concept of the doctrine of the Objective Spirit, which in turn is the negation and thus only a necessary transitional point for the doctrine of the Absolute Spirit. But neither the section on marriage nor *Philosophy of Right* as a whole can, according to Hegel's fundamental concept, have any validity isolated from the system as a whole, or apart from its principles, its method, its conclusion.

In Judge William's first epistolary essay to the young esthete A, we cannot discover any corresponding foundation for his main point of view, nor has he set for himself the same goal as that of Hegel. The method that was all important for Hegel is employed only occasionally by Judge William. The agreements and parallels on particular points that we can mention here and there consequently cannot be granted essential significance.

Just by his choice of literary form alone, Judge William is un-Hegelian; he is also anti-Hegelian not only in his view on individual points but by the justification for his notion of the aesthetic validity of marriage, a justification that is certainly expressed more clearly in his second epistolary essay but that is nevertheless also the foundation for the first.

Specific examples help to show the correctness of these statements.

"The Aesthetic Validity of Marriage" is the part of *Either/Or* that was written first, i.e., shortly after Kierkegaard's defense of his thesis,[7] and this external circumstance contributes to an explanation of the fact that we find some reflections of Kierkegaard's reading of Hegel.

Judge William holds (*Either/Or*, II, 22ff.) that his own era has turned away from the romantic version of love, either mocking its naïve chivalry, fidelity, and especially marriage, or embracing the notion that marriage is a purely civil or rational arrangement, a marriage of convenience, thus ignoring the significance of love. While we may describe the romantic interpretation as "immediate," the two distinct interpretations of Judge William's contemporaries are to be described as "reflected." Frequently people speak of a marriage of convenience, Judge William says (*Either/Or*, II, 27); but if we want "to respect linguistic usage" (i.e., contemporary Hegelian), we really ought to call it a marriage of common sense, which belongs to the "sphere of reflection." In opposition to these two opinions, Judge William maintains that Christianity resolves the conflict between immediate and reflected love in marriage, which "essentially belongs to Christianity" (p. 29).

That this reasoning follows Hegel's pattern requires no further demonstration, nor that the Judge uses Hegelian terminology. At the same time, however, the question of the relation between the attitudes expressed by Judge William and by Hegel is not satisfactorily answered.

We can put the matter thus: if Judge William had been a genuine and consistent Hegelian, he would hardly have needed to bother producing either the first or the second letter in order to convince his young esthetical friend of the inadequacy of his stage and of the advantage of his own, because then the esthete would necessarily (in the Hegelian sense) by himself have intuited the provisional and temporary validity of his own stage and with the

[7] On the relative dates of composition reference is made to P. A. Heiberg's *Nogle Bidrag til Enten-Ellers Tilblivelseshistorie* [Some Contributions to the History of the Genesis of *Either/Or*] (1910), whose main conclusion, which can scarcely be disputed, is that Kierkegaard wrote the esthetic portion after he wrote the ethical portion. That is, *Or* was written before *Either*.

same necessity he would have passed on to the ethical. According to Hegel, this law would have been operative both in the world historical and individual development, as, indeed, the Judge's treatise had to come into existence and to have had its effect on the unfolding of the Concept precisely in the year of Our Lord 1843. If one embraces this notion, then one is a genuine Hegelian; but Judge William is just not a spokesman for this notion. His whole reasoning process proceeds in the sphere of freedom, not in that of necessity, where the possibilities of choice are genuine, not illusory as in Hegel. Hence he must be described as essentially an un-Hegelian ethician, even though he does use Hegelian patterns and means. Moreover, neither does the fact that he is an optimist like Hegel, although more controlled (cf. his statements on p. 341 and "The Ultimatum" itself) mean that he can be described as a Hegelian, since optimism is not sufficient to qualify a view as Hegelian. Johannes de Silentio's statement about *Fear and Trembling* "This is not the system, it has nothing whatever to do with the system" (p. 24) applies to Judge William's position even in his first essay.

In a continuation of this sequence of thought Judge William offers some comments that quite directly show him to be un-Hegelian. He says that "every generation and each individual in the generation to a certain extent begin afresh," which is unquestionably incompatible with Hegel's philosophy of history, in which every generation (and the individuals in it) simply does not begin afresh, but continues the development in which the preceding must yield.[8]

We could then ask whether Judge William's opinion that Christianity is mankind's highest development (p. 31) and that it alone makes possible the union of "all of the first erotic of love" and "Marital love" is not the same as Hegel's view. Both in Hegel's *Encyclopedia* and in his *Philosophy of Religion* Christianity is interpreted as "the absolute religion," and since for Hegel the development of mankind is identical with the self-unfolding of the divine Idea in time, the harmony, indeed, identity between Judge William's opinion and Hegel's on this main point should be evident.

In response to this, it must be pointed out that neither the harmony nor the identity between the two opinions is established merely by the designation of Christianity as the highest point of

[8] There is a parallel here with Kierkegaard's criticism of Martensen's view on baptism in *Papirer*, V A 11 (not in Hong).

development when this conceptual designation is not especially Hegelian[9] and when it does not include any specification of the content of the Christianity identified in this way.

While it is not difficult to specify the content of Hegel's notion of Christianity, especially on the basis of his philosophy of religion, in the case of Judge William one is referred to individual utterances not only in his first essay but also in his second in *Either/Or*. Only this much can be said here in a summary way: the Judge's stage is so undifferentiated that it is able harmoniously to contain within it the esthetic, the ethical, and the religious (A and B, according to the designations in the *Postscript*). The explanation for this situation must be partly that Kierkegaard had still not worked out his theory of stages as precisely and distinctly as he did later, and partly that from his "higher" ethical stage the Judge was in a position to survey the esthete's "lower" stage and present a more adequate understanding of it than the esthete A's understanding. So too, the Judge could not have had a complete insight into the religious stage, which is higher than his own, but only, as is also suggested in his introductory comments for "The Ultimatum," an understanding that his own stage was not the highest. Hence there is nothing peculiar in the fact that it is not possible to write Judge William's dogmatic theology, at least not just on the basis of his essay on "The Aesthetic Validity of Marriage," whose purpose is clearly expressed in the title, which certainly cannot be rephrased either as "The Religious (Christian) Validity of Marriage," for example, or as "The Notion of Christianity Which Must Be Presupposed So That Marriage Can Be Religiously (Christianly) Sanctioned."

If we turn now from Judge William's first epistolary essay to his second, longer, and weightier, on "The Equilibrium Between the Aesthetical and the Ethical in the Composition of Personality" (*Either/Or*, II, 161-338, hereinafter referred to as "The Equilibrium"), we again discover, as expected, the same characteristics regarding form and content as in his first; but there are several additional items of significance—significant in themselves and in relation to Hegel.

Although it is not explicitly indicated, the essay is clearly arranged into three main sections, the first of which deals with the choice, the second concerns the esthetic attitude toward life in the ethical

[9] On this point cf., e.g., Troeltsch's treatise *Christentum und Religionsgeschichte*, 1897 (reprinted in his *Gesammelte Schriften*, II, 1913, 328ff.).

light, and the third, the ethical attitude toward life in its relation to the esthetic.[10] As in Judge William's first essay so it is in the second that it is first and foremost estheticism, not Hegelian speculation, he turns against, even though at several points along the way he takes a position on the latter. In this study it is these positions which are of primary interest.

The Judge's claim, rendered against the esthete, is that rather than cultivating his mind [*Aand*] the important thing is to mature his personality (p. 166), and for the content of the personality the choice is not the esthete's indifferent either/or, but the decisive either/or (pp. 166f. and *passim*). Postponement of, or failure to make the ethical choice only entails that "then the personality chooses unconsciously, or the choice is made by obscure powers within it" (p. 168). The esthetic choice is no genuine choice (p. 171), since it is not an absolute ethical choice between good and evil. Thus the choice stands between ethical decisiveness and indecisiveness, indifference; but then it follows, the Judge continues (p. 171), that in choice it is not so much a matter of choosing the right as of the energy, the earnestness, the pathos with which it is chosen. In Kierkegaard's *Papirer* terminology, that is the same as saying that Judge William asserts a pathos-filled transition (in the sphere of freedom), not just a dialectical one (in the sphere of necessity); he demands a leap. By this requirement alone Judge William separates himself completely from Hegel, in whose philosophy this does not come up at all and it is impossible for it to come up without destroying the method as well as the system. The Judge further asserts optimistically that if one has brought a man into the situation that the only way out of it consists in a choice, then that man chooses the right, i.e., he determines himself to choose ethically instead of not choosing at all or at most doing so esthetically, and then, when he has chosen to make ethical choices, he chooses rightly between good and evil (pp. 172-173).

Having come thus far, Judge William draws a significant parallel between the esthete's indifferent ethical attitude and "modern philosophy's pet theory, that the principle of contradiction is annulled" (p. 174). The esthete, he says, mediates opposites in a higher madness, philosophy (i.e., the speculative) in a higher unity; but the result is the same—the absolute opposition between good and evil illegitimately disappears for them. Surely there is this difference

[10] The division is given by Hirsch in *Kierkegaard-Studien*, II (1933), 614-615.

between the esthete and the speculative philosopher, that the first is turned forward toward existence, the latter is turned backward toward history. Viewed ethically, this difference means nothing since neither the esthete nor the speculative philosopher undertakes the ethical choice. Even if one now suggests that speculative philosophy is correct in its assertion that the principle of contradiction has been annulled as far as the past is concerned (insofar as the world historical development has proceeded according to the Hegelian dialectic's rule of the resolution of relative oppositions in a higher unity, which is the point of departure for the next movement of the Idea), still this cannot hold true for the future, the Judge says, because the oppositions must first exist before they can be mediated. If the claim that the principle of contradiction has been annulled can apply only to the past, not the future, this means that the possibility of choice enters each instant and, note well, the possibility of ethical choice.

Here there is also clearly enough a complete break with Hegel's philosophy of history, which in the system follows the philosophy of right (including ethics), and in principle it could be continued with a prophecy of history, since it would be inconsistent to suggest the presence of a definite set of laws in the past until A.D. 1830, but not in the time thereafter. Judge William does not offer any counterpart to Hegel's philosophy of history in this context—that first appeared in the Climacus text *Philosophical Fragments* a good year later. But there are grounds for noting that the Judge's objection against the speculative philosophy of history, that for it "world history is concluded, and he [the speculative philosopher] mediates" is already found suggested in the previously discussed (Chapter IV, section 4) draft for a play "The Conflict Between The Old and The New Soap-Cellar" (II B 19). It is likely that Judge William alludes to the historical basis and persons satirized in this play with the later familiar quotation about the pet philosophy [*Yndlingsfilosofi*] of the age which becomes the juvenile philosophy [*Ynglingsfilosofi*] of the age (p. 176).[11]

Judge William also objects to philosophy (i.e., speculative philosophy) because, in his view, it has confused the modern era with absolute time, and thus has also mistaken relative mediation with

[11] This locution was used with approval by, among others, H. N. Clausen in his *Optegnelser om mit Levneds og min Tids Historie* [Notes on the History of My Life and Times] (1877), p. 213.

absolute mediation, which cannot take place until world history is completed. If Judge William is right in holding that this confusion has taken place, this means that mediation, the vital nerve of the dialectical method and of the Hegelian system, is cut, speculation is discarded, and the system is not completed but is constantly coming into existence, which amounts to saying that the system is not a system at all but a hypothesis that cannot possibly be verified until the end of the ages. Here again Judge William's criticism adumbrates the later Authorship. This is reflected especially in the *Concluding Unscientific Postscript* (pp. 106ff.), just as in his subsequent objection (which Kierkegaard had prepared for in the *Papirer* and worked out in more detail in the Authorship) to the effect that it seems that they, the speculative philosophers, have confused the two spheres of thought and of freedom with each other (*Either/Or*, II, 177ff.). While ethical conflict cannot exist for thought, it does exist in the realm of freedom—which is entirely left out of consideration in Hegel's philosophy, where there is, to be sure, much discussion of freedom, but only of the freedom of the absolute spirit to follow its own dialectical law, so that for Hegel freedom is identical with metaphysical necessity.

After these objections, the Judge takes the opportunity to maintain that the spheres that properly concern the philosopher are logic, nature, and history. Here necessity reigns, he says (p. 178), although he imagines that there is some difficulty with history (cf. especially the "Interlude" in *Philosophical Fragments*), a difficulty he resolves here by suggesting that the philosophy of history has as its objects only external events, not "the inward work [which] is the genuine life of freedom" (p. 178). This solution also points toward the *Postscript* (pp. 119ff.), and—just as Climacus does later—Judge William maintains that freedom, i.e., that which is the given actuality as a task for every existing individual, is a fact that speculative philosophy has nothing to do with (p. 179), it knows nothing about the impending ethical choice. In this respect there is a similarity between the esthete and the speculative philosopher: they have not discovered the reality of the fact of choice. The Judge then passes on to a more detailed account of what he understands by the ethical choice (pp. 180ff.).

In the following main section, dealing with the esthetic stage from the perspective of the ethical (pp. 180-223), Judge William once more draws a parallel between the esthete and the speculative philosopher (pp. 215ff.)—and at this point also briefly reflects a theme developed at length in *De Omnibus Dubitandum Est* (cf. *supra*, Chapter VII, section 3).

Having described the esthete's stage as despair and urged the esthete to choose his despair and thereby choose himself "in his eternal validity," i.e., as created, concrete person with reality as the object of ethical position and activity, not as the object of speculative conceptualization and description, the Judge distinguishes between doubt [*Tvivl*] and despair [*Fortvivlelse*]: whereas doubt belongs to the realm of thought (that of logical necessity), despair is an expression of the whole personality and hence belongs to the realm of freedom, where there can be choice. The speculative philosophers, he continues, confused doubt with despair. They themselves suffer from a form of despair, which is apparent from the fact that they "divert themselves with objective thinking" (p. 216), and thereby, like the esthete, escape ethical choice, which is also a choice, albeit the wrong one. Their only possibility for a cure of the sickness of despair (from the Christian perspective a sin, which the Judge does not point out here since he is reasoning on another level) is to become revealed to oneself, i.e., to see into one's factual situation and embrace it in earnest. The Judge expresses this by saying that the task is to choose the absolute, i.e., to choose oneself in his eternal validity, which again means to choose that which is at once the most abstract and the most concrete of all: freedom (p. 218). Accepting this will lead the esthete to repentance for his sinful despair. The consequence of the Judge's thought process must be that while the esthete has, as it were, the opportunity to carry his estheticism over into the ethical stage as a mastered moment (cf. the Judge's first essay), so the speculative philosopher can save himself as a personality only by turning over his whole edifice of thought to a museum of misconceptions as a cautionary example of what existing humans ought not concern themselves with. This is almost like comparing the building of the system with the building of the Tower of Babel. Johannes de Silentio preferred to compare it with a public omnibus. (*Fear and Trembling*, p. 25).

Again in the final and largest main section (pp. 222-337), where the Judge develops the positive exposition of his ethical-religious attitude toward life in its relation to the esthetic attitude toward life, there are occasional direct criticisms of Hegel and the Hegelians; but the objections here, weighty as they are, bear the character of parting shots, as the Judge passes on to the next point on his schedule.

It is said (p. 227) that philosophy—which here as always in the essay means speculative philosophy—could seem to have abolished the principle of contradiction. It could surely have done this in the realm of thought, but not in the sphere of ethical reality. Even if philosophy cannot conceive of an absolute contradiction, it does not follow that there is no such thing, and if there is such a thing—as Judge William insists throughout—then this is sufficient proof that the chief thesis of Hegelian philosophy, the identity of thought and being, has been refuted by an ethical fact that belongs to the sphere of freedom, not that of necessity.

With that, on every point that was important to him, Judge William has directly criticized, not just corrected Hegel. It becomes abundantly clear that as thinkers they are totally divergent in points of departure, methods, and conclusions.

Just as at the end of his thesis Kierkegaard let it be known that he had deliberately dealt with his topic only within a sharply limited point of view, so also both from Judge William's Introduction to "The Ultimatum" and from the sermon itself we get an unmistakable manifestation of the—optimistic—ethical stage the Judge is a spokesman for, which is the only one, or the highest one.

If we have observed how the Judge distances himself not only from the esthete but also from speculative philosophy, it must appear strange that several scholars over the years have wished to maintain that there are important similarities between the points of view in the "The Equilibrium" and those of Hegel,[12] particularly in the notion of how the transition from the esthetic position to the ethical occurs and the notion of "the universal." Knud Hansen, in particular, in his large critical exposition *Søren Kierkegaard, Ideens Digter* (1954, pp. 82ff.) has presented this interpretation, which seems plausible indeed, although it can hardly withstand criticism.

A single little word in Knud Hansen indicates that he has understood neither Hegel nor Kierkegaard correctly, i.e., according to their own meaning. That word is "only," which apparently for Knud Hansen should signify something less essential. What is for him less essential was for Kierkegaard, at least, all important.

Knud Hansen asserts that, in "The Equilibrium," it is not said

[12] Valter Lindström in *Stadiernas teologi* (1943), pp. 243ff., mentions a few of the earlier scholars.

"how there is a passage from the negative to the positive, from despair over the temporal self [the esthetical] to the conception of the self in its eternal validity." This is not said, Knud Hansen continues, because it obviously did not need to be said:

> The thought seems to be [that] when only the will oppressed with despair strains itself to the utmost by despairing completely, the change comes of itself: the negative changes into the positive.

Thus, just as Diem in his book (1929), Knud Hansen finds that this dialectic of the will of the Judge is "very strongly related to the dialectic of thought in Hegel." To be sure, notice is correctly taken of the fact that Kierkegaard later rejected this notion of the process by which a person finds himself according to his eternal condition; but the conclusion is drawn there that Kierkegaard (here in "The Equilibrium") is "depending on the Hegelian dialectic which he combats; he has only moved it from one area to another, from thought over to passion."

This "moving" of the problematic from the sphere of necessity to that of freedom, to use Kierkegaard's terminology again, is quite important, for it implies the change from a quantitative to a qualitative dialectic, which means that we can speak only of a pathos-filled transition, i.e., a leap, no longer of the dialectic, and that rules out that "the change comes of itself." The Judge does not assert that either, and Knud Hansen also says quite correctly that "The thought seems [for Knud Hansen] to be . . ." etc., to which we can respond that certainly Kierkegaard sketches Judge William as someone with not a little optimism and confidence in his own convincing and persuasive capacities. But Judge William does not express the notion that any esthete (in the Kierkegaardian sense) at all after reading the Judge's essay will necessarily become convinced and turn into an ethician of the Judge's fashioning, so that the conversion must needs come from himself. He says that it can happen and ought to happen *if* the esthete himself chooses and wills it. We can add, *unless* this is the Judge's meaning, then all his talk about choice and responsibility in the strict sense is meaningless—just as it is in Hegelian philosophy, which, according to Kierkegaard's later objection, has no ethics because everything without exception happens with an inviolable metaphysically grounded necessity.

The next point, the designation of the ethical as "the universal" also belongs to a disputed area in Kierkegaard scholarship. Here, as is generally the case with studies of Kierkegaard's relation to Hegel, if one isolates individual words, concepts and more restricted conceptual contexts in Kierkegaard and in Hegel, one can without the slightest difficulty find a multiplicity of verbal correspondences, simply because Kierkegaard to a large degree still used the speculative vocabulary of his contemporaries, and one can from the terminological similarities draw hasty conclusions from verbal to real correspondences. In addition, while Kierkegaard scholars who obviously try to incorporate suitable hermeneutical references not only to the more immediate context but also of the wider context in Kierkegaard (that is: the word, the sentence, the section, the chapter, the works as a whole, the work's situation and its thus given function in the Authorship), we find only rarely the same reference taken in their understanding of Hegel.

Knud Hansen's exposition can again be mentioned as an example, and with respect to this point as an example of a presentation of Judge William's (Kierkegaard's) conception of the ethical, which is certainly clear and correct in a great many things, but which suffers from a slight defect that leads to a not quite accurate determination of the relation to Hegel.

Like earlier scholars,[13] Knud Hansen says (*Kierkegaard*, p. 83) that the very expression "the universal" is derived from Hegel, "who by the universal understands human moral conduct as it takes shape in family life, civil society, and above all in the state." Naturally, he is thinking of *Philosophy of Right* here. He goes on to say, quite admirably, that in Judge William's essay the expression is used in two senses, viz., both in reference to the universal validity of the ethical claim and the life of civil society as a representative of that claim. So far, so good. Then Knud Hansen carries this out further when he emphasizes (p. 86) quite correctly that the relation to the universal in Judge William is different from what it is in Hegel: "While this relation in Hegel is determined in a purely compulsory way from the demand for the individual's immersion in 'the common life of civil society' " as it is called with a quote from Kuno Fischer's presentation of Hegel's philosophy, "the Kierkegaardian ethician understands how to use the relation to win freedom for himself," and a little further on Knud Hansen correctly asserts (pp. 90-91) that it is a mistake to think of Judge William as a representative of Hegel's ethics.

[13] E. g., Himmelstrup in *Terminologisk Ordbog* . . . (2nd ed., 1964), p. 13.

Here is the slight defect previously mentioned. It is quite correct that Judge William cannot rightly be said to be a representative of Hegel's ethics. But strictly speaking no one can be said to be a representative of Hegel's ethics, simply because in Hegel's system there is no ethics and none can be discovered there. Earlier in the present study (Chapter V, section 3b) it was said of Hegel, by way of interpretation, that his system is correctly seen as a reasoning process built out of an experience of the divine cosmos, hence a description that reports in direct form, "direct communication" as Kierkegaard put it, and consistently is communicated in the indicative. Only as an inconsistency can Hegel use the imperative, without which there can be no talk of ethics, but only of moral psychology and moral sociology. In addition, one must distinguish between the origin of the ethical requirement and the point (the situation) wherein it demands fulfillment. On this point Valter Lindström's previously mentioned presentation is clearer than Knud Hansen's.

Judge William himself says in his little introduction to "The Ultimatum" that the Jutland pastor "in this sermon [has] apprehended, what I said . . . [and] expressed it more felicitously than I find myself capable of doing."

What the sermon insists upon is "the edification contained in the thought that against God we are always in the wrong" (p. 343). The text for the sermon is Luke 19:41ff.: just as we must understand that the destruction of Jerusalem was a punishment that severely afflicted both guilty and innocent people at that time, so also all men must learn not to approach God as if we were in the right but accept the fact that against God we are always in the wrong. Only in this way can we designate the perfection of man as man, man's special position within creation. But at the same time it is made clear that the certainty of the fact that God is always right, man wrong, is not gained by the way of contemplation, the way of thought. It is gained only by means of love, i.e., that of freedom, by which the infinite qualitative difference between God and man becomes clear. And because certainty is achieved in this way of love and freedom, doubt is excluded and action is stimulated, and it is stressed that the thought that as against God we are always in the wrong means that God's love is always greater than human love (*Either/Or*, II, 354-355), which is an edifying truth, i.e., a truth that builds up a human's existence.[a]

[a] In the Danish there is an obvious connection between the adjective *opbyggelig* (which I have translated as "edifying") and the verb *at bygge*

This sermon quite closely parallels Judge William's insistence that the esthete should choose himself in his eternal validity, namely as a responsible creature with a concrete existence as a task. The sermon contains a point of view that would later be more precisely developed by Kierkegaard and which is as un-Hegelian, indeed indirectly anti-Hegelian, as possible, both in the concept of God that dominates it and in the view of man to which it gives expression. For Hegel—as for all idealistic thinkers—there was no infinite qualitative difference between God and man. For Hegel man's perfection was not to be seen in his unrighteousness (and impotence) but in his righteousness (and omnipotence).

Finally, there is reason to note that in the preparatory work for *Either/Or* (*Papirer*, III B 31-192)[b] there are individual remarks in this context. Reference is made (III B 41, 8, p. 130)[c] to Karl Rosenkranz's *Kritische Erläuterungen des Hegel'schen Systems* [Critical Elucidation of the Hegelian System] (1840), in connection with the discussion of woman as an imperfect being (*Either/Or*, II, 49-50). In the place cited, Rosenkranz polemicizes against J. H. Pabst's *Der Mensch und seine Geschichte* [Man and His History] (1830), to whose obviously very narrow-minded discussion of the sexual aspect of marriage Rosenkranz took strong exception: "The Holy Ghost" Rosenkranz says (p. 309),

> is certainly neither male nor female; we Protestants know that as well as Herr Pabst; but we men cannot deny the sexual life, and marriage exterminates lust in it, is subordinated to the spiritual relation and sanctifies the life of nature.

Shortly after the above entry in the *Papirer* (at III B 41, 22, p. 132)[d] there is a reference to Hegel's *Phenomenology of the Spirit* "Introduction," pp. 135f., where Hegel discusses doubt. Judge William distinguishes (*Either/Or*, II, 96-97) between a personal and a scientific doubt, and thinks (in the draft III B 41, 22) that it is only the latter that Hegel advocates, on which point he may be right, although in the place cited Hegel speaks of "the way of doubt . . . or more properly a way of despair" for the science that is about to

---

op, or *opbygge*, to construct, build up, or edify. Professor Hong prefers to translate *opbyggelig* literally, and quite correctly, as "upbuilding," but I consider this inelegant in English.

[b] A few of these entries will be found in various volumes of Hong, *Journals and Papers*.

[c] Not in Hong.

[d] Not in Hong.

manifest itself. Two other entries in the drafts (III B 179, 60, p. 206, and III B 179, 63, pp. 208-209)[e] on the tautology and on the principle of contradiction are dealt with by Kuhr in the work referred to previously (cf. *supra*, Chapter III, section 5, note 11). III B 192[f] contains a devastating description "of the present condition of philosophy": whereas the rationalists in "The first epoch worked toward the sound understanding of man and achieved it as well," then "philosophy today abandons more and more this relative superficiality in order to reach something higher."

Just as in the preparatory drafts for *Either/Or* we discover individual comments of interest in this context, so in the more complete entries Kierkegaard made after its publication (IV B 19-59)[g] we find important statements of how he himself wished the work to be understood. Kierkegaard had been extremely irritated by Heiberg's discussion of *Either/Or* in *Intelligensblade*, as a series of witticisms and attacks (IV B 26-59)[h] shows; but it is mainly "Victor Eremita's" lengthy "Post-Scriptum" (IV B 59, March 1844)[i] which is important. He takes particular notice there of

> a deception in the book: a movement is attempted, which cannot be made, or at least not in that way; the Judge has undoubtedly noticed it himself, I cannot believe otherwise. Since he had it as a task only to delimit an ethical view, such a deception was unavoidable.

The deception spoken of is elucidated later in *Concluding Unscientific Postscript* (pp. 229-231) as follows: The Judge gave the impression that man in despairing can in that very despair find himself without divine aid. But the truth is that by himself man can undertake only one part of the double movement, not the other. "Victor Eremita" does not pass up the opportunity to ironize over the fact that the reviewers of *Either/Or* have not noticed this limitation in Judge William's position.

3. THE *Eighteen Edifying Discourses*

Just as there was little intention under the preceding points of this

[e] Neither of these are in Hong.

[f] Hong, III, #3288. This entry is another fine example of the extraordinary satirical talent of Kierkegaard.

[g] A few of these will be found in Hong, vols. IV and V.

[h] A few of these will be found in Hong, vols. III, IV, and V.

[i] Hong, V, #5710.

study to present a complete treatment of the esthetic and ethical stages according to *Either/Or*, so also under the present heading we do not intend to give an exhaustive account of the religious stage such as it is sketched in Kierkegaard's collection of edifying discourses. Only that which directly and indirectly has significance for an understanding of the relation to Hegel and speculative idealism as a school of thought within the philosophy of religion will be considered here.[14]

If we wish to compare the *Eighteen Edifying Discourses*, which Kierkegaard published in 1843 and 1844, three sets each year with two, three, or four discourses in each, and which he then collected under a common title page in 1845, with others, then in the present study it would be most relevant to take Hegel's few extant sermons from his Tübinger period (1792-1793),[15] if it would not be somewhat unfair to compare the quite young Hegel's first—and not continued—efforts in this area with the expert and masterful preacher Kierkegaard was from the start. There is no satisfactory reason for including other preachers here. If one wished to do that, we should first and foremost discuss Mynster, and secondly Martensen.[16] Even if we do not find any originality evident in Kierkegaard's *Edifying Discourses* either in style or form, in their calm, progressive reflections on the themes chosen, it would be quite incorrect to think that Kierkegaard was a pedantic writer of sermons [*Postilrytter*]. He could have been outstanding.

Nor is there reason to devote much attention to the question of the correct designation for these discourses. In the first draft of the preface for the first two, Kierkegaard called them simply sermons (IV B 143);[j] but because he was not ordained and, as he constantly

[14] In neither the earlier nor in the more recent Kierkegaard scholarship has anyone devoted to these collections of edifying discourses approximately as much attention as to the pseudonymous Authorship. Hirsch in his *Kierkegaard-Studien*, II (1933), 623ff., 649ff., 658ff., and 719ff., was the first to have analyzed them. The first two discourses were very perspicaciously treated by Sløk in the article "Das Verhältnis des Menschen zu seiner Zukunft" [Man's Relation to His Future] (in *Orbis Litterarum*, XVIII, 1963, 60-79).

[15] These are printed in Johannes Hoffmeister's edition of *Dokumente zu Hegels Entwicklung* [Documents on Hegel's Development] (1936), 175-192.

[16] Kierkegaard's collection of sermons (Ktl. 211-252) was not large and contained no rarities; earlier editions of St. John Chrysostom, Tauler, and Luther, contemporaneous editions of Bindesbøll, Grundtvig (*Søndags-Bog*), Martensen, Mynster, Schleiermacher, and of his acquaintance, P. J. Spang, are the most important.

[j] Not in Hong.

said of himself, "without authority," he changed the designation to "edifying discourses." Here is already an indication of the notion of the ordination that he later amplified. There is another equally important reason for not using the designation "sermons" for these discourses, that is, as it is said in the *Postscript* (p. 229) that the discourses "only employ ethical categories of immanence, not the doubly reflected religious categories in the paradox." Hirsch was not inclined to recognize these explanations (*Kierkegaard-Studien* II, 623ff.), especially not that of Climacus in the *Postscript*; to which it can be said, with regard to the first point, that it does not indicate any penetrating understanding of Kierkegaard's notion of ordination and of the priestly office at that time when Hirsch writes that SK means by this "the external [consideration], that he is still without ordination and office." Kierkegaard did not have the prevailing concept of ordination and office as something only external, which in the context must mean unimportant formalities. Kierkegaard's reflections throughout several years on whether he ought to and dared to become a priest shows that his conception was different from the usual. Just one entry like VIII 1 A6 (1847):[k] "a sermon presupposes a priest (ordination), [while] the Christian discourse [that is, not just the edifying] can be [delivered or written by] an ordinary man," says enough in this context against accepting Hirsch's explanation. With regard to the second point, we can say of Hirsch's comment that "now here there is . . . a fog to be lifted, which Johannes Climacus has blown over the state of affairs" that even if Climacus's explanation is later and reflects the fully developed theory of stages, still it is quite erroneous to call it a smoke screen that might obscure the actual situation. The designation "edifying discourses" is neither an expression of false modesty on the part of Kierkegaard nor a false description of the contents. On the contrary it is a quite accurate description of the contents when we consider that, for Kierkegaard, "to edify" simply means to build the individual's existence up in authenticity. Thus it is an expression situated within the same sphere of meaning as Judge William's imperative that one should choose himself in his eternal validity.

As a motto over all eighteen edifying discourses we could, in line with Kierkegaard's often free style of writing, put the statement that strength is perfected in powerlessness. The discourses lead up to and include religiousness A, to use the language of the *Postscript*, and

[k] Hong, I, #638.

they point toward and give a fleeting glimpse of religiousness B, which provides an absolute standard and gives the full explanation of the interpretation of existence contained in the eighteen edifying discourses, and which is such—and this is what is significant for the purpose of the present study—that it excludes the view of Hegelian philosophy about man's actual situation, its goal and its inherent possibility of reaching that goal. Some examples will be sufficient to show this.

The discourses are completely devoid of direct polemic.

If we read the first two, which appeared on May 16, 1843, then it is correct, as Sløk says in a more recent terminology than Kierkegaard's ("Das Verhältnis . . . ," p. 60), that both discourses will disclose the fundamental traits of human existence, that it is immersed in time and that man is human, rightly understood, only when he sees his own future before his eyes, engages himself in it, but does not lose himself in it. Faith alone can rescue him from perdition—or the aimlessness of an uncertain future, and in that way faith is the only unconditioned good, qualitatively distinct from all other goods, and for the same reason faith is the only thing that one can desire unconditionally—but not give—for another human.

It is enough to mention these features here. Sløk says, quite correctly, in the conclusion of his article (p. 79) that the first two discourses give the edifying solution to the problem that Judge William had failed to notice; but that is less significant in the present context.

Now had, if not Hegel himself, then a speculative author of edifying pieces written on the same theme as Kierkegaard, everything would have been different: human existence would not have been interpreted as immersed in time but as a necessary moment in the world-historical, inexorable unfolding. The future would not be understood to be unknown, but as foreseen, and faith would not be explained as the only unconditioned good, but as an imperfect dimension that is to become automatically superseded by the speculative concept.

If we next take the second discourse in the set Kierkegaard issued on December 6, 1843,[1] for which the text is the one he so frequently

---

[1] *Edifying Discourses*, 2 vols., trans. David F. Swenson and Lilian Marvin Swenson (Minneapolis, Minn.: Augsburg Publishing House, 1962), I, 150-167. In the sequel, volume and page references will be to this edition. For conversion to the pagination of the earlier four-volume edition of the same translation, see Alastair McKinnon, *The Kierkegaard Indices*, I (Leiden:

preferred (James 1:17-22; Every good and every perfect gift is from above, etc.), we can make a similar observation.

It is said that the condition of Paradise was ruptured by the Fall into sin, when man ate from the tree of knowledge, and "what happened then in the beginning of the days is repeated constantly in every generation and in the individual" (I, 152—cf. *The Concept of Dread*, p. 26). Man became frightened, fell into doubt and found no escape before it was revealed, again, that only God can really console, which also became a seed of doubt. The question is raised anew: what, then, is the good? and the answer resounds that God is the immutable love who gives good gifts. Doubt has no place here, it is not overcome by man himself, by neither intellect nor will, but only by the divine miracle. To need a good and perfect gift thus entails a perfection in man, i.e., it belongs to the definition of man to need a good and perfect gift, which man cannot give himself or any other man. This first becomes clear to a man after an upheaval, a new beginning, which man cannot accomplish himself (cf. *Philosophical Fragments*, pp. 23f.). In harmony with this it is said of doubt in this discourse (I, 165) that "the untrue doubt doubts about everything, only not about itself, the salvific doubt doubts only about itself with the aid of Faith."

The following discourse (I, 168-189)—on the same text—emphasizes, consistently enough, all men's similarity in the relation to God, especially the similarity that all men have the humble fate that they must receive and only be able to respond with thanksgiving, and in the fourth and last discourse in this set (I, 190-210) on the text: secure your souls in patience (Luke 21:19). This verse is interpreted along the same lines as Judge William's invitation to choose oneself in one's eternal validity. But the significant point in this discourse is the emphasis on the fact that the rightful owner of a man's soul is God, and that man's task is to acquire his soul from the unrightful owner ("the world") through God by himself (I, 199), and that the patience is not brought along as a postulate but comes into existence during the acquisition.

What is meant by patience is probed in greater depth in the two following discourses, which appeared on March 5, 1844 (I, 211-239; II, 25-51). For the purposes of the present treatment, we can highlight the emphasis in these two discourses on the fact that "the

E. J. Brill, 1970), xii. A selection of some of the *Discourses* (but not including the one presently under discussion) will be found in *Edifying Discourses* (New York: Harper Torchbooks, 1958).

error of the doubter or despairer does not lie in knowledge, for knowledge can decide nothing with certitude . . . the error lies in the will" (II, 36). In the set of three edifying discourses that appeared on June 8, 1844, a few days before *Philosophical Fragments* and *The Concept of Dread*, we should especially note (in the discourse on II Corinthians 4:17-19; the expectation of an eternal blessedness) that this expectation should help a man to understand himself in temporality (II, 83-84; cf. the first of the eighteen discourses). Quite in line with the other discourses it is said furthermore (II, 95) that eternal blessedness is expected by God's grace, which does not have any finite condition, as for example deeds, definite manifestations, or feelings, but only the faith as a non-finite condition.

That man's perfection consists in his powerlessness over against God resounds repeatedly and very strongly in this discourse, which especially points forward to the Christian, the discourse on John the Baptist's statement as recorded in John 3:30: my joy is complete, he must increase, I must decrease (II, 101-119), completely in harmony with the first discourse in the last set issued (August 31, 1844), in which it is stressed that to need God is man's highest perfection (II, 120). In the case of earthly things it holds true that we should minimize our needs as much as possible, and the less we need, the more perfect we are. In relation to God, however, it is precisely the opposite: the more we need God, the more perfect we are (II, 128). This relation makes life more difficult, but insofar as a man does not know himself in such a way that he realizes that he is capable of almost nothing, he really does not, in a deeper sense, acknowledge that God exists (II, 154).

The last discourses in the group from August 31 carry forward and make more precise the ideas in the previous ones: in the discourse on the thorn in the flesh (II, 161-185), Kierkegaard does not offer consolation, but the horror of the thorn in the flesh as an inward suffering, which in each and every person is the contradiction of the spirit's ineffable blessedness.

In the following discourse (II, 186-222), he speaks against cowardice, a mistaken type of self-love. Finally, in the last discourse (II, 223-253) he treats the righteous man praying—he strives in prayer and conquers—in that God conquers. God is immutable and immutably the same, man can be changed. This is in line with the theme in "The Ultimatum" that against God man is always in the wrong, which is neither a scientific nor a philosophic (speculative) truth, but an edifying truth for the individual—which is every individual, i.e., all and each. There is a clear and straight line from this theme to the thesis of the *Postscript*, that subjectivity is untruth (p. 185).

There is actually not one single directly polemical statement against Hegelian speculation in the eighteen edifying discourses. But the whole understanding of the transcendent, omnipotent, and all-loving God and of the powerless human expressed in the discourses is such that the way of speculation means for Kierkegaard the broad road to perdition, since it proceeds from a theory of man's omnipotence, which is totally incompatible with the anthropology expressed by Kierkegaard. *Either/Or* and the eighteen edifying discourses can be said to correspond to the stream of thought in the Epistle to the Romans 1:18-3:20—the whole world stands in a condition of guilt over against God, and no man is truly innocent. Just as little as Paul stopped with that conclusion, did Kierkegaard stop there. The continuation was plotted out and already begun before the last edifying discourses appeared.

Indications of what direction the continuation would take are already found in Kierkegaard's trial sermon (*Papirer* IV C 1,[m] delivered on March 24, 1844, in Trinity Church on I Corinthians 2:6-9) and the *Three Discourses on Imagined Occasions*[n] he published the day before the appearance of *Stages on Life's Way*, i.e., April 29, 1845. In the *Three Discourses* there is good reason to call attention to the penetential address [*Skriftetalen*] on the theme "What it Means to Seek God";[o] but just as in the edifying discourses it is entirely devoid of polemic, and as in the edifying discourses it speaks from a position that excludes the possibility of a speculative understanding of God and of man.

4. *Fear and Trembling* AND *Repetition*

The main purpose of *Either/Or* was not to combat Hegel but estheticism, and to set forth an ethical view that even in its given confines could be employed critically against both estheticism and speculative idealism, which eventually Kierkegaard variously labeled "modern philosophy," "Speculation," or simply "the System."

[m] Hong, IV, #3916.

[n] Published in English as *Thoughts on Crucial Situations in Human Life*, trans. David F. Swenson (Minneapolis: Augsburg Publishing House, 1941).

[o] Pages 1-41.

The reflections in the two books, which came out on the same day, *Fear and Trembling* and *Repetition*, lie—according to the criterion in the *Postscript*—on a higher plane than *Either/Or*. In the two later books issues are raised and solutions are given into which Judge William could have no insight on his stage.

Both books are polemical against Hegel and his adherents; but they are so mainly indirectly, clearly only by their form and style, although direct criticism is also expressed.

Briefly it can be said that neither of the two books seems to show that before and while he was writing them Kierkegaard had enlarged or deepened his purely factual knowledge of Hegel's own works. What he already knew was enough for him, and he only occasionally consulted one or another of them, for the sake of confirmation, as it were. The explanation for this situation is probably simply that the more he became occupied with the development of his own Authorship, the less other thoughts and sets of problems meant to him in reality: they lost interest for him since he found very little he could positively use himself. An original mind like Hamann he could respect, and likewise Lessing; but only Socrates impressed him unqualifiedly.[17]

In its problematic itself *Fear and Trembling* is un-Hegelian and in its solutions anti-speculative,[18] so that it is evident that these questions have no place in the total system.

The polemical tendency is already clear in the preface, which was not sent out without an intended recipient, but was especially meant for Martensen.

It had been Martensen, in his lectures on the introduction to spec-

[17] Perhaps it would be appropriate to point out that through the years this became a more notable tendency—that only now and then did Kierkegaard concern himself seriously with other thinkers. But this is not a trait unique to Kierkegaard. We can find the same tendency in other authors, for example, Karl Barth, whose *Prolegomena zur kirchlichen Dogmatic* is filled with polemics against nearly everything and everybody, whereas the last volume of his *Dogmatics* is indirectly polemical and only occasionally takes direct account of one or another recent book.

[18] With regard to details, reference is made to my notes on Jungbluth's German translation in the volume *Die Krankheit zum Tode und Anderes [Sickness unto Death and Other Works]*, (1956), pp. 654ff., as well as to the notes in my Danish edition of the book (2nd edition, 1963). In the Introduction to the latter edition I have provided a discussion (pp. 7-22) of the book's relation to Hegel, to which reference is made here. Since I have nothing important to change or add to this Introduction, this book is discussed quite briefly in the present work.

ulative dogmatics (cf. *supra*, Chapter III, section 4), who had stressed Descartes and his methodical doubt. Kierkegaard's first encounter with this attempt at a speculative interpretation of the history of modern philosophy was sketched in his "Battle Between the Old and the New Soap Cellar" (*supra*, Chapter IV, section 4). Kierkegaard's first reaction after having read Descartes himself we have in *De Omnibus Dubitandum Est* (*supra*, Chapter VII, section 3), and his approximately simultaneous resolution of the problem of doubt (and despair) is to be found in Judge William's second essay in *Either/Or*, volume II. Here in the preface to *Fear and Trembling* new significant comments emerge. The first (p. 22) says that Descartes—unlike his late parroters—"did what he said and said what he did." The second points out that Descartes did not doubt in matters of faith (so as to grasp it speculatively later) and finally, the last says that Descartes modestly acknowledged "that his method had importance only for himself"ᵖ—and not without qualification for others, for posterity.

It was Martensen, above all whom Kierkegaard knew, who was unwilling to remain stationary at either doubt or faith, but who wanted "to go further," namely to a secure knowledge and a speculative conceptualization of faith, which would be set forth as something given.

Johannes de Silentio also permits himself the luxury to doubt, not about faith, but about the speculative theologians' right to refer to Descartes, of their right to go further than Hegel himself, of their speculative conceptualization of faith. His response is that their right to appeal to Descartes is mighty dubious, their attempt to go further than Hegel himself is a hopeless misunderstanding since Hegel himself pursued this road to its end, and a speculative concept of faith is a concept of something other than authentic faith and is therefore an explaining away. Thus, their supposed advance was a retreat. The speculative theologians, especially Martensen, overturned the proper rank order so that they placed faith lower than (speculative) knowledge. On the contrary, Johannes de Silentio maintains that the faith he speaks of, the pre-Christian as we may call it, is already higher than knowledge. This faith is paradoxical, and only faith so understood can contain the possibility of an exception, which Abraham is, and the intelligibility [*Forstaaelse*] of the double movement of infinity, which Judge William still thought

ᵖ Cf. Descartes, *Discourse on Method*, parts I and III.

could be undertaken by man himself in the penitence of choosing oneself in his eternal validity, as has been said.

If faith is such, and if there is such a believer (Abraham), then we can raise the three questions, as Johannes de Silentio formulates them, of whether there is a teleological suspension of the ethical, whether there is such a thing as an absolute duty toward God, and whether Abraham's silence was ethically defensible, and we can, as Johannes de Silentio does, answer all three affirmatively. If we do not share his interpretation of faith, of the possibility of a special revelation, and of the possibility of man's becoming an isolated exception, then with Hegel we should have to answer the same questions negatively.[19] We can add that if speculative thought cannot explain the case of Abraham, that which otherwise maintains that it is able to conceive absolutely everything without any exception whatsoever, then it is not actual reality that something is wrong with, it is the system that is incomplete and the method that is faulty, as artistically perfect as both parts are elaborated. We can add furthermore, that the individual's, the existing man's task then becomes not to go beyond faith to a speculative concept, but, on the contrary, to return back. Especially in *Philosophical Fragments* and in *The Concept of Dread* Kierkegaard showed how this return was to be undertaken. In the present context, however, *Fear and Trembling* has the special significance that it looks away from the way of speculation as a way of delusion only in the domain of ethics, not to mention that of faith.

Repetition is an attack on speculation from another angle and with other weapons.[20]

The book is deliberately confusing, with its lengthy segments speaking of inauthentic types of repetition, their possibility and impossibility. Only in short passages and comments does it speak of

[19] Even if obviously from positions other than that of Hegel we can also answer especially the first one negatively, cf. for example, the otherwise mutually diverse responses of Martin Buber (in the article "Upphävande av etiken" [The Annulment of Ethics] in the anthology edited by R. N. Anshen translated into Swedish with the title *En etik, en värld* [One Ethics, One World], 1956, pp. 93-97), and of Søren Holm in his *Kristelig Ethik* [Christian Ethics] (1963), pp. 188f.

[20] I have given information about details in this work in note 18 *supra* (referring to pp. 683ff. of the German translation). The best introduction to the problematic of this book with particular reference to the relation to Hegel is given by Gregor Malantschuk in his edition of the work (1961), pp. 5-10.

genuine repetition, the religiously motivated sort, while at the same time the chief character of the book, the young man, although he tends toward the religious stage, is existing on a poetic level with a problematical relation to the ordinary everyday reality as a task and at the same time the pseudonymous author, Constantine Constantius, does not stand on a stage where repetition in its genuine meaning is possible either, although he understands what conditions it requires.

Repetition is important in the present context both for the fact that we find a new category developed there and for the fact that it was discussed by Heiberg in such a way that Kierkegaard seized the opportunity in a detailed draft of a response to Heiberg (*Papirer*, IV B 100-124)[q] to develop his theory of repetition more completely than in the book itself and to do it in such a way that the difference from a Hegelian notion was made clear.[21]

Most of *Repetition* deals with inauthentic forms of repetition, their impossibility, and the various unsuccessful attempts to obtain them pursued nevertheless whether by the book's hero, the young man, or by its author, Constantine Constantius. The explanation for the hopelessness of the inauthentic repetitions is suggested at the beginning of the book and at the end.

The young man in love, for whom Constantine became a confidant, could undertake only the movement of recollection, not that of repetition, i.e., he remained in the Greek "ethnic" sphere, remained a "poetic existence," an esthete, who was not—to use the language of Judge William now—able to choose himself in his eternal validity and realize the universal, and was thereby, in this respect, no further advanced than the speculative thinkers who distracted themselves from the given reality as a task. The young man

[q] Only one small portion of these entries (IV B 118:1) will be found in Hong, II, #1246.

[21] Although Hegel's (and the Hegelians') concept of philosophy and science, including their anthropology, generally speaking is quite different from modern concepts, for example, that of empiricism or philosophy and science, and Kierkegaard's is again different, in his development of the category of repetition there is precisely a point where Kierkegaard's objections to using "the categories of nature" in the sphere of freedom implies criticism of any modern thought, which like Hegel's wishes to employ what are, according to Kierkegaard's interpretation, unsatisfactory and irrelevant categories to define and explain phenomena that simply cannot be explained within a total view like the idealistic or the empiricistic. A psychology on biological foundations would, by that very fact, be a chimera for Kierkegaard.

"did not understand repetition" Constantine says with a regretful, matter-of-fact statement (p. 49). Then Constantine himself attempted a repetition, i.e., a repetition in an inauthentic sense (= a reliving) through a journey to Berlin, where he had been before (like Kierkegaard himself). Everything was a disappointment for him: the journey (p. 54), his former lodgings (pp. 54-56), the visit to the theater (pp. 73-74), the restaurant (p. 75) where everything was so terribly unchanged that here a horrible type of repetition was possible, and because of spring cleaning his home was so frightfully changed that repetition was entirely impossible here. The journey was not worth the trouble. There is no repetition, Constantine says (pp. 76, 77).

These attempts at (inauthentic types of) repetition were obviously doomed to fail from the start. Just as recollection triumphed in the young man (p. 49) and thereby cut him off from genuine repetition, so recollection stifled the counterfeit attempt at repetition for Constantine (p. 75).

Then follows the second half of the work, titled again "Repetition" (p. 82ff.), and twice, but also only these two times, it is said explicitly that repetition has taken place, namely, first for Job, who became reconciled and received everything back twofold: "this is what is called a *repetition*" (p. 117), and the second time when the young man read in the newspaper that the girl to whom he had been engaged had married someone else: "here I have the repetition" (p. 125).

On the question of when this (genuine) repetition occurs, the young man answers quite candidly that it cannot be said easily in human terms (p. 117). It comes like a "thunderclap" for Job as for himself, "when all conceivable human certitude and probability pronounced it impossible"—then it became the reality. Through repetition Job was restored to his old reality, as the young man was restored to his, which was and remains a poetic existence—although he had hoped for another. If he had had a deeper religious background, Constantine says in his explanation (p. 136), then he would not have become a poet, an exception, albeit not a genuine exception, i.e., a religious exception (p. 134). The unjustified exception will evade the universal, the justified exception is reconciled with it.

Thus *genuine* repetition is described in the poetic parts of the work as a thunderstorm. In Constantine's theoretical elucidations, as well as in Kierkegaard's rejoinders to Heiberg in the *Papirer*, it is described in other terms—"repetition is and remains a transcendence" (p. 90). The meaning is the same, and repetition in this sense is inconceivable within the Hegelian system, in which the transcendent is made immanent—as Heiberg's article on "Det astronomiske Aar" [The astronomical year],[22] among others, presents it.

Heiberg says there, after having quoted Constantine's introductory remarks, that this is "very true and very beautiful, if we understand it with the appropriate qualification," which Goethe provided for him. This qualification consists precisely in only wishing to call repetition in the world of nature (the cycles, the seasons of the year, etc.) repetition, and to confine man's ("subjectivity's") task to reliving, thus—according to Constantine's (and Kierkegaard's) meaning —only to speak of fatuous [*aandsforladte*] repetitions in nature and to speak inauthentically of repetition in the human. In this way then, the qualification claimed becomes an expression of an unjustified extension of the mechanistic interpretation of nature so as also to include man as a totality. In Kierkegaard's view this is the fundamental mistake in Heiberg, regardless of the source of the mistake: whether he had produced it himself or unthinkingly derived it from Goethe or from Hegel himself. Repetition as "a transcendence," as "a thunderclap," as it actually took place in two instances, cannot be incorporated into the Heibergian (Hegelian) conceptual world at all, which means (cf. *Fear and Trembling*) that speculative philosophy comes up short against reality, which it asserts it will and can conceive completely without anything left out [*begribe restløs*].

In *Repetition* (as well as in the rebuttal to Heiberg's criticism) the sphere of speculative knowledge is delimited in relation to the sphere of faith. In that respect this work points toward *The Concept of Dread*, whose introduction describes the contents of the two spheres in more detail.

5. *The Concept of Dread* AND *Philosophical Fragments*

The direct and indirect polemic against Hegel was continued and elaborated in the two major works, *Philosophical Fragments*, which appeared on June 13, 1844, and *The Concept of Dread*, which came out on June 17 in the same year. The chronological sequence here

[22] The article (in *Urania*, 1844) was reprinted in Heiberg's *Prosaiske Skrifter*, IX (1861), 53-131.

is not crucial, and it is natural to deal with *The Concept of Dread* first, since its content comes before that of *Philosophical Fragments* systematically.

Even though there are various places in *The Concept of Dread* where Kierkegaard engages in direct polemic against Hegel,[23] yet it is the case that the indirect polemic is the most significant. Just as in the writings discussed in the previous section it is true of both *The Concept of Dread* and *Philosophical Fragments* that, while writing them, Kierkegaard again consulted various works of Hegel and to that extent deepened his knowledge of Hegel. But his use of these works resulted almost exclusively in criticism both against Hegel's main tendency and against individual points in his system. On the contrary, it must be noted here, as was done in the earlier Kierkegaard scholarship,[24] that certain writings of the German Hegelians, especially Rosenkranz and Erdmann, at least in the formal respect had had some importance for Kierkegaard. It is noteworthy in the highest degree, that in the very important introduction to *The Concept of Dread* (p. 18) Kierkegaard praises, at the expense of Hegel, Schleiermacher's immortal services to dogmatics, and [that] he develops his own structure of the sciences [*Videnskabssystematik*] similar to that of Schleiermacher. It is thereby not only different from but incompatible with Hegel's attempt to develop the unified science of his time.

The book's whole anti-Hegelian perspective is indicated clearly enough on the reverse of the title page, where Socrates and Hamann are singled out because they undertook an important distinction which "the system's" originator and adherents did not undertake; in the dedication to Poul Martin Møller;[25] in the Preface, where Vigilius Haufniensis describes himself as "a layman, one who speculates, it is true, but stands nevertheless far removed from Speculation" (p. 5); in the Introduction's powerful polemic against the speculative confusion of tongues (and as a positive counterpart to

[23] I have identified individual instances in my notes on R. Løgstrup's German translation (in the volume cited in note 18 *supra*), pp. 701ff.

[24] For example, Bohlin in *Kierkegaards dogmatiska åskådning* [Kierkegaard's Dogmatic Viewpoint], 1925 p. 106 and *passim*, and critical opposition to Bohlin's interpretation—Lindström in *Stadiernas teologi* [Theology of the Stages] (1943), pp. 73 and 216. Henriksen in *Kierkegaards Romaner* [Kierkegaard's Novels] (1954), pp. 61ff., in the digression on anthropological definitions mentions Rosenkranz's *Psychologie* (1837) and Erdmann's *Leib und Seele* [Life and Soul] (1837) as works Kierkegaard utilized.

[25] On this, cf. Malantschuk's article in *Kierkegaardiana,* III (1959), 7ff.

that, the outline of a classification of the sciences and their concepts);
and last but not least, in the work itself. This, by its existence and
treatment of the issues alone, which simply do not occur, and in
principle cannot occur in Hegel's system, is a unique protest against
Hegel and his disciples' unsatisfactory, superficial and confusing
chatter, which in Kierkegaard's estimate mingled philosophy and
theology in such a way that their products were neither one nor the
other, but simply a series of meaningless groupings of words, or—to
use an expression of Hegel which Kierkegaard later severely criticized—an exemplification of the bad infinity.

Thus, *The Concept of Dread*, in addition to whatever else the
book is, is a contribution to conceptual clarification. This clarification was not necessary for Kierkegaard himself, since he had already
undertaken it in his private notes (see Chapter VII *supra*). In his
view, however, the clarification was far from superfluous for his
esteemed contemporaries. Entirely the same intention is found in
Philosophical Fragments and in *Concluding Unscientific Postscript*,
and just as in these works, so also in *The Concept of Dread* in a
conspicuous degree at that, Kierkegaard employed his opponents'
terminology and form.[26] He even remarked later that this was the
reason why *The Concept of Dread* was the only one of the pseudonymous writings that "found a little favor in the eyes of the
Docents."[27]

The introduction to *The Concept of Dread* has particular importance for the present study with its emphasis on the linguistic
(and thus, topical) confusion in Hegel and his philosophical and
theological disciples, and with the draft of a new classification in
part formally undertaken in harmony with Schleiermacher.[28]

If "reality" is treated in such a way in logic, i.e., in Hegel's logic,
then Kierkegaard maintains that both reality and logic are confused,
at least as he (Vigilius Haufniensis) understands these two dimensions, that is, reality as containing the fortuitous, the accidental, the
irregular event (and with this concept of reality he is at odds with

[26] Sløk, in *Die Anthropologie Kierkegaards* (1954), has particularly emphasized Kierkegaard's anti-idealist intention in his tripartite anthropological
definitions.

[27] *Concluding Unscientific Postscript*, p. 241. Cf. Nordentoft's comment on
Heidegger's relation to Kierkegaard in *Heideggers Opgør med den filosofiske
Tradition* [Heidegger's Confrontation with the Philosophical Tradition]
(1961), p. 102.

[28] Cf. Lars Bejerholm's *Meddelelsens Dialektik* [Dialectic of Communica-
tion] (1962), pp. 48ff., on the misuse of language.

Hegel, for whom necessity is the controlling factor), and logic as classical formal logic, which has nothing to do with empirical reality, whereas for Hegel logic is basically ontology.[29] The same holds true of the concept of faith: if faith is understood as the immediate without any further precision, i.e., as the first and lowest level (on the way to the higher, speculative science), then faith (understood as Christian faith) is deprived of its indispensable historical principle (the Incarnation, which is treated in *Philosophical Fragments*), and thus dogmatic theology is confused. Kierkegaard's sequential and hierarchical arrangement is quite clearly the reverse of Hegel's for whom knowledge (metaphysics) is higher than faith (dogmatics). For Kierkegaard, on the contrary, faith is higher than knowledge, and while it can, to be sure, be called immediacy, it is important to note that it is a later immediacy, not the first. The same is the case with the concept of reconciliation (or redemption) and the concept of the negative: according to Kierkegaard's interpretation they have been misused by being employed outside of the domain where they really belong, and the misuse had led to a conceptual [saglig] confusion.

The explanation for the fact that Kierkegaard criticizes speculation for misuse of language and conceptual confusion is partly his concept of language (of which Bejerholm has given an account in his previously cited book), partly his classification of the sciences, in which the distinctions are of particular importance in the present context, as the reverse of the title page of *The Concept of Dread* indicates ("The age of distinctions is over, the System has overcome it"), and as is expressed with the help of language.

The Concept of Dread is, as the subtitle says, a "simple," that is non-speculative, psychologically oriented deliberation directed toward the dogmatic (thus not, for example, directed toward a metaphysical) problem of original sin. The discussion has "the dogma of original sin in mind [as an indisputable given] and before its eye," states the Introduction (p. 13). The final chapter of the book, "Dread as salvific through faith," concludes, consistently enough, with these words: "As soon as psychology is finished with dread, it remains only to turn it over to dogmatics"—not to the speculative philosophy of religion, the anthropological (psychological) presuppositions of which are totally different from the ones sketched in *The Concept of Dread*, from the sole fact that the concept of dread

[29] In his *Philosophische Propädeutik* (SW III, 172), Hegel plainly calls his first section on logic "ontological logic."

is entirely absent from the speculative philosophy of religion, as little as in Hegel's philosophy taken as a whole.

While dread can be described psychologically and in direct communication, sin cannot be dealt with in the same way in psychology, since in that case it must be treated as a state. Nor can sin be handled, but only mishandled, in metaphysics, "which thinks sin through as something which cannot withstand thought" (p. 14). Sin does not rightly belong in any science: it is the theme of the sermon. Surely sin belongs to a certain extent to ethics, i.e. humanistic ethics, inasmuch as sin points out the limits of ethics. But original sin makes everything still more desperate for such ethics (pp. 16-17), and the difficulty is resolved only with the aid of dogmatics, and "the new ethics," i.e., the Christian, which has dogmatics as its prerequisite.

Here, too, the difference from Hegel is evident. The system has fundamentally no ethics (as little, for example, as Schelling's philosophy contains), and sin is considered by Hegel to be only a necessary evil, which is an intermediate link for the triumphant good. Certainly a disciple of Hegel such as Martensen could write a moral philosophy first and then much later a Christian ethics. But precisely in Martensen's *Grundrids til Moralphilosophiens System* [The Fundamental Principles of a System of Moral Philosophy], which appeared in 1841, the difference between humanistic and Christian ethics fades (or is reconciled, as it is said in Hegelian terms). It is legitimate to suppose that although here as elsewhere in the pseudonymous Authorship where Martensen is never identified by name, Kierkegaard did not entirely unintentionally include him, among others, in his salvo against the fortress of speculation.[30]

On the one side, then, is "the immanent science," which begins with metaphysics and in which the "first" ethics has its place; on the other side is "the new science," which begins with dogmatics, which is the presupposition for "the new ethics." It is in this context that Schleiermacher's "immortal service" to dogmatics is emphasized in the Introduction.

The situation now is not that Hegel's system represented for Kierkegaard an acceptable elaboration of what he calls the immanent science; if it were acceptable, it would need only to be corrected here and there as well as supplemented (as, among others,

---

[30] P. P. Jørgensen has correctly pointed out Kierkegaard's "crypto-polemic" against Martensen (*H. P. Kofoed-Hansen*, 1920, p. 137 and *passim*).

Martensen wished to do by "going further"), not to be destroyed, as Kierkegaard had in mind. On the contrary, for him it represented a totally unacceptable, confused backward step (see *Papirer* IV C 73, among others).[r] Kierkegaard did not consider it his responsibility to develop the correct "Immanent science," any more than he engaged in writing a dogmatics; but it was a matter of great urgency for him to specify that Hegelian speculation was unjustified in both places with respect to its principles, goal, and method, condemned as unjustified on the basis of the anthropology developed in *The Concept of Dread*, which again has dogmatics as its presupposition. Here as elsewhere, dogmatics is not understood in the speculative sense.

The Introduction to *The Concept of Dread* contains enough to make clear the work's relation to Hegel: Kierkegaard's thought and that of Hegel appear, the further along we go in the Authorship, as entirely incompatible positions [*Størrelser*]. Not only are there disagreements on one or several individual points, for such discords could possibly derive from their different environments, but a total disagreement on the presuppositions, point of departure, goal, and method of thought which then emerges naturally in individual points and spheres: logic, metaphysics, anthropology, ethics, understanding of Christianity. We must not, then, let ourselves be distracted by the many purely verbal (terminological) similarities between Kierkegaard and Hegel, any more than, as for example, by his tripartite anthropological definitions in *The Concept of Dread* and in other writings,[31] which to a cursory view could bring to mind the famous Hegelian triads.

In the present study it is not absolutely necessary to go through the presentation of the concept of dread from beginning to end so as to determine its relation to Hegel and to the whole Hegelian speculation. The complete disharmony is evident in every point, and only a single example is sufficient to illustrate it.

In *The Concept of Dread*, Chapter 1, §4 (pp. 34-37), the concept of the Fall is treated. Kierkegaard's understanding of it can obviously only be understood as he desired it to be in connection with

[r] Hong, II, #1601.

[31] Cf. note 26 *supra*. Arild Christensen in several penetrating and valuable analyses, as for example "Om Søren Kierkegaards Inddelingsprincip" [On SK's Principle of Classification] in *Kierkegaardiana*, III, 1959, pp. 21-37) has investigated the relation in individual aspects and emphasized Kierkegaard's uniqueness.

what has gone before (and what follows it) where the thought process is as follows.

In §1 it is his intention to combat the various attempts he is familiar with to explain original sin by "fantastically" putting Adam outside of the history of the human race[32] instead of maintaining, in the first place, that "man is an individual and as such is at once himself and the whole race" and, in the second place, that "Adam is the first man, he is at once himself and the race" (p. 26). If this is not maintained, Kierkegaard asserts, then everything is distorted. On the concept of the first sin (§2), he claims, in conjunction with this, that both Adam's and every man's first sin represents a qualitative leap, by which sin enters the world. He then says (p. 28, note) that Hegel "affirmed the leap . . . in logic," where according to Kierkegaard's concept of logic it just does not belong. Against Hegel's interpretation of the account of the Fall in Genesis as a myth[33] Kierkegaard maintains that this account quite precisely says everything that, on the whole, can be said about the matter, namely that sin came into the world through a sin. Since the

[32] N. M. Plum's demonstration "Lidt om SKs Citationsmaade" [A Little on SK's Manner of Quotation] in *Teologisk Tidsskrift*, 1927, pp. 42-49) of Kierkegaard's extensive use of Hase's *Hutterus redivivus* (as well as the creedal books, naturally) has been corrected and supplemented by Arild Christensen in "Søren Kierkegaards Individuationsprincip" (DTT, 1953, p. 217 note 2), who—as the first—very correctly mentions, that Kierkegaard could also have used Aug. Hahn's *Lehrbuch des Christlichen Glaubens* (Ktl. #535), which is very rich in quoted material. The latter article particularly emphasizes that it is demonstrable that Kierkegaard used his notebooks from Clausen's lectures on dogmatics (II C 34). [Hong, I, #36, translates only the abbreviated portion of this entry found in the original 1910 edition of the *Papirer*. The full text of this entry is in volume XIII (2nd Supplementsbind) of the second edition (1968).] We can add to this that particularly during the composition of Chapter 1, §§1-4 Kierkegaard was thinking of Marheineke's lectures, which he heard during the winter semester 1841-1842 in Berlin, on "Dogmatic Theology with Particular Reference to Daub's System" (III C 26 [Hong, V, #5514]), whereas he does not seem to have known Carl Daub's own great work *Judas Ischariot oder das Böse in Verhältniss zum Guten* [Judas Iscariot: or, Evil in Relation to Good] (1816-1818). Aage Kabell (*Kierkegaard-Studiet i Norden*, 1948, p. 212) mentions a single quotation Kierkegaard might have used from *Libri Symbolici Ecclesiae Orientalis* [Creedal Books of the Eastern Church] (ed. J. Kimmel, 1843, p. 272); but unfortunately Kabell quotes the Greek even more inaccurately than Kierkegaard.

[33] Hegel himself says in his *Philosophy of Religion* (I, 276) that the Fall is "the eternal, necessary history of mankind, expressed in external, mythical fashion," so Kierkegaard need not have thought of Strauss.

human race does not begin anew with each individual, then the sinfulness of the race acquires a history (as has been traditionally maintained). This history, however, advances in "quantitative determinations," which for Kierkegaard means that there can be no talk of responsibility in this history, seen in isolation. When "the individual by the qualitative leap" participates in this history, then responsibility follows with, so to speak, a qualitative leap.

The whole thought process is in complete opposition to that of Hegel, in which history can be considered only under what Kierkegaard calls quantitative determinations.

With this background, which on literally every point is different from Hegel's understanding (particularly in his philosophy of religion), Kierkegaard begins §3 by saying that "it holds true here as usual that if one in our day would have a dogmatic definition, one must make a beginning by forgetting what Hegel invented to help dogmatics," because he has "weakened every dogmatic concept just so much that it retains a reduced existence [i.e. for a Hegelian dogmaticist such as Marheineke or Martensen] as a spiritual expression for the logical" (p. 32). After this, just as in the Introduction, Kierkegaard "calls to order" and requires every concept to be handled in the science to which it belongs. Immediacy is a concept that belongs to logic, innocence to ethics; and he asserts that the speculative dogmaticists confuse both concepts by commingling them.[34] Then innocence is defined as ignorance, and in §4 he develops the theme of how innocence is lost. The explanation of how it is lost is not given through "ingenious and foolish hypotheses," concocted by "thinkers and schemers" who ride in furious but futile competition with a witch on a broomstick outside of history. Here, perhaps, Kierkegaard wants to describe Marheineke on the basis of his Berlin lectures—or more correctly, Schelling. However that may be related to the present topic, in any case it is as clear as one could wish that Kierkegaard parts company with any speculative explanation, whether Schelling's or Hegelian. In this passage (p. 36) he

[34] The editors of the Danish edition add in a note on this passage [2de udg. SV IV, til p. 341; 3de udg. Bind 6, p. 132; this note is absent from the English translation] "Innocence simply does not appear in [Hegel's] logic." But it does appear, however, in a single place, which in all likelihood Kierkegaard knew and remembered precisely when he wrote these pages, namely, in Hegel's *Logic* [the first part of *The Encyclopedia of the Philosophical Sciences*, trans. William Wallace (Oxford: The Clarendon Press, 1892), p. 55] in the "Preliminary Notion" where "the first condition of man" is discussed.

refers first to Usteri and then in a note to Baader, emphasizing that even a psychological explanation of the Fall can only be an explanation "toward the explanation," i.e., one that points to ethics, that explains it by presupposing it through dogmatics, which does not explain, but authoritatively declares how innocence was—and is —lost.

This example is sufficient to show both Kierkegaard's own thought process and his direct and indirect dissociation from Hegel. His anthropology ("Man is a synthesis" etc., p. 39) could also be chosen as an example; but that has been thoroughly analyzed by others,[35] also with reference to its relation to Hegel, so that it will be sufficient simply to refer to them here. Similarly his theory on the instant [or moment—*Øjeblikket*]—developed in explicit opposition to Hegel (pp. 73ff.)—could be taken as an example; but it is also true that its problematic structure has been clarified in the most recent scholarship, so that it is not necessary to add anything here.

The drafts for *The Concept of Dread* (*Papirer*, V B 42-72, 33)[s] contain relatively little of importance here. Just as in the drafts for the other pseudonymous works, especially for the *Postscript*, Kierkegaard identifies his Danish opponents by name. In the printed book the names, especially Heiberg and Martensen, are left out.

Thus, the note in the Introduction to *The Concept of Dread* (p. 12) was originally considerably longer (*Papirer*, V B 49, 5),[t] and it contains a sharp criticism of Heiberg's "Det logiske System" (in *Perseus*, 2. Hefte):

> In our little Denmark, too, one has come to the aid of logical movement. In his "Logical System" which in spite of everything does not extend further than §23 . . . Prof. Heiberg has got everything to go—except the System, which stalled at §23, in spite of the fact that we are supposed to believe that by an immanent movement it must go by itself.

A little further on he mentions Magister A. P. Adler's *Populaire*

---

[35] Especially Valter Lindström in *Stadiernas teologi* (1943), pp. 44-127; by Sløk in the previously cited book; by Arild Christensen in the articles mentioned as well as in "Zwei Kierkegaardstudien" (in *Symposion Kierkegaardianum*, 1955, pp. 36-49; and by Malantschuk in his *Kierkegaard's Way to the Truth*.

[s] Many (but not all) of these entries will be found in various volumes of Hong, *Journals and Papers*. The interested reader should consult the "Collation of Entries" at the end of each volume for particular items.

[t] Not in Hong.

Foredrag over Hegels objective Logik [Popular Lectures on Hegel's Objective Logic] (1842), and—as, a counterpart, Trendelenburg's *Die logische Frage in Hegel's System* (1843) with its criticism of the illegitimate use of the negative in logic. In this connection it can be remarked that although Kierkegaard acquired works of other German critics of Hegel, such as F. A. Staudenmaier's large *Darstellung und Kritik des Hegelschen Systems* [Exposition and Criticism of the Hegelian System] (1844), they seem not to have played any particular role for him, probably because he did not think he needed support for his criticism of Hegel, apart from Trendelenburg's treatment of Hegelian logic.

If we go from *The Concept of Dread* to *Philosophical Fragments*, as far as the relation to Hegel is concerned, the matter has been, if possible, more simply clarified.[36] Just as in *The Concept of Dread*, Kierkegaard's clash with Hegel and his adherents is not a traditional (or, if you will, trivial) refutation of Hegel's view point by point, although some directly critical expressions are there. In the main it is an indirect clash, which by its experimenting presentation simply will show that Hegel's alleged reconciliation of Christian faith and speculative knowledge is impossible, a reconciliation which in its Hegelian version can be correctly understood only in the light of Hegel's principles, goal, and method as they have been schematically presented in the foregoing.

We can select only three items in *Philosophical Fragments*—his theory of paradox, his theory of contemporaneity, and his philosophy of history—and simply by clarifying some of the content of these theories we can discern not only the difference from Hegel's philosophy but the total incompatibility with it.

It is not possible at once to compare immediately here Kierkegaard's theories with the corresponding ones in Hegel, because for at least two of them there is simply no counterpart in Hegel: he says nothing about paradox or of the theory of contemporaneity. If we want to find something corresponding to the latter, then it is the speculative concept; but that is—according to Hegel's philosophy of history—precisely bounded by the contemporary (i.e., that point in

---

[36] I have treated the issues in the Introduction and the Commentary for my edition of the work (1955) [trans. into English by Howard V. Hong in *Philosophical Fragments,* 2nd ed. (Princeton: Princeton University Press, 1962)]. Since I have nothing essential to correct or add to what I have presented there, the treatment here will be quite brief, taking into account particularly questions that have been dealt with in the most recent years.

the course of historical development where Hegel himself found himself) and for Hegel it must not under any circumstances "skip the 1800 years," as Kierkegaard said. On the contrary, according to Hegel the historical development should be grasped in its necessity as the unfolding of the spirit in time. The situation was somewhat different with the philosophy of history. On this Hegel has a large (albeit only posthumously published) work, Kierkegaard only some few pages.

It is not our task to analyze Kierkegaard's theory of paradox in detail[37] just as it is developed in *Philosophical Fragments*. All that

[37] The theory of paradox is one of the most frequently treated topics in Kierkegaard scholarship. Among the recent contributions the following can be singled out: Kl. Schilder's *Zur Begriffsgeschichte des "Paradoxon"* [On the History of the Concept of "Paradox"] (1933), contains good observations in the chapter on Kierkegaard (pp. 89-118). He takes account especially of Bohlin's, Diem's, and Geismar's earlier books and occasionally of Per Lønning, who treats the concept of paradox extensively—and with reference to all of any importance in the earlier Kierkegaard scholarship in *Samitidighedens Situation* [The Situation of Contemporaneity], (1954), pp. 118-154—has summarized his understanding in *Symposion Kierkegaardianum*, 1955, pp. 155-165, where K. Olesen Larsen (pp. 130-147) treats the same concept with particular reference to *Philosophical Fragments* and the *Postscript*. In his book on Kierkegaard (1954) Knud Hansen treats the Socratic paradox (pp. 145-157) and the Christian paradox (pp. 245-258). N. H. Søe's "Soren Kierkegaards Lære om Paradokset" appeared in *Nordisk Teologi*, [*Festskrift*] *till Ragnar Bring* (1955), pp. 102-121 (English translation: "Kierkegaard's Doctrine of the Paradox" in Howard Johnson and Niels Thulstrup, editors, *A Kierkegaard Critique*, New York, Harper & Row, 1962), and was severely attacked by H. M. Garelick in *The Anti-Christianity of Kierkegaard* (1965). J. Heywood Thomas analyzes the concept in *Subjectivity and Paradox* (1957), pp. 103-134, and H. Schröer has given a most thorough presentation of it in *Die Denkform der Paradoxalität als theologisches Problem* (1960), pp. 55-97. Although G. Malantschuk in his article "Das Verhältnis zwischen Wahrheit und Wirklichkeit in Sören Kierkegaards existentiellem Denken" [The Relation between Truth and Reality in SK's Existential Thought] (*Symp. Kierk.*, 1955, pp. 166-177) has a certain tendency to draw quite far-reaching conclusions from isolated expressions and suggestions in Kierkegaard (e.g., in *On the Concept of Irony*) there can hardly be any doubt that his claim that just as Kierkegaard developed his theory of stages for human existence, so also he worked with a series of degrees of knowledge, namely: 1. mythological thought, 2. metaphorical thought, 3. represented (abstract) thought, 4. scientific thought, and 5. the thought of the absurd, is in the main correct, and if so, then simply by the specification of the level on which paradox appears we have a clear indication that Kierkegaard's theory of the paradox (apart from its genesis and some different formulations of it in various places in the Authorship) is incompatible with Hegel's philosophy, in which that which is called here scientific

is necessary in the present context is to give its content and, together with that, to describe what function this theory has in the book's indirect polemical experiment.

The absolute paradox in *Philosophical Fragments* is not primarily a category of thought but a philosophical definition of a single person, Jesus Christ, who as God is absolutely different from man, and who as Man is different from every other man in that He was sinless. Sin is the difference (p. 58), and man himself is guilty of this crucial difference in the factual situation. If sin is of total significance and not just a defect in a particular respect, then a tight limit is placed not only on man's ethical effort and ability but also on man's capacity with regard to knowledge. That which human knowledge cannot grasp and which thus indicates the limit of knowledge can, then, be defined philosophically as the paradox.

These imperfect and provisional definitions of the paradox understood as the Incarnation can now be compared with a definite thought process in Hegel's *Philosophy of Religion* (III, 76f.).

Hegel says there: "In the Church Christ has been called the God-Man—it is this extraordinary combination that directly contradicts the Understanding." We may observe that Hegel explicitly says that the statement conflicts with the Understanding, not the Reason (speculative reason, for which there are no contradictories). He continues immediately after this, saying that

> the unity of the divine and human natures has thereby been brought into human consciousness, has become a certainty for it, so that the otherness, or, as it is also expressed, the finitude, the weakness, the frailty of human nature is not incompatible with this unity, just as in the eternal Idea otherness in no way detracts from the unity which God is. This is the extraordinary combination the necessity of which we have seen. It is thereby established that the divine and human natures are not inherently [*an sich*] different.

Two things should be noted here. The first is that Hegel does not

---

thought represents the highest level, in which all thinkable (and thus, for Hegel, all real) oppositions are subsumed in the highest unity: the Absolute Spirit. This incompatibility of Kierkegaard's theory of paradox with speculative idealism, especially in the version of Hegel, is, of course, emphasized by all of the above named Kierkegaard scholars; but from a systematic perspective Malantschuk's article is the most clarifying in giving the place and rank of the paradox in Kierkegaard's world of thought.

assert any qualitative difference between the divine and human natures; hence their conjunction is not deemed paradoxical either. Second, according to Hegel's interpretation, the Incarnation took place necessarily. These two points are sufficient to demonstrate not only the differences between Kierkegaard's and Hegel's views but their incompatibility. In addition, whereas for Kierkegaard sin is the important difference, in Hegel's development of thought it plays no essential role as an obstacle for the speculative conceptualization of that which for Kierkegaard is beyond conceptualization. For Hegel, sin is the negative, the antithesis, which as a necessary evil pushes the speculative unfolding of the concept in historical form onward.

Hegel's philosophy of history can be read as a kind of philosophical "salvation history," which is understood by his history of philosophy. In both of these historical works (as they may be called here for the sake of convenience, although we have them only as posthumously published lectures), we get the same explanation as in the purely systematic *Encyclopedia* and the *Phenomenology of the Spirit*, which, as was stressed earlier (Chapter V, section 3b), can be read with just as great justification and just as great profit as a historical and as a systematic endeavor: the individual and the world historical development, the microcosm and the macrocosm as they can be called, proceed with metaphysical, inexorable necessity through the same development from the immediate, through the reflected to the speculative condition—which is a standstill. If we were to ask Hegel whether, according to his interpretation, this alleged dialectical unfolding is determined by nature (causally determined); or determined by human feelings, will, and intellect; or determined by a divine decree, his answer would be that these three determining factors are only three ways (the objective, the subjective, and the absolute) of expressing the same thing: the Idea.

Kierkegaard's philosophy of history is totally different.[38] "The Interlude" in *Philosophical Fragments* shows this with desirable clarity. Whereas Hegel answered the question "Is the past more necessary than the future?" (*Philosophical Fragments*, p. 89) by

[38] This has been presented with a great deal of clarity in Søren Holm's *Søren Kierkegaards Historiefilosofi* [SK's Philosophy of History] (1952).

I have given a brief account of Søren Holm's interpretation of Kierkegaard's relation to (and dependence on) Idealistic philosophy in my Introduction to the *Philosophical Fragments* (2nd ed., pp. xc f.). Holm's *Religionsfilosofi* (1955), *Dogmatik* (1962), *Kristelig Ethik* (1963), and his *Ontologi* (1964) give a comprehensive explanation of his interpretation of Kierkegaard (and of the evaluation that has come to be expressed about it).

maintaining that both are equally necessary, Kierkegaard answers that neither part has happened or will happen with necessity. Kierkegaard bases his response on his theory of becoming [*Tilblivelsen*], in which the transition from possibility to actuality "takes place with freedom" (p. 93), where something (whose essence is unchanged) alters its form of being [*Værensform*]. Necessity is a category of eternity, which, according to Kierkegaard's theory, Hegel has illegitimately wished to transfer from the sphere of eternity to the sphere of time (history).[39] Consequently, Kierkegaard comes to understand the historical as well as the interpretation of it in a way that is quite incompatible with Hegel's philosophy of history, which he thus also completely rejects. Again it is evident that the incompatibility between Kierkegaard and Hegel manifests itself in a series of discords on individual points and areas. If we wish to understand this series of particular discords, however, we must see it as the consequence of their quite different notions of the point of departure, the task, and the mode of procedure of thought (or, in Kierkegaardian terms: of the existing thinker). As far as the philosophy of history is concerned, for a speculative thinker such as Hegel it was an indisputable given [*Udgangspunkt*] that the divine Idea's unfolding in time had taken place, and it was for him an obvious responsibility to describe how this occurred, just as his procedure in this description was the utilization of the dialectical method, after which he came to the conclusion criticized by Kierkegaard that necessity is the unity of possibility and actuality (Hegel, *Science of Logic*, II, 178). On the other hand, neither in *Philosophical Fragments* nor elsewhere in the Authorship was it Kierkegaard's task to elaborate a philosophy of history, but rather to furnish a conceptual clarification in place of the speculative conceptual confusion and unjustified commingling of philosophical and Christian self-understanding. In the course of this work of clarification there then arose the

[39] It is not our concern here to exhibit what Kierkegaard understands by "time," "eternity," "the moment," or "the instant," "transition," "change," "leap," "possibility," "actuality" or "reality," "necessity," etc. On these reference may be made to Søren Holm's book (*supra cit.*) as well as to the relevant passages of Sløk's *Die Anthropologie Kierkegaards* (1954). That these two authors do not understand Kierkegaard's concepts in quite the same way hardly needs demonstration here, where the issue is to clarify Kierkegaard's relation to Hegel on a definite point. Sløk's criticism of Holm's interpretation of Kierkegaard is expressed directly in his article on Holm's, Løgstrup's, and Knud Hansen's "tre Kierkegaardtolkninger" [Three Interpretations of Kirkegaard] in *Kierkegaardiana*, 1955, pp. 89-102.

occasion in the "Interlude" and elsewhere to put the furniture of the philosophy of history in the right place. Kierkegaard saw it as his job to show in experimental fashion what philosophical Idealism ("The Socratic") has to say about man's (i.e., every man's) relation to the truth, and what that implies, if it is maintained that the truth is not innate in man (as is maintained by Christianity, which, however, in the *Fragments* is presented as an experiment which on every point should be different—and which appears to be quite different). Speculative Idealism, in the version of Hegel and the right-wing Hegelians, thus appeared to Kierkegaard to be an untenable and pernicious commingling of two incompatible dimensions [*Størrelser*]. Concerning Kierkegaard's procedural approach to demonstrate this, the conceptual analysis in *Philosophical Fragments*, it is sufficient to mention that it is not identical nor compatible with Hegel's dialectical method, since the logic Kierkegaard uses is not the speculative logic and the only real criterion he recognizes for the understanding of Christianity, and therewith of man and man's relation to the truth, is the New Testament. For him, the indisputable point of departure was Christianity as a given dimension (not a doctrine in the philosophical sense, but an existential communication, as he put it later in the *Postscript*, especially in his footnote on p. 339) and the individual human as a given dimension. The task, then, was to show how these two givens can come into the correct mutual relation and what consequences this produces, not for Christianity —which the speculative thinkers and their ilk wanted only to improve and thereby abolish—but for man.

According to Kierkegaard, the correct mutual relation between these two givens is obtained in only one way, in the situation of contemporaneity,[40] in which God Himself gives man the necessary condition that man himself neither has nor can procure.

Here again, on the last of the three points in *Philosophical Fragments* where the basic relation between Kierkegaard and Hegel should be characterized, it appears that their positions are not only different but incompatible.

There is no theory of contemporaneity (in Kierkegaard's sense) in Hegel. Apart from what Kierkegaard otherwise thinks of contemporaneity as the requirement, man himself does not have nor can he bring it about that he enters into the right relation with the

[40] P. Lønning's book (1954) with this title [*Samtidighedens Situation*] together with Lindström's comments on it in *Kierkegaardiana* (1955), pp. 102-113, are especially important in this connection.

Incarnate Truth. Inasmuch as this is an indispensable condition for man's genuine understanding of himself, then—simply from a philosophical perspective alone—the theory preserves (on the level of existence, not just on the level of theoretical knowledge) a distinction between subject and object, as it is called in traditional terminology. We do not find, nor ought we to seek the identity of subject and object, since that would entail a fatal misconception of the situation of man and his confinement in temporal existence. In Hegel, on the other hand, precisely the identity of subject and object in the speculative concept is maintained,[41] which indicates that the theory of contemporaneity in Kierkegaard and the speculative concept aided by the dialectical method mutually exclude each other.[42]

If the differences are situated in this way on the three points mentioned, it is of no importance that both Kierkegaard and Hegel, although in different ways and with different basic principles, emphasize the significance of the Incarnation, for there is nothing in that which is particularly Hegelian or particularly Kierkegaardian. Nor does it entail anything of significance that we can find in the writings of both men other traditional dogmatic concepts (in Kierkegaard's sequence: sin, salvation, redemption, judgment, the fulness of time, rebirth, etc.), since both their content and their function are different: in Kierkegaard they are all-important; for Hegel they are really unimportant, since the same result can be obtained for man in another way, namely with the help of the dialectical method and the system.

6. *Prefaces*

As a rule Kierkegaard did not identify his speculative targets by name in his pseudonymous writings, but only spoke of the topic, not its representatives, corresponding to the pseudonymity he preserved for himself until he came out in the open with his "first and last declaration" at the end of the *Postscript*. Yet Nicolaus Nota-

[41] It can be noted in passing that Heidegger's theory of the solidarity of subject and object (in *Being and Time*, I, §§12-13 and *passim*) and his later philosophy of being can be understood in concord with Hegel's philosophy; on the other hand, it has only isolated and peripheral connection with Kierkegaard's thought.

[42] Bohlin, in *Kierkegaards dogmatiska åskådning* (1925), pp. 354-440, has given the most complete treatment to date of the problem of revelation and history in Hegel's philosophy of religion and in Kierkegaard.

bene's "Light Reading for Individual Conditions According to Time and Opportunity," i.e., *Prefaces*, which appeared on the same day as *The Concept of Dread* (June 17, 1844) is more straightforward, especially in his many jibes at Heiberg.

Kierkegaard employed different weapons against speculation here than he did in his other writings. He neither developed his own positive view, as he did in the books he published under his own name, nor did he argue psychologically, philosophically, or theologically against Hegel and his enthusiastic followers, as in the pseudonymous works. Now he began (and continued soon after in the *Postscript*) to do as Poul Møller did at the end: he showed the comical aspect of their energetic system building, but, of course, this was the comical according to his own concept of the comical, such as he developed it in the *Postscript*.

Even in the first "Preface"[t] there is an outburst against those who only make promises about the system—without living up to them, and in the fourth he gives a hint of what Heiberg—whose discussions of *Repetition* in *Urania* he had not forgotten—could expect. Heiberg's philosophical efforts had come to a standstill, and now Nicolaus Notabene will kindly entrust to experts the judgment of the value of Heiberg's "later astronomical, astrological, chiromantic, necromantic, horoscopic, metroscopic, chronological studies" (SV, V, 32; 5, 217); but it is not until the seventh "Preface" that Kierkegaard really gets down to business, and then in the last "Preface," the eighth, he draws up his own plan for a philosophical periodical.

The criticism in the seventh "Preface" is directed against "mediation," against the Hegelian imitators, unoriginal minds, who only put together an eleventh book after ten previous ones on the same topic, or who cannot push further than the well-known thought "of the prospect of the hope of the system" (SV, V, 47; 5, 229). Nicolaus Notabene cannot himself push it far enough so as to understand all mankind, but he will at least try to understand himself. He cannot omit a sour remark about the science (i.e., speculative philosophy), which in his time has completed everything, although it has unfortunately forgotten the point of the whole thing (SV, V, 52; 5, 233). On the other hand he is quite sure that "our Systematizers and philosophical optimists" will not waste their time on him, who "has only taken a domestic journey within his own consciousness, and thus in no way intrudes" on their speculations (SV, V, 52-53; 5,

[t] There is no English translation of this book of Kierkegaard, which consists entirely of a series of prefaces.

234). His devout request that no one "with the aid of mediation" bring him into "the Systematic peddler's box" was not entirely respected. Martensen did not pass up the opportunity for making condescending unsympathetic remarks which, without mentioning him by name, were clearly directed against Kierkegaard in the preface (p. iii) of his *Den Christelige Dogmatik* (1849),[u] and then in *Den Christelige Ethik* [Christian Ethics] (esp. I, 275) to arrange Kierkegaard systematically [*at sætte K. paa Paragraf*]. Finally, Nicolaus indicates that he knows very well that "the history of modern philosophy begins with Descartes, and the philosophical fairy tale of how being and nothing amalgamated their deficit, so that becoming came out of it" (SV V, 53; 5, 235).

In close harmony with *De Omnibus Dubitandum Est*, the eighth "Preface" says that the difficulty with beginning a philosophical periodical in Denmark (see Chapter VI, section 2 *supra* on V A 100-101) is that he, Nicolaus Notabene (alias Kierkegaard) cannot manage to doubt everything so he concentrated on the more practicable task "to doubt all that the philosophizers understood, what they said and what came to be said. This doubt is not overcome in the System, but in life" (SV, V, 57; 5, 238). Indeed, it helps nothing that philosophy conquers all doubt, if doubt remains whether people really understand philosophy, and this doubt cannot be entirely a matter of indifference to people or to philosophy. Directly against Martensen (cf. his lectures on dogmatics, discussed *supra* Chapter III, section 4) it is said that, at that time, it was surely maintained that it was necessary for a theologian to be a philosopher "in order to be able to satisfy the demands of the time" (SV V, 58; 5, 238), but Nicolaus himself doubts whether the demands of the time are also what the age requires, and it is this doubt of his own that he desires eradicated—by beginning a periodical whose viewpoint he wishes to be defeated. He feels that his desire can be fulfilled if the Hegelian philosophy that has flourished for some time in Denmark (SV V, 65; 5, 244) and has explained absolutely everything, will go a step further and explain itself, and explain itself for him so that he may understand that which he has not been able to understand so far. If the pure Hegelians (Heiberg!) cannot perform this function, then he is consoled by the fact "that in the land of my birth there are also philosophers who have gone beyond Hegel.

[u] The English translation (of Martensen's own German version) *Christian Dogmatics* (Edinburgh: T. & T. Clark, 1886) does not seem to have these remarks.

Just as soon as they [Martensen and his followers], by a little telegraphic bulletin, explain just where they have arrived, then my confidence in them will be unshakable" (SV, V, 65; 5, 245). This expresses precisely the attitude toward Martensen that Kierkegaard adopted several years earlier (II A 7, written in 1837).[v] With direct aim at Martensen it is said in addition that Hegel had "known how to edit the whole of modern philosophy in such a way that it looked as though he had completed everything, and everything that went before tended toward him. Another [Martensen] now gives a similar presentation, a presentation that is indistinguishable from Hegel's even to a hair's breadth ... and then he adds a concluding paragraph in which he testifies that he has gone beyond Hegel" (SV, V, 66; 5, 245). This startling information paralyzes Nicolaus Notabene's mind. It is not said why, nor should an answer to this be demanded: if one shares Hegel's view that his own philosophy, the all-inclusive in which the whole and complete truth is conceived and presented in the only completely valid philosophical form, is not just the intermediary, but the absolute and finally valid conclusion and high point of the unfolding, then one simply cannot go beyond Hegel, "go further" along Hegel's path, for it stops with him. One can only, as shown in the form of the experiment in *Philosophical Fragments*, advance by going back, i.e., by completely abandoning the way of speculation, which only leads the individual existing human astray. The highest thing attainable for philosophy is not speculative insight but the Socratic wisdom—of one's own ignorance.

Nicolaus Notabene, who thus wishes to take on speculative philosophy, is, according to what he says himself, possibly so stupid that philosophy will hardly bother about him. The question then is, what influence does this possible stupidity have, in the first place, on his existence as human and, in the second place, on his relation to salvation. He comes to the conclusion that possibly the philosopher achieves salvation by his philosophy; but this salvation is accidental. There must be something higher than speculative philosophy, and this something "is higher by virtue of the fact that it includes me and similar poor wretches." If that is correct, how—Nicolaus asks —can one continue to call philosophy the absolute? If it is not that, then it must in any event give an account of where its boundaries extend.

A second possibility is that Nicolaus Notabene is not stupid but

[v] Hong, V, #5200.

stubborn, and thus philosophy will have nothing to do with him. If one assumes that philosophy possesses the truth, then all defiance will be in vain against the power of the truth. He reasons further about this possibility and arrives at the same conclusion as with the postulate of his stupidity: speculative philosophy is perhaps not the highest.

Finally, he could imagine a third possibility, namely, that philosophy condescended to speak with him, this philosophical outsider, only to tell him that philosophy is for the elite, to whom Nicolaus does not belong. To this Nicolaus would reply (SV, V, 73; 5, 250-251) that it would be most desirable to obtain a revision of its worst adherents' theory that it is necessary for every man, even the most stupid or the most obstinate, to understand philosophy. But if there is no need to grasp it then one can with peace of mind let the elite grasp it while remaining without oneself—and start a philosophical periodical, which certainly cannot become either speculative or orthodox. Nicolaus has certainly not doubted about everything; but he will address himself to those who at least claim that they have done so, and who presumably on at least some points have gone further and won certainty, not about everything, but about something.

Kierkegaard did not begin such a periodical and no rich dialogue between him and the Danish speculative thinkers emerged, which could scarcely have been expected after such a "Preface." He spoke in the east, they spoke in the west, and "the mediation" was and remained an impossibility.

Instead of a periodical, Kierkegaard issued first *Stages on Life's Way*[43]—which simply does not sketch stages along the way of speculative knowledge, such as Hegel presented it in the *Phenomenology of the Spirit*. After this, Kierkegaard published the *Concluding Unscientific Postscript* as the work in which all the threads of the previous pseudonymous Authorship are gathered together, and in which in constant indirect and direct confrontation with speculation in every conceivable version he made his theology and anthropology more precise in their absolute incompatibility with Hegel's and his disciples' views.

---

[43] This work, whose poetic-philosophical description of the three chief stages is a deeper and more precise treatment (especially of the religious stage) in comparison with that of *Either/Or* is by its very presence an indirect protest against Hegelian philosophy, in which its problems simply have no place; but it is not necessary to discuss it further here.

7. *Concluding Unscientific Postscript*

In each of the foregoing pseudonymous works, Kierkegaard dealt with a single main theme, with the result that along the way he directly and indirectly took up related questions for discussion and came to overall conclusions that did not agree with those of speculative thought. In the *Postscrpit* there is also only one single main question, namely, how man must be constituted so that there can be any problem at all of how man enters into the correct relation to Christianity. But while working out the solution for this main question Kierkegaard discusses so many other problems of logic, metaphysics, ethics, and the philosophy of history that the work is a confrontation not just with Hegel but with the two traditions Hegel sought to coalesce in his system, and—in its positive content —the point of departure not only for Kierkegaard's own further work as a thinker but also for the philosophical and theological work of later times.[44]

As in the foregoing pseudonymous works so in the *Postscript* Kierkegaard is completely unsympathetic toward Hegel. In only a very few places, to be sure, does he mention Hegel and the Hegelians by name, but speaks instead of "speculation," "the modern speculation," "the System," "Christian speculation," "the science." These terms mean basically the same thing, and the designation "Unscientific" in the title was obviously chosen to underscore the difference.

That Kierkegaard is completely unsympathetic toward "speculation" is so frequently and strikingly emphasized in the *Postscript*, both in the work itself and in the literature about Kierkegaard, that it would be superfluous to describe it in more detail one more time. On the other hand, it is perhaps not superfluous to seek clarification of why he was unsympathetic.

This question can be answered in two ways: one way is to investigate all of the many specific instances where the text of the

[44] In the Introduction and Commentary to my [Danish] edition of the *Concluding Unscientific Postscript*, II (1962), I have stated my understanding of the origin and history of the speculative philosophy of religion as well as of Kierkegaard's anti-speculative position and its presuppositions, and specific details are brought out in the Commentary. In this edition the reader will be able to find, if not all, then at least some of what he might miss in the present treatment, which I do not wish to burden with a repetition of the Commentary volume's information and contributions to interpretation of the *Postscript's* totality and details.

work has direct or indirect contact with one or another specific item in Hegel and in his followers. This way is followed in the Commentary cited in note 44. The second way to deal with this question is to pose three simple questions for Kierkegaard's work, read the answers we find in the work, and then pose the same three questions for Hegel and ascertain his answers. The answers contain the determination of the basic relation between the two thinkers, but since the answers in each case are given from definite presuppositions and positions, we must, in order to understand the questions completely, make these presuppositions clear. If these questions are clarified first, then we can understand specific points in the correct perspective. This procedure was followed in the Introduction mentioned in note 44 (*supra*).

Even if these questions have already been pursued in both ways, this does not mean that the answers we find say all that can be said in response, nor does this mean that this is the only possible way of investigating the matter.

Three questions can be posed in order to clarify the problem, if it still is a problem, of why Kierkegaard is so totally hostile to speculation and all its deeds and all its odious practices: what chief presuppositions do Hegel and Kierkegaard have, respectively? What goals did they set for themselves in their work as authors? and What procedures did they employ to obtain their goals?

In the case of Hegel these questions have been answered above (Chapter V, section 3b). Kierkegaard's position in the *Postscript* shall be considered here.

Kierkegaard's main presuppositions can be delineated quite briefly: traditional logic is his formal principle; for Hegel, it is speculative logic; Kierkegaard's concrete principle is Christianity understood as the absolute communication of existence; for Hegel, Christianity is an imperfect version of the same truth that receives its perfect formulation in the speculative system, and man is regarded as a created but destroyed synthesis, who, as existing, does not possess the capacity for recreating the synthesis.

Kierkegaard's aim in the *Postscript* (with which the previous Authorship is included), is to answer the question of how every single individual can enter into the correct relation to Christianity, which is not considered a doctrine in the philosophical sense, but as a quite definite Kerygma, a communication of existence, as he called it.

To obtain this goal, he first answers the so-called objective problem of the truth of Christianity and comes to the conclusion that on the way of objectivity an existing person can scarcely see the subjective problem of the individual's relation to Christianity. In the main portion of the work he deals with the subjective problem itself, at the same time deepening his anthropology and his theology and placing them in constant conflict with Hegel and the right-wing Hegelians, especially Martensen, whose name, however, he does not mention except in the drafts for the work.

The procedure employed by the subjective thinker, who is constantly seen in opposition to the objective, i.e. the speculative thinker, does not utilize the Hegelian dialectical method, but as the subtitle expresses, is mimic, pathetic, and dialectic. The result is not, and was not supposed to be "scientific," i.e., objective and speculative, but precisely in opposition thereto: an unscientific existential contribution, which corresponds exactly with man regarded as existing (on one of the stages outlined) in untruth until the moment when Christianity communicates to man existence in truth, and thereby both explains and judges the lower stages of existence.

If we compare the presuppositions, goals, and methods of Hegel and Kierkegaard only insofar as they have been briefly described here and in what has already been said, it becomes evident that the two thinkers as thinkers basically have nothing in common. Obviously, this relationship does not exclude a multitude of contacts on particular points on the part of Kierkegaard, as for example, in terminology, in the interpretation of historical and individual philosophical phenomena and the like; but if the relation is basically as it has been presented here, then it is inherently obvious why Kierkegaard so tirelessly and relentlessly, directly and indirectly undertook his confrontation with Hegel and his disciples. He did so because, in his view, their speculation represented a distorted concept of man and a distorted concept of Christianity. Even if speculation could speculatively apprehend everything possible other than the individual man and his correct relation to Christianity, Kierkegaard found it at best trivial and at worst, distracting from what was for him the only essential thing.

Now is the relationship actually as it has been sketched and claimed here? This question can best be answered from the *Concluding Unscientific Postscript* itself, not by presenting once more and interpreting its whole thought content but by making clear its reasoning with particular emphasis on the aspects that have direct significance for understanding the relation to Hegel.

Immediately, the Introduction says that if the problem of the single, existing individual's relation to Christianity is raised, and it is maintained that the individual's transition to it can happen only by a leap, then neither historical scholarship, spiritual rhetoric, nor philosophical speculation (especially the latter, which claims to go beyond the faith as a given point of departure, not as a culmination as it was for Kierkegaard) can help.

For the objective point of view, there is the problem of the truth of Christianity in itself, not its truth for the existing man. Thus the objective account can either be historical, so that one seeks "to obtain an entirely reliable account of what the Christian doctrine really is" (*Concluding Unscientific Postscript*, p. 25), or it can be speculative, so that one seeks through the way of thought to conceptualize and thereby philosophically validate the truth of Christianity. But the problem of the existing man's relation to Christianity does not emerge at all for the objective account, whether it is historical, because on the path of historical research we cannot reach beyond probability to certainty, or speculative, because the speculative approach misunderstands both what Christianity is and what it is to be human.

After this brief, sharp clash, which results in a complete rejection of Hegelian speculation (in which what is for Kierkegaard the crucial problem, the subjective problem of the individual's relation to Christianity, cannot emerge), the question of how man must be understood must be answered, and this must be done so that the subjective problem can appear. In this connection, the problem of *Philosophical Fragments*, how Christianity should be defined, is taken up again.

In what follows Lessing is taken as a type of subjective thinker who isolates himself and sets forth neither a system nor finished conclusions at all, but who as a subjective thinker is interested both in his own uncompleted existence which is still in a process of becoming [*vordende*], and in the way of thought. Like every existing human, the subjective thinker has the eternal within him, while he is in temporality; but he does not, unlike the objective thinker, become addicted to the supposition that time is only becoming eternal. The paradox for the subjective thinker arises from the fact that Christianity claims that it brings an absolute truth into time and demands the decision of every individual existing human also in time. There can be no talk of any straightforward transition from historical reliability to the eternal decision. If a transition is to take place it must happen by a leap—which objective, speculative philosophy does not recognize.

If existence as human is an uncompleted existence, in the future, in process within time, and if logic is essentially atemporal, then certainly a logical, philosophical system can be formulated, but not a system of being. The existence to which every human is bound is dynamic. Logic, on the other hand, is static. Hence Hegel's attempt to bring movement into logic, so as thereby to be able to work out a logical system of being, is an impossible endeavor. If existence as human is an unfinished endeavor, then the effort must in all circumstances be an effort toward one or another goal, and consequently ethics becomes crucial. The existing man's endeavor is simply an expression of his ethical attitude (p. 110) provided by whatever goal he strives for. Hegel's attempt (in the *Philosophy of Right*) to neutralize the ethical endeavor by declaring its ethical goal achieved only shows, then—in a field other than the logical—the impossibility of the system: it holds that it is all-inclusive, but it lacks the most important thing, ethics. The subjective thinker must, in the final analysis, interpret the whole speculative endeavor as a comical attempt to do what is impossible for an existing human.

In general, speculation does not recognize the problems of existence, for they are evidently only pseudo-problems.[45] It has confused things in logic by trying to incorporate movement into it, while ignoring ethics. All of its guidance has been misleading. The existing man's decision, his ethical choice, is not recognized by speculation. Instead, it loses itself in the world-historical. The situation is no better even with the concept of truth, with which the existing man has a duty to come into the right relation. This concept can be defined empirically or idealistically; but in either case it is defined as something objective. In neither of these two instances is truth sought in the way that the existing individual must seek it, namely truth as subjectivity, in which the existing subject has a duty to immerse himself. The recognition of truth that can be

[45] In the *Postscript* quite frequently the expression "modern science" is used synonymously with "speculation." If we used the designation "modern science" everywhere and understood it in the contemporary sense, not in Kierkegaard's, then there would be no great difficulty in making the *Postscript* contemporaneous with us; but—as tempting as it might be to make this little change—it is not the purpose of this study to update Kierkegaard, an updating that could hardly surprise others than those who—like Martensen in connection with Hegel—have gone further than Kierkegaard and thus have engaged in a kind of progress by which one goes backward.

obtained in this way is defined as essential, whereas all other knowledge is unimportant because it does not concern existence. Knowledge gained in the rational way, as, for example, mathematical knowledge, as well as knowledge obtained in the empirical way, such as historical knowledge, must thus be classified as unimportant, while the alleged speculative knowledge is neither important nor unimportant, but simply an expression of fantasy.

Even without taking Christianity directly into consideration, one can come so far, as Socrates did, that one may say that subjectivity is truth.

On the other hand, from the Christian perspective subjectivity is untruth, i.e., the existing man is in sin, whereas the truth that by entering into time becomes the paradox (cf. *Philosophical Fragments*) cannot now emerge through man's self-knowledge (which in its highest development results in Socratic, not speculative, self-knowledge), but emerges through a divine revelation of the eternal truth, which has become present in time.

The truth of this revelation, the paradox in the Christian sense, cannot be understood speculatively either. That is, speculation, by denying the absolute difference between God and man, wishes to abolish the paradox and therewith that on which Christianity stands or falls. Similarly, speculation wishes to abolish the paradoxicality of sin, faith, and the forgiveness of sin.

The conclusion of these reflections up to this point, if in spite of Climacus's (i.e. Kierkegaard's) admonition against speaking of conclusions in a subjective thinker, we can so speak, is, then, that speculation has misconstrued what it means to be human, since it understands man, at least the speculative man, as simply eternal, which no existing man is or can be. Quite in the same way it has misunderstood what Christianity is, since speculation wishes to conceive the inconceivable. If it has misunderstood these two dimensions, then its determination of their mutual relation as a given and harmonious relation is a distorted determination.

Thus in the *Postscript* there is no evidence that Kierkegaard benevolently intends to employ certain viewpoints and ingredients from the Hegelian system, to modify them, complete them, similarly to the way systematic theologians through the ages have done with other philosophers—as for example, Aristotle, Kant, Heidegger[w]—

---

[w] One might also recall the *"pie exponenda,"* or "belevolent interpretation" technique which the Christian scholastics of the later middle ages developed

on the contrary, the rejection is complete and is based on his anthropology as well as on the theology that gives his anthropology its meaning and justification.[46]

Then it is shown in the *Postscript* how Kierkegaard's whole previous Authorship contains a sustained indirect polemic against speculation. Speculation has ignored the problems of existence and misconstrued the relation to Christianity by understanding it as harmonious instead of disharmonious.

After this (pp. 267ff.) he develops in greater detail the theory of ethical subjectivity and the subjective thinker in a continued direct and indirect clash with Hegel in such a way that it is one continuous corroboration of the chief contention of the present study, that at bottom Hegel's and Kierkegaard's thought have nothing in common, even though there are many contacts that clearly show Kierkegaard's studies and his taking of positions first with regard to the Hegelians alone, then with regard to Hegel himself, and finally in the same degree toward both the master and his disciples equally included in the common designation "speculation" or "the system."

The process of clarification—or the story of a cure, as P. A. Heiberg has called it in another connection—was continued. There is no need to mention more than a few typical instances of it so as to give an insight into its course and result.

The *Postscript* maintains that abstract thinking is undertaken under the perspective of eternity, and it looks away from existence, which cannot be in the tranquility of eternity, but is always in process, in becoming, as is the world in which the task of existence is to be solved. Then it maintains that thinking existence, subjective thought, so far from being easier than abstract thinking is, on the contrary, more difficult, since its task is to think (and in faith to relate oneself to) the individual, not the universal. If one thinks of the universal in a purely abstract way, one can speak only in principle of, for example, immortality; but on the basis of abstract thinking (and for Kierkegaard this is a genuinely comical situation, pp. 270f.) one cannot express himself concerning a single, existing man's im-

---

into a highly sophisticated way of resolving conflicts between opinions of various "authorities" and/or between their own thought and that of the tradition.

[46] If one wishes to criticize his theology and anthropology, one will have to try to find inconsistencies and gaps therein. If one wishes to evaluate them, one will have to try to follow the objective path, historically or speculatively.

mortality. Correspondingly, Hegelian philosophy maintains that the principle of contradiction has been overcome, and in that respect it can be correct in the realm of pure thought and pure being; but no existing man finds himself in these pure spheres, so that the abrogation of the principle of contradiction is really without interest.[47] However, if one maintains that the abrogation of the principle of contradiction is also valid in the sphere of existence, then this assertion is fatal, since in this case it means the abolition of the difference between good and evil and thus of all ethics, and consistently enough the system has no ethics in the traditional sense either, whereas for the existing man, the subjective thinker, the ethical is the only important reality, his absolute interest, as he puts it.

A little later he asserts that even if one grants legitimacy to speculation (here represented by Rosenkranz's *Psychologie* and Hegel's *Phenomenology of the Spirit*) in its mockery of the ancient threefold division of man into body, soul, and spirit, and concedes to it the merit of having defined man as spirit, and within this explains the elements of soul, consciousness, and spirit as developmental levels in the same subject, still it does not follow from this that we can, without further ado, transfer this from the world-historical development to the individual (pp. 308-309). When, without further qualification, someone asserts that the unfolding of world history and of the individual proceed identically this must indicate that in each generation only imperfect copies of man are born— who together in all their imperfection should produce the perfect world history.

Significantly, it is said that the subjective thinker's task is to understand himself in his existence (p. 314), and in order to fulfill this task he must use imagination as well as feeling and thinking, that is, he does not accomplish the task "scientifically" (speculatively) but, as the title of the work also says, unscientifically, as an artist. To understand oneself in existence was the Greek principle, personified in Socrates, as it is the Christian principle, except that in and with Christianity the self has obtained far deeper determinations than Greece had the capacity to give it. However, the speculative principle, if it should be similarly formulated, is prepared to ignore self-understanding for the sake of an understanding of every-

[47] Here, as always in the careful reading of the *Postscript*, it may be seen that Kierkegaard has actually performed like the innocent boy in "The Emperor's New Clothes."

thing else possible, especially the world-historical, and if one ignores self-understanding, then one can attain to conclusions in the traditional sense, while as distinct from that, what is characteristic of the subjective thinker is that he cannot furnish conclusions at all in the same sense.

Now speculative thought, it is asserted, has come to the conclusion that it has understood Christianity both in its world-historical legitimacy and in its fundamental truth, to which is added the remark that it seems almost to have done a still greater work of art, namely to go further on the other side of Christianity so that it has nearly returned to heathendom: one has got a so-called Christian speculation on the theoretical level just as on the practical level we have reached the point that everybody thinks that he is Christian.

Set over against this confused state of affairs, it must first be made clear what Christianity and heathendom are in their pure state, before there can be any possible talk of "mediating" them—as speculative thought has done too hastily. This clarification was undertaken in the *Philosophical Fragments*. The conclusion was that the central point of Christianity is paradoxical, that it is not any doctrine in the speculative-philosophical sense (see especially the note on p. 339 of the *Postscript*), but it expresses an existential contradiction, namely, that an existing man's eternal salvation is worked out in time, through the fact that he relates himself to something that paradoxically has become historical, together with the fact that Christianity is communication of existence (Kerygma, as it is frequently called nowadays), i.e., it causes one to participate in the true existence, which is an irreconcilable contrast to speculation, since to follow the path of speculation means to flee from the ethical reality of existence in quite the same way as the esthetic attitude toward life is a flight from reality.

There is no continuous or gradual transition from non-Faith to Faith; this transition can take place only by a leap, so this also involves saying that the way of speculation cannot be followed by an existing man. Speculation cannot incorporate the problem of the *Postscript* at all. If in speculative philosophy there is any talk of a leap, what is meant by it is something entirely different. If there is any talk of Faith, what is meant by it is something entirely different. If there is any talk there of pathos, what is meant by it is something entirely different from the existing man's infinite anxiety for his eternal salvation. If they speak of dialectic, what is meant there is something entirely different from the qualitative dialectic of faith, which belongs within the sphere of freedom, which is unknown to speculation, but to which sphere all problems of existence belong. That an existing man's passionate concern transforms this man's whole existence cannot come within the purview of speculation. Thus, the possibility objective thinkers devote themselves to speculating about cannot be spoken of at all except as a mistaken possibility of a type similar to the disinterested esthete's pseudopossibility, about which speculation knows nothing.

Speculative thought is unaware of and cannot incorporate existential pathos; nor is it aware of, nor can it include existential dialectic, which is the second moment of Faith, as pathos is its first moment. This dialectic is present from the fact that the existing man should relate himself to the paradoxical revelation of Christ and express this relation in his own existence, which even before the encounter with the revelation of Christ is paradoxical in the wider sense by being put together as a synthesis. Upon the encounter with this revelation it becomes paradoxical in a narrower sense by being bound to what neither can nor should be revealed—as Judge William from his lower ethical stage demanded it—but living in the hidden interiority, attempt the cloister movement inward, relating oneself relatively to the relative, absolutely to the absolute.

Speculative thought knows about the stages on the way of knowledge; but it does not know and cannot include the stages on the way of existence, life's way—which means the way to the true life, that of Faith. Certainly speculative thought recognizes guilt and sin, but not as existentially crucial elements, only as relative components in the all-relativizing system, where nothing is stable, where everything is in flux. Speculative thought is hopeless as philosophy simply by the strength of its special logic, and it is impossible as theology from the fact that it wishes to conceive that which is humanly impossible to conceive, namely the paradox. In Kierkegaard's view, speculative thought, especially in Hegel's version, belongs in a museum for comical and useless discoveries.

Briefly described, such is Kierkegaard's understanding and evaluation of Hegelian speculation in *Concluding Unscientific Postscript*, and it is on the basis of this overall interpretation that the many individual points where criticism is rendered against one or another thing in Hegel must be understood. It is not absolutely necessary to follow these individual items point for point in the present study, since such a pursuit has already been undertaken at least for the majority of them in the edition of the work already mentioned.

8. Conclusion

The conclusion of the investigation in this chapter can be briefly stated.

Corresponding to the examination of Kierkegaard's *Papirer* from this period (Chapter VII *supra*), scrutiny of the *Works* reveals that Kierkegaard did not in any particularly extensive degree seem to have continued any genuine study of Hegel during these years. Although in this area we can make only more or less well-founded conjectures, it can—with these necessary reservations—be said that there is very little to indicate that Kierkegaard read Hegel's "seventeen whole volumes" from beginning to end. On the contrary, the many quotations and allusions,[48] show that he particularly intensively and with never-slackening critical attention read *in* the seventeen whole volumes, in *Phenomenology of the Spirit*, in *The Science of Logic*, in both the little *Philosophische Propädeutik* and the large *Encyclopedia of the Philosophical Sciences*, in the *Philosophy of Right*, in the *Lectures on Fine Art*, on *Philosophy of Religion*, on the *Philosophy of History*, and on the *History of Philosophy*. Only the section on the philosophy of nature in the *Encyclopedia* seems to have left no mark on Kierkegaard. Perhaps he did not read it at all, perhaps he thought that Sibbern had spoken about it sufficiently. In addition to these there would be his reading of the writings of the Hegelians, together with the anti-Hegelian logician Trendelenburg's works and articles especially.

Nor can we say that Kierkegaard's overall interpretation of Hegel himself changed significantly during this period. It became more striking, and on various points (logic, philosophy of history, ethics, etc.) it became more profound; but Kierkegaard did not wish to be, nor was he, a historian of philosophy. His efforts were not primarily directed toward understanding and presenting Hegel's philosophy—as Chalybäus, Erdmann, Michelet, and others in his time did—and nowhere in his works (any more than in his *Papirer*) do we find even an outline of a coherent presentation of Hegel's philosophy. We find quotations, allusions, accounts of Hegel's views on individual topics and problems, most often very closely connected with a critical evaluation. The natural explanation for this is that the main thing for Kierkegaard was to work out his own Authorship and to clarify the problems that appeared to him as existing thinker.

---

[48] Insofar as possible identified and explained in the previously mentioned editions of Kierkegaard's works with commentaries.

Both the direct, and the at least equally important indirect clashes with Hegelian speculation are, as it were, concomitant circumstances in the Authorship. He found this clash called for mainly on the basis of the fact that according to his interpretation of Hegel's philosophy it contained a wrong anthropology and a reprehensible theology, and partly on the basis of the fact that the right-wing Hegelians, especially Martensen, employed the methods and alleged results of Hegelian philosophy in theology, which thereby, in Kierkegaard's estimate, was completely corrupted. Thereupon Kierkegaard undertook both an evaluation of Hegel's own system as a totality, especially with reference to its method and intention, but without noteworthy reference to (or knowledge of) this system's general and special principles, and an evaluation of the Hegelians', especially the right-wing Hegelians', attempt to go further than Hegel. In both cases the evaluation was completely negative.

NOTE: Distinctive letters of the Danish and Swedish alphabets are alphabetized as if they were English. Thus, å = a, ä = a, æ = ae, ø = o, and ö = o.

A. PRIMARY SOURCES (HEGEL AND KIERKEGAARD)

1. Danish and German

Barfod, H. P., ed., *Kierkegaards Efterladte Papirer* (1869-1881).

Hegel, Georg Wilhelm Friedrich, *Sämtliche Werke, Jubiläumsausgabe*, ed. Hermann Glockner, 20 vols. (Stuttgart: Frommann, 1927-1939, 3rd ed. 1957).

Kierkegaard, Søren, *Afsluttende uvidenskabelig Efterskrift*, udgivet med indledning og Kommentar af Niels Thulstrup, 2 vols. (Copenhagen: Gyldendal, 1962).

———, *Samlede Værker*, ed. A. B. Drachmann, J. L. Heiberg, and H. O. Lange, 2nd ed., I-XV (Copenhagen: Gyldendalske Boghandel, 1920-1936).

———, *Samlede Værker*, ed. A. B. Drachmann, J. L. Heiberg, and H. O. Lange, 3rd ed. revised by Peter P. Rohde, 1-20 (Copenhagen: Gyldendal, 1968-1978).

———, *Søren Kierkegaards Papirer*, eds. P. A. Heiberg and Victor Kuhr, 2nd expanded edition, ed. Niels Thulstrup, with index (vols. XIV-XVI) by Niels Jørgen Cappelørn, 25 vols. (Copenhagen: Gyldendal, 1968-1978).

Thulstrup, Niels, ed., *Breve og Aktstykker vedrørende Søren Kierkegaard*, 2 vols. (Copenhagen: Munksgaard, 1953-1954).

2. English Translations

Hegel, Georg Wilhelm Friedrich, *Aesthetics: Lectures on Fine Art*, 2 vols., trans. T. M. Knox (Oxford: Clarendon Press, 1975).

———, *Early Theological Writings*, trans. T. M. Knox (Chicago: University of Chicago Press, 1948; reprinted, University of Pennsylvania Press, 1971).

———, *Lectures on the History of Philosophy*, 3 vols., trans. E. S. Haldane and Frances H. Simson (London: Routledge & Kegan Paul, 1963).

——, *Lectures on the Philosophy of Religion*, 3 vols., trans. E. B. Speirs and J. Burdon Sanderson (New York: Humanities Press, 1962).

——, *Hegel's Logic* [Part 1 of the *Encyclopedia*] trans. William Wallace (Oxford: Clarendon Press, 1892).

——, *The Phenomenology of Mind*, trans. J. B. Baillie (London: Allen & Unwin, 1949).

——, *The Philosophy of Fine Art*, 4 vols., trans. F.P.B. Osmaston (New York: Hacker Art Books, 1975).

——, *The Philosophy of History*, trans. J. Sibree (New York: Dover Publications, 1956).

——, *Hegel's Philosophy of Mind* [Part 3 of the *Encyclopedia*] trans. William Wallace (Oxford: Clarendon Press, 1894, 1971).

——, *Philosophy of Right*, trans. T. M. Knox (London: Oxford University Press, 1953).

——, *Hegel's Science of Logic*, 2 vols., trans. W. H. Johnston and L. G. Struthers (London: Allen & Unwin, 1929).

——, *Hegel's Science of Logic*, trans. A. V. Miller (London: Allen & Unwin, 1969).

Kierkegaard, Søren, *Armed Neutrality and An Open Letter*, trans. Howard V. Hong and Edna H. Hong (Bloomington, Indiana: Indiana University Press, 1968).

——, *Attack Upon "Christendom,"* trans. Walter Lowrie (Princeton: Princeton University Press, 1944).

——, *Christian Discourses*, trans. Walter Lowrie (Princeton: Princeton University Press, 1940).

——, *The Concept of Dread*, trans. Walter Lowrie (Princeton: Princeton University Press, 1957).

——, *The Concept of Irony*, trans. Lee M. Capel (New York: Harper & Row, 1965).

——, *Concluding Unscientific Postscript*, trans. David F. Swenson and Walter Lowrie (Princeton: Princeton University Press, 1941).

——, *Crisis in the Life of an Actress*, trans. Stephen Crites (London: Collins; New York: Harper Torchbooks, 1967).

——, *Edifying Discourses*, 2 vols., trans. David F. Swenson and Lillian Marvin Swenson (Minneapolis: Augsburg Publishing House, 1962).

——, *Edifying Discourses*. A selection, trans. David F. Swenson and Lillian Marvin Swenson (New York: Harper Torchbooks, 1958).

Kierkegaard, Søren, *Either/Or*, 2 vols., trans. Walter Lowrie (Princeton: Princeton University Press, 1944, 1959).

————, *Fear and Trembling* and *The Sickness Unto Death*, trans. Walter Lowrie (Princeton: Princeton University Press, 1954).

————, *Johannes Climacus: or, De Omnibus Dubitandum Est* and *A Sermon*, trans. T. H. Croxall (Stanford, California: Stanford University Press, 1958).

————, *The Journals of Kierkegaard*, selected and trans. Alexander Dru (New York: Harper Torchbooks, 1959).

————, *Søren Kierkegaard's Journals and Papers*, 7 vols., ed. and trans. Howard V. Hong and Edna H. Hong (Bloomington, Indiana: Indiana University Press, 1967-1978).

————, *Letters and Documents*, trans. Henrik Rosenmeier, *Kierkegaard's Writings*, vol. XXV (Princeton: Princeton University Press, 1978).

————, *On Authority and Revelation* [The Book on Adler], trans. Walter Lowrie (Princeton: Princeton University Press, 1955; reprinted, Harper Torchbooks, 1966).

————, *Philosophical Fragments*, introduction and commentary by Niels Thulstrup, trans. David Swenson and Howard V. Hong, 2nd revised ed. (Princeton: Princeton University Press, 1962).

————, *The Point of View for My Work as an Author*, trans. Walter Lowrie (New York: Harper Torchbooks, 1962).

————, *The Present Age* and *The Difference Between a Genius and an Apostle*, trans. Alexander Dru (New York: Harper Torchbooks, 1962).

————, *Purity of Heart Is to Will One Thing*, trans. Douglas V. Steere (New York: Harper Torchbooks, 1938, 1948).

————, *Repetition*, trans. Walter Lowrie (Princeton: Princeton University Press, 1941).

————, *Stages on Life's Way*, trans. Walter Lowrie (Princeton: Princeton University Press, 1940).

————, *Thoughts on Crucial Situations in Human Life*, trans. David F. Swenson (Minneapolis: Augsburg Publishing House, 1941).

————, *Training in Christianity*, trans. Walter Lowrie (Princeton: Princeton University Press, 1941).

————, *Two Ages*, ed. and trans. Howard V. Hong and Edna H. Hong, *Kierkegaard's Writings*, vol. XIV (Princeton: Princeton University Press, 1978).

——, *Works of Love*, trans. Howard V. Hong and Edna H. Hong (New York: Harper Torchbooks, 1964).

B. Secondary Sources

Abbagnano, Nicola, *Storia della Filosofia*, 2nd ed., III (1963).

Adler, A. P., *Den isolerede Subjectivitet i dens vigtigeste Skikkelser* (1840).

——, *Populaire Foredrag over Hegels objective Logic* (1842).

Althaus, P., *Die Theologie Martin Luthers* (1962).

Ammundsen, Valdemar, *Søren Kierkegaards Ungdom* (1912).

Andersen, Oskar, *Biskop Hans Lassen Martensen, Hans Liv, Udvikling og Arbejde* (1932).

Andersen, Vilhelm, *Goethe*, 2 vols. (1915-1916).

——, *Illustreret dansk Litteraturhistorie* vol. III (1924).

——, *Poul Møller: Hans Liv og Skrifter*, 3. Udg. (1944).

——, *Tider og Typer af dansk Aands Historie* (1916).

Aquinas, Thomas, *Expositio super librum Boethii De Trinitate* (Rome, Turin: Marietti, 1934).

——, *Summa Contra Gentiles* (Rome, Turin: Marietti, 1934).

——, *Summa Theologiae*, 5 vols. (Madrid: Biblioteca de Autores Cristianos, 1951).

Arildsen, Skat, *H. L. Martensen* (1932).

Baagø, K. *Magister Jacob Christian Lindberg* (1958).

Bagge, Povl, *D. G. Monrads Statstanker* (1936).

Barth, Heinrich, "Kierkegaard, der Denker" *Zwischen den Zeiten* (Munich, 1929).

Barth, Karl, *Die protestantische Theologie im 19. Jahrhundert* (1947).

Baur, F. C., *Die christliche Lehre von der Versöhnung in ihrer geschichtlichen Entwicklung von der ältesten Zeit bis auf die neueste* (1838).

Bejerholm, Lars, *Meddelelsens Dialektik* (Copenhagen: Munksgaard, 1962).

Benktson, B. E., *Den naturliga teologiens problem hos Karl Barth* (1948).

Beyer, W. R., *Hegel-Bilder, Kritik der Hegel-Deutungen* (1964).

Billeskov Jansen, F. J., *Danmarks Digtekunst* vol. III (1958).

Bochenski, I. M., *A History of Formal Logic*, trans. and ed. Ivo Thomas (Notre Dame, Indiana: University of Notre Dame Press, 1961).

Bohlin, Torsten, *Kierkegaards dogmatiska åskådning i dess histo-riska sammanhang* (Stockholm: Diakonistyrelses Förlag, 1925).

——, *Søren Kierkegaards etiska åskådning med särskild hänsyn till begreppet "Den enskilde"* (Stockholm: Diakonistyrelses Förlag, 1918).

Borup, Morten, *Christian Molbech* (1954).

——, *Johan Ludvig Heiberg* I-III (1947).

Brandt, Frithiof, *Den unge Søren Kierkegaard* (Copenhagen: Levin & Munksgaards Forlag, 1929).

Brandt, Frithiof, and Rammel, Else, *Søren Kierkegaard og Pengene* (Copenhagen: Levin & Munksgaard, 1935).

Bréhier, Emile, *History of Philosophy*, vol. VI, *The Nineteenth Century* (Chicago: University of Chicago Press, 1968).

Bryar, William, and Stengren, George L., *The Rebirth of Learning* (New York: Putnam, 1968).

Buber, Martin, "Upphävande av etiken," *En etik, en värld*, ed. R. N. Anshen (1956), pp. 93-97.

Bugge, K. E., *Skolen for Livet* (1965).

Chevalier, Jacques, *Histoire de la Pensée* I-IV (1955-1966).

Christensen, Arild, "Zwei Kierkegaardstudien," *Symposion Kierke-gaardianum* (1955), pp. 36-49.

——, "Om Søren Kierkegaards Inddelingsprincip," *Kierkegaard-iana*, III (1959), pp. 21-37.

——, "Søren Kierkegaards Individuationsprincip," *Dansk teolo-gisk Tidsskrift* (1953).

Christensen, Villads, *Søren Kierkegaards Vej til Kristendommen* (Copenhagen: Munksgaard, 1955).

Clausen, H. N., *Det Nye Testaments Hermeneutik* (1840).

——, *Optegnelser om mit Levneds og min Tids Histories* (1877).

Connell, Desmond, *The Vision of God: Malebranche's Scholastic Sources* (New York: Humanities Press, 1967).

Copleston, Frederick, *A History of Philosophy*, vol. III, "Fichte to Nietzsche" (Westminster, Maryland: The Newman Press, 1963).

Cornford, F. M., *The Origin of Attic Comedy* (1961).

Daub, Carl, *Judas Ischariot oder das Böse in Verhältnis zum Guten* (1816-1818).

——, *Vorlesungen über die philosophische Anthropologie* (1838).

Diem, Hermann, *Kierkegaard: An Introduction* (Richmond, Vir-ginia: John Knox Press, 1966).

——, *Kierkegaard's Dialectic of Existence* (1959).

————, *Philosophie und Christentum bei Søren Kierkegaard* (Munich: Kaiser, 1939).

Dilthey, Wilhelm, *Die Jugendgeschichte Hegels* (Berlin, 1905).

Erdmann, Johann Eduard, *Grundriss der Geschichte der Philosophie*, 3rd ed. (1878).

————, *Leib und Seele nach ihrem Begriff und ihrem Verhältnis zueinander* (Halle, 1837).

Fichte, Immanuel Herman, *Beitrage zur Charakteristik der neueren Philosophie* (1828); 2nd ed. (1841).

————, *Ueber Gegensatz, Wendepunkt und Ziel heutiger Philosophie*, 3 vols. (1832-1836).

————, "Aphorismen über die Zukunft der Theologie, in ihrem Verhältnisse zu Spekulation und Mythologie," *Zeitschrift für Philosophie und spekulative Theologie* (1839).

Fischer, Kuno, *Geschichte der neuern Philosophie*, 2nd ed. (1911).

Forchhammer, Peter Wilhelm, *Die Athener und Sokrates: Die Gesetzlichen und der Revolutionär* (1837).

Friis, Oluf, *Dansk Litteraturhistorie* IV (1965).

Garelick, Herbert M., *The Anti-Christianity of Kierkegaard* (The Hague: Martinus Nijhoff, 1965).

Geismar, Eduard, *Søren Kierkegaard, hans Livsudvikling og Forfattervirksomhed*, 6 vols. (Copenhagen: G.E.C. Gads Forlag, 1926-1928).

Gilson, Etienne, *The Christian Philosophy of St. Thomas Aquinas* (New York: Random House, 1956).

Graus, G. G., *Die Selbstauflösung des christlichen Glaubens, eine religions-philosophische Studie über Kierkegaard* (1963).

Graves, Robert, *The Greek Myths* (New York: George Braziller, 1955).

Hahn, August, *Lehrbuch des christlichen Glaubens* (1828).

Hartmann, Nicolai, *Philosophie des deutschen Idealismus*, 2nd ed. (1960).

Hase, Karl, *Hutterus redivivus oder Dogmatik der evangelisch-lutherischen Kirche*, 4th revised ed. (Leipzig, 1839).

Hauge, Sv., *Studier over D. G. Monrad som religiøs Personlighed* (1944).

Heiberg, Johan Ludvig, "Det logiske System. Første Afhandling, indeholdende Paragrapherne 1-23," *Perseus*, No. 2 (1838). Reprinted in: Johan Ludvig Heibergs *Prosaiske Skrifter*, vol. 2 (Copenhagen: C. A. Reitzels Forlag, 1861).

Heiberg, Johan Ludvig, *Prosaiske Skrifter* 11 Bind (Copenhagen: C. A. Reitzels Forlag, 1861).

――, *Breve og Aktstykker Vedrørende Johan Ludvig Heiberg* ved Morten Borup, 5 Bind (1946).

Heiberg, P. A., *Nogle Bidrag til Enten-Ellers Tilblivelseshistorie* (1910).

――, *Et Segment of Søren Kierkegaards religiøse Udvikling; Kierkegaard Studier*, III (Copenhagen: Gyldendal, 1918).

――, *Søren Kierkegaards religiøse Udvikling* (Copenhagen: Gyldendal, 1925).

Heidegger, Martin, *Being and Time*, trans. John Macquarrie & Edward Robinson (Oxford: Basil Blackwell, 1967).

Heimann, B., *System und Methode in Hegels Philosophie* (1927).

Heinsius, Th., *Sokrates nach dem Grade seiner Schuld* (1839).

Henriksen, Aage, "Kierkegaard's Reviews of Literature," *Symposion Kierkegaardianum* (1955), 75-84.

――, *Kierkegaards Romaner* (Copenhagen: Gyldendal, 1954).

Himmelstrup, Jens, *Søren Kierkegaard: International Bibliografi* (Copenhagen: Nyt Nordisk Forlag, Arnold Busck, 1962).

――, *Søren Kierkegaards Opfattelse af Sokrates* (Copenhagen: Arnold Busck, 1924).

――, *Sibbern* (1934).

――, *Terminologisk Ordbog til Søren Kierkegaards Samlede Værker*. Also in vol. XV of SK's *Samlede Værker*, 2nd ed. (Copenhagen: Gyldendal, 1920-1931), and in vol. 20 of SK's *Samlede Værker*, 3rd ed. (Copenhagen: Gyldendal, 1962-1964).

Hirsch, Emanuel, *Geschichte der neuern evangelischen Theologie* vol. 4 (1954).

――, *Kierkegaard-Studien*, 2 vols. (Gütersloh: C. Bertelsmann, 1930-1933).

Høffding, Harald, *A. History of Modern Philosophy*, 2 vols., trans. B. E. Meyer (New York: Dover Publications, 1955).

――, *Danske Filosofer* (1909).

――, *Philosofien i Tydskland efter Hegel* (1872).

Hoffmeister, Johannes, *Dokumente zu Hegels Entwicklung* (1936).

Høirup, H., *Grundtvigs Syn paa Tro og Erkendelse* (1949).

Holm, Søren, *Religionsfilosofi* (Copenhagen: Munksgaard, 1955).

――, *Religionsfilosofiske Essays* (1943).

――, *Dogmatik* (1962).

――, *Kristelig Ethik* (1963).

――, *Ontologi* (1964).

————, *Søren Kierkegaards Historiefilosofi* (Copenhagen: Nyt Nordisk Forlag, Arnold Busck, 1952).

Holmer, Paul L., "Kierkegaard and Logic," *Kierkegaardiana,* II (1957), 25-42.

Hyppolite, Jean, *Genèse et structure de la Phénomenologie de l'esprit de Hegel,* 2 vols. (Paris: Aubier, 1946).

Iljin, Iwan, *Die Philosophie Hegels als kontemplative Gotteslehre* (1946).

Jaspers, Karl, *Schelling* (1955).

Jensen, Hans, *De danske Stænderforsamlingers Historie* (1931).

Jensenius, Knud, *Nogle Kierkegaardsstudier* (Copenhagen: Nyt Nordisk Forlag, 1932).

deJong, K.H.E., *Hegel und Plotin* (1916).

Jørgensen, Jørgen, *A Treatise of Formal Logic,* 3 vols. (New York: Russell, 1962).

Kabell, Aage, *Kierkegaardstudiet i Norden* (Copenhagen: Hagerup, 1948).

Kimmel, J., ed., *Libri Symbolici Ecclesiae Orientalis* (1843).

Knittermeyer, H., *Schelling und die romantische Schule* (Munich: Reinhardt, 1929).

Koch, Hal, *Den danske Kirkes Historie* (1954).

Koktanek, A. M., *Schellings Seinslehre und Kierkegaard* (1962).

Kornerup, Bjørn, ed., *J. P. Mynsters Visitatsdagbøger, 1835-1853,* (1937).
————, *Vor Frue Kirkes og Menigheds Historie* (1930).

Kühle, Sejer, *Søren Kierkegaard: Barndom og ungdom* (Copenhagen: Aschehoug, 1950).

Kuhr, Victor, *Modsigelsens Grundsætning; Kierkegaard Studier,* II (Copenhagen: Gyldendal, 1915).

Larsen, J., *H. N. Clausen* (1945).

Leisegang, Hans, *Denkformen,* 2nd ed. (1951).

Lind, W., *Das Ringen Luthers um die Freiheit der Theologie von der Philosophie,* 2nd ed. (1955).

Lindström, Valter, "Eros och agape i Kierkegaards åskådning, reflexioner kring Per Lønning, *Samtidighedens Situation,*" *Kierkegaardiana,* I (1955), 102-112.
————, *Stadiernas teologi* (1943).

Løgstrup, K. E., "Christentum ohne den historischen Jesus," *Orbis Litterarum,* XVIII (1963), 101ff.

Lønning, Per, *Samtidighedens Situation* (1954).

Lowrie, Walter, *Short Life of Kierkegaard* (Princeton: Princeton University Press, 1942).

Lund, H.C.A., *Studenter-Foreningens Historie* (1896).

Mackey, Louis, *Kierkegaard: A Kind of Poet* (Philadelphia: University of Pennsylvania Press, 1971).

Malantschuk, Gregor, "Das Verhältnis zwischen Wahrheit und Wirklichkeit in SK's existentiellem Denken," *Symposion Kierkegaardianum* (1955).

———, "Søren Kierkegaard og Poul M. Møller," *Kierkegaardiana*, III (1959), 7-20.

———, "Søren Kierkegaards Teori om Springet og hans Virkelighedsbegreb," *Kierkegaardiana*, I (1955), 7-15.

———, "Begrebet Fordoblelse hos SK," *Kierkegaardiana*, II (1957), 43-53.

———, "Frihedens Dialektik hos SK," *Dansk teologisk Tidsskrift* (1949), 193ff.

———, *Indførelse i SKs Forfatterskab* (Copenhagen: Munksgaard, (1953). English translation: *Kierkegaard's Way to the Truth* (Minneapolis, Minnesota: Augsburg Publishing House, 1963).

Marc-Wogau, Konrad, "Der Zweifel Descartes," *Theoria*, XX (1954), 128ff.

Marheineke, Philip, *Die Grundlehren der christlichen Dogmatik als Wissenschaft*, 2nd ed. (Berlin, 1827).

Martensen, Hans Lassen, *Christian Dogmatics* trans. (from Martensen's German) William Urwick (Edinburgh: T. & T. Clark, 1886).

McKinnon, Alastair, *The Kierkegaard Indices*, I (Leiden: E. J. Brill, 1970).

Mesnard, Pierre, *Le vrai visage de Kierkegaard* (Paris: Beauchesne, 1948).

Michelet, K. L., *Geschichte der letzen Systeme der Philosophie in Deutschland von Kant bis Hegel*, 2 vols. (Berlin, 1833-1836).

Michelsen, W., *Tilblivelsen af Grundtvigs Historiesyn* (1954).

Mitchell, P. M., *A History of Danish Literature* (Copenhagen: Gyldendal, 1957).

Möhler, Johan Adam, *Athanasius der Grosse und die Kirche seiner Zeit*, 2 vols. (Mainz, 1827).

Møller, Poul, *Efterladte Skrifter*, vol. 1-6, 3rd ed. (1856).

Müller, Julius, *Die Christliche Lehre von der Sünde*, 3rd ed. (1849).

Nedergaard-Hansen, Leif, *Bayle og Leibniz' Drøftelse af Theodicé-Problemet*, 2 vols. (Copenhagen: Munksgaard, 1965).

Newman, John Henry, *An Essay in Aid of a Grammar of Assent* (New York: Catholic Publication Society, 1870. South Bend, Indiana: University of Notre Dame Press, 1978).

Nilsson, Martin P., *Geschichte der griechischen Religion*, 2nd ed. (1955).

Nordentoft, Kresten, *Heideggers Opgør med den filosofiske Tradition* (1961).

Nyholm, Asger, *Religion og Politik, en Monrad Studie* (1947).

Ørsted, Børge, *J. P. Mynster og Henrich Steffens*, 2 vols. (1965).

Paulus, H.E.G., *Die endlich offenbar gewordene positive Philosophie der Offenbarung* (1843).

Pivčević, E., *Ironie als Daseinsform bei Sören Kierkegaard* (1960).

Plum, N. M., *Jakob Peter Mynster som Kristen og Teolog* (1938).

——, "Lidt om SKs Citationsmaade," *Teologisk Tidsskrift* (Copenhagen, 1927), pp. 42-49.

——, *Schleiermacher i Danmark* (1934).

Rehm, Walther, *Kierkegaard und der Verführer* (Munich: Rinn, 1949).

Reuter, Hans, *S. Kierkegaards religionsphilosophische Gedanken im Verhältnis zu Hegels religionsphilosophischem System* (Leipzig, 1914).

Reyburn, H. A., *The Ethical Theory of Hegel* (Oxford, 1921).

Rode, Vilhelm, "Bidrag til den danske Studenterforenings Historie," *Nordisk Universitets-Tidsskrift* (1854).

Rohde, H. P., *Auktionsprotokol Over Søren Kierkegaards Bogsamling* (Copenhagen: Det Kongelige Bibliotek, 1967).

——, "Om Søren Kierkegaard som Bogsamler," *Fund og Forskning i Det Kongelige Biblioteks Samlinger*, VIII (1961), 79-127.

Rohde, Peter, *Søren Kierkegaard*, trans. Alan Moray Williams (London: Allen & Unwin, 1963).

Rohde, Sven Eduard, *Zweifel und Erkenntnis*, Lunds Universitet Årsskrift, N.F., Avd. 1, vol. 41, No. 4 (1945).

Rome, Beatrice K., *The Philosophy of Malebranche* (Chicago: Henry Regnery Company, 1963).

Roos, Carl, *Kierkegaard og Goethe* (1955).

Roos, H., *Søren Kierkegaard and Catholicism*, trans. Richard M. Brackett (Westminster, Maryland: The Newman Press, 1954).

Rosenkranz, Karl, *Encyclopädie der Theologischen Wissenschaften* (Halle, 1831).

——, *Hegel's Leben* (1844).

Rosenkranz, Karl, *Psychologie oder die Wissenschaft vom subjektiven Geist* (Königsberg, 1837).

Rothe, Valdemar Henrik, *Læren om Treenighed og Forsoning* (Copenhagen: Qvist, 1836).

Rubow, Paul V., *Dansk litterær Kritik i det nittende Aarhundrede* (1921).

Ruttenbeck, Walter, *Søren Kierkegaard: Der christliche Denker und sein Werk* (Berlin: Trowitzsch & Sohn, 1929).

Scharling, C. I., *Grundtvig og Romantikken belyst ved Grundtvigs Forhold til Schelling* (1947).

Schasler, Max, *Kritische Geschichte der Aesthetik*, 2 vols. (1872).

Schilder, Kl., *Zur Begriffsgeschichte des "Paradoxon"* (1933).

Schleiermacher, Friedrich Ernst Daniel, *Kurze Darstellung des theologischen Studiums* (1811); ed. H. Schotz (Hildesheim, 1961).

——, *On Religion: Speeches to its Cultured Despisers*, trans. John Oman (New York: Harper Torchbooks, 1958).

Schmidt, Erik, *Hegels Lehre von Gott* (1952).

Schnurr, G., *Skeptizismus als Theologisches Problem* (1964).

Schröer, H., *Die Denkform der Paradoxalität als Theologisches Problem* (1960).

Schulz, Walter, *Die Vollendung des deutschen Idealismus in der Spätphilosophie Schellings* (1955).

Sløk, Johannes, "Das Verhaltnis des Menschen zu seiner Zukunft," *Orbis Litterarum*, XVIII (1963), 60-79.

——, *Die Anthropologie Kierkegaards* (Copenhagen: Rosenkilde og Bagger, 1954).

——, "Religionsfilosofi," *Teologien og dens Fag* (1960).

Søe, N. H., *Religionsfilosofi* (2. Udg., 1963).

——, "S.K.'s lære om paradokset," *Nordisk teologi: Idéer och Män* [festskrift] till Ragnar Bring (Lund, Sweden: C.W.K. Gleerups Förlag, 1955), pp. 102-121. English trans.: "Kierkegaard's Doctrine of the Paradox," in Howard Johnson and Niels Thulstrup, eds., *A Kierkegaard Critique* (New York: Harper & Row, 1962. Republished, Chicago: Gateway Editions, 1967), pp. 207-227.

Stengren, George L., "Connatural Knowledge in Aquinas and Kierkegaardian Subjectivity," *Kierkegaardiana*, X (1977), 182-189.

——, "Malebranche's Version of the Ontological Argument," *Analecta Anselmiana*, IX (1975), 231-237.

Stenzel, Julius, *Hegels Auffassung der griechischen Philosophie: Kleine Schriften zur griechischen Philosophie* (1956).

Stephan, Horst, *Geschichte der deutschen evangelischen Theologie seit dem deutschen Idealismus*, (1938), rev. ed. Martin Schmidt (1960).

Stilling, P. M., *Philosophiske Betragtninger over den Speculative Logiks Betydning for Videnskaben* (1842).

Strohschneider-Kohrs, I., *Die romantische Ironie in Theorie und Gestaltung* (1960).

Thaning, K., *Menneske først* vol. I-III (1963).

Thomas, J. Heywood, *Subjectivity and Paradox* (Oxford: Basil Blackwell, 1957).

Thomsen, Anton, *Hegel, Udviklingen af hans Filosofi til 1806* (1905).

Thomsen, Oluf, *F. G. Howitz og hans Strid om "Villiens Frihed"* (1924).

Thomte, Reidar, *Kierkegaard's Philosophy of Religion* (Princeton: Princeton University Press, 1948).

Thulstrup, Niels, "Incontro di Kierkegaard e Hamann," *Studi Kierkegaardiana* (Brescia, Italy, 1957), pp. 325-357.

————, *Kierkegaards Verhältnis zu Hegel: Forschungsgeschichte* (Stuttgart: Verlag W. Kohlhammer, 1969).

————, *Søren Kierkegaards Bibliotek: En Bibliografi* (Copenhagen: Munksgaard, 1957).

————, "Die historische Methode in der Kierkegaard-Forschung durch ein Beispiel beleuchtet," *Symposion Kierkegaardianum* (1955), 280-297.

————, "Kierkegaards Verhältnis zu Hegel," *Theologische Zeitschrift* (Basel, 1957), 200-226.

————, "Kierkegaard og den filosofiske Idealisme," *Kierkegaardiana* IV (1962), 88ff.

Thulstrup, Niels, ed., *Kierkegaardiana* (Copenhagen: Søren Kierkegaard Selskabet, 1955-   ).

Tielsch, E., *Kierkegaards Glaube* (1964).

Trendelenburg, Friedrich A., *Logische Untersuchungen* (1840).

Ueberweg, Friedrich, *A History of Philosophy*, trans. from the 4th German edition by George S. Morris, 2 vols. (New York: C. Scribner & Company, 1872-1874).

————, *Grundriss der Geschichte der Philosophie,* 13th ed. (1951).

Vedel, Valdemar, *Guldalderen i dansk Digtning* (1890; 2nd ed., 1948).

Weltzer, Carl, *Grundtvig og Søren Kierkegaard* (Copenhagen: Gyldendal, 1953).

Werder, Karl, *Logik* (1841).

Witt-Hansen, Johannes, *Om Generalisation og Generalisationsproblemer i de matematiske og historiske Videnskaber* (1963).

Zeller, Eduard, *Geschichte der deutschen Philosophie seit Leibniz* (1872).

INDEX

Hegel and Kierkegaard are not listed except in connection with a few specific topics. Distinctive letters of the Danish and Swedish alphabets are alphabetized as if they were English.

LIBRARY OF CONGRESS CATALOGING IN PUBLICATION DATA

Thulstrup, Niels.
  Kierkegaard's relation to Hegel.

  Translation of Kierkegaards forhold til Hegel og
til den spekulative Idealisme indtil 1846, which was orig-
inally presented as the author's thesis, Copenhagen, 1967.
  Bibliography: p.
  Includes index.
  1. Kierkegaard, Søren Aabye, 1813-1855.   2. Hegel,
Georg Wilhelm Friedrich, 1770-1831.   3. Idealism.
I. Title.
B4377.T51813   198.9   79-3233
ISBN 0-691-07243-4
ISBN 0-691-10079-9 pbk.